PERMEABILITY AND FUNCTION
OF BIOLOGICAL MEMBRANES

PERMEABILITY AND FUNCTION OF BIOLOGICAL MEMBRANES

Proceedings of the 1969 meeting of the
International Conference on Biological Membranes

NATO ADVANCED STUDY INSTITUTE

Editors

Liana Bolis
Institute of General Physiology
University of Rome, Italy

A. Katchalsky, R.D. Keynes, W.R. Loewenstein,
B.A. Pethica

1970

NORTH-HOLLAND PUBLISHING COMPANY – AMSTERDAM · LONDON
AMERICAN ELSEVIER PUBLISHING COMPANY, INC. – NEW YORK

Library of Congress Catalog Card Number 75-114582

ISBN North-Holland   7204 4065 3
ISBN American Elsevier 0444 10031 8

Publishers:
NORTH-HOLLAND PUBLISHING COMPANY – AMSTERDAM
NORTH-HOLLAND PUBLISHING COMPANY, Ltd. – LONDON

Sole distributors for the U.S.A. and Canada:
AMERICAN ELSEVIER PUBLISHING COMPANY, INC.
52 Vanderbilt Avenue
New York, N.Y. 10017

PRINTED IN THE NETHERLANDS

EDITORIAL PREFACE

The papers assembled in this volume are based on the material presented at the International Conference on Biological Membranes devoted to the permeability and function of biomembranes. While numerous meetings were devoted to the chemical structures and organization of protoplasmatic membranes and intercellular reticulum, less attention has been paid to cell surfaces. This conference considered the mechanical properties of cellular covers, and devoted much of its time to the surface forces, intercellular contacts and to cell communication. Since it is realized that the surfaces of cells are not geometrical boundaries between phases but active structures endowed with immunological properties and responsible for cellular recognition, several sessions were devoted to the interaction of the membranes with anesthetics, to their immune reactions, their antigen recognition as well as to the role played by cell membranes in histocompatibility.

In an attempt to interpret biomembrane behavior in physical terms, a couple of sessions were devoted to the thermodynamics analysis of membrane transport and to a discussion of the physical chemistry of monolayers and bilayers, liposomes and black films as models for membrane behavior. The last part of the meeting was devoted to the ever-exciting field of excitable membranes. There is a growing tendency to interpret the phenomena of nerve excitation in terms of clear-cut molecular processes which were discussed rather extensively.

It is not possible to reproduce in this volume the friendly atmosphere and the intellectual stimulus of the discussions which went on after the sessions, during round-table talks, and late into the night. These discussions were inspired not only by the stimulating material presented by the lecturers but also by the serene atmosphere of the Lago Maggiore and by the cordial reception of the Italian Organizing Committee. The efforts of the secretary-general, Professor Liana Bolis, and her co-workers have made out of this conference an unforgettable scientific and personal experience.

A.Katchalsky
Honorary Chairman

LIST OF CONTRIBUTORS

CONTENTS

Part 5. *Structure of excitable membranes*

Contributions to the general discussion

Part 1

MECHANICAL PROPERTIES OF CELL MEMBRANES

THE STRETCHING OF 'PORES' IN A MEMBRANE

Alan C.BURTON

Department of Biophysics, University of Western Ontario, Canada

1. Introduction

This paper is little more than the presentation of some basic ideas, with a few crude experiments on inanimate membranes. Even fewer experiments were made on biological material, that might suggest that these ideas may apply to the physiological behaviour of living membranes; even though the 'models' used in the logic are very far from representing living membranes. In that the ideas have apparently not had much attention, they may serve to stimulate those capable of making relevant measurements on living membranes. Whatever the outcome when this is done, the crude ideas will have served their purpose of suggesting worthwhile investigations.

Our interest in the subject of stretching of holes in elastic membranes arose in the very real problem of the permeability behaviour of the membrane of the red cell, which has been an object of our experimental research for some years. The problem is emphasized in the facts of hemolysis of the erythrocyte in hypotonic solutions.

When the red cell is placed in a hypotonic solution, water enters very rapidly under osmotic gradient, and the cell swells from its biconcave disc shape, through the 'planar' disc shape, to the biconvex, and finally to the spherical shape (Rand and Burton [1]). It has been possible to make quite accurate statistical estimates of the volume of the cell, and of the surface area of the membrane, by computation from photographs of profiles of single cells hanging on edge, because they retain, in all the shapes assumed in swelling, a quite remarkable axial symmetry [2]. There is no doubt that from the initial normal biconcave shape to the sphere, while the volume increases by 60 to 140% (depending on the initial shape, which is best characterized by the 'sphericity index' [2]), the surface area of the membrane has not significantly changed. (This has long been the view of the authorities.) Once the spherical shape is reached, however, any further swelling necessitates an increase in area of the membrane, and the membrane is stretched.

1

The cell then becomes remarkably rigid, and displays a relatively high resistance to stretch of the membrane. (The Young's modulus is of the order of 10^7 dyne/cm^2, from the work of Katchalsky [3] as well as of Rand [4].)

In very violent rapid osmotic hemolysis, as in distilled water, the membrane is obviously 'torn' (irreversibly damaged) and hemoglobin can be observed to leave in 'blobs' (seen by using a precipitating agent outside). The idea that, in slow osmotic hemolysis, holes sufficiently large to permit the egress of hemoglobin have been 'torn' in the membrane is quite untenable. In slow hemolysis the optical contrast of the whole cell diminishes uniformly, and Hb is apparently leaving through the membrane at all points. Moreover, the membrane after hemolysis behaves as if intact, and the ghost has a permeability, to ions like Na$^+$ and K$^+$, of the same order of magnitude as the unhemolysed normal cell [5,6].

We are forced to wonder if it is possible that the pre-existing 'pores', which according to the excellent work of Dr. Solomon and his colleagues [7,8] are functionally of diameter about 7 Å in the normal erythrocyte from data on water, Na$^+$ and K$^+$ permeabilities, could be stretched sufficiently to permit the passage of Hb molecules (diameter of at least 60 Å would be required) at the time of hemolysis, and then return to their original diameter in the ghost. An increase of diameter of pores at least 9 or 10 times could be required. Seeman [9] in his work in the laboratory of Dr. Palade, studied with the electron microscope the passage into and out of the interior of red cells at the time of osmotic hemolysis of particles of 100 μ or more. His photographs show discontinuities (holes) in the membrane up to 300 Å in diameter, if the cells were fixed within a few seconds of becoming spherical. Just 30 sec later, when hemolysis was complete, the holes were 'closed', and there was no entrance of the large particles later than this. He adduces evidence that these 'holes' were those through which the Hb had left. In more gentle hemolysis, perhaps these very large holes would not be seen, but in any case they must have reached at least 60 Å in diameter. Could we imagine that mechanical stretching of the membrane could expand the holes as much as this?

To answer this question, the degree of increase of area of the membrane required for hemolysis is critical. Rand and I [1] were sure, from the increase in diameter of sphered cells before hemolysis that 10% was sufficient. Seeman [10] considers that 5 to 7% increase in area is enough, at least in his cells whose membrane has been 'stabilized' by drugs. In order that hemolysis could be explained by 'stretching pores' therefore, we must have a 10-fold increase in diameter of 'pores' for a linear stretch of the membrane of only about 6%. The ratio of linear expansion of the hole to the membrane (we call this the

'expansion ratio') must be of the order of 900%/5% or 180. Is this conceivable?
We share the growing scepticism about the model of fixed cylindrical pores as representing the reality of living biological membranes, but we should know all of the possibilities of this model before we forget it, particularly when it has proved so useful in stimulating ideas.

2. Classical mechanics of stretching an isolated hole in an elastic membrane

About this time, I was very lucky that a colleague in Applied Mathematics, Dr. Don Miller, came to my office to borrow a journal that I had kept out of the Library. I asked him if he could solve the problem of how much a hole in a uniform elastic membrane increased in size when the membrane was stretched. Next morning he left on my desk a very neat solution, of course for the idealized case of an isotropic Hookean membrane, submitted to uniform stretch, i.e. with an equal tension in all directions (below). The solution is astonishing to me.

The relative displacement U_r/r of a point on the membrane, distant r from the centre of the hole, when the uniform tension in the membrane is T, Young's modulus is E, and Poisson's* ratio is σ, is given by:

$$\frac{U_r}{r} = \frac{T}{E}\left[(1+\sigma)(1-2\sigma) + \frac{(1+\sigma)r_0^2}{r^2}\right]. \tag{1}$$

For a point on the membrane very distant from the hole, put $r \to \infty$. This will give the stretch of the membrane itself:

$$\left.\frac{U_r}{r}\right|_{r\to\infty} = \frac{T}{E}(1+\sigma)(1-2\sigma). \tag{2}$$

For the edge of the hole, $r = r_0$, and

$$\left.\frac{U_r}{r}\right|_{r_0} = \frac{T}{E}(1+\sigma)(2-2\sigma). \tag{3}$$

* Poisson's ratio is the ratio of the fractional decrease in width of a strip, to the fractional increase in length, when a purely longitudinal stress is applied.

∴ Expansion ratio:

$$N = \frac{2-2\sigma}{1-2\sigma}. \tag{4}$$

Thus the 'expansion ratio' depends only on the value of Poisson's ratio for the membrane. It is independent of the stiffness of the membrane, or the size of the hole. With multiple holes in the membrane that are far apart relative to their diameter ($> 10\times$) (this is certainly true for the 'pores' of the red cell membrane), eq. (1) shows that the stretching of the membrane is negligibly affected by the presence of the holes.

Poisson's ratio for an isotropic material can be expressed in terms of the two fundamental elastic moduli, the rigidity n, and the bulk modulus k (reciprocal of compressibility):

$$\sigma = \frac{3k-2n}{6k+2n}.$$

Since n and k are essentially positive, σ could theoretically lie between -1 and $+\frac{1}{2}$. For a liquid, n is zero or very small indeed compared to k, which is very large, so that σ approaches $\frac{1}{2}$. For a solid, with some rigidity, σ must be less than $\frac{1}{2}$ but may approach this value. Another relation between the constants, involving k and Y, the Young's modulus is:

$$\sigma = \frac{1}{2} - \frac{Y}{6k}. \tag{6}$$

Now for the red cell membrane, Young's modulus is of the order of 3×10^7 dyne/cm^2 [3,4]. The bulk modulus of water is about 2×10^{10} dyne/cm^2. If the bulk modulus of the red cell membrane were as high as that of water (it may be much less), Poisson's ratio could be as high as 0.499.

It is the interesting property of the expression in eq. (4) for the expansion ratio that this ratio approaches infinity as σ approaches $\frac{1}{2}$. Table 1 illustrates this.

Table 1

Expansion ratio, $N = (2-2\sigma)/(1+2\sigma)$, for different values of σ

σ	0.3	0.35	0.40	0.43	0.46	0.48	0.49	0.495	0.50
N	2.00	4.33	6.00	8.13	12.5	26.0	51.0	100	∞

A hole in a membrane is thus very much a *'focus of stress'*. It seems possible that in biological membranes, very large 'expansion ratios' might exist if σ is close to $\frac{1}{2}$, so that in stretching the membranes we might very greatly increase the diameter of a pore. However, an expansion from 7 to 60 Å for a stretch of only 5% would seem very unlikely. For the selective permeability of smaller molecules like Na^+ and K^+ however, the fact of the much greater

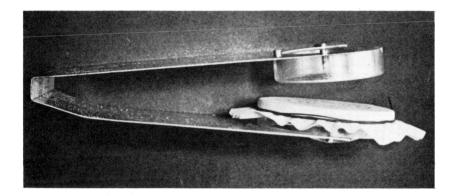

Fig. 1. Simple demonstration that when an elastic membrane (here rubber dam) is uniformly stretched, the linear dimensions of a hole in the membrane increase much more than those of the membrane. The hole obviously increases in diameter by 2 to 3 times, while the rings on the rubber far from the hole increase only 10–20%.

expansion of pores when the membrane is stretched must be taken into account, for here expansion ratios of 10–50 could very significantly affect the ratio of transport of different ions, even with a small degree of stretch of biological membranes.

A simple demonstration of the high expansion ratio for rubber dam is illustrated in fig. 1. The apparatus is based on grandmother's 'embroidery frame'.

3. The expansion ratios of some non-living 'membranes'

The theoretical result for the 'expansion ratio' has been tested on some inanimate membranes. A uniform tension of a membrane of, for example, rubber-dam was easily achieved by mounting it on a 'manometer capsule' between a brass face and a brass ring. Small holes of different diameter were cut in the centre of the membrane, and compressed air blown through the capsule, escaping through the hole. The rubber took the shape of a spherical cap where the pressure in the capsule was sufficient to make the leak through the hole equal to the rate of supply of air. Simple geometry shows that the area of the curved surface of the membrane, when the central part has risen by height h, is given by

$$A = \pi(a^2 + h^2) , \tag{7}$$

where a is the radius of the original, flat, membrane. The linear dimensions of the membrane have, therefore, been increased in the ratio $(1+h^2/a^2)^{1/2}$. The height h was measured by the change in the height of a low-powered microscope required to keep the edges of the hole in focus, while the diameter D of the hole was measured by an eye-piece scale. If the 'expansion ratio', N, is a constant

$$\frac{dD}{D_0} = N \frac{dL}{L_0} \tag{8}$$

where L is the linear dimension of the membrane. Integrating:

$$D/D_0 = (L/L_0)^N ,$$

or

$$\log (D/D_0) = N \log (L/L_0) . \qquad (9)$$

Accordingly the logarithm of D/D_0 was plotted against the logarithm of L/L_0 (fig. 2). The slope of the line on the graph gave the expansion ratio N. (This is a better plot than $\Delta D/D_0$ versus L/L_0 since the absolute value of $\Delta D/D_0$ depends critically on D_0, the diameter of the hole when the membrane is unstretched, which is the least reliable of the measurements of diameter.) Fig. 2 shows results for three different sized holes in dental rubber dam. The slopes are identical and indicate an expansion ratio of 17, which would correspond to $\sigma = 0.47$. Many such measurements were made on other samples of rubber, giving expansion ratios of from 10 to 30. Dental rubber dam is 'rolled' in manufacture, so the elastic constant at right angles to the surface is probably very different from that in the surface, and even in the plane of the membrane it was found that there was a 30% difference in Young's modulus, longitudinal versus transverse. For a more isotropic material, and because it represents a different structure, a thin sheet was cut from a block of 'cellular rubber' (giving $N = 10$). To represent 'fibres' rather than 'continua', material of a cotton shirt and 'elastic stockings' were used. In the cotton fabric, the fibres move to increase the size of the hole. Only a small degree of stretch (5%) was possible, but the expansion ratio was high (50). For the elastic stocking where the fibres themselves were stretched the expansion ratio was 30.

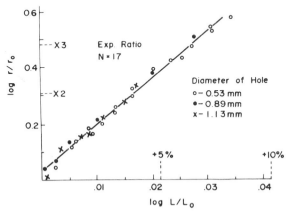

Fig. 2. Verification of the theory for uniform stretch for rubber dam. The 'expansion ratio' (see text) is the same for the three holes of different size.

A.C.BURTON

4. Test on some biological membranes with artificial 'holes'

Table 2
Expansion ratios for some living membranes

Membrane	N	Max stretch used (%)	Remarks
Frog skin	10–31	5	Different from different areas of skin
Dog mesentery	12	10	Not very homogeneous
Dog pericardium	25	10	Decreases at higher stretch
Rabbit bladder	9	10	

We then tested a few 'biological membranes', with a small hole cut in them (table 2). In many cases the maximum stretch possible was not great, and, in some, at higher degrees of stretch the expansion ratio tended to decrease, a feature not predicted in the idealized theory.

We conclude that expansion ratios of from about 10 to 50 might be expected, at least for macroscopic holes in biological membranes.

5. Living biological membranes with natural pores

There has already been discussion in the literature of 'stretched pores' in the blood capillaries, in the extensive work of Meyerson and his colleagues [11] in which they measured the rate of formation and flow of lymph in the hind limb of the dog, and the passage of plasma proteins and dextran molecules of different sizes from blood stream to lymph. The stretching of the capillaries was the result of increasing the blood volume by transfusion, up to 40% above normal. They found not only an increase of many times in the rate of filtration, but a marked increase in the appearance of large molecules in the lymph. The increase was more marked for the large molecules than for the smaller. They concluded that the only explanation was an increase in the effective diameter of the pores by stretching. Opening up of new capillaries, without such an increase in pore-size would not be an adequate explanation. Unfortunately in these experiments there was no measure of the degree of increase in the area of the capillary membrane.

It happened that, in two quite different researches proceeding in our laboratory, there was an opportunity to see how the permeability to water of biological 'membranes' was affected by stretch. Dr. Derek Boughner is studying in detail the distensibility and elastic behaviour of the wall of human iliac arteries obtained from autopsy (his interest is in the effect of vibration on these properties). He measures the increase in volume of an arterial segment as the transmural pressure is increased. A small artefact in his measurement, for which correction can be made, is the leakage, or filtration, of the perfusing fluid through the wall. I asked him to measure how this filtration altered with increasing transmural pressure, as the wall was stretched. Since these arteries resist stretch much more strongly in the longitudinal direction than circumferentially, the stretch is 'one-way' rather than 'uniform'.

Fig. 3 shows the result for the filtration constant, i.e., the filtration rate divided by the driving transmural pressure, versus the increased circumferential stretch. Two features are of interest: (a) There is evidence of increase in size or number of 'pores', since the filtration increases 3 or 4 times, but the 'expansion ratio' is very much less than found for uniform stretch of the materials tried. (b) There seems to be a maximum filtration at a stretch of about 30%. No such maximum was predicted or found in 'uniform' stretch.

A second possibility of measuring the effect of stretch on permeability to water, but again confined to one-way stretch, was offered by a simple experi-

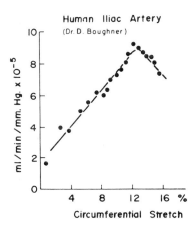

Fig. 3. Filtration constant (leakage/transmural pressure) as affected by circumferential stretch of a segment of human iliac artery (data of Dr. D.R.Boughner). Note the maximum at about 30% stretch.

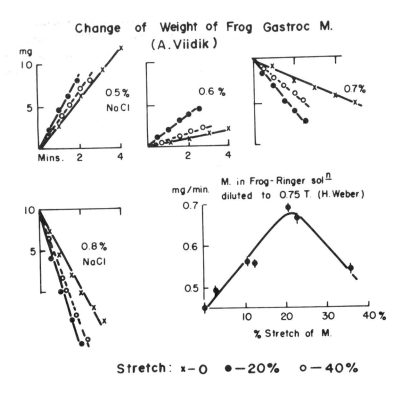

Fig. 4. Changes in weight of frog gastrocnemius muscle when put in Ringer's solutions of different tonicity, and the effect of stretch of the muscle on this. Above is shown how the rate of change of weight (unstretched - crosses) increases for 20% stretch (black dots), but in every case increases less for 40% stretch (open circles). Below, the same tonicity of solution was used in each case, with different degrees of stretch. The existence of a maximum for a certain degree of stretch is verified.

ment we use in our undergraduate Biophysics laboratory. An isolated frog muscle is left in Ringer's or salt solutions of different tonicity, and the gain or loss in weight is recorded by removing, blotting, and weighing. The operation of the simple osmotic laws is demonstrated, and the effective tonicity of the muscle can be determined. The slope of the lines (fig. 4) measures the filtration constant or permeability.

I asked two undergraduates, Mr. Anthony Viidik, and later Mr. Hans Weber, to repeat such measurements with the muscle stretched on a frame to different degrees. Viidik's results (fig. 4) consistently showed an increase in filtration constant for 20% stretch, but for 40% stretch the filtration was less than for 20% stretch, though still greater than for unstretched muscle. This was true for all concentrations of saline used to produce the shift of water. Mr. Weber used a constant tonicity of Ringer's solution, but a larger number of degrees of stretch. He verified that there was a maximum effect of stretch on the permeability, at about 25% stretch, and that it was quite reversible (not a permanent tearing of a membrane). As with the arteries, the maximum increase in filtration constant was 3 or 4 times, suggesting a rather low linear expansion ratio.

The unexpectedly smaller effect of stretch on pores in 'one-way' compared to 'uniform' stretch prompted me to ask my colleagues in Applied

Mathematics to solve the problem of 'one-way' stretch for the idealised Hookean, isotropic elastic membrane. Dr. E.Lewis (Dr. D.Miller having left) supplied the answer, which is as remarkable in its independence of many of the elastic constants as is the solution for uniform stretch.

6. Theory of one-way stretch

The problem of one-way stretch is more difficult than the case of uniform stretch solved by Dr.Miller, where radial symmetry could be assumed, and a circular hole remained circular, but larger, when the membrane was stretched. In the case of stress in one direction only, Cartesian rather than polar coordinates must be used, and the boundary conditions at the edge of the hole, which becomes elliptical, are now that the stress at each point normal to this ellipse must vanish.

The solution for the semi-major axis 'a' of the elliptical hole (in the direction parallel to the stretching force), and the minor axis 'b', are given below. If L and B denote the distance between two points on the membrane distant from the hole, parallel and perpendicular to the force, we have the expansion ratio, N, given by:

$$N = \frac{\mathrm{d}a/a}{\mathrm{d}L/L} = 1 + 2b/a \ . \tag{10}$$

We also have the 'contraction ratio'

$$N^1 = \frac{\mathrm{d}b/b}{\mathrm{d}B/B} = \frac{1-\sigma}{\sigma} \ . \tag{11}$$

Eq. (10), which does not contain Poisson's ratio σ explicitly, shows that if we start from an unstretched circular hole, where $a \equiv b \equiv r$, *the expansion ratio will initially* always be 3, but will *decrease to unity* where the ellipse has been stretched very greatly $(a \gg b)$. This is to be contrasted with the solution for uniform stretch, where the expansion ratio can approach infinity if σ approaches $\frac{1}{2}$.

Eq. (11) shows that the minor axis 'b' will decrease a little more than the width of the membrane itself. For example for $\sigma = 0.5$, N^1 will be unity, for $\sigma = 0.4$, N^1 will be 1.5.

The theory has been verified with membranes of rubber dam (fig. 5), with an initially circular hole. Measurements were made of the dimensions of the hole (major and minor axes of the ellipse) and of the distance between ink marks drawn on the rubber at some distance on each side of the hole, to give values of B/B_0 and L/L_0. The expansion ratio (fig. 5) was 2.8, close to the

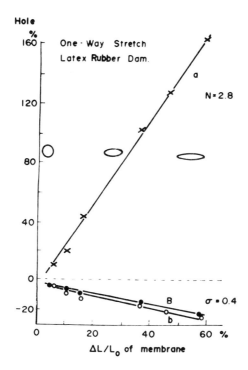

Fig. 5. Results of measurement of effect of unidirectional stretch on an initially circular hole in a sheet of dental rubber dam. The theory given in the text is verified.

value of 3 predicted by theory, and the minor axis of the hole decreased slightly more than the breadth of the rubber. Similar tests with a sheet of rubber cut perpendicular to this with respect to the 'rolling' give $N = 3.7$ and $N^1 = 1.5$. It was also easy to verify that at high values of one-way stretch, when the ellipse was very long and narrow, the expansion ratio approached unity.

It was of great interest whether the theory of one-way stretch would predict a maximum filtration constant at a given stretch, as found experimentally in the human arteries and the frog muscle. Fortunately the eqs. (10) and (11), plus the relation

$$\sigma = \frac{dB/B}{dL/L},$$ (12)

permit integral equations for the major and minor axes of the ellipse as a function of the stretch L/L_0. The filtration constant for a tube of elliptical cross section, according to Lamb [11], is given by:

$$F \propto \frac{2a^3 b^3}{a^2 + b^2}$$

compared to $F \propto r^4$ for a circular cross section (Poiseuille's law). As the stretch L/L_0 increases, while a increases, the width of the elliptical hole, b, decreases to a very small value, so that further stretch actually decreases the value of F. Numerical analysis of the solutions given below shows that a maximum is to be expected at from 40 to 80% stretch, depending on the value of Poisson's ratio, and that the filtration constant might be increased, at the maximum, to 2 or 3 times its original value. If we start with pores that are already elliptical in the unstretched case, the maximum will, of course, occur at a smaller degree of stretch. Considering that the theory is for the ideal case of isotropic membranes following Hooke's law, the agreement with theory seems satisfactory.

7. Discussion — The physiological importance of stretched pore theory

The problem of hemolysis of the red cell by swelling in hypotonic solutions, from which this enquiry started, can hardly be considered 'physiological' in view of the narrow range of osmotic pressure maintained in body fluids. However, we believe that hemolysis of old erythrocytes in the circulation is basically due to stretching of the membrane (eq. (2)), not because the volume of the cell increased but because of drastic change of shape when the cells pass through narrow cylindrical channels, probably in the spleen. If so, stretched pore theory is relevant to normal physiological hemolysis. However, even though the expansion ratio to be expected for the membrane is high, it seems unlikely, though not impossible, that it is high enough to explain how pores of diameter about 7 Å can expand to more than 60 Å (i.e. 9 times) for a stretch of only 6%, i.e. the expansion ratio would have to be of the order of 150. Until someone measures the Poisson's ratio for the red cell membrane, we cannot be sure. Measurement of the bulk modulus for a collection of membrane material would make the estimate of σ possible.

However, there is a possibility of reducing the value of expansion ratio that would be required, which at least deserves some attention. It is possible that pores existing in the normal red cell membrane are, geometrically, of considerably greater diameter than the effective diameter of 3.5 Å deduced from studies of permeability. There is suggestive evidence that the red cell membrane and other biological membranes may be covered with a mono-layer of absorbed protein. Long continued washing of red cells in protein-free solutions has been observed to increase the permeability to water consider-ably. We know that the A and B agglutinins that are responsible for blood groupings are loosely absorbed, for they can be removed onto a liquid-air interface and re-absorbed on other red cells. According to Adam [12], protein monolayers, at gas-liquid interfaces, average about 7.5 Å in thickness. Such monolayers are freely mobile, and can be 'plated' into solid surfaces, as Blod-gett [13] first demonstrated.

Let us suppose that a monolayer of protein covers the surface of the red cell and extends into the 'pores' as a cylindrical lining (fig. 6), restricting the area through which water and electrolytes could move freely. To offer an ef-fective diameter of 7 Å for transport, the actual diameter of the pore would have to be 22 Å (adding the thickness of the absorbed layers). It is shown from the experiments where monolayers are transferred from the air-water interface to 'plate' a metal bar thrust into the surface, that a degree of sur-face-pressure is required in the monolayer, or the protein will not coat the metal. Conversely a monolayer on the metal will retract and enter the inter-face if the area of the film on the tray is increased. We would expect from physical-chemical considerations of repulsion between the tails of the oriented molecules that, if there was space on the surface of the membrane, a mono-layer coating the pore would retract and occupy the surface. This would leave the pore presenting the full diameter (22 Å) for transport. Now we would need an expansion ratio of only 60 to expand the hole, (with the 6%

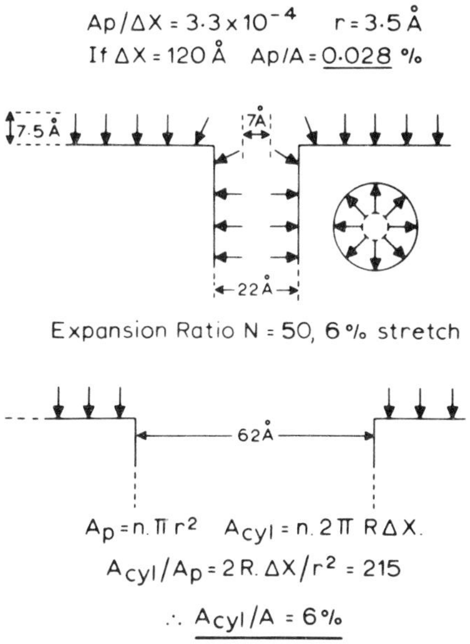

$A_p/\Delta X = 3.3 \times 10^{-4}$ $r = 3.5 \text{ Å}$
If $\Delta X = 120 \text{ Å}$ $A_p/A = \underline{0.028}$ %

Expansion Ratio N = 50, 6% stretch

$A_p = n.\pi r^2$ $A_{cyl} = n.2\pi R \Delta X$.
$A_{cyl}/A_p = 2R.\Delta X/r^2 = 215$
$\therefore A_{cyl}/A = \underline{6 \%}$

Fig. 6. Model of pores in a membrane with absorbed molecules lining the pores as well as on the membrane surface. If the surface area is increased, those molecules lining the pores could retract to the surface, leaving the pore effectively of greater diameter. The calculation below shows that for the red cell, the area of the walls of the pores may be 6% of the total surface area.

increase in area of membrane in osmotic hemolysis) sufficiently to allow Hb to leave. The key question is whether it is reasonable to suppose that 6% increase in membrane area could accommodate the monolayers that had lined the pores. Let us estimate the total area of the cylindrical walls of the pores, supposing them to be geometrically of 22 Å diameter, though only 7 Å effectively.

$$A_{pd} = n\pi r^2$$

$$A_{cyl} = n2\pi R \Delta x$$

$$\therefore A_{cyl}/A_{pd} = \frac{2R\Delta x}{r^2},$$

using $R = 11 \text{ Å}, r = 3.5 \text{ Å}, \Delta x = 120 \text{ Å}$,

$A_{cyl}/A_{pd} = 235$.

The work of Paganelli and Solomon [11] on the permeability of the red cell membrane gives the ratio $A_{pd}/\Delta x$. Assuming $\Delta x = 120$ Å (they took the thickness as 50 to 500 Å) one finds a value of A_{pd} which is 0.025% of the area of the membrane. The area of our 'enlarged' pores would be 235 times this, i.e., 6% of the membrane area. At least the idea is not contradicted by such quantitative estimates as are available.

Of course, one can juggle successfully with such figures as long as facts are not known that might prevent it. The order of magnitudes involved in this theory combining 'lining of pores' with 'stretching of holes' seems right.

8. The role of stretching of pores in receptor organs

Many of the biological transducers can be classified as 'deformation receptors', that initiate nervous impulses when the 'end-bulb', usually a naked ending of the sensory nerve enclosed in a membranous capsule (e.g. tactile organs, Paccinian capsules, tendon receptors), is deformed. It has been suggested by Loewenstein [14,15] and doubtless by many others, that mechanical deformation of these membranes might alter their selective permeability to ions, change the flux of these driven by 'metabolic pumps', and so initiate a generator potential. As long ago as 1936, Hoagland [16] showed that mechanical stimulation of frog skin released K^+, and later related this to adaptation in the tactile receptors. It is to be noted that if the membrane is spherical, the slightest deformation must result in an increase in area, i.e., in a stretching of the membrane. With an 'expansion ratio' of the magnitude we find in biological membranes, a very small deformation (e.g. increase area by 1%) indeed might change the effective pore size from say 7 to 10 Å, and this would significantly alter the ratio of Na^+ to K^+ permeability. This paper can serve only to point out that classical mechanics, applied to the current 'pore theory', could explain the remarkable sensitivity of mechano-receptors to very slight deformations.

9. Dynamic models

This paper started with the model of the membrane as an elastic structure with cylindrical 'pores' in it. In sect. 7 we added a molecular layer to the surface and to the pores. Of course, one can go to the other extreme, and

think of the membrane as having no structure at all, except as a double surface layer of oriented molecules. 'Pores' in such a double film could be completely dynamic, here one moment, gone the next. My friend, Dr. J.Clements,
of surfactant-of-the-lung fame, worked out for me that a mono- or double
film of phospholipid, at a liquid-gas interface, would have the following
properties:

(1) When the 'membrane' was unstretched the rate of formation of holes
of a given diameter (e.g. 60 Å for egress of Hb) would be remarkably small.

(2) When the membrane is stretched, hole formation would be very frequent.

The basis of his calculation is absolute reaction rate theory for the rate is:
$k'(\sec^{-1}) = (kT/h) \exp(-\Delta\epsilon/kT)$ where $\Delta\epsilon$ is the difference in energy per
hole, no hole. His estimates for ϵ are 280 kT units for the unstretched and
7 kT units for the stretched. For intermediate, small degrees of stretch, the
rate of formation of 'holes' would be remarkably sensitive to slight increase
in area, so that $d(\log k')/d(\log A)$ would be of the order of 10^3 (i.e. analogous
to an expansion ratio of more than 1000).

This is, of course, for a phospholipid film at a water-air interface. Perhaps
the calculation could be made for the red cell surface if we could estimate
the difference in energy per hole from the energy of the surface of the membrane, and utilize, say, the Boltzmann relation, to give us the probability for
the area occupied by 'holes' of a given size, and how it would depend on the
total area of the 'membrane'. I am certainly not competent as a theoretical
physical-chemist to attempt this. The point is that whether our model is the
elastic structure with pores; nothing but a combination of molecular monolayers; or a combination of surface molecular layers with an underlying elastic structure; we would conclude that 'holes' will be likely to increase in size
a very great deal more than does the membrane area under conditions of uniform stretch.

Summary

1) The hemolysis of red cells when the surface area of the membrane is
increased by only a few percent poses a difficult problem in 'pore theory',
since pores normally of 7 Å diameter must expand, reversibly, to at least 60 Å
diameter.

2) Classical theory of elasticity indicates that a hole (pore) in an elastic
membrane is very much a 'focus of stress'. When the linear dimensions of the
membrane are increased by uniform stretch, the diameter of the hole in-

creases by much more than the membrane dimensions (expansion ratio).

3) For 'uniform' stretch of an isotropic Hookean membrane the linear expansion ratio is given by $(2-2\sigma)/(1-2\sigma)$, where σ is the Poisson's ratio. If σ is close to 0.5, as it is in many materials, this ratio approaches infinity.

4) The theory for uniform stretch was verified for rubber dam, some fabrics and sbme biological membranes in which small holes were cut. Expansion ratios from 10 to 50 were found.

5) The filtration constant for water moving into or out of frog muscle under osmotic gradients was found to increase to a maximum for about 20% linear stretch of the muscle, but decrease for further stretch. A maximum for about 15% stretch was also found for the filtration constant of segments of human iliac artery submitted to circumferential stretch by transmural pressure. The classical idealized theory for one-way stretch, together with the theoretical filtration constant of an elliptical 'pore', predicts that there should be a maximum for a certain degree of stretch.

6) The probable role of stretching of pores, with a high expansion ratio, in the function of 'deformation receptors', is discussed.

7) The problem of hemolysis can be explained if a high expansion ratio (e.g. of 60) exists for the red cell membrane, and in addition the pores are larger than thought, but transport is restricted by lining of the pores by a monolayer (e.g. protein), which retracts to the surface when the area there is increased.

8) It is concluded that whether one uses a model for the membrane of an elastic structure with cylindrical pores, a combination of this with an added monolayer of molecules, or at the other extreme, a dynamic model of nothing but two associated monolayers, one would expect that a small increase in area of the membrane would result in an astonishingly great increase in the size of either static or dynamic 'pores'.

Acknowledgements

The author is indebted to the Medical Research Council of Canada for support in this research, as well as to Drs. D.Miller and E.Lewis of the Department of Applied Mathematics, Dr. D.Boughner, Mr. A.Viidik and Mr. H.Weber of our own department.

References

[1] R.P.Rand and A.C.Burton, J. Cell. Comp. Physiol. 61 (1963) 245–253.
[2] P.B.Canham and A.C.Burton, Circ. Res. 22 (1968) 405-422.
[3] A.Katchalsky, O.Kedem, C.Klebansey and A.de Vrez, in: Flow Properties of Blood and Other Biological Systems, eds. A.L.Copley and G.Stainsby (Pergamon Press, Inc., New York) 5.
[4] R.P.Rand, Biophys. J. 4 (1964) 303-316.
[5] T.Teorell, J. Gen. Physiol. 52 (1952) 669-701.
[6] J.F.Hoffman, J. Gen. Physiol. 45 (1962) 837-859.
[7] A.K.Solomon, J. Gen. Physiol. Suppl. 51 (1968) 335-364.
[8] C.V.Paganelli and A.K.Solomon, J. Gen. Physiol. 41 (1957) 259-277.
[9] P.Seeman, J. Cell Biol. 32 (1967) 55-70.
[10] P.Seeman, Biochim. Biophys. Acta (in press).
[11] H.H.Shirley Jr., C.G.Wolfram, K.Wasserman and H.S.Meyerson, Am. J. Physiol. 190 (1957) 189-193.
[12] N.K.Adam, The Physics and Chemistry of Surfaces, 3rd ed., (Oxford Univ. Press, London, 1941) p. 87.
[13] K.B.Blodgett, J. Amer. Chem. Soc. 57 (1935) 1007-1022.
[14] W.R.Loewenstein, Sci. Am. 208 (1960) 99-108.
[15] W.R.Loewenstein, J. Physiol. 133 (1965) 588-602.
[16] H.Hoagland, J. Gen. Physiol. 19 (1936) 939-942.

A THERMODYNAMIC CONSIDERATION
OF ACTIVE TRANSPORT

A.KATCHALSKY

Polymer Department, Weizmann Institute of Science,
Rehovoth, Israel

1. Introduction

1.1.
Active transport is a universal property of cells and tissues. It determines the selective influx and outflow of substances and is intimately connected with the cybernetic system of the cells. By its regulatory function, active transport plays an important role in osmoregulation and in the adaptation of organisms to their environment. It seems, therefore, that the evolution of suitable mechanics for active transport was the prerequisite for the evolutionary transition from the sea to sweet water and from rivers to land.

A pronounced expression of active transport is found in biological desalination and ion separation, which to the uninitiated physical chemist seem to be operated by Maxwell's demon. Salt excretion by the glands of desert plants and by the tear glands of reptiles and sea birds, and the accumulation of potassium in certain bacteria against a very large concentration gradient (a three thousand-fold accumulation during the growth phase of Escherichia coli; and an accumulation of 5 moles K^+ from a 1 mM solution in the *Halobacterium valium* of the Dead Sea) are dramatic examples of the "demonic powers" of active transport.

In its high selectivity, its competitive inhibition, its poisoning by specific metabolic inhibitors and its saturation kinetics of flow, active transport is closely related to facilitated transport. If the rate of local reaction coupled to transport is denoted by J_r (in moles/cm^{3}sec) the total turnover per unit membrane per unit time is

$$J_r^{tot} = \int_0^{\Delta x} J_r \, dx \;,$$

where x is a coordinate perpendicular to the membrane surface and Δx the membrane thickness. In facilitated transport $J_r^{tot} = 0$, while in active transport $J_r^{tot} \neq 0$.

1.2.

The conventional method for establishing the existence of active transport is by the study of contra-gradient flows, which proceed from a range of lower to higher chemical potentials. Such ionic flows were found in erythrocyte ghosts, where the contra-gradient pumping of potassium and sodium is clearly due to membrane activity. Since the movement of matter from a lower to a higher potential against the concentration and electrical potential gradients reduces the entropy of the system, active transport would seem to violate the second law of thermodynamics. In the words of Henri Bergson in "Creative Evolution": 'Life is an effort to remount the decline that matter descends, it is riveted to an organism that subjects it to the general laws of inert matter - but everything happens as if it were doing its uttermost to set itself free of these laws'.

To resolve the mystery of active transport we start by writing the entropy change of any system dS as

$$dS = d_eS + d_iS , \tag{1}$$

where d_eS, which may be either positive or negative, is the entropy exchanged with the surroundings and d_iS is the entropy formed *in* the system by irreversible processes. The essence of the second law of thermodynamics is that d_iS is positive definite, or

$$d_iS \geqslant 0 . \tag{2}$$

It is convenient to consider the entropy production per unit time, d_iS/dt, or preferably the dissipation function

$$\phi = T\frac{d_iS}{dt} , \tag{3}$$

which represents the degradation of free energy due to irreversible processes.

As the methods of non-equilibrium thermodynamics show

$$\phi = \sum_i J_iX_i \geqslant 0 , \tag{4}$$

where the J_i's are flows and the X_i's conjugate forces. The flows may be vectorial, such as the flow of electricity and diffusional fluxes, or scalar, such as the progress of chemical reactions. The conjugate forces must have dimensions such that their product with the corresponding flows gives free energy degradation per unit time. Thus, the force driving a flow of electricity is the electrical field $E = (- \text{grad } \psi)$ and the forces driving diffusion are the negative gradients of electrochemical potentials

$$X_i^d = - \text{grad } \tilde{\mu}_i .$$ (5)

An important set of forces driving chemical flows are the affinities A_k, which are given by the difference between the sum of chemical potentials of the reactants and the corresponding sum of the chemical potentials of the reaction products. Consequently the affinity of the kth reaction is

$$A_k = - \sum_{i=1}^{n} \nu_{ik} \mu_i ,$$ (6)

where the ν_{ik}'s are the stoichiometric coefficients of the ith component in the kth reaction, and n is the number of components participating in the reaction.

For a single diffusional flow across a membrane *coupled* with a chemical-metabolic process, eq. (4) may be written as

$$\phi = J_d X_d + J_r A \geqslant 0 ,$$ (7)

which represents the simplest thermodynamic description of active transport. It is worth noting that eq. (7) does not require that both the terms $J_d X_d$ and $J_r A$ be positive - if one is *positive and sufficiently large*, the other may be *negative*. But if, say, the term $J_d X_d$ is negative, the signs of J_d and X_d are opposite, implying that the diffusional flow is in a direction *opposite* to that dictated by the conjugate driving force. Since this is the case of active transport, we may state that coupling with entropy-increasing metabolic processes allows the permeation flow to proceed in an entropy-reducing direction, without contradicting the second law of thermodynamics. Thus the Platonic legacy that the role of the scientist is "to save the phenomena", is fulfilled by the thermodynamics of irreversible processes.

2. Coupling in active transport

2.1.

To make the coupling between chemical reactions and diffusional flows explicit and amenable to quantitative treatment, it is assumed, following Onsager [1], that all the flows are linear functions of all the driving forces. Thus, in the case of a two-flow, two-force system, for which $\phi = J_1 X_1 + J_2 X_2$, we may write

$$J_1 = L_{11} X_1 + L_{12} X_2$$

$$J_2 = L_{21} X_1 + L_{22} X_2 \, , \tag{8}$$

where L_{11} and L_{22} are the straight coefficients relating X_1 to J_1 and X_2 to J_2 respectively, while L_{12} and L_{21} are the coupling coefficients. The coefficient L_{12} expresses the dependence of the flow J_1 on the coupled force X_2, while L_{21} describes the dependence of J_2 on X_1, and, as shown by Onsager, in the linear range $L_{12} = L_{21}$. The set of eqs. (8) may be transformed to an equivalent form

$$X_1 = R_{11} J_1 + R_{12} J_2$$

$$X_2 = R_{21} J_1 + R_{22} J_2 \, , \tag{9}$$

where the thermodynamic resistances R_{ij} also obey the Onsager symmetry relation $R_{12} = R_{21}$.

For active transport in which a single diffusional flow is coupled to a chemical reaction, we may write for the local behavior at a point within the membrane

$$\phi = J_d \, \text{grad} \, (-\mu) + J_r A \tag{10}$$

and for the flow-force relations, according to eq. (9),

$$\text{grad} \, (-\mu) = R_{11} J_d + R_{12} J_r$$

$$A = R_{12} J_d + R_{22} J_r \, . \tag{11}$$

This expression was used by Kedem [2] to define active transport as the non-vanishing of R_{12}.

Equation (11) has two difficulties when applied to real systems. It will be observed that J_d is vectorial while J_r is scalar; since grad $(-\mu)$ is a vector, R_{11} is a scalar function while R_{12} must be a vector. This observation leads to the conclusion that R_{12} has to vanish in an isotropic medium, hence diffusion and reaction can only be coupled locally in anisotropic media. Thus in order to derive the *local* coupling underlying active transport, biological membranes have to be endowed with structural anisotropy in the direction of diffusional flow. It seems that this condition is actually fulfilled in the case of biomembranes, which are two-dimensional operators, endowed with a topological organization which determines the pattern of flow across the membrane, so that eq. (11) is applicable. The other difficulty is more serious, and stems from the fact that we have no information about the local flows and forces in biomembrane systems, so that eq. (11) cannot be used in its exact form. If we are to utilize eq. (11), we should integrate the expression over the membrane thickness and introduce as flows and forces other parameters such as the chemical potentials and flows in the cell or in the surrounding medium. As will be shown below, this can be done if the flows are steady so that the parameters of state do not alter with time. A more general treatment was given by Katchalsky and Oster [3], as well as by Sauer [4] and by Caplan et al. [5]; a simpler derivation based on a discussion with Oster, Lavenda and Perelson is given in the appendix.

The integration procedure leads to a dissipation function which comprises only extra membrane quantities

$$\phi = \sum_i J_i^{in} \Delta\tilde{\mu}_i + \sum_k J_r^k A_k^c , \qquad (12)$$

where the J^{in}'s denote permeation flows entering the cell from the *outside* and the $\Delta\tilde{\mu}_i$'s are the differences of electrochemical potential across the membrane. The J_r^k's denote the *total* chemical turnover of the kth reaction taking place *within* the membrane, and the A_k^c's are the conjugate affinities within the cell.

2.2.

The natural procedure is to write the equivalent of eq. (11) for the external flows and forces, where for a single diffusional flow and a single chemical reaction the phenomenological equations assume the form

$$\Delta\mu = R_{11}J_d^{in} + R_{12}J_r^{tot}$$

$$A = R_{21}J_d^{in} + R_{22}J_r^{tot} \ . \tag{13}$$

Moreover, the Onsager symmetry relations, $R_{12} = R_{21}$, can be shown to also hold for the overall flows and forces [3,4] . The condition of stationarity makes the overall R_{12} a non-vanishing quantity, even if for isotropic membranes the local $R_{12} = 0$. Since most of the studies of active transport were carried out at steady state, the possibility of *stationary state coupling - which does not reflect intrinsic dependencies between chemical and permeation flows -* should be borne in mind.

2.3.

To demonstrate the utility of the phenomenological eqs. (13) let us apply them to the analysis of sodium flow in the frog skin. From the classical work of Ussing and Zerahn [6] it is well known that in the transport of sodium chloride across the skin it is the flow of sodium ions (J_{Na}) which is coupled to the metabolic process (J_r^{tot}), while the flow of the chloride ions (J_{Cl}) may be assumed to proceed in a passive manner.

The driving forces for the sodium, the chloride and the metabolic flows are $\Delta\tilde{\mu}_{Na}$, $\Delta\tilde{\mu}_{Cl}$ and A, respectively. It will, however, be noted that the driving forces for the ionic flows are not the differences in the chemical potential $(\Delta\mu_i)$ but in the electrochemical potential $\Delta\tilde{\mu}_i$, which comprises both the difference in concentration and in the electrical potential. In simple cases it may be written as

$$\Delta\tilde{\mu}_i = RT(\ln c_i^I - \ln c_i^{II}) + z_i F(\psi^I - \psi^{II}) \ , \tag{14}$$

where I and II denote the compartments adjacent to the membrane, z_i is the valence of the ion, ψ the electrical potential and F the Faraday.

Eqs. (13) may now be written explicitly as

$$\Delta\tilde{\mu}_{Na} = R_{Na}J_{Na} + R_{Na\,r}J_r^{tot}$$

$$\Delta\tilde{\mu}_{Cl} = R_{Cl}J_{Cl}$$

$$A = R_{Na\,r}J_{Na} + R_r J_r^{tot} \ . \tag{15}$$

In eqs. (15) we have assumed that no hydrodynamic coupling exists between sodium and chloride flows.

Equations (15) may now be applied to two experimental cases.

2.3.1. Short circuit

Two electrodes inserted one in each compartment are short circuited so that the potential difference $(\psi^I - \psi^{II})$ is made zero and an electrical current I is allowed to flow across the membrane. The experiment is carried out at equal salt concentrations in I and II so that $\ln c^I - \ln c^{II} = 0$. Thus by eq. (14)

$$\Delta\tilde{\mu}_{Na} = 0 \qquad \text{and} \qquad \Delta\tilde{\mu}_{Cl} = 0 \tag{16}$$

and the only driving force of the process is the affinity A of the metabolic reaction.

Inserting eq. (16) into (15) we find that

$$J_{Na} = -\frac{R_{Na\,r}}{R_{Na}} J_r^{tot} , \qquad J_{Cl} = 0 . \tag{17}$$

Since the flow of electricity is determined by the ionic fluxes

$$I = (J_{Na} - J_{Cl})F , \tag{18}$$

which with eq. (17) gives

$$I = -\frac{R_{Na\,r}}{R_{Na}} J_r^{tot} F . \tag{19}$$

Thus under short circuited conditions the electrical current is linearly proportional to the overall rate of the reaction and the existence of a non-vanishing proportionality coefficient depends on the fact that the coupling coefficient $R_{Na\,r} \neq 0$.

2.3.2. Open circuit

In the case of a potentiometric experiment, in which $I = 0$, both J_{Na} and J_{Cl} vanish so that

$$\Delta\tilde{\mu}_{Na} = R_{Na\,r} J_r^{tot}$$

$$\Delta\tilde{\mu}_{Cl} = 0 . \tag{20}$$

To reach a steady state the concentrations and electrical potentials in compartments I and II have to be different. From eqs. (14) and (20) we learn that

$$RT \ln \frac{c_{Na}^{I}}{c_{Na}^{II}} + F(\psi^{I}-\psi^{II}) = R_{Na\ r} J_{r}^{tot}$$

$$RT \ln \frac{c_{Cl}^{I}}{c_{Cl}^{II}} - F(\psi^{I}-\psi^{II}) = 0 ,$$

which upon addition give the distribution of salt in both compartments

$$RT \ln \frac{c_{Na}^{I} c_{Cl}^{I}}{c_{Na}^{II} c_{Cl}^{II}} = R_{Na\ r} J_{r}^{tot} ,$$

or, since $c_{Na}^{I} = c_{Cl}^{I}$ is the salt concentration in compartment I, c_{s}^{I}, and the same holds for compartment II, we finally obtain

$$2RT \ln \frac{c_{s}^{I}}{c_{s}^{II}} = R_{Na\ r} J_{r}^{tot} . \tag{21}$$

Equation (21) shows that the non-equal salt distribution in an open circuit experiment is again due to the existence of a non-vanishing coupling coefficient $R_{Na\ r}$. If the rate of reaction J_{r}^{tot} is known the comparison of the results obtained in experiments 2.3.1 and 2.3.2 allows the explicit evaluation of the coupling and of the straight coefficients.

3. An alternative treatment of chemico-diffusional coupling. The relaxation length

3.1.

It may be advantageous to reconsider from an alternative point of view the coupling of diffusional flow with chemical reaction which underlie active transport. The starting point of our consideration is the equation of continuity, which expresses the local conservation of mass. Without attempting a rigorous derivation it is clear that the change with time of the local concentration of the ith component, $\partial c_i/\partial t$, is due to the net inflow of substance i by diffusional flows $(-\mathrm{div}\,J_i)$ and the change due to chemical reaction $(\nu_i J_r)$, i.e.

$$\frac{\partial c_i}{\partial t} = - \operatorname{div} J_i + v_i J_r .$$ (22)

If the diffusional flow proceeds only in one direction - e.g. along the x-coordinate perpendicular to the surface of the membrane - eq. (22) reduces to the simpler form

$$\frac{\partial c_i}{\partial t} = - \frac{dJ_i}{dx} + v_i J_r .$$ (23)

In aged systems for which a steady state is attained the local parameters of state do not vary with time so that

$$\frac{\partial c_i}{\partial t} = 0 \quad \text{and} \quad \frac{dJ_i}{dx} = v_i J_r .$$ (24)

Equation (24) shows that a stationary state imposes a relation between diffusion and reaction - even if there exists no intrinsic local coupling between the processes. This relation is of special interest in isotropic membranes for which the coupling coefficients R_{12} in eq. (11) vanish.

3.2.

In homogeneous and isotropic media the phenomenological equations may be written as the uncoupled system:

$$- \frac{d\mu_i}{dx} = \sum_k R_{ik} J_k$$

$$A = R_r J_r .$$ (25)

• Let us now assume that the R's are for the most part independent of position so that dR_{ik}/dx is negligible compared to other quantities. If the first equation of (25) is differentiated with respect to x and eq. (24) inserted, it follows that

$$- \frac{d^2\mu_i}{dx^2} = \sum_k R_{ik} \frac{dJ_k}{dx} = \left(\sum_k v_k R_{ik} \right) J_r .$$

Multiplying both sides by ν_i and summing over i

$$-\sum_i \nu_i \frac{d^2\mu_i}{dx^2} = \left(\sum_{i,k} \nu_i\nu_k R_{ik}\right) J_r .$$

From the definition of the affinity, $A = -\sum_i \nu_i\mu_i$, we find that

$$\frac{d^2A}{dx^2} = -\sum_i \nu_i \frac{d^2\mu_i}{dx^2} ,$$

and further inserting J_r from the second of eqs. (25) we finally get

$$\frac{d^2A}{dx^2} = \left(\sum_{i,k} \frac{\nu_i\nu_k R_{ik}}{R_r}\right) A . \tag{26}$$

The expression

$$\sum_{i,k} \frac{\nu_i\nu_k R_{ik}}{R_r}$$

has the dimensions of cm^{-2} and will be denoted as λ^{-2} so that

$$\frac{d^2A}{dx^2} = \lambda^{-2}A . \tag{27}$$

Equation (27) describes the *field* of the affinities within the membrane. The characteristic parameter λ was denoted by Friedlander and Keller [7] as the "relaxation length" of the coupled chemico-diffusional process within the membrane. If the thickness of the membrane is Δx then the pure number $\lambda/\Delta x$ is closely related to the Thiele [8] modulus used for many years by the chemical engineers for the characterization of heterogeneous reaction columns. It may be shown that if the relaxation time of the chemical reaction is τ_r and the average relaxation time of the diffusional processes occurring in the membrane is $\langle\tau_d\rangle$ then

A.KATCHALSKY

$$\left(\frac{\lambda}{\Delta x}\right)^2 = \frac{\tau_r}{2\langle\tau_d\rangle} .$$ (28)

Equation (28) clarifies why λ was denoted the relaxation length. If the reaction relaxes much quicker than the time for diffusion across the membrane, i.e. if $\tau_r < \langle\tau_d\rangle$, then the relaxation length λ will be smaller than Δx, and the reaction will reach equilibrium after the reactants have diffused only a short distance within the membrane. In this case the reaction may be assumed to attain equilibrium on the surface of the membrane. If on the other hand Δx is very small - which is generally the case in biological membranes - τ_r and $\langle\tau_d\rangle$ may be of the same order of magnitude, so that an equilibrium treatment is not possible.

A fuller treatment of membrane behavior utilizing the field equation (27) is given in the paper of Katchalsky and Oster [3].

4. Dissipative structures

If several simultaneous reactions proceed within the membrane, the continuity equation (23) should be generalized to the form

$$\frac{\partial c_i}{\partial t} = -\frac{dJ_i}{dx} + \sum_k \nu_{ik} J_r^k .$$ (29)

In order to relate the numerous coupling coefficients to relaxation lengths, a single relaxation length is insufficient and a matrix of λ's is required to describe the distribution of concentrations and affinities within the system. There is no intention to involve the reader in the intricacies of the calculations needed to solve chemico-diffusional coupling for these more complex - though more realistic systems. It is, however, interesting to observe that for multireaction processes some of the stationary states are unstable and that some of the solutions are of an oscillatory nature. The unstable stationary states undergo a spontaneous transition to stable stationary states which are often characterized by a non-isotropic symmetry. The first person to recognize the existence of unstable stationary states was Turing [9] who foresaw the possibility of symmetry breaking and spatial structuring through coupled chemical and diffusional processes.

Dynamic flow structures based on dissipative processes were recently denoted by Prigogine [10] as "dissipative structures" and their biophysical significance in morphogenetic and kinetic phenomena is now being studied in several laboratories. In addition also Gmitro and Scriven [11] pointed out that some of the periodic solutions of eq. (29) lead to propagating waves which may be involved in the transport of substances. Though the relation of these theoretical predictions to active transport is still unknown, it is of interest to look for dissipative waves as biological transport agents.

5. Appendix

Consider a three compartment system comprising two external baths (I and II) and a membrane compartment (m). For the sake of simplicity, it is assumed that the temperature is the same throughout the system and that the volumes of the compartments are constant so that $dV_I = dV_{II} = dV_m = 0$.

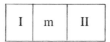

The Gibbs equations for the three compartments are in this case:

$$dU_I = TdS_I + \sum_i \mu_i^I dn_i^I$$

$$dU_{II} = TdS_{II} + \sum_i \mu_i^{II} dn_i^{II}$$

$$dU_m = TdS_m + \sum_i \mu_i^m dn_i^m . \qquad (1a)$$

It is assumed that reaction takes place only in the membrane compartment so that

$$dn_i^m = dn_i^{exch} + dn_i^{react} , \qquad (2a)$$

where dn_i^{exch} is the number of moles of the ith component exchanged with the surroundings, while dn_i^{react} is the number of moles of i produced by chemical reaction. Denoting the degree of advancement of the kth chemical process by ξ_k, we may write for dn_i^{react}

$$dn_i^{react} = \sum_k \nu_{ik} \, d\xi_k \, , \tag{3a}$$

where the ν_{ik}'s are the same as in eq. (6). Inserting (2a) and (3a) into the Gibbs equation for the membrane compartment, and using eq. (6), we obtain

$$dU_m = T dS_m + \sum_i \mu_i \, dn_i^{exch} - \sum_k A_k^m \, d\xi_k \, , \tag{4a}$$

where A_k^m is the affinity of the kth reaction *within the membrane.*

Now since I, II and m constitute a closed system

$$dU^I + dU^{II} + dU^m = 0$$

and

$$dn_i^I + dn_i^{II} + dn_i^{exch} = 0 \, . \tag{5a}$$

Further, upon summing the entropy contributions of the three compartments, the exchangeable terms ($d_e S$ in eq. (1)) cancel, and only the terms due to the irreversible processes in the three compartments remain. Denoting their sum as $d_i S$ we find

$$dS_I + dS_{II} + dS_m = d_i S_I + d_i S_{II} + d_i S_m = d_i S \, . \tag{6a}$$

Hence, by adding the expressions in eq. (1a) and utilizing eqs. (4a), (5a) and (6a), we obtain

$$T d_i S + \sum_i (\mu_i^I - \mu_i^m) \, dn_i^I - \sum_i (\mu_i^m - \mu_i^{II}) \, dn_i^{II} - \sum_k A_k^m \, d\xi_k = 0 \, . \tag{7a}$$

Dividing by dt we obtain an expression for the dissipation function of the system, $\phi = T(d_i S/dt)$.

The introduction of several new symbols is found to be useful. If we regard compartment I as the surroundings of the cell, $-dn_i^I$ is the number of moles of the ith component lost by the surrounding and *gained by the membrane* through diffusional processes. It follows that the *input* flow to the membrane of the ith component is

$$J_i^{in} = -\frac{dn_i^I}{dt} \, .$$

Similarly, dn_i^{II} denotes the number of moles of species i *lost by the membrane* and transported into the cell by diffusion. We denote the *output* flow of the component i from the membrane into the cell by

$$J_i^{out} = \frac{dn_i^{II}}{dt} .$$

Further,

$$\Delta\mu_i^{in} = \Delta\mu_i^{I} - \Delta\mu_i^{m}$$

is the macroscopic driving force for the input flow, while

$$\Delta\mu_i^{out} = \mu_i^{m} - \mu_i^{II}$$

is the overall driving force for the outflow from the membrane into the cell. Finally, noting that the total rate of the kth chemical process within the membrane is

$$J_r^k = \frac{d\xi_k}{dt} ,$$

we can rewrite eq. (7a) in the form

$$\phi = T\frac{d_iS}{dt} = \sum_i J_i^{in}\Delta\mu_i^{in} + \sum_i J_i^{out}\Delta\mu_i^{out} + \sum_k A_k^m J_r^k . \qquad (8a)$$

Although eq. (8a) is written in terms of inputs and outputs to the membrane, we still need to know the magnitudes of the chemical potentials within the membrane, μ_i^m, in order to evaluate $\Delta\mu_i^{in}$, $\Delta\mu_i^{out}$ and A_k^m.

In order to overcome this difficulty, we utilize the fact that under steady state conditions the difference between the diffusional output and input flows of the ith component equals the amount of the ith component transformed in all chemical processes, or

$$J_i^{out} - J_i^{in} = \sum_k \nu_{ik} J_r^k . \qquad (9a)$$

Writing the last term of eq. (8a) and inserting (9a) we find:

$$\sum_k A_k^m J_r^k = - \sum_k \left(\sum_i \nu_{ik} \mu_i^m \right) J_r^k = - \sum_i \mu_i^m \sum_k \nu_{ik} J_r^k$$

$$= - \sum_i \mu_i^m (J_i^{out} - J_i^{in}) \tag{10a}$$

which upon introduction into (8a) gives

$$\phi = \sum_i J_i^{in} \mu_i^I - \sum_i J_i^{out} \mu_i^{II} . \tag{11a}$$

Equation (11a) is based on external parameters alone; however, since chemical potentials are unmeasurable and only their difference can be determined, eq. (11a) must be transformed further. Introducing the affinity of the kth reaction *in the cell* or in compartment II, by the symbol A_k^c, where

$$A_k^c = A_k^{II} = - \sum_i \nu_{ik} \mu_i^{II} , \tag{12a}$$

and inserting J_i^{out} from (9a) we finally get

$$\phi = \sum_i J_i^{in} (\mu_i^I - \mu_i^{II}) + \sum_k J_r^k A_k^c , \tag{13a}$$

or

$$\phi = \sum_i J_i^{in} \Delta\mu_i + \sum_k J_r^k A_k^c$$

where $\Delta\mu_i = \mu_i^I - \mu_i^{II}$ is the measurable, cross-membrane difference of chemical potentials.

The dissipation function (13a) will be used in the thermodynamic consideration of active transport.

References

[1] L.Onsager, Phys. Rev. 37 (1931) 405; 38 (1931) 2265.
[2] O.Kedem, in: Membrane Transport and Metabolism, eds. A.Kleinzeller and A.Kotyk (Academic Press, New York, 1961) p. 87.
[3] A.Katchalsky and G.Oster, in: Molecular Basis of Membrane Function, ed. D.C. Tosteson (Prentice Hall, New York, 1969).

[4] F.Sauer, Stationärer Stoff Transport durch Membranen von Makroskopischer Dicke (to be published).

[5] S.R.Caplan, J.N.Weinstein and B.Bunnow, Coupling Phenomena in Synthetic Membranes, Saline Water Conversion Report (1968), OSW U.S. Department of the Interior, Washington, D.C.

[6] H.H.Ussing and K.Zerahn, Acta Physiol. Scand. 23 (1951) 110.

[7] S.K.Friedlander and K.H.Keller, Chem. Eng. Sci. 20 (1965) 121.

[8] E.W.Thiele, Ind. Eng. Chem. 31 (1939) 916.

[9] A.M.Turing, Phil. Trans. Roy. Soc. London Ser. B237 (1952) 37.

[10] I.Prigogine, in: Theoretical Physics and Biology, ed. M.Marois (North-Holland, Amsterdam, 1969) p. 23.

[11] J.L.Gmitro and L.E.Scriven, in: Intracellular Transport, ed. K.B.Warren (Academic Press, New York, 1965) p. 221.

TRANSPORT PROPERTIES AS RELATED TO CONFORMATIONAL CHANGES OF PROTEINS*

A.GLIOZZI, V.VITTORIA and A.CIFERRI

Physics Department, University of Genoa, Genoa, Italy
and *Research Laboratory for Polymer Technology and Rheology,*
National Research Council, Arco Felice, Naples, Italy

The possibility that conformational changes of proteins are important in the functioning of biological membranes [1,2] has stimulated our interest in the transport properties of model systems undergoing phase transition. Previous work [3] includes the characterization of transport properties for cross-linked collagen films undergoing phase transition at the near isoelectric pH in the presence of neutral salts. Herein, we report a characterization of the transport properties of cross-linked collagen films in the case of a charge-induced phase transition.

It has already been demonstrated that, on lowering pH, the increase of the net number of fixed charges on the collagen molecules is adequate to bring about a melting transition (shrinkage) in the case of collagen tendons [4], or a helix-random coil transition in the case of soluble tropocollagen [5]. In the former case [4], a large increase of swelling occurs on lowering pH as a result of both the Donnan effect and the conformational transition.

In the present experimental conditions, doubly-oriented collagen films (25 μ thick), obtained by casting a dispersion of steer tendon fibrils and cross-linking with p-benzoquinone [3], were analyzed while in equilibrium swelling with a 10^{-2} M KCl solution in H_2O at $T = 52°C$.

The variations of length and volume with pH (determined as described elsewhere [4]) are reproduced in figs 1a and 1b respectively. These results (as well as independent optical and elasticity measurements [4]) indicate that the phase transition occurs within the pH range 3.1 to 2.2. Above and below this pH range, the membrane is, respectively, in the crystalline and in the amorphous state.

---

* This is a contribution to the discussion of A.Katchalsky's paper "A thermodynamic consideration of active transport", and presented by A.Katchalsky.

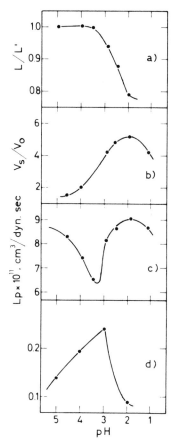

Fig. 1. (a) Variation of length (relative to the value at pH = 5) with pH for a collagen film (cross-linked by exposure to a 0.1% p-benzoquinone solution [3] for 5 min) immersed in a 10^{-2} M KCl solution. $T = 52°$C. (b) Corresponding variation of the degree of swelling (relative to the dry volume) with pH. (c) Corresponding variation of the filtration coefficient with pH. (d) Corresponding variation of the reflection coefficient with pH.

The pH-variation of the filtration coefficient L_p (determined [3] by clamping the membrane between two half-cells with identical solutions on both sides and following the rate of flow due to a pressure gradient across the membrane) is reported in fig. 1c. Although some hyperfiltration properties of the membrane were found, the rate of flow was constant with time, owing to the great volume of the two half-cells as compared to the volume flowing through the membrane. The filtration coefficient was thus obtained by simply dividing [3] the volume flow J_v by the difference of pressure ΔP. The results indicate an increase of L_p during the phase transition. Moreover, comparison of figs. 1b and 1c indicates that the trend of $\partial L_p/\partial$pH and of $\partial(V_s/V_o)/\partial$pH is similar when the membrane is amorphous and opposite when the membrane is crystalline. Similar features were already observed in previous work [3], where the transport properties of collagen membranes were investigated as function of salt concentration at the near isoelectric pH.

Thus, when the degree of swelling increases, L_p *decreases* if the membrane is in the crystalline state. However, in the amorphous state and during the transition an increase of swelling is accompanied by an *increase* of L_p. Since the electrical characteristics of the membrane do not primarily affect L_p (only a 5% variation in L_p can be due to streaming potential), the above results suggest that swelling in the crystalline state improves the homogeneity of the membrane (perhaps by closing up structural voids [3]). In the amorphous state, instead, swelling (or deswelling) produces an increase (or a decrease) of the filtration coefficient, as can be expected in a homogeneous membrane.

The electrical properties of the membrane are here described by the reflection coefficient σ, defined by the phenomenological equations of irreversible thermodynamics [6] as

$$\sigma = (\Delta P/\Delta\pi)_{J_v=0} = -L_{pd}/L_p , \qquad (1)$$

where $\Delta\pi$ is the osmotic pressure difference between the two half-cells and L_{pd} is the diffusional cross-coefficient of the phenomenological equation of flow. In the present experiments, σ was measured using two different KCl solutions (10^{-2} and 5×10^{-3} M) in the two half cells and measuring the hydrostatic pressure difference needed to make the volume flow vanishing. One can observe, from fig. 1d, an inversion in the trend of σ as a result of the phase transition.

In order to interpret the latter result we consider the expression of σ for a monovalent salt [6]

$$\sigma = 1 - \omega V_s/L_p - C_s\varphi_W/Xt_1^0 , \qquad (2)$$

where ω is the diffusion coefficient of the salt, V_s is the partial molar volume of salt, C_s is the mean concentration between the two external solutions, t_1^0 is the transport number of the counter-ion in free solution, φ_W is the volume fraction of water inside the membrane and X the fixed charge concentration.

In the present case, an independent measure of ω with tracers [3] gives values in the range of 10^{-13} to 3×10^{-14} mol/dyn $\times$ sec. Thus, the second term in eq. (2) is in the range 5×10^{-2} to 3×10^{-2}. As C_s and t_1^0 depend only on the properties of the external solutions and can be considered constant with pH, one can see that σ (which is in the range 0.1 to 0.2, cf. fig. 1d) is primarily determined by the ratio φ_W/X or, in other terms, by the competition between swelling and charge concentration X. In the crystalline state the charge concentration X increases more than φ_W does, thus leading to the observed increase of σ. During the phase transition, however, swelling increases far more than X does, thus leading to the observed decrease of σ.

References

[1] I.Tasaki, Nerve Excitation (Springfield, Illinois, 1968).
[2] J.P.Changeux, J.Thiery, Y.Tung and C.Kittel, Proc. Natl. Acad. Sci. 57 (1967) 335.
[3] A.Gliozzi, R.Morchio and A.Ciferri, J. Phys. Chem. 73 (1969) 3063.
[4] A.Ciferri, L.Rajagh and D.Puett, Biopolymers 3 (1965) 461.
[5] E.Bianchi, A.Ciferri, G.Conio, D.Puett and L.Rajagh, J. Biol. Chem. 242 (1967) 1361.
[6] A.Katchalsky and P.F.Curran, Non Equilibrium Thermodynamics in Biophysics (Harvard University Press, Cambridge, Mass., 1965).

MEMBRANE EXPANSION AND STABILIZATION BY ANESTHETICS AND OTHER DRUGS

Philip SEEMAN

Department of Pharmacology, University of Toronto, Toronto, Canada

1. General property of membrane stabilization by drugs

The term "membrane stabilization" was introduced into neurophysiology in 1940 by Guttman, who found that alkaline earth metals prevented or stabilized the nerve membrane resting potential from depolarization by potassium or veratrine. The work of Shanes [40,41] broadened this idea of membrane stabilization; any compound which inhibited a change in the membrane resting potential was termed a "stabilizer".

It is possible to extend this idea of membrane stabilization further to include the action of a wide variety of drugs on many types of cell and subcellular membranes. It is possible that the comparison of many different types of membrane-drug interactions may help elucidate some of the events involved in the action of anesthetics on nerve membranes.

The data in figs. 1 and 2 represent a partial review of the literature on this subject [32,35,38]. It can be seen that a wide variety of drugs at very low concentrations protect or stabilize cellular or subcellular membranes from disruption or release of their enclosed contents.

The top parts of figs. 1 and 2 show that low concentrations of steroids (testosterone, pregnanolone), tranquilizers (butyrylperazine), phospholipids (lysolecithin), fat-soluble vitamins (vitamin A), anesthetics (nonanol), and anti-inflammatory compounds (flufenamic acid, indomethacin, phenylbutazone, chloroquine and sodium acetylsalicylate) all reduce the amount of osmotic hemolysis of erythrocytes [14,32,21]. The ordinate value of 1.0 represents approximately 50% hemolysis that occurs in the absence of any drugs.

High concentrations of all these compounds, except the salicylates, cause lysis, and the dose-response curve, therefore, is in general biphasic. Saponin and filipin, which both have an extremely high affinity for membrane cholesterol, only cause lysis without any stabilizing effect at low concentrations.

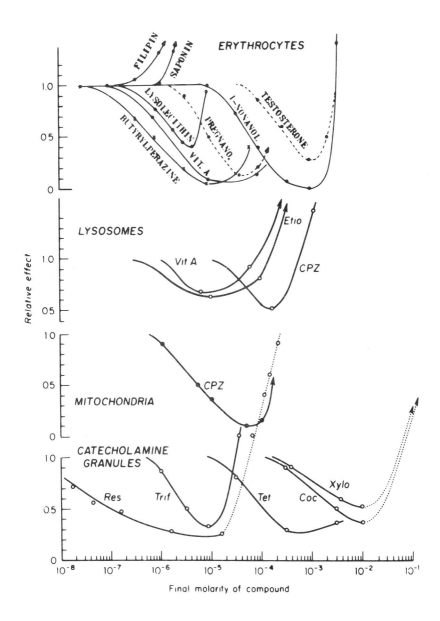

Fig. 1. Showing that low concentrations of many drugs stabilize membranes and that high concentrations lead to the opposite effect. See text for details.

The membranes of such subcellular particles as lysosomes, mitochondria and secretion granules are also protected or stabilized at low concentrations of these drugs. Fig. 1 shows that the spontaneous release of acid hydrolases from secondary lysosomes is reduced by vitamin A [16], chlorpromazine [11] and etiocholanolone [56]. As with erythrocytes, high concentrations of these compounds have an opposite effect, and the enzyme release-rate is enhanced. The swelling rate of mitochondria is reduced by low concentrations of chlorpromazine, but accelerated at high concentrations [45].

The bottom part of fig. 1 shows that the spontaneous release-rate of adrenaline from chromaffin granules is reduced by tranquilizers (trifluperazine, reserpine) and anesthetics (tetracaine, xylocaine, cocaine) at low concentrations but accelerated at higher concentrations [55,49-53]. It is interesting to note that Grobecker et al. [9] have found that prenylamine protects erythrocytes from hypotonic hemolysis in about the same low drug concentration region as that which inhibits the spontaneous release of catecholamines from granules of sympathetic nerves [53] and ganglia [27].

The work of Tanaka and Iizuka [46] on the effect of anti-inflammatory compounds (flufenamic acid, indomethacin, phenylbutazone and sodium acetylsalicylate) on the release of lysosomal enzymes is shown in fig. 2. These results are in qualitative and almost quantitative agreement with the findings of Inglot and Wolna [14] on the erythrocyte.

Recent work by Lee et al. [20] indicates that the drug SKF-525-A (beta-diethylaminoethyl-diphenylpropyl acetate HCl), which is an inhibitor of protein and cholesterol biosynthesis, as well as an inhibitor of many liver microsomal enzymes, also stabilizes erythrocytes at low concentrations and causes lysis at high drug concentrations.

Deuticke [7] has found that compounds which reduce osmotic fragility also induce shape changes of the erythrocyte at drug concentrations which are approximately 10 times higher than those required for anti-hemolysis. Deuticke has found that cup-shaped cells are induced by cationic compounds, and crenated shapes by anionic and non-ionic substances.

2. Correlation between membrane stabilization and anesthesia

The concentrations of various anesthetics which protect erythrocytes against osmotic hemolysis are virtually identical to the concentrations required to anesthetize isolated frog sciatic nerves. This is shown in fig. 3 where the minimal blocking concentrations [43] are plotted on the ordinate and where the concentrations which produce 50% reduction in osmotic hemolysis are plotted

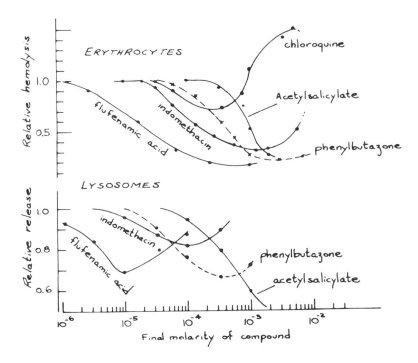

Fig. 2. A comparison of the membrane stabilizing effects of anti-inflammatory compounds on erythrocyte membranes and lysosome membranes. Modified from Inglot and
Wolna (1968) and from Tanaka and Iizuka (1968).

on the abscissa. The inhibition of the tadpole response by alcohols [22] also
correlates with the erythrocyte protective concentrations.

   A large number of drugs have now been tested, and it has been found that
all compounds which are anesthetics can protect the erythrocyte. The only
exception is tetrodotoxin. Tetrodotoxin is also an exception to the fact that
most anesthetics act on both sides of the neurolemma while tetrodotoxin only
acts on the exterior of the membrane [25,26].

   Because of the fact that anesthetics stabilize nerve membranes and erythrocyte membranes at the same concentrations, and because just about all anesthetics stabilize both membranes, the erythrocyte membrane may be a useful
model for studying the property of membrane stabilization in general and
membrane anesthesia in particular.

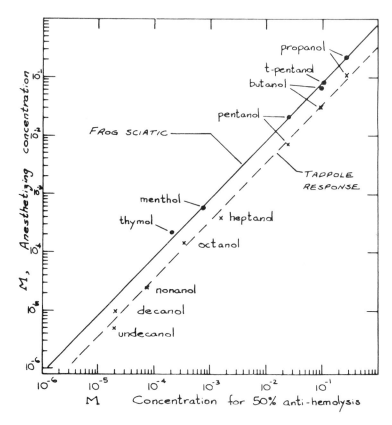

Fig. 3. Showing that alcohol anesthetics stabilize erythrocyte membranes and nerve membranes at almost identical concentrations. Data from Skou (1958) and from Meyer and Hemmi (1935).

3. Membrane expansion by anesthetics

It is known that monolayers of lipid, protein and lipo-protein spread on a Langmuir trough can be penetrated and expanded by drugs added to the subjacent bulk phase [6,4]. Both Shanes [42] and Skou [44] have predicted that an expansion of biomembranes would occur in the presence of anesthetics, on the basis that such an expansion does occur in a lipid monolayer at the air/water interface.

The mechanism for the anesthetic-induced protection of erythrocytes

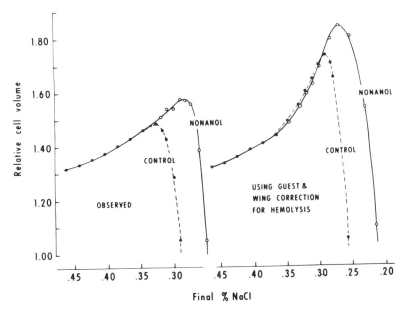

Fig. 4. Nonanol increases the critical hemolytic volume of erythrocytes.

against osmotic hemolysis appears to be that the drug expands the area of the membrane. The area/volume ratio of the cell is thus increased and the cell can harbour more water before bursting.

An example of this anesthetic-induced increase in critical hemolytic volume is shown in fig. 4. It can be seen that nonanol shifted the osmotic fragility and increased the critical hemolytic volume. The concentration of nonanol is that shown in fig. 3. The data on the right of fig. 4 were obtained after a Guest and Wing correction [10].

The increase in hemolytic volume is not because the membrane is more slowly stretched in the presence of the anesthetic. Fig. 5 shows that if the membrane is stretched more slowly (injecting hypotonic solution into the hemolysis tube at a slow rate of 0.34 ml/min), the osmotic fragility is indeed shifted [15] but there is no increase in critical hemolytic volume. The explanation for the shift in osmotic fragility in slow hemolysis is that the cells lose about 20% of the intracellular potassium ions in the brief pre-lytic phase; normally, in fast hemolysis only about 10% is lost. This is shown in fig. 6.

It is also possible to measure the expansion of erythrocyte ghost mem-

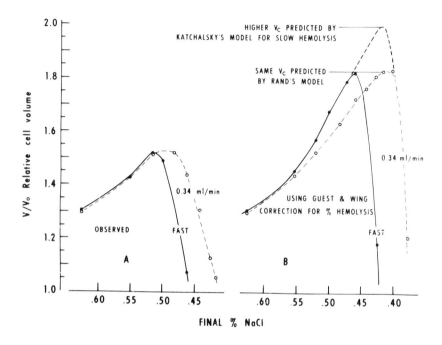

Fig. 5. Slow hemolysis (0.34 ml/min) shifts the osmotic fragility curve compared to fast hemolysis (about 100 ml/min) but does not increase the critical hemolytic volume.

branes by anesthetics. It has been shown [38] that erythrocytes (about 80.000 cells/ml), hemolysed in 0.9% NaCl, 10 mM sodium phosphate buffer, pH 7, re-seal and re-swell to become spherical ghosts of mean cell volume of about 145 cubic microns (135 μ^2 in area).

The addition of an anesthetic to these spherical ghosts makes the cells irregular at first. Two hours later, however, the cells re-sphere and it is found that the mean cell volume increases. This is shown in fig. 7.

4. The hydrophobic nature of the anesthetic-membrane interaction

The nature of the bond between the anesthetic molecule and the membrane was studied [29,18]. The absorption of radioactive isotopes of chlor-

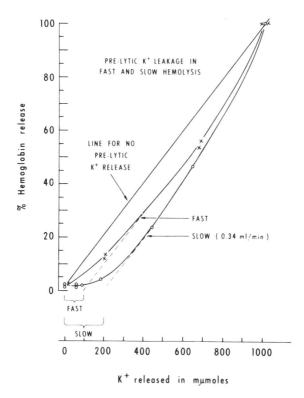

Fig. 6. In fast hemolysis about 10% of the intracellular leaks out prelytically; in slow
hemolysis this increases to about 20%.

promazine and the alcohols to hemoglobin-free erythrocyte membranes was
measured.

The results in fig. 8 show the adsorption isotherms for octanol, nonanol and
decanol. The values were obtained by measuring the radioactivity remaining
in the supernatant after the ghosts were centrifuged at 39,600 × g for 15 min
at 20°C. Dry weight determinations of the stock ghost suspension were made
and these were usually around 1 g dry membranes per 100 ml of ghost suspension. The amount of alcohol bound to the membrane is expressed as
moles of alcohol bound per liter of hydrated membrane. If the density of
the normally hydrated membrane is 1.17 [23,1] and if the degree of membrane hydration is 30% at 20°C [5], then the density of the dry membrane
is 1.24 g/ml. The concentration of drug in the hydrated membrane, therefore,

P.SEEMAN

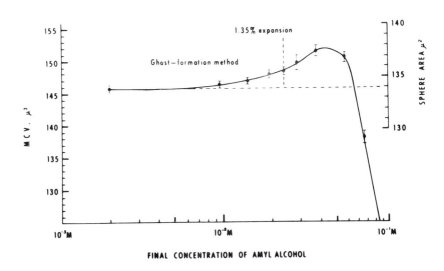

Fig. 7. The expansion of erythrocyte ghosts by amyl alcohol. The mean cell volumes are
measured using a Coulter counter and mean cell volume computer.

will be 70% × 1.24 × $C_{dry\ membrane}$, where $C_{dry\ membrane}$ is the amount of
drug bound per kg of dry membrane.

The data in fig. 8 indicate that the alcohols have a similar number of
binding sites on the membrane since they have a common intercept on the
ordinate. The affinity constants of the alcohols for the membranes were calculated, and the free energy of adsorption was derived by the equation $F =
-RT \ln K$. The free energies of absorption are shown in fig. 9.

The results in fig. 9 indicate that the free energy of adsorption per methyl
group is 820 cal/mole $-CH_2$ group. This is the value (about 809 cal/mole) predicted by Schneider [31] for the anesthetic-membrane bond. It is quantitatively in agreement with the value for a hydrophobic bond, which is for example, about 900 cal/mole $-CH_2$ for the adsorption of alcohols to polystyrene
[30].

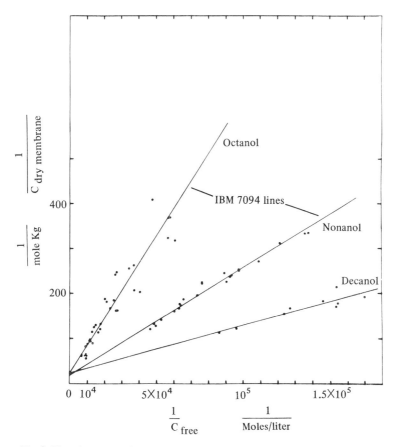

Fig. 8. The adsorption of alcohols to hemoglobin-free erythrocyte membranes.

5. The membrane concentration of anesthetic is between 0.02 to 0.06 M

The data in fig. 10 [19] indicate that the membrane concentration of chlorpromazine is of the order of 5000 to 10,000 times higher than the free concentration in the extracellular water. A comparison of the data in figs. 8 and 10 indicates that the membrane concentration of the anesthetic is always of the order of 0.03 to 0.06 M. Surprisingly, this is the value predicted by the classical partition theory of anesthesia of Overton and Meyer [13].

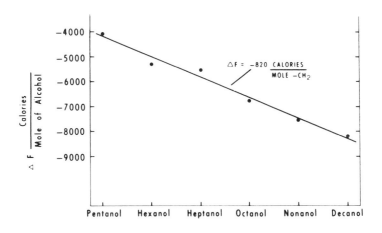

Fig. 9. The free energy of adsorption of the alcohols for erythrocyte membranes.

6. The molecular parameter important in membrane stabilization

The membrane concentrations of alcohol at equal membrane effect (i.e. at equal degrees of erythrocyte protection) are plotted in fig. 11. Correcting the membrane concentrations for molecular volume on the assumption that "equal volumes of anesthetic in the membrane exert equal effects" [24] does not lead to a universal constant value for membrane stabilization. Further multiplication by the molecular polarizability [2] leads to a universal constant.

7. The displacement of membrane-bound Ca^{++} and ATP

It has been suggested by Feinstein [8] and by Blaustein and Goldman [3] that anesthetics may act by displacing membrane calcium ions. Fig. 12 shows that chlorpromazine displaces calcium ions from erythrocyte membranes. Calculations [19] of the adsorption isotherms of calcium in the presence of chlorpromazine indicate that it requires two chlorpromazine molecules inside the membrane to displace one calcium ion inside the membrane. Alcohols, however, do not displace membrane calcium.

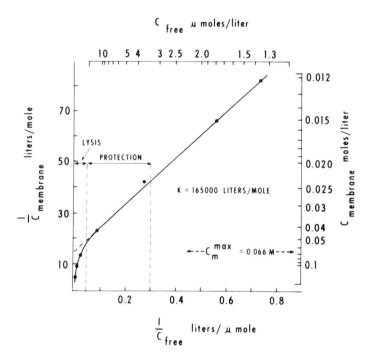

Fig. 10. The adsorption of chlorpromazine to erythrocyte membranes. The region marked protection is the membrane-stabilizing region for this drug.

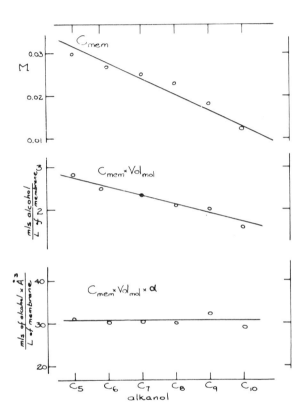

Fig. 11. Showing the membrane concentrations of the alcohols at equal membrane effect (top), the volume fraction (middle) and the correction for molecular polarizability (bottom).

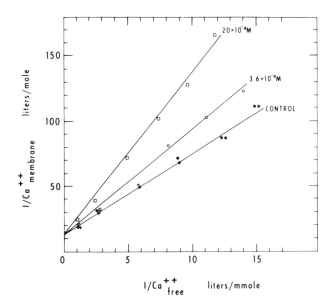

Fig. 12. The displacement of membrane-bound calcium ions by chlorpromazine.

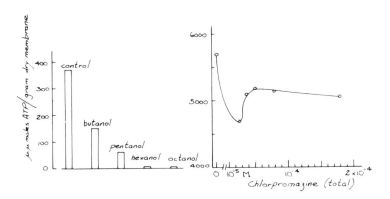

Fig. 13. The displacement of membrane-bound ATP by alcohols and chlorpromazine.

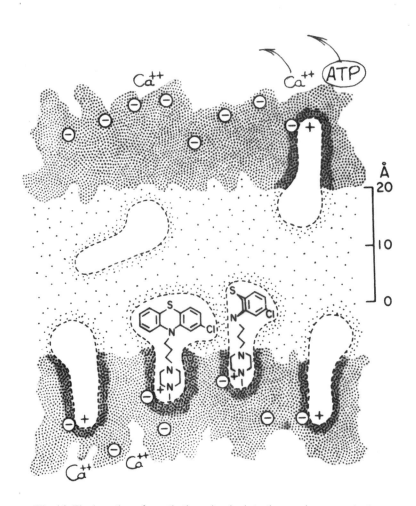

Fig. 14. The insertion of anesthetic molecules into the membrane; see text.

The results in fig. 13 (Chau and Seeman, in preparation) indicate that alcohols and chlorpromazine displace the membrane-bound ATP (adenosine tri-phosphate). This chlorpromazine-induced displacement of ATP is interesting since Kuperman et al. [17] found that ATP can reverse the nerve block of procaine; this reversal requires calcium ions.

Fig. 14 summarizes the findings discussed in this paper. The anesthetic molecules are buried in a hydrophobic region while the polar ends of the molecules are at the same time competing for calcium sites. The molecules are imbedded into the membrane and partly expanding it. These events are in some unknown way associated with an inhibition of the development of the sodium conductance of the membrane action potential.

References

[1] M.Barclay, R.K.Barclay, E.S.Essner, V.P.Skipski and O.Terebus-Kekish, Science 156 (1967) 665.

[2] S.W.Benson and J.W.King Jr., Science 150 (1965) 1710.

[3] M.P.Blaustein and D.E.Goldman, Science 153 (1966) 429.

[4] J.A.Clements and K.A.Wilson, Proc. Natl. Acad. Sci., U.S. 48 (1962) 1008.

[5] J.Clifford, B.A.Pethica and E.G.Smith, in: Membrane Models and the Formation of Biological Membranes, eds. L.Bolis and B.A.Pethica (North-Holland, Amsterdam, 1968) p. 19.

[6] R.A.Demel and L.L.M.Van Deenen, Chem. Phys. Lipids, 1 (1966) 68.

[7] B.Deuticke, Biochim. Biophys. Acta 163 (1968) 494.

[8] M.B.Feinstein, J. Gen. Physiol. 48 (1964) 357.

[9] H.Grobecker, P.Holtz, D.Palm, I.J.Bak and R.Hassler, Experientia 24 (1968) 701.

[10] G.M.Guest and M.Wing, J. Clin. Invest. 21 (1942) 257.

[11] P.S.Guth, O.Z.Sellinger and L.Elmer, Biochem. Pharmacol. 14 (1965) 769.

[12] R.Guttman, J. Gen. Physiol. 23 (1940) 346.

[13] V.E.Henderson, Physiol. Rev. 10 (1930) 171.

[14] A.D.Inglot and E.Wolna, Biochem. Pharmacol. 17 (1968) 269.

[15] A.Katchalsky, O.Kedem, C.Klibansky and A.De Vries, in: Flow Properties of Blood and other Biological Systems, eds. A.L.Copley and G.Stainsby (Pergamon Press, New York, 1960) p. 155.

[16] H.Keiser, G.Weissmann and A.W.Bernheimer, J. Cell Biol. 22 (1964) 101.

[17] A.S.Kuperman, M.Okamoto, A.M.Beyer and W.A.Volpert, Science 144 (1964) 1222.

[18] W.Kwant, S.Roth and P.Seeman, Fed. Proc. 28 (1969) 614.

[19] W.O.Kwant and P.Seeman, Biochim. Biophys. Acta, in press (1969).

[20] I.P.Lee, H.I.Yamamura and R.L.Dixon, Biochem. Pharmacol. 17 (1968) 1671.

[21] J.C.Metcalfe, P.Seeman and A.S.V.Burgen, Mol. Pharmacol. 4 (1968) 87.

[22] K.H.Meyer and H.Hemmi, Biochem. Z. 277 (1935) 39.

[23] C.D.Mitchell and D.J.Hanahan, Biochem. 5 (1966) 51.

[24] L.J.Mullins, Chem. Rev. 54 (1954) 289.

[25] T.Narahashi and J.W.Moore, J. Gen. Physiol. 51 (1968) 93S.

[26] T.Narahashi and M.Yamada, Fed. Proc. 28 (1969) 476.

[27] A.Philippu, R.Pfeiffer and H.J.Schumann, Naunyn-Schmiedebergs Arch. Exp. Path. Pharmak. 258 (1967) 251.

[28] R.P.Rand, Biophys. J. 4 (1964) 303.

[29] S.Roth and P.Seeman, Proc. Can. Fed. Biol. Soc. 12 (1969) 9.

[30] H.Schneider, G.C.Kresheck and H.A.Scheraga, J. Phys. Chem. 69 (1965) 1310.

[31] H.Schneider, Biochim. Biophys. Acta 163 (1968) 451.
[32] P.Seeman, Int. Rev. Neurobiol. 9 (1966a) 145.
[33] P.Seeman, Biochem. Pharmacol. 15 (1966b) 1632.
[34] P.Seeman, Biochem. Pharmacol. 15 (1966c) 1753.
[35] P.Seeman, Biochem. Pharmacol. 15 (1966d) 1767.
[36] P.Seeman and J.Weinstein, Biochem. Pharmacol. 15 (1966) 1737.
[37] P.Seeman, J. Cell Biol. 32 (1967) 55.
[38] P.Seeman, in: Metabolism and Membrane Permeability of Erythrocyte and Thrombocytes, eds. E.Deutsch, E.Gerlach and K.Moser (Georg Thieme Verlag, Stuttgart, 1968) p. 384.
[39] P.Seeman, T.Sauks, W.Argent and W.Kwant, Biochim. Biophys. Acta, in press (1969).
[40] A.M.Shanes, Pharmacol. Rev. 10 (1958a) 59.
[41] A.M.Shanes, Pharmacol. Rev. 10 (1958b) 165.
[42] A.M.Shanes, Proc. 22nd Int. Congr. Physiol. 1 (1962) 93.
[43] J.C.Skou, Biochim. Biophys. Acta 30 (1958) 625.
[44] J.C.Skou, J. Pharm. Pharmacol. 13 (1961) 204.
[45] M.A.Spirtes and P.S.Guth, Biochem. Pharmacol. 12 (1963) 37.
[46] K.Tanaka and Y.Iizuka, Biochem. Pharmacol. 17 (1968) 2023.
[47] J.Traube, Biochem. Z. 10 (1908) 371.
[48] U.S.Von Euler and F.Lishajko, Science 132 (1960) 351.
[49] U.S.Von Euler and F.Lishajko, Acta Physiol. Scand. 52 (1961) 137.
[50] U.S.Von Euler and F.Lishajko, 1st Intern. Pharm. Meeting, eds. O.H.Lowry and B. Uvnas, Vol. 5 (Macmillan, New York, 1963a) p. 77.
[51] U.S.Von Euler and F.Lishajko, Acta Physiol. Scand. 59 (1963b) 454.
[52] U.S.Von Euler and F.Lishajko, Intern. J. Neuropharmacol. 2 (1963c) 127.
[53] U.S.Von Euler and F.Lishajko, Proc. 2nd Intern. Pharm. Congr., eds. G.B.Koelle, W.W.Douglas, A.Carlsson and V.Trcke, vol. 3 (Macmillan, New York, 1964) p. 245.
[54] U.S.Von Euler, L.Stjarne and F.Lishajko, Life Sci. 3 (1964) 35.
[55] H.Weil-Melherbe and H.S.Posner, Biochem. Pharmacol. 13 (1964) 685.
[56] G.Weissmann, Biochem. Pharmacol. 14 (1965) 525.

RECOGNITION BY MACROPHAGES
OF ALTERATIONS IN THE MEMBRANES
OF OLD RED CELLS AND EXPELLED NUCLEI

David DANON

Section of Biological Ultrastructure,
The Weizmann Institute of Science,
Rehovoth, Israel

It is generally conceded that the aging of mammalian red blood cells is as-sociated with biochemical [1,2] and biophysical [3] changes, resulting final-ly in sequestration of the old cell in the reticuloendothelial system, phago-cytosis by macrophages and disintegration of the phagocytized cells within the phagocytic ones.

Under normal physiological conditions, old cells do not die in the circula-tion; the fact that they are old and may display low enzymatic activity does not seem to interfere with their capacity to circulate or to fulfill their task in gas transport.

Our notion concerning age of red blood cells is based on our knowledge that the human erythrocyte, for example, circulates only for 120 days and therefore it must be very old on the 119th day. These cells circulate until they are stopped in the spleen and phagocytized by the macrophages. The question arises: How does the macrophage recognize the senescent cell that is to be phagocytized? It is a very unlikely assumption that the macrophage, by contacting the red cell surface is capable of titrating the levels of enzyma-tic activities within the cell, thereby recognizing any marked drop in the ac-tivity of some enzyme associated with old age. The same improbability holds as regards the ATP levels, which have often been indicted as the conditio sine qua non for red cell survival. Even if the ATP level is critical, which is still open to discussion, it is hard to imagine the macrophage titrating ATP levels before deciding to phagocytize the senescent red cell.

It seems much more probable that the biophysical alterations that take place in the aging red cell are recognizable by direct contact of the macro-phage membrane with the red cell surface. Macrophages are known to recog-nize a non self; the question is, how does the macrophage recognize an altered or a deteriorated self?

57

Of all the biophysical characteristics that change with aging of the mammalian red blood cell [3] the surface charge which is markedly reduced in older cells [4–6], seems to us the most likely feature to be recognized by the macrophage. Separated fractions of old red cells move more slowly in an electric field than do cells from the young fraction taken from the same blood sample.

Adsorption of myxovirus, followed by elution, results in a marked decrease in the electric mobility of red cells [7]; the degree of reduction depends on the myxovirus type [8]. Incubation of red blood cells with receptor-destroying enzyme (RDE) derived from *Vibrio cholerae* cultures almost completely removes the negative charge from the cells [8].

The substrate for the receptor-destroying enzyme on the red cell surface is neuraminic acid [9], and treatment with neuraminidase reduces the electric mobility of red cells [10]. It has been demonstrated that the negative charge on the red cell surface can be ascribed almost entirely to the carboxylic group of neuraminic acid [11–13]. N-acetyl neuraminic acid (NANA) was also found to be the major component in the reaction of the negatively charged red cell surface with the positively charged poly-L-lysine [14]. A correlation was demonstrated between the rate of agglutinability with poly-L-lysine and the electric mobility as well as the absence of agglutinability and reduction of electric mobility in neuraminidase-treated red cells [5,15].

These features provide a system in which we can reduce the surface charge on the cell thus facilitating attempts to establish a correlation between surface charge and survival. Another model system in which the macrophage recognizes an altered or deteriorated entity would be helpful in establishing whether a low surface charge on the membrane is a common feature in both recognition processes. Such a model is presented by the nucleus of the late erythroblast, which on expulsion is surrounded by a narrow rim of cytoplasm and membrane.

It has been pointed out, that if the nucleus is always expelled, more free nuclei would be present in the circulating blood than are actually found [16]. However, we can assume that the rarity of free nuclei in the hemopoietic centers may be ascribed to the avidity with which the macrophages phagocytize the expelled nuclei [17–23]. It is interesting to query [22] in what respect does the membrane surrounding the expelled nucleus differ from that which envelopes the reamining future reticulocyte? What makes it recognizable by the macrophage? Direct measurement of the electric mobility or of the agglutinability of expelled nuclei, in order to estimate their electric charge, is not feasible because of the fact that they are very rarely, if ever, found in the circulation while it is practically impossible to separate them from the

bone marrow. We have therefore employed a system whereby we can analyse
the differences in charge density on the various membrane surfaces using positively charged colloidal ferric oxide particles visualized on the membrane
surface by electron microscopy, as described by Gasic et al. [24]. This approach has also allowed us to compare the surface charge on marrow cells
and circulating cells.

The techniques for preparation of the red cells, their separation into age
groups, their preparation for measurements of the agglutination kinetics, for
labelling of bone marrow, and the methods used for counting the colloidal
iron particles on micrographs were described in two recent papers by Mari-
kovsky and Danon [25] and by Skutelsky and Danon [26]. Most of the il-
lustrations and tables presented in this paper are taken from these two publications. If not, the different origin is noted.

Table 1 shows our first demonstration of the reduced electric mobility of
old red blood cells as compared with cells of the young fraction. In these experiments of 1961 [4] the cells were separated into old and young fractions
by centrifugation according to Prankerd [27]. Our modifications of a later
technique for separating cells of different density by differential flotation
[28] enabled us subsequently to separate red cells into age groups more effi-
ciently. With this method - using a battery of twenty separating phthalate
ester mixtures of decreasing specific gravity (Gravikit Miles Yeda, P.O.B. 1122,

Table 1

Electric mobility (μ/sec/V/cm) of separated young and old red cells from 10 different
human blood samples. Electric mobility of 30 cells in each direction were measured and
the average of each blood sample calculated

Blood sample no.	Young erythrocytes (top fraction)	Old erythrocytes (bottom fraction)
1	1.34	0.94
2	1.47	0.97
3	1.42	1.12
4	1.51	1.16
5	1.29	1.06
6	1.42	1.10
7	1.47	1.18
8	1.47	1.04
9	1.47	1.04
10	1.26	1.14
Mean	1.412	1.075

Table 2
Correlation between electric mobility of red blood cells and the density of colloidal iron oxide particles counted on electron micrographs*, for comparative evaluation of surface charge

Blood sample	No. of particles per micron length of membrane		Electric mobility (μ/sec/V/cm)	
Human red blood cells		Decrease (%)		Decrease (%)
Young	20.4		1.32	
Old	12.6	35.0	1.03	24
10 U/ml RDE	11.8	38.0	0.96	28
20 U/ml RDE	0.0		0.27	80
Rabbit red blood cells				
Young	17.8		0.70	
Old	12.0	32.5	0.60	14
10 U/ml RDE	10.8	39.0	0.57	18
20 U/ml RDE				

* From each sample, the membranes of 25 cells were measured on the micrograph in the parts where the membrane is perpendicularly sectioned. On these parts the iron particles were counted.

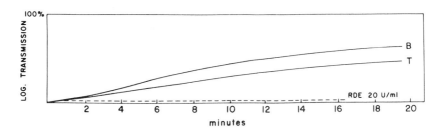

Fig. 1. The rate of agglutination of human red blood cells by poly-L-lysine, n = 100. Agglutination curves of young red cells from a top fraction (T), old red cells from a bottom fraction (B) and a whole population of red cells treated with 20 U/ml RDE (------). Note that at any time after onset of agglutination the old cells are agglutinated in a rate approximately 30% higher than that of the young cells. No agglutination occurs after RDE treatment.

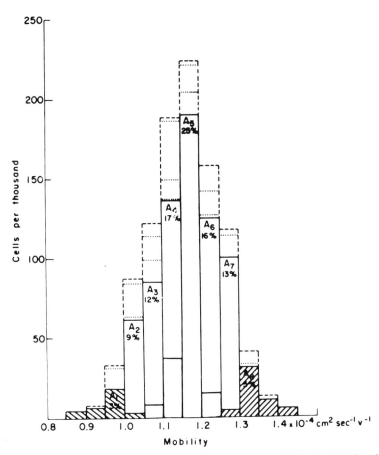

Fig. 2. Bar graph illustrating the mobility of cells in an electric field in the eight fractions separated according to their density. On top of each bar which constituted the peak of a fraction, its fraction number, as well as the percentage it constituted of the whole population, is given. Each bar indicates the ‰ of cells that migrated at the speed noted in the abscissa. Since the various fractions had overlapping migration speeds, the additive effect from other fractions at each migration speed is shown on top of the column indicating the appropriate values in dotted lines. Fractions no. 1, 5 and 8 are shadowed to illustrate the distribution of migration speeds within these three representative fractions.

Rehovot, Israel) - we were able to confirm our early data and show that there is a correlation between electric mobility and agglutination kinetics, or agglutination by the positively charged poly-L-lysine molecules [5,15]. With both

techniques we could demonstrate that cells from the old fraction are less
negatively charged than cells from the young fraction (table 2 and fig. 1).
These data were confirmed by Yeari [6] who fractionated a red cell population into eight age groups (fig. 2). Using the new method of labelling the
surface charge on cell membranes with colloidal iron, it can be seen that
while the young human red blood cells are densely labelled (plate 1), the old
red cells are less labelled, showing patches devoid of colloidal iron particles
(plate 2).

Treatment of young cells with neuraminidase in amounts and under incubation conditions such that about 30% of the surface charge is removed,
shows that the electric mobility is reduced accordingly, and the Fragiligraph
recordings of agglutinability by poly-L-lysine reveal a higher and more rapid
deflection, like that of old cells (see fig. 1). Electron microscopy reveals practically the same density and distribution of colloidal iron particles adsorbed
to the cell membrane in such cells as in old cells (plate 3). If a more severe
treatment with neuraminidase, using higher doses, is applied on the cells, practically no surface labelling can be detected (see plate 4) and the Fragiligraph
recording of agglutinability by poly-L-lysine shows no deflection. In electric
mobility measurements, only about 20% of the original mobility is observed.
Plates 5 and 6 show that similar differences exist between old and young
rabbit erythrocytes.

Assuming that this reduction in surface charge demonstrated by three different methods, is recognized by the macrophage, let us now look at what
happens to the nucleus that is expelled from the late erythroblast and is also
recognized as an undesirable self and phagocytized by the macrophage. In
fig. 9 the series of events that result in the expulsion of the nucleus, surrounded by a narrow rim of cytoplasm and plasma membrane, are summarized.
This plasma membrane, or at least part of it, was a few moments ago a part
of the erythroblast that was occasionally in close contact with the macrophage, but was not phagocytized. It was apparently recognized by the macrophage not only as a self but as an undamaged desirable self. In the time lapse
of a few minutes, a part of this late erythroblast is separated – as seen in plate
7 – and, at this stage, it is approached by the macrophage and recognized as
an undesirable self or deteriorated self. The expelled nucleus is phagocytized
as seen in plate 8. What is different on the part of the membrane that envelopes the nucleus from the rest of the cell which makes it recognizable by the
macrophage? The labelling with colloidal iron demonstrated in plates 9 and
10 suggests at least a partial answer to the question. The colloidal iron particles on the surface of the membrane that envelopes the nucleus are much
less numerous than on the membrane of the future reticulocyte. This visual

Plate 1. Human red blood cells from a young fraction separated by differential flotation, fixed in glutaraldehyde and labelled with a non-dialyzed positive colloidal iron suspension. Colloidal particles are uniformly distributed along the membrane surface. X 16,000.

Plate 2. Human red blood cells from an old fraction separated by differential flotation, fixed in glutaraldehyde, labelled with a non-dialyzed positive colloidal iron suspension. Iron particles are deposited irregularly, leaving unlabelled gaps on the membrane surface. X 16,000.

Plate 3. Unseparated human red blood cells treated with RDE (10 U/ml) and labelled with non-dialyzed positive colloidal suspension. Deposition of colloidal iron particles is similar in amount and disposition to that of an old human red blood cell (see fig. 4).
X 16,000.

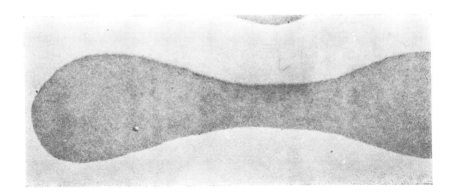

Plate 4. Unseparated human red blood cells treated with RDE (20 U/ml) and labelled with non-dialyzed positive colloidal iron suspension. There is practically no deposition of colloidal particles on the membrane surface. X 16,000.

Plate 5. Young rabbit red blood cells, labelled with a non-dialyzed positive colloidal iron suspension, showing a deposition similar to that of young human red blood cells. × 16,000.

Plate 6. Old rabbit red blood cells, labelled with a non-dialyzed positive colloidal iron suspension, showing particles deposited irregularly, leaving unlabelled gaps on the membrane surface. × 16,000.

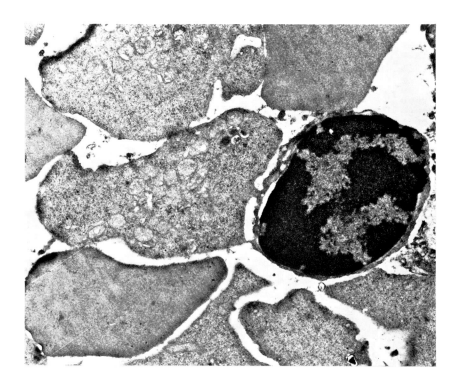

Plate 7. Electron micrograph showing the separation of the expelled nucleus and its surrounding plasma membrane from the remaining future reticulocyte. The nucleus which has reassumed its typical rounded form, is now connected to the main bulk of cytoplasm by a wide bridge. Some vacuoles appear within this bridge. These openings become elongated thus resembling the cleavage furrow which appears at the equatorial plane at the telophase of mitotic division of erythroblasts. The vacuoles continue to elongate parallel to the nuclear membrane until the extruded nucleus is attached to the cytoplasm by only one or two tiny connections. X 12,700.

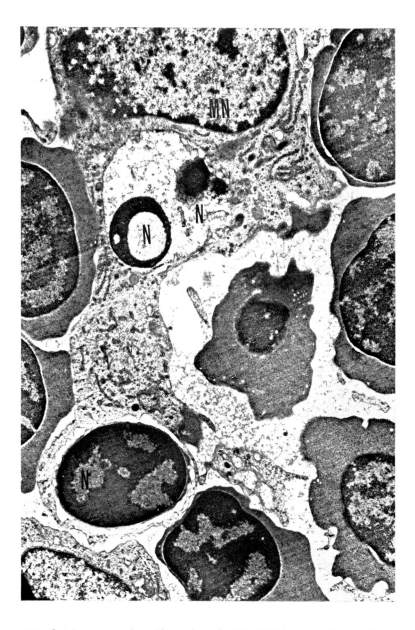

Plate 8. A large macrophage, the nucleus of which (MN) is seen at the top of the micrograph contains three extruded erythroid nuclei (N) at different degrees of disintegration. It is in close proximity to some late erythroblasts. × 9,800.

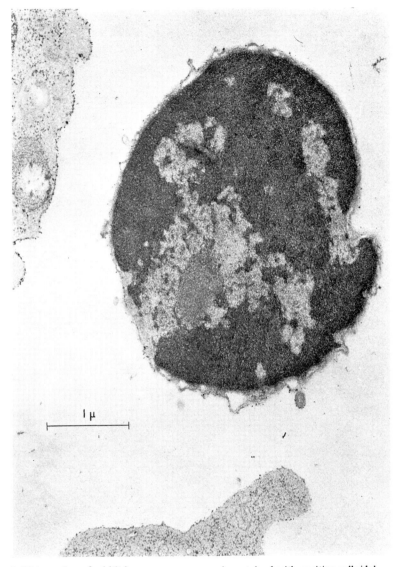

Plate 9. Thin section of rabbit bone marrow suspension, stained with positive colloidal iron suspension. An extruded nucleus, surrounded by a narrow rim of cytoplasm and plasma membrane, is seen in the vicinity of an erythroid (bottom) and leukoid elements. Heavy deposits of the colloid appear on the leukoid cell membrane as compared to those on the membrane of the erythroid cell. Almost no colloidal deposits appear on the free nucleus. × 34,000.

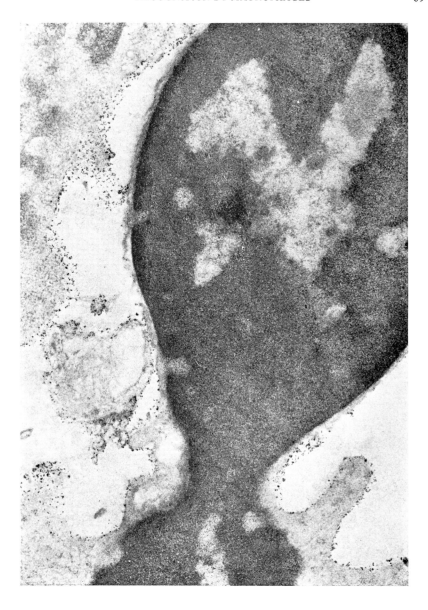

Plate 10. Bone marrow cells stained with the positive colloid. A late erythroblast is shown representing an early stage in the nuclear expulsion process in which a part of the nucleus is situated outside the main bulk of cytoplasm, surrounded by a rim of cytoplasm and membrane. The positive colloid on the erythroblast surface is present mainly on that part of the membrane which surrounds the remaining cytoplasm. A part of leukoid cell (top) shows a membrane heavily coated with dense particles. X 34,000.

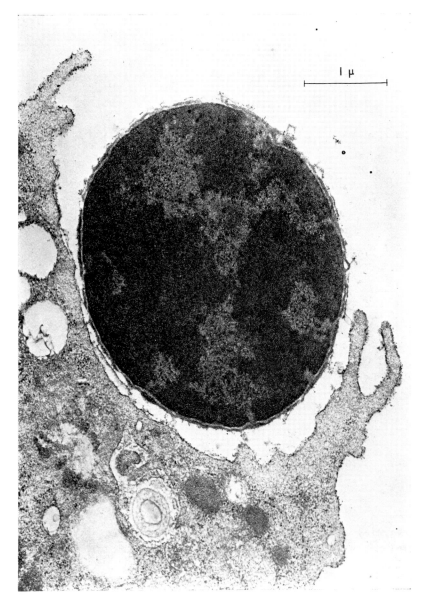

Plate 11. Thin section of rabbit bone marrow suspension, stained with the positive colloid. Free erythroid nucleus, situated in proximity to a macrophage, is partly surrounded by the cytoplasmic protrusions of the macrophage. The colloid black dots are abundant on the macrophage membrane and scarce on the membrane surrounding the erythroid nucleus.

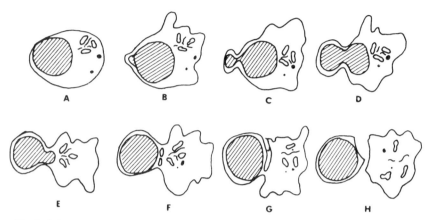

Fig. 9. Schematic representation (A–H) of the sequence of events occurring in the process of extrusion of the nucleus from the late erythroblast.

impression was confirmed by counting the number of particles per micron of perpendicularly sectioned membrane on micrographs at a magnification of X 30,000. It was thus shown that the density of colloidal iron particles on the membrane that envelopes the expelled nucleus is only about 50% of that on the reticulocyte membrane. The macrophage apparently recognizes this reduced surface charge (plate 11).

The apparent similarity in charge density between rabbit and human red cells, as estimated by the density of colloidal iron particles is rather surprising, in view of the marked lower electric mobility of rabbit red cells [29]. Furthermore, poly-L-lysine, $n = 1000$, was required to agglutinate rabbit red cells, while the shorter polymer, of $n = 100$, agglutinated human red cells [15]. However, it was estimated that the iron particle covers 5–16 molecules of sialic acid [30], and even if only 10% of these molecules are ionized, there would be sufficient charge to interact with the iron particles [24]. Assuming that these charges are uniformly distributed, the equal density of iron particles on the surface of both human and rabbit young red blood cells would be understandable. Apparently, in spite of the difference in their over-all surface charge, both contain sufficient charges to saturate the surface with iron particles. The reduction in mobility, in density of labelling with colloidal iron, and the increased rate of agglutination in old cells and in RDE-treated cells can therefore be attributed to the depletion of negative charges in areas on the red cell surface as visualized by the unlabelled gaps on the membrane surfaces in the electron micrographs. In this connection, it is interesting to note

that if human red cells are labelled with ^{51}Cr and injected into rabbits, they
disappear from circulation within the first hour after injection, despite the
fact that their surface charge is three times that of rabbit red cells. The recognition of non self seems to overwhelm the charge density signal. On the other
hand, ^{51}Cr-labelled rabbit red cells treated with neuraminidase and injected
into rabbits disappear from the circulation within a day or two [31]. The
avidity of macrophages in phagocytizing neuraminidase-treated red cells *in
vitro* has been reported [32]. It is interesting to note that the neuraminidase-
treated cells do not demonstrate any significant changes in other biophysical
parameters, like osmotic fragility, mechanical fragility or density distribution
of cells or at any rate no more than cells incubated without neuraminidase.
These findings, together with the reduced labelling by positively charged colloidal iron particles of the membrane that envelopes the nucleus that is being
extruded, lead us to believe that the reduction in surface charge of senescent
cells and extruded erythroid nuclei is a major recognition signal that helps the
macrophage to sort out the undesirable altered or deteriorated self cells.

References

[1] P.A.Marks, Nouvelle Rev. Franc. Hematol. 1 (1960-61) 900.
[2] Ch.Bishop and D.M.Surgenor, The Red Blood Cell, Academic Press (1964).
[3] D.Danon, Bibliotheca Haematol. 29 (1968) 178.
[4] D.Danon and Y.Marikovsky, Compt. Rend. (Paris) 253 (1961) 1271.
[5] Y.Marikovsky, D.Danon and A.Katchalsky, Biochim. Biophys. Acta 124 (1966)
154.
[6] A.Yeari, Blood 33 (1969) 159.
[7] M.Honig, Proc. Soc. Exptl. Biol. Med. 68 (1948) 385.
[8] J.D.Stone and G.L.Ada, Brit. J. Exptl. Pathol. 33 (1952) 428.
[9] A.Gottschalk and P.E.Lind, Nature 164 (1949) 232.
[10] G.M.Cook, D.H.Heard and G.V.F.Seaman, Nature 191 (1961) 44.
[11] R.M.Glaeser and H.C.Mell, Biochim. Biophys. Acta 79 (1964) 606.
[12] D.A.Haydon and G.V.F.Seaman, Arch. Biochem. Biophys. 112 (1967) 126.
[13] P.Sachtleben and G.Ruhenstroth-Bauer, Nature 192 (1961) 982.
[14] D.Danon, C.Howe and L.T.Lee, Biochim. Biophys. Acta 101 (1965) 201.
[15] D.Danon, Y.Marikovsky and A.Kohn, Experientia 25 (1969) 104.
[16] L.Heilmeyer and H.Bergeman, Blut und Krankheiten (Springer Verlag, 1951).
[17] F.R.Campbell, Anat. Record 160 (1968) 593.
[18] D.Orlic, A.S.Gordon and J.A.G.Rhodin, J. Ultrastruct. Res. 13 (1965) 616.
[19] D.C.Pease, Rev. Hematol. 10 (1955) 300.
[20] M.Seki, T.Yoneyama and H.Shirasawa, Acta Pathol. Japon. 15 (1965) 295, 303.
[21] M.Seki, T.Yoneyama and H.Shirasawa, Acta Pathol. Japon. 15 (1965) 387.
[22] E.Skutelsky and D.Danon, J. Cell Biol. 33 (1967) 25.
[23] Z.Zamboni, J.Ultrastruct. Res. 12 (1968) 525.

[24] G.J.Gasic, L.Berwick and M.Sorrentio, Lab. Invest. 18 (1968) 63.
[25] Y.Marikovsky and D.Danon, J. Cell Biol. 43 (1969) 1.
[26] E.Skutelsky and D.Danon, J. Cell Biol. 43 (1969) 8.
[27] T.A.J.Prankerd, J. Physiol. 143 (1958) 325.
[28] D.Danon and Y.Marikovsky, J. Lab. Clin. Med. 64 (1964) 668.
[29] E.H.Eylar, M.A.Madoff, O.V.Brody and J.L.Oncley, J. Biol. Chem. 237 (1962) 1992.
[30] P.M.Kraemer, J. Cellular Comp. Physiol. 67 (1966) 12.
[31] D.Danon and Y.Marikovsky, unpublished results.
[32] E.Gardner, C.S.Wright and B.Z.Williams, J. Lab. Clin. Med. 58 (1961) 743.

EFFECT OF SODIUM ON PASSIVE PERMEABILITY
OF NON-ELECTROLYTES THROUGH
THE INTESTINAL WALL

G.ESPOSITO, A.FAELLI and V.CAPRARO
Istituto di Fisiologia Generale, Milan, Italy

1. Introduction

It is well known that sodium concentration in the bathing mucosal fluid strongly affects glucose and amino acid transport through the isolated intestinal barrier [1]. This may be explained by supposing an influence of sodium on the entry of sugars [2] and of amino acids into the epithelial cells. Actually there is a decrease in the unidirectional influx of L-alanine into the intestinal cells in the absence of sodium in the perfusing fluid [3]. According to Crane [4], the transported substance interacts with a binding site on a carrier and this interaction is enhanced by the binding of sodium with a second site present on the same carrier.

In a recent paper [5] our aim was to investigate whether, besides the hypothetical above-mentioned specific mechanism of sodium effect, there was another unspecific effect on the resistance of the intestinal barrier to the passage of non-actively transported molecules. From the results collected in that paper some evidence was appearing that by lowering sodium concentration, the passive flux of acetamide or thiourea is decreased. To avoid the criticism to which our indirect method of evaluation of the test substance concentration in the intestinal sac was exposed, another set of experiments was performed by using a continuous circulation of the perfusion fluid through an open and everted intestinal tract. Such a perfusion method provides a direct control of the inside and the outside concentrations of the tested substance throughout the period of the experiment.

2. Methods

Sprague-Dawley albino male rats, initially weighing about 250 g, semi-

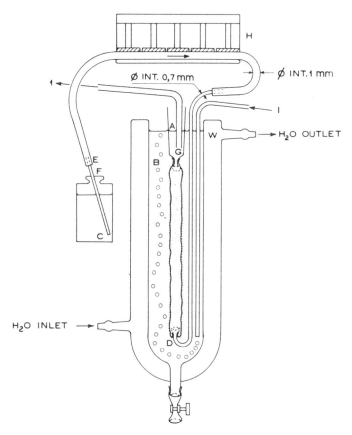

Fig. 1. Apparatus used for the incubation of the intestinal tract. The intestine is kept at constant temperature (28°C) in the container W. The intestinal tract is previously washed with the incubation fluid C via the peristaltic pump H (Tygon tube E) and the polythene tube D.

starved over a 15 day period and with a final percent weight decrease of 24–26% were used. Under these conditions, transport activities of isolated jejunum are enhanced in comparison with unstarved condition [6,7].

A tract of small intestine 15 cm long was removed from the animal at about 10 cm from the pylorus, under barbituric narcosis. Each tract was everted according to the Wilson and Wiseman technique [8] and connected at one end with a reservoir and at the other with a tube and a peristaltic pump. The intestinal tract was dipped into the perfusion fluid at a constant temperature of 28°C. The Krebs-Henseleit bicarbonate solution added with glucose 13.9 mM and saturated with a gas mixture of 95% O_2 and 5% CO_2 was employed as a basic incubation fluid. This fluid was added with the tested substance (acetamide or thiourea) at a concentration of 10 mM. After a convenient washing period (5 min) via the peristaltic pump (fig. 1) the reservoir was emptied and filled with 5 ml of the above final solution, added with a trace amount of the labelled (^{14}C) compound and of tritiated inulin; 40 ml of the same non-radioactive fluid was used as a mucosal incubating medium.

By shifting the reservoir a position was reached where no hydrostatic pressure was present between the fluid level inside the reservoir and the level of the mucosal fluid. At this moment the recirculation of the serosal fluid (fig. 2) and the experimental observation were beginning.

After 20 min and then every 10–20 min for 60 min small samples (100 μl) were withdrawn from the mucosal and the serosal spaces and the ^{14}C and ^{3}H radioactivities were measured with a liquid scintillation spectrometer (Tri-Carb Packard, mod. 3003). From these values the volume increase of the serosal space (transepithelial volumetric flux), the concentration of the tested substance and its unidirectional flux from the serosa to the mucosa could be calculated. One serosal sample was used to determine the D-glucose concentration (enzymatic method of Hugget and Nixon [9]). The mobility coefficients and the net glucose transport (from mucosa to serosa) were at first calculated for all the 10 or 20 min periods and then the mean values between all the single data belonging to one experiment (1 hr) were obtained.

In another set of experiments we have tried to determine the water content of the mucosal epithelial cells and the cellular concentration of acetamide. In this case tritiated inulin was added at the beginning of the experiment only to the serosal fluid as before or both to the serosal and the mucosal ones. After 30 min of perfusion the mucosal layer of the intestinal tract was scraped off following the Dickens and Weil-Malherbe technique [10]. The cells were broken up by osmotic shock followed by freezing and subsequent thawing [11]. The liquid so obtained as well as the incubating fluids were deproteinized and then analyzed for ^{3}H and ^{14}C radioactivities. The difference between wet and dry weight of the scraped mucosa is the total water content of the tissue. The quantity of tritiated inulin in the extracellular serosal medium and its concentration in the serosal medium give us the extracellular serosal volume. The quantity of tritiated inulin in both the extracellular serosal and mucosal media and its concentration in the serosal and the mucosal media give us the total extracellular volume. The total extracellular volume is about twice as much as the serosal extracellular volume only. From these data the intracellular water content of the mucosal epithelial cells

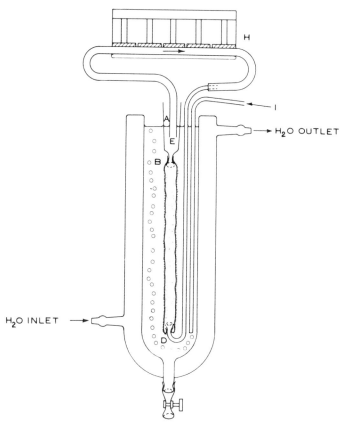

Fig. 2. Same apparatus and conditions as in fig. 1. The experiment begins. The intestinal tract is incubated in the mucosal fluid B. The serosal fluid present in the reservoir A is continuously removed and recirculates via the same peristaltic pump through the intestine. The gas mixture bubbles with the polythene tube I in the mucosal space B.

and the intracellular acetamide concentration can be calculated. The concentration difference of acetamide between the cellular space and the mucosal medium is a rather constant fraction of the total transepithelial difference.

The first set of experiments was repeated by replacing NaCl in the Krebs-Henseleit bicarbonate fluid with Tris-Cl or LiCl in an iso-osmotic quantity.

The second set of experiments was repeated by replacing NaCl with Tris-Cl.

Knowing the fluxes ($\dot{n}$), and supposing a constant volume of the system spaces, the mobility ω was calculated according to the following equation (12):

$$\dot{n} = \omega RT \Delta c_s ,$$

where Δc_s is the mean of the concentration differences between the serosal and the mucosal medium at the beginning and at the end of the experimental period.

Actually the volumes are not constant, because there is a contemporary net volumetric flux from the mucosa to the serosa, so that a drag effect must be taken into account. But under our experimental conditions the presence of a drag effect of water on the tested substance increases the mobility difference between NaCl and Tris-Cl or LiCl experiments, because the volumetric net flow has a direction opposite to that of the observed unidirectional flux and because this volumetric flux is higher under the first condition than under the second one. Therefore we have reported on the tables the mobilities across the whole intestinal barrier disregarding the drag effect.

On the other hand, to represent more exactly the relationship between the mobility coefficient of acetamide and the net transport of glucose, we have calculated the mobility through the brush border (ω_b) by disregarding the drag effect, as well as by assuming a reflection coefficient equal to zero. In the first case we have utilized the simple above reported equation:

$$\dot{n} = \omega_b RT \Delta c_s ,$$

where Δc_s is the mean of the concentration differences between the cellular (c_c) and the mucosal medium (c_m). The cellular concentration may be considered equal to the mucosal one added with a fraction of the total transepithelial concentration as resulted from the experiments carried on for this special purpose.

In the second case $\dot{n}$ must be corrected by subtracting from the previously reported term the following one:

$$\dot{v} \bar{c}_s ,$$

where $\dot{v}$ is the net transepithelial fluid flux; the theoretical c_s is equal to:

$$\bar{c}_s = \frac{c_c - c_m}{\ln (c_c/c_m)} ;$$

Table 1

Decrease of the mobility of thiourea through the intestinal barrier (ω) in the absence of water drag effect, and of the amount of glucose transferred to the serosal space by replacing NaCl of the Krebs-Henseleit bicarbonate bathing fluid (NaCl Krebs) with equi-osmotic quantities of Tris-Cl (Tris-Cl Krebs). ω and glucose are referred to 1 g of dry intestinal tissue. The mean values ± S.E. are reported. n = number of experiments

Bathing fluid	Substance	ω μ Moles g^{-1}h^{-1}At^{-1}	Transp. gluc. (μ Moles g^{-1}h^{-1})
NaCl Krebs + gluc. 13,9 mM	Thiourea 10 mM	342 ± 10 n = 5	102 ± 7 n = 5
Tris-Cl Krebs + gluc. 13,9 mM	Thiourea 10 mM	216 ± 26 n = 4	36 ± 10 n = 4

Table 2

Decrease of the mobility of acetamide through the intestinal barrier (ω) in the absence of water drag effect, and of the amount of glucose transferred to the serosal space by replacing NaCl of the Krebs-Henseleit bicarbonate bathing fluid (NaCl Krebs) with equi-osmotic quantities of Tris-Cl or LiCl (Tris-Cl Krebs, resp. LiCl Krebs). ω and glucose are referred to 1 g of dry intestinal tissue. The negative values in the glucose transport mean that the glucose total quantity in the serosal space is decreased during the experiment instead of being increased. The mean values ± S.E. are reported. n = number of experiments.

Bathing fluid	Substance	ω μ Moles g^{-1}h^{-1}At^{-1}	Transp. gluc. (μ Moles g^{-1}h^{-1})
NaCl Krebs + gluc. 13,9 mM	Acetamide 10 mM	584 ± 82 n = 6	178 ± 39 n = 6
Tris-Cl Krebs + gluc. 13,9 mM	Acetamide 10 mM	233 ± 25 n = 4	− 4 ± 24 n = 4
LiCl Krebs + gluc. 13,9 mM	Acetamide 10 mM	177 ± 6 n = 4	− 13 ± 8 n = 4

the calculated $\dot{v}\,\bar{c}_s$ is the mean between the value of $\dot{v}\,\bar{c}_s$ calculated at the beginning and the value at the end of the experimental period.

3. Results and discussion

The results collected in tables 1 and 2 allow us to confirm the previous ones [5] and to conclude that a decrease in sodium concentration of the bathing fluid not only inhibits the net uphill transfer of glucose from the mucosa to the serosa, but seems to inhibit also the passive unidirectional passage of uncharged hydrosoluble molecules with a low molecular weight such as acetamide and thiourea.

The observed inhibition is obviously non-specific; a physical modification of the intestinal membrane may presumably account for this decrease in permeability.

Apparently these data do not agree with those presented by Lauterbach [13] concerning the transmural movement of urea across the intestinal bag and with those of Clark et al. [14] concerning the movement of thiourea through the intestinal membrane. However, in Lauterbach's experiments urea concentration only is provided, and the amount of urea crossing the intestinal epithelium may vary according to the concentration as well as to the volume of fluid present in the sac. Clark et al. do not report numerical data, and calcium was absent in the bathing fluids they used in their experiments.

Our data do not agree also with those concerning the permeability of molecules with a higher molecular weight such as non-actively transported sugars [15,16] and creatinine (unpublished data of ours); the permeability of these substances is very poor and is Na^+-independent. Maybe these substances cross the luminal intestinal barrier prevailingly in a place other than the brush border.

In the semi-starved rat intestine the basic oxygen consumption is by far prevailing over the oxygen consumption due to sodium active transport, and lactic acid production is independent of the sodium pump [7], so that the total oxygen consumption and lactic acid production may be considered good indexes of the basic metabolism. As we have already reported [5], in the absence of sodium chloride in the perfusion fluid, the total oxygen consumption and lactic acid production are not substantially altered. Therefore no basic metabolism or pH modifications should be taken into account to explain the lowering of passive permeability.

The resistance to diffusion seems to be due, to a greater extent, to the serosa facing membrane of the epithelial cells rather than to the brush border.

Table 3

Acetamide concentration difference between serosal and cellular space, and between cellular and mucosal space, and acetamide unidirectional fluxes (from serosa to mucosa), under basal incubation conditions (NaCl Krebs), and by replacing NaCl of the Krebs-Henseleit bicarbonate fluid with equi-osmotic quantities of Tris-Cl (Tris-Cl Krebs). Fluxes are referred to 1 g of dry intestinal tissue. The mean values ± S.E. are reported. n = number of experiments

Bathing fluid	Substance	Unidir. flux (ser. to muc.) (μ Moles g^{-1}h^{-1})	Conc. diff. betw. ser. a. cells (μ Moles/ml)	Conc. diff. betw. cells a. muc. (μ Moles/ml)
NaCl Krebs + gluc. 13,9 mM	Acetamide 10 mM	88,5 ± 9,8 $n = 6$	4,84 ± 0,17 $n = 8$	0,87 ± 0,09 $n = 8$
TrisCl Krebs + gluc. 13,9 mM	Acetamide 10 mM	68,7 ± 5,4 $n = 8$	5,37 ± 0,21 $n = 8$	1,63 ± 0,04 $n = 8$

In fact the concentration difference is higher through the serosal membrane than through the brush border (table 3). By lowering sodium concentration in the bathing fluid the resistance of the brush border is proportionally more affected than that of the serosal membrane, because the concentration difference across the former barrier increases more than that across the latter (table 3).

If we plot the mobility coefficients across the brush border (the coefficients calculated disregarding the solvent drag or those calculated by including a maximal theoretical drag effect) against the glucose net transport we obtain a linear highly significant correlation (fig. 3). The active transport capacity of the epithelial absorbing cells of the intestinal mucosa surviving in the normal Krebs-Henseleit bicarbonate fluid seems to be directly or indirectly correlated to the passive permeability of the brush border. A similar behaviour is appearing also if we compare the modifications of the active transport capacity and of the passive mobility which occur throughout a single experiment (fig. 4).

As far as the mechanism of the dependence of passive mobility on sodium content of bathing fluids is concerned, a possible explanation is that sodium substituents Tris, choline [5], lithium directly affect the physico-chemical properties of the cell brush border, decreasing the rate of the glucose entry and increasing the resistance to the thermal diffusion of small molecules, so that glucose transport and the mobility of acetamide or thiourea are simul-

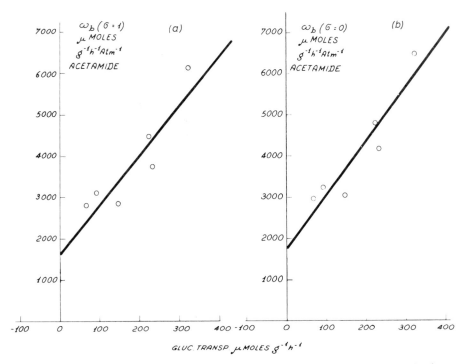

Fig. 3. The mobility coefficients of acetamide across the brush order (ω_b, μMoles g^{-1} h^{-1} At^{-1}), the coefficients calculated disregarding the solvent drag (fig. 3a) and those calculated by including a maximal theoretical drag effect ($\sigma = 0$) (fig. 3b) are plotted against the glucose net transport on the abscissa. ω_b and glucose transport are referred to 1 g of dry intestinal tissue.

taneously reduced by the replacement of sodium with these cations. The glucose entry and the mobility of permeating small molecules may be reduced as a consequence of the fact that the primary effect of cations on the membrane may be the causing of a different degree of swelling of its protein framework. In the presence of sodium the degree of swelling is higher, the interaction of glucose with the carrier is easier, the mobility of the carrier-glucose complex is greater and the membrane pores are larger than in the presence of Tris or choline. Assuming this hypothesis, the lithium effect is not easy to understand, because the hydration layer of lithium is larger than that

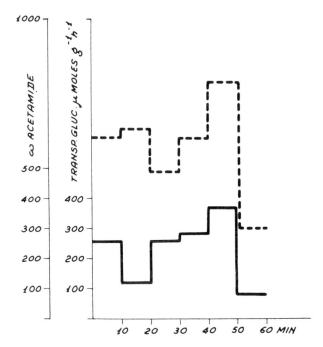

Fig. 4. Behaviour of the mobility coefficient through the intestinal barrier (ω, μMoles g^{-1} h^{-1} At^{-1}), in the absence of water drag effect (broken line), and of the net transport of glucose in one single experiment in the course of time. ω and glucose transport are referred to 1 g of dry intestinal tissue.

of sodium [17]. Another working hypothesis would be compatible with our experimental findings. The rate of accumulation of glucose in the epithelial cells is subject, whatever the mechanism, to a spontaneous variability in the different intestinal preparations and furthermore it depends on the relative concentration of sodium ions in the medium. The accumulated sugar causes cellular swelling which in turn may mechanically increase the permeability; on the other hand, glucose transport depends on the rate of intracellular sugar accumulation. Consequently, by reducing sodium concentration in the medium, the rate of glucose accumulation and transport, the cellular swelling and permeability will also be diminished.

As a matter of fact, if we examine the water content of the mucosal cells (table 4) we find it significantly higher in the normally incubated epithelium than in that bathed with a Tris-Cl Krebs-Henseleit bicarbonate solution.

Table 4
Decrease of the mobility of acetamide through the intestinal barrier (ω) in the absence
of water drag effect and decrease of the intracellular water content by replacing NaCl of
the Krebs-Henseleit bicarbonate bathing fluid (NaCl Krebs) with equi-osmotic quantities
of Tris-Cl (Tris-Cl Krebs). ω is referred to 1 g of dry intestinal tissue. The mean values ±
S.E. are reported. n = number of experiments

Bathing fluid	Substance	ω μ Moles $g^{-1}h^{-1}At^{-1}$	intracell. H_2O (μl/mg dry weight)
NaCl Krebs + gluc. 13,9 mM	Acetamide 10 mM	584 ± 82 $n = 6$	5,79 ± 0,15 $n = 12$
Tris-Cl Krebs + gluc. 13,9 mM	Acetamide 10 mM	233 ± 25 $n = 4$	4,72 ± 0,13 $n = 13$

4. Conclusions

1) The thermal diffusion of small molecules such as acetamide and thiourea through the intestinal barrier is reduced together with the active transport of D-glucose, when NaCl of the incubating medium is replaced by equi-osmolar quantities of Tris-Cl, choline-Cl or LiCl.

2) The reduction of the passage of small molecules, almost partially, is due to an increase of the resistance offered by the brush border.

3) The replacement of NaCl with Tris-Cl in the bathing fluid is paralleled by a significant shrinkage of the epithelial cells.

4) The mechanism of the correlation between the mobility of small molecules and the active transport of D-glucose through the intestinal barrier is discussed. The working hypothesis is advanced that the swelling of the epithelial cells due to glucose accumulation mechanically increases the passive permeability.

References

[1] T.Z.Csaky and M.Thale, J. Physiol. 151 (1960) 59;
T.Z.Csaky, Am. J. Physiol. 201 (1961) 999;
V.Capraro, A.Bianchi and C.Lippe, Experientia 19 (1963) 347;
H.E.Harrison and H.C.Harrison, Am. J. Physiol. 205 (1963) 107.
[2] R.K.Crane, Fed. Proc. 21 (1962) 891.

[3] R.E.Fuisz, S.G.Schultz and P.F.Curran, Biochim. Biophys. Acta 112 (1966) 593;
S.G.Schultz, P.F.Curran, R.A.Chez and R.E.Fuisz, J. Gen. Physiol. 50 (1967) 1241.
[4] R.K.Crane, Federation Proc. 24 (1965) 1000.
[5] G.Esposito, A.Faelli and V.Capraro, Experientia 25 (1969) 603.
[6] J.T.Hindmarsh, D.Kilby, B.Ross and G.Wiseman, J. Physiol. 188 (1967) 207.
[7] G.Esposito, A.Faelli and V.Capraro, Arch. Intern. Physiol. Biochim. 75 (1967) 601.
[8] T.H.Wilson and G.Wiseman, J. Physiol. 123 (1954) 116.
[9] A.S.G.Hugget and D.A.Nixon, Biochem. J. 66 (1957) 12P.
[10] F.Dickens and H.Weil-Malherbe, Biochem. J. 35 (1941) 7.
[11] A.Faelli, G.Esposito and V.Capraro, Arch. Sci. Biol. (Bologna) 50 (1966) 234.
[12] O.Kedem and A.Katchalsky, Biochim. Biophys. Acta 27 (1958) 229.
[13] F.Lauterbach, Biochim. Biophys. Acta 135 (1967) 256.
[14] L.Clark, H.Helbock and P.Saltman, Arch. Biochem. Biophys. 122 (1967) 807.
[15] A.M.Goldner, J.J.Hajjar and P.F.Curran, Biochim. Biophys. Acta 173 (1969) 572.
[16] I.Bihler, Biochim. Biophys. Acta 183 (1969) 169.
[17] A.Frey-Wyssling, Submicroscopic Morphology of Protoplasma and its Derivatives
(Elsevier Publishing Co., Amsterdam, 1948) pp. 98–102.

Part 2

CELLULAR COMMUNICATIONS AND SURFACE INTERACTIONS

ON DECIDING WHETHER A MEMBRANE PROTEIN IS INVOLVED IN TRANSPORT*

Arthur B.PARDEE
Department of Biology, Moffett Laboratories,
Princeton University, Princeton, New Jersey 08540, USA

1. Introduction

As work on membranes progresses, membrane proteins are being isolated. One of their most important and evident possible functions will be involvement in specific transport systems. Indeed, there are already numerous candidates for such roles [23]. The question to which I wish to address myself in this paper is what criteria we can use to decide whether an isolated protein is involved in a transport process. At first glance this seems to be a very difficult problem, since disruption of a cell eliminates the possibility of measuring its ability to transport. But several tests are available to relate a protein with a transport mechanism. Each test is liable to uncertainties of various sorts; no one gives sure proof of the relationship. This is a problem similar to the one, of two decades ago, to identify the role of an enzyme in a metabolic pathway [1]. By a combination of the tests to be discussed, it should be possible to determine whether involvement of a protein in a transport system is very likely.

2. Location of proteins in the cell

When we talk about a membrane protein we first must ask whether the protein is indeed located in or on the membrane of the living cell. This question is relatively easy to answer if the protein is so firmly bound that it remains with the membrane during isolation. Thus, the "M-protein" of *Escherichia coli* is released from the isolated membrane by detergents [9]. Components of the "enzyme II" complex of *Salmonella typhimurium* are released

* This work was aided by a Grant AI-04409 from the U.S. Public Health Service.

by urea-butanol [28]. Binding of such proteins is so firm that it is hard to imagine that they become associated with the membrane by adsorption after the cells are broken.

Another class of proteins is proposed to be located in or on the membrane, even though these proteins do not remain with the purified membrane preparations. These proteins seem to be loosely held. They are generally characterized by being released by osmotic shock, a procedure that depends on first removing the cells from a concentrated sucrose solution and then rapidly suspending them in low osmotic pressure medium [15]. There are many such osmotic-shock released proteins; those that appear to be related to transport are able to bind sulfate, leucine, galactose, arabinose, and arginine, respectively. Most of them are from *E. coli* or *S. typhimurium*, but recently a shockable phenylalanine binding protein from a *Pseudomonas sp.* has been studied by Guroff and Bromwell [12].

The property of being released by osmotic shock has itself been suggested to indicate a surface location [15]. Other results support this hypothesis. One approach is to determine whether small, non-penetrating molecules can reach these proteins. Certain *S. typhimurium* mutants cannot use sulfate even though they possess all the necessary enzymes, and yet they are capable of combining with sulfate [8]. This is consistent with a membrane barrier between the binding site and the internal enzymes; in current terms the sulfate binding protein is located outside of the membrane. Brockman and Heppel [5] have recently used a similar argument for the location of shockable phosphatases of *E. coli*. The enzymes can split phosphorylated substrates that presumably cannot penetrate the cell membrane owing to their charge.

A similar principle depends on ability of a non-penetrating protein reagent, diazo-naphthalene disulfonate, to inactivate the sulfate binding protein in intact *S. typhimurium* [25]. This procedure also inactivates β-galactoside transport by *E. coli*. A new nonpenetrating reagent, N-*p*-phenyl-sulfonic acid-maleimide had no effect on β-galactoside transport in contrast to the effect of N-ethyl-maleimide; both reagents inactivated β-galactosidase of broken cells [7]. M-protein is known to be inactivated by N-ethylmaleimide [9]; it is presumably buried sufficiently deeply in the membrane (or is otherwise modified in the intact cell) so that it cannot react with the larger, more charged sulfanilic derivative. Other reagents of this sort should be useful for mapping protein locations at various depths in membranes.

A final approach to locate easily released proteins is inactivation by antibodies specific to them. Neither the sulfate binding protein [25] nor the leucine binding protein of *E. coli* [26] are inactivated in intact cells by their antibodies. But the latter reacts in fixed preparations, and has been located by an ingenious staining technique as being near the cell surface [21].

3. Reconstitution

The most direct test of involvement of a protein probably is to determine if the protein has a unique ability to elicit a specific transport activity when added to cells previously lacking this activity. The potentially most interesting work of this sort has been done by Kaback [17] with membrane vesicles of *E. coli*. These vesicles were shown to accumulate several compounds above their concentrations in the medium, when they were properly supplemented. In particular, transport of α-methyl-glucoside was greatly stimulated by addition of phosphoenolpyruvate. This confirms the data obtained by Roseman and his colleagues [28] which show that the transport of numerous sugars and their derivatives depends on phosphoenolpyruvate, on two soluble proteins (enzyme I and HPr), and on a group of membrane bound proteins ("enzyme II"). In Kaback's experiments, there seemed to be sufficient quantities of these proteins associated with the vesicles so as not to limit the sugar's uptake. Vesicles made from a mutant that lacks enzyme I do not take up α-methyl-glucoside.

Reconstitution has been reported by Kundig et al. [19] for the uptake of thiomethyl-β-galactoside and α-methyl-glucoside by intact *E. coli*, although success was only occasional. Shocked cells lost about 70% of their transport activity, and this was completely and specifically restored when HPr protein was added. Anraku [3] has reported success in reconstituting transport of galactose or leucine (but not glucose or glycerol) by shocked *E. coli*. Not only the galactose binding protein but also an unidentified fraction of the shock fluid was required; in fact addition of the latter was the more important. Reconstitution of arginine transport has recently been reported [36]. In contrast, several other systems could not be reconstituted by other investigators who used shocked cells and purified binding proteins, in spite of repeated attempts.

The loss of transport by osmotic shock itself provides some evidence for a role of the shock-released proteins. This has been observed for sulfate, leucine, galactose, arginine, and arabinose. But uncertainty as to which lost protein is required or whether some other damage to the cell is responsible for the loss of transport makes this an uncertain test.

Reconstruction might appear at first sight to provide the most convincing evidence for the role of a protein in transport. However, the difficulties with this approach are underlined by the variable results reported, even those which claim successful reconstitution. Transport is a complex process that requires integrity of the entire cell. Damage to the membrane or energy supply, for example, could greatly reduce the rate of transport, and repair of these lesions could restore transport. Thus, conditions where transport loss is caused uniquely by the loss of binding protein are difficult to find. One must demonstrate that the addition of the specific protein restores transport.

4. Genetic tests

The basic idea of the genetic test is that the membrane protein is made inactive by a mutation; then the cells should not be able to carry out transport if this protein is an essential part of the transport system. A clearly documented example is mutation of the LacY gene of *E. coli* which has long been known to determine the ability to transport β-galactosides. Mutations in this gene prevented the appearance of the M-protein [10]. A temperature sensitive LacY mutant made a temperature sensitive M-protein. This result is particularly good evidence that the gene determines the structure of the protein.

Extensive tests have also been made on the HPr system for multiple sugar transport. Mutations of *S. typhimurium* that prevent appearance of HPr or enzyme I are defective in sugar transport [20]. Genetic data with *Aerobacter aerogenes* [33], with *E. coli* [31], and with *Staphylococcus aureus* [14] lead to the same conclusion. Enzyme II for mannitol of this system is lacking in a mannitol-transport defective mutant [32].

A mutant of *E. coli* defective in galactose transport lacks a shockable galactose binding protein [4]. Transport-negative mutants that are low in sulfate binding protein [24,22] or arabinose binding protein [16] have been found, but they are not mutated in the corresponding structural gene. Similarly, a mutant with low galactose binding activity used by Anraku [2] is also defective in two enzymes of the galactose pathway, and so is probably a regulatory mutant. These results indicate the need for caution in interpreting genetic tests: a mutation that simultaneously stops both transport and the formation of a membrane protein might be a regulatory mutant that also blocks formation of other components, and these might be necessary for transport. At least, a regulatory mutation of this kind strongly suggests that the regulated protein is part of the regulated pathway.

Another problem with the genetic test arises when a mutation that blocks a transport process requiring a membrane protein also blocks a second transport process. This result does not prove that the known protein of the first process is also required for the second; clearly, still another unknown component might be involved. This is indicated by the studies with *E. coli* of Wang and Morse [34] and of Fox and Wilson [11]. Pleiotropic mutants de-

fective in transport of the many sugars that require the HPr system were also
defective in lactose transport, even though this particular sugar is presumably
not dependent on the HPr components (being transported by HPr- or enzyme
I-negative mutants, and not being found in the cell as the phosphorylated
derivative, unlike other sugars [18]).

Connections between the HPr and other transport systems might exist.
Hanson and Anderson [13] have discovered a protein from *A. aerogenes* that
is soluble and of low molecular weight, similar to binding proteins, which increases the affinity of an enzyme II component of an HPr system for fructose.
This protein is absent in a mutant that transports and utilizes fructose poorly.
Simoni et al. [29] have found possibly similar essential and specific soluble
protein components III of the *S. aureus* HPr systems for thiomethyl-galac-
toside and for mannitol.

Mutants that lack a protein are still sometimes able to transport. Transport
of fructose is only diminished by one-third, not eliminated, in the mutant
lacking the fructose "affinity" protein [13]. Similarly, Hogg and Englesberg
[16] have reported mutations which greatly diminish arabinose binding without completely abolishing its transport. One possible explanation for this result is that derepressible or inducible binding proteins can be made in enor-
mous excess, and a small amount in the mutants is still quite adequate for
good transport. Another explanation comes from the results of Tanaka et al.
[32] in which an *A. aerogenes* mutant which lacks enzyme II for mannitol
can still transport mannitol. The reason is that the system is replaced by an
arabitol transport system whose specificity overlaps. Thus, transport in the
absence of a membrane protein does not prove the latter's non-involvement.

Inability of a mutant to transport in spite of its possessing a particular
protein merely suggests that some other part of the transport system is missing. It of course does not prove that the protein is not required for transport.

5. Co-regulation by nutrition

Transport systems are often inducible or repressible: their activities depend
greatly on nutritional conditions. Some membrane proteins are also inducible.
The result that the two can be made to change in proportion suggests that the
protein functions in the rate limiting step of transport. Penrose et al. [26] give
a nice example of proportionality over about a 20-fold range for the leucine
binding protein and leucine transport by *E. coli*. When a binding protein can
be made in excess, as with highly derepressed cells, one expects proportionality only in the lower ranges of derepression. This is the case with the sulfate
binding protein of *S. typhimurium* [22].

Interesting examples of qualitatively related changes are seen in the work of Fox and Kennedy [9] who showed that β-galactoside binding and transport by *E. coli* are both inducible; and by Hogg and Englesberg [16] who demonstrated that the arabinose binding protein and transport are inducible, and that a constitutive mutant for transport is also constitutive for binding. Wasserman [35] has demonstrated that both Ca^{++} transport and its binding protein from animal tissues are "induced" by vitamin D.

Again, one must be cautious in interpreting such results. Induction conditions can produce changes in amounts of many proteins of a cell; the change of the one under observation might fortuitously correlate with increased transport activity.

6. Kinetic measurements

Correlation of kinetic parameters such as a binding constant and a saturation constant for transport can be considered evidence for relation of the two phenomena. Data of this sort are greatly strengthened if some changed condition causes both to change in the same way. An example of this is the 10-fold difference of both K's, of leucine binding and transport, between two *E. coli* strains [27,26]; the transport and binding constants to one protein are similar for each of several neutral amino acids. The binding and transport constants are also similar for the arabinose [16], arginine [36] and galactose (2 components) systems [4]. In making these comparisons it is essential that experimental conditions be the same. For example, at low ionic strength K of sulfate binding is three orders of magnitude lower than that of transport but at the ionic strength of the growth medium the two are similar at about 0.03 mM (Pardee, unpublished).

Actually these two constants are not strictly comparable, since binding has an equilibrium constant but the transport half-saturation constant is a kinetic value which depends on dissociation of the complex in the process of transport, very much as the Michaelis constant of an enzyme is not a true measure of affinity of enzyme and substrate.

Studies of inhibition of binding and transport also can be compared, and similar results can be taken as evidence for a relation of the two processes. A series of anions had similar effects on transport and binding of sulfate by *S. typhimurium* [24]; several sugars inhibited these processes similarly for the galactose systems [4]. Again, one must recognize that dissimilar processes are being compared. Extra steps in transport can alter the apparent inhibitory power of a compound. For example, thiosulfate inhibits sulfate transport more

strongly than it does binding, probably because it is metabolized by the
cell and hence only blocks flow of sulfate inward.

A curious observation is that while one substrate of the β-galactoside
transport system, thiodigalactoside, blocks combination of the active site
with the protein reagent N-ethylmaleimide, other substrates such as isopro-
pyl- or methyl-thiogalactosides do not prevent this reaction [6]. The significance of this result is obscure in view of all the other data that strongly support a role of the M protein in transport of these galactosides.

6. Enzymic activity

A protein with enzymic activity can be related to a transport system in
which this activity is involved. The catalysis of sugar phosphate formation by
the HPr system correlates well with the finding that these sugars are found
intercellularly only as phosphates [28]. This hypothesis is confirmed by
Kaback's [17] demonstration that membrane vesicles convert the sugars to
their phosphates, using phosphoenolpyruvate, as an obligatory part of their
transport. Another case is the implication of a membrane bound ATPase in
Na^+ transport. Many kinetic parameters of the two processes such as K's for
Na^+ and K^+ and for inhibition by ouabain support this conclusion [30].

The enzymic activity of a transport protein makes a powerful tool available for further studies, as the recent work of Roseman [28] demonstrates.

Summary

The best evidence for a role of a membrane protein in transport is obtained
from the totality of several different sorts of experiments. This follows from
the complexity of processes carried out by intact cells and from our very
recent and fragmentary knowledge of transport mechanisms in general.

Evidence is already good that the HPr system is used for sugar transport
by several organisms, and that the M-protein is part of the galactoside transport system of *E. coli*. Probably it is fair to say that while the evidence for
involvement of any single shockable binding protein in its transport system
is not absolutely conclusive, the sum-total of results with these proteins
definitely gives them such a role.

References

[1] E.A.Adelberg, Bacteriol. Rev. 17 (1953) 253–267.
[2] Y.Anraku, J. Biol. Chem. 242 (1967) 793–800.
[3] Y.Anraku, J. Biol. Chem. 243 (1968) 3128–3135.
[4] W.Boos, Europ. J. Biochem. 10 (1969) 66–73.
[5] R.W.Brockman and L.A.Heppel, Biochemistry 7 (1968) 2554–2562.
[6] J.R.Carter, C.F.Fox and E.P.Kennedy, Proc. Natl. Acad. Sci. U.S. 60 (1968) 725–732.
[7] E.V.Craig and J.P.Guthrie, unpublished.
[8] J.Dreyfuss and A.B.Pardee, Biochim. Biophys. Acta 104 (1965) 308–310.
[9] C.F.Fox and E.P.Kennedy, Proc. Natl. Acad. Sci. U.S. 54 (1965) 891–898.
[10] C.F.Fox, J.R.Carter and E.P.Kennedy, Proc. Natl. Acad. Sci. U.S. 57 (1967) 698–705.
[11] C.F.Fox and G.Wilson, Proc. Natl. Acad. Sci. U.S. 59 (1968) 988–995.
[12] G.Guroff and K.E.Bromwell, Federation Proc. 28 (1969) 667.
[13] T.E.Hanson and R.L.Anderson, Proc. Natl. Acad. Sci. U.S. 61 (1968) 269–276.
[14] W.Hengstenberg, J.B.Egan and M.L.Morse, J. Biol. Chem. 243 (1968) 1881–1885.
[15] L.A.Heppel, Science 156 (1967) 1451–1455.
[16] R.W.Hogg and E.Englesberg, J. Bacteriol. 100 (1969) 423–432.
[17] H.R.Kaback, J. Biol. Chem. 243 (1968) 3711–3724.
[18] E.P.Kennedy and G.A.Scarborough, Proc. Natl. Acad. Sci. U.S. 58 (1967) 225–228.
[19] W.Kundig, F.D.Kundig, B.Anderson and S.Roseman, J. Biol. Chem. 241 (1966) 3243–3246.
[20] M.Levinthal and R.D.Simoni, J. Bacteriol. 97 (1969) 250–255.
[21] P.K.Nakane, G.E.Nichoalds and D.L.Oxender, Science 161 (1968) 182–183.
[22] N.Ohta, Thesis, Princeton University, 1968.
[23] A.B.Pardee, Science 162 (1968) 632–637.
[24] A.B.Pardee, L.S.Prestidge, M.B.Whipple and J.Dreyfuss, J. Biol. Chem. 241 (1966) 3962–3969.
[25] A.B.Pardee and K.Watanabe, J. Bacteriol. 96 (1968) 1049–1054.
[26] W.R.Penrose, G.E.Nichoalds, J.R.Piperno and D.L.Oxender, J. Biol. Chem. 243 (1968) 5921–5928.
[27] J.R.Piperno and D.L.Oxender, J. Biol. Chem. 241 (1966) 5732–5734.
[28] S.Roseman, J. Gen. Physiol. 54 (1969) 138–184.
[29] R.D.Simoni, M.F.Smith and S.Roseman, Biochem. Biophys. Res. Commun. 31 (1968) 804–811.
[30] J.C.Skou, Physiol. Rev. 45 (1965) 596–617.
[31] S.Tanaka, D.G.Fraenkel and E.C.C.Lin, Biochem. Biophys. Res. Commun. 27 (1967) 63–67.
[32] S.Tanaka, S.A.Lerner and E.C.C.Lin, J. Bacteriol. 93 (1967) 642–648.
[33] S.Tanaka and E.C.C.Lin, Proc. Natl. Acad. Sci. U.S. 57 (1967) 913–919.
[34] R.J.Wang and M.L.Morse, J. Mol. Biol. 32 (1968) 59–66.
[35] R.H.Wasserman, B.A.Corradino and A.N.Taylor, J. Gen. Physiol. 54 (1969) 114–137.
[36] O.H.Wilson and J.T.Holden, J. Biol. Chem. 244 (1969) 2743–2749.

CELL ADHESION AND SOME IONIZED
GROUPS AT THE CELL SURFACE*

Leonard WEISS

Department of Experimental Pathology,
Roswell Park Memorial Institute, Buffalo, New York, USA

1. Introduction

It would appear from the very nature of chemical and physical bonds, that if two surfaces can approach closely enough to each other, they can form a whole spectrum of adhesive bonds [1]. For this reason, a key problem in analyzing cell adhesion is not the adhesion mechanism itself, but in understanding the approach of two surfaces closely enough to form adhesive bonds. From the practical viewpoint of the formation of stable adhesive bonds, the surfaces may not be separated by more than approximately 5 Å.

As all cells from vertebrates so far examined carry net negative surface charges, the problem of contact between them has been treated in terms of colloid theory, as described by Derjaguin and Landau [2] and Verwey and Overbeek [3]. Essentially, DLVO-theory considers contact as being dependent on the balance between electrostatic forces of repulsion which tend to keep cells apart, and attractive interactions of the London–Van der Waals' type which tend to bring them together. On the one hand, in spite of its recognized shortcomings (discussions of Faraday Soc. 42, 1966), use of DLVO-theory has led to considerable clarification of the physical bases of cell contact phenomena; on the other hand, failure to appreciate the dynamic properties and heterogeneity of the cell surface, and the complexity of the biological situation, have led to considerable confusion.

In this paper, I propose to discuss some of the ionogenic groups associated with RNA at the cellular electrokinetic surface as these are least familiar, the dynamic nature of these and other ionized groups, and their possible effects on cell contact phenomena.

* Partially supported by Grant No. P403-B from the American Cancer Society.

2. RNase-susceptible groups at the cell surface

Treatment of a variety of cells with mammalian ribonuclease A, produces significant reductions in the net negativity of *some* of them [4–6]. It is well-known that RNase A is a highly basic protein which readily adsorbs to many surfaces, and it is also well known that it acts specifically on pyrimidine nucleoside linkages of ribonucleic acid. Evidence showing that the loss in cell net surface negativity after incubation with RNase was *not* due to enzyme adsorption, would therefore also indicate that the loss was due to enzyme activity, which in turn would suggest that the substrate for RNase, namely RNA, is a constituent of the cell periphery.

A compelling argument against nonspecific adsorption of RNase reducing net cell surface negativity, comes from the observation [6,7] that the electrophoretic mobilities of a variety of cells are *unchanged* after incubation with RNase. If nonspecific adsorption were involved, then it would be expected that the anodic mobilities of all negatively charged cells would be reduced following exposure to the enzyme.

Another strong argument against the nonspecific adsorption of RNase A, comes from the repeated observation that in the different types of cells in which the active enzyme produced a reduction in net surface negativity, no detectable change was produced by enzyme inactivated by the technique of Barnard and Stein [8], in which histidine residue 119 is carboxymethylated [9]. As of the 19 positively charged groups present in the native enzyme, 18 are unaffected by inactivation, both active and inactive forms have isoelectric points close to pH 9.6, and cannot be separated on ion-exchange columns [10]. In addition, small angle X-ray diffraction studies at 3 Å resolution, reveal only minor conformational changes around the active centre of the inactivated enzyme (Kartha, personal communication) which are not expected to offer steric hindrance to its adsorption by substrate. Thus, if the reductions in electrophoretic mobility produced by incubation of cells with active RNase A were simply due to adsorption, they should also occur after incubation with the inactivated enzyme. The fact that they do not, therefore argues against the adsorption hypothesis.

Further experiments have been made [6,11] in which a number of different cell types showed similar loss of net surface negativity to that produced by RNase A, following incubation with T_1 RNase isolated from *Aspergillus oryzae*. As T_1 RNase molecules carry a net negative charge, the observed reduction in surface negativity of cells incubated in their presence, cannot be attributed to adsorption.

Finally, the adsorption hypothesis is rejected on the grounds that the temperature dependence of reduction of cellular electrophoretic mobility by RNase, follows the time course of enzyme activity, rather than adsorption [6].

The effect produced by RNase on cell surfaces is not associated with the adsorption of released intracellular materials. Although the liberation of oligonucleotides by cells following RNase-treatment, has been demonstrated spectrophotometrically, this in itself is not very informative, since the material may well represent the breakdown products of intracellular and peripheral RNA. Attempts to deliberately contaminate the surfaces of cells which are non-susceptible to RNase, by incubating them in cell sap, in an effort to make them RNase-susceptible, have been unsuccessful. Attempts to make RNase-susceptible cells non-susceptible by repeated washing, have also been unsuccessful. The RNase-susceptible material is not due to viral or mycoplasmal contaminants.

Incubation of RNase-susceptible cells with purified venom phosphodiesterase, which hydrolyses nucleotides with free 3'-hydroxyl end groups to liberate mononucleoside-5'-phosphates, produced no change in cell electrophoretic mobility. This may well indicate that the RNA within the cell periphery has terminal ionized phosphates, as these would inhibit the enzyme.

In addition to the electrokinetic evidence, which shows the presence of RNase-susceptible anionic groups at the electrokinetic surfaces of a number of cells, RNA has been detected chemically in membrane fractions isolated from cells [12–14]. This evidence is not as good in my opinion, as that obtained from electrokinetic studies, because of the problem of contamination, and because they do not indicate where the RNA is, with respect to the membrane.

To sum up, ribonuclease-susceptible material - RNA - appears to be firmly attached to the peripheries of *some* cells; it moves with the cell periphery in an electrophoresis apparatus; it is present when cells grow *in vivo* and *in vitro*, and is to be functionally regarded as part of the cell periphery. On minimal evidence it seems possible that RNA-phosphates are present at the electrokinetic surface of cells; however, as RNA in other regions of cells is usually found in association with other macromolecules, including mucopolysaccharides [15], the ionogenic groups of these materials may also contribute to zeta potential.

3. Dynamic aspects of peripheral RNA

The sialic acid moieties at the cellular electrokinetic surface, show an increase in density at the G2 phase of the mitotic cycle [16]. However, studies of parasynchronous cultures have failed to reveal changes in the surface density of RNase-susceptible ionogenic groups related to the mitotic cycle *per se* [17].

Another indication that cellular activity might influence cellular electrophoretic mobility came from the work of Eisenberg et al. [18] which showed the mobilities of cells isolated from regenerating and neonatal rat livers were higher than in controls. It was also observed [19] that the electrophoretic mobilities of some cells increased with their environmental temperature and oxygen consumption, and it was tentatively suggested that the increase in mobility was due to metabolically linked conformational changes in the cell periphery. More recent work [20] indicated that severe depression of oxygen utilization, anaerobic glycolysis, and uncoupling of oxidative phosphorylation can occur, with no appreciable alteration in cellular electrophoretic mobility over periods of approximately 30 min.

In apparent contrast to the studies made over a few minutes, longer term observations, in which similar cells were grown at different rates *in vitro*, over periods of days, showed that the higher the growth-rate the higher the negative charge density at the cell surface. It was also shown that the increased net negativity was due to an increased density of RNase-susceptible ionogenic groups at the cellular electrokinetic surface, whereas the density of sialic acid moieties in this region remained constant [21]. In other studies of mouse lymphoid cells, grafted into irradiated allogeneic or syngeneic recipients, rapid proliferation was found to be associated with significant increases in RNase-susceptible net surface negativity [11].

Thus, the cell surface density of sialic acid carboxyl groups and RNase-susceptible anionic groups may vary very considerably in any cell or group of cells, depending on their proliferative and mitotic status.

As a late result of cell contact and adhesion may be synthesis of specialized junctional regions such as desmosomes, it is pertinent to ask whether changes in the surface density of ionized groups can influence synthetic processes. Mayhew and Levinson [22] have shown that the cardiac glycoside, ouabain, reversibly inhibits not only cation transport in Ehrlich ascites cells, but also division. This association of the two cellular functions is interesting in view of the speculations of Bygrave [23] and Lubin [24], among others, that changes in intracellular cationic levels and ratios may control cell metabolism and growth. As it has often been suggested that ion-binding to carriers is an essential preliminary to their transmembrane movement, the possibility was examined that neuraminidase- and/or ribonuclease-susceptible ionogenic groups at the cell periphery influenced ion transport [25]. Treatment of Ehrlich ascites cells with either neuraminidase or RNase, which reduced their

net surface negativity by 30 to 45% and 30%, respectively, did not appreciably affect their Na^+ or K^+ content, i.e., net flux. Experiments with ^{42}K revealed a reduction of 10 to 17% in unidirectional K^+ flux following incubation of the cells with neuraminidase, but not with RNase. The data therefore
suggested that ionized sites susceptible to these two enzymes are not of major
quantitative importance in regulating Na^+ and K^+ flux. The results did not
enable us to determine whether ion-binding to an anionic cell surface carrier
in fact occurred through the agency of those anionic groups accounting for
the residual 40% of net surface negativity remaining after treatment with the
two enzymes.

4. Ionogenic groups and contact

The total energy of interaction, V_T, between two charged particles is the
sum of their attractive, V_A, and repulsive, V_R, interactions. In the case of
two similar spherical particles, DLVO-theory predicts that:

$$V_R = \tfrac{1}{2}\psi_0^2 a \ln\left(1 + \exp\left(-\kappa H\right)\right),$$ (1)

and,

$$V_A = -\frac{1}{12}\frac{Aa}{H}$$ (2)

where,

ψ_0 = surface potential,
a = particle radius of curvature,
ϵ = dielectric constant,
$1/\kappa$ = the Debye-Hückel parameter,
H = distance between approaching particle surfaces,
A = the Hamaker constant.

Some of the biophysical problems associated with applying these, and
similar formulae, to the contact between cells have been discussed by Curtis
[26], Weiss and Woodbridge [27], and Weiss [28,29], among others. Although
there are many difficulties in attributing numerical values to the terms given
in eqs. (1) and (2), the general form of the interaction energy/distance plot is
not disputed. In essence, such plots indicate that when two negatively charged
cell processes approach each other, an electrostatic repulsion barrier tends
to prevent their close apposition. If this repulsion barrier can be overcome,
the processes will move into an attractive minimum at distances permitting
the formation of mutual adhesive bonds.

In view of the confusion apparent in this field, it must be emphasized that distances are calculated from the plane of the ionized groups at the cell surface, and that this plane does not coincide with the outer dense line of the well-known trilaminar structures representing the unit membrane seen when conventional preparations are examined under the electron microscope. As the critical distances involved are only of the order of 10 Å or less, and as preparative artefacts and interpretative problems pose currently insuperable difficulties, it seems unlikely that the problems of initial contact reactions between cells as discussed here, can be resolved by present electron micrographic techniques.

In the region of the repulsion barrier to contact, it can be seen from eq. (1) that electrostatic repulsion will be reduced, and contact favoured, by reduction in either surface potential, ψ_0, or radius of curvature, a. Although reduction in dielectric constant, and $1/\kappa$ (by increasing ionic strength and/or valency) will also reduce V_R, these variables cannot usefully be discussed further at the moment. Variations in cellular electrophoretic mobility may be associated with other events, and such variations in surface negativity are expected to affect the electrostatic barrier to contact as indicated in eq. (1). Bangham and Pethica [30] noted that one effect of cells making contact by means of low radius of curvature probes, is that energetically this is easier, as also indicated in eq. (1). A causal relationship between cell surface potential and the ability of a cell to bend into low radius of curvature probes is suggested by the observation that treatment of cells with neuraminidase enables them to be more easily sucked into micropipettes. This is explained in terms of the mutual electrostatic repulsion between peripheral ionized sialic acids contributing to the rigidity of the cell periphery, and their enzymatic removal facilitating deformation of this region [31]. The expectation that incubation with neuraminidase would promote contact interactions has been supported by the observation that such treatment promoted the phagocytosis of negatively charged particles by human monocytes [32]. Some proteolytic enzymes also render the cell periphery more deformable [33], and it may be speculated that sublethal release of enzymes, such as the lysosomal cathepsins [34], can affect cell contact interactions by peripheral autolysis.

It was observed that following incubation of a number of different cell types with RNase, in spite of significant decreases in their electrophoretic mobilities, no change was observed in the pressures required to deform them. However, neuraminidase-treatment, causing similar decreases in mobility to that produced by RNase, enabled the cells to be deformed by significantly lower pressures. This finding, along with others, was used as the basis for an electromechanical model of the cell periphery, in which the distribution of the ionogenic groups associated with sialic acids and RNA, is different [35].

As will be discussed shortly, I think that the problem of the spatial location of ionized groups in the cell periphery is central to an understanding of the physical bases of contact phenomena between cells.

Detailed studies were made of two types of cells maintained in suspension cultures, from whence they could be sampled without isolation trauma. One cell type, D, adhered to its fellows and in glass *in vitro*, the other, type M, did not. Examination of many surface properties of the two cell types revealed no differences which accounted for their different biological behaviour [36]. Families of curves were computed for the approximate interaction forces between the two cell types and glass surfaces, and attempts were made to measure them by direct experiments. Briefly, the computed curves indicated that a repulsion barrier equivalent to more than 10^{-3} dynes prevented both cells from making contact with glass; this force is equivalent to a relative centrifugal force in excess of 13,000 g, when the cells are centrifuged towards the glass under cultural conditions [37]. The main point of interest emerging from this work is that when two electrokinetically similar types of cell were confronted by similar formidable electrostatic barriers preventing their contact with glass coverslips, the non-adhesive M cells could not be centrifuged into an adherent location with respect to the glass by forces of up to 5000 g, whereas the D cells sedimented onto the glass under the influence of 1 g. The question of main interest is *not* why the M cells did not adhere, this was expected from the computed interaction forces; the interest lies in explaining how the D cells overcame the barrier to contact. The explanation which seems most attractive at the moment is based on the fact that as pointed out previously in this context [38], measurements of cell electrophoretic mobility, on which so many of our calculations and arguments depend, give at most an index of the *average charge density*, σ, at the cell electrokinetic surface, as indicated by the Helmholtz-Smoluchowski equation:

$$V = \frac{\sigma}{\kappa \eta} \tag{3}$$

where
V = electrophoretic mobility,
η = dynamic viscosity near to the cell shear plane and
$1/\kappa$ = the Debye-Hückel parameter.

Measurements of electrophoretic mobility thus describe an average situation, and cannot in themselves indicate charge distribution at the cellular electrokinetic surface. Thus, the charge densities in some regions will be higher or lower than the average for the whole cell. If biological behaviour is to be correlated with cell surface potential, then it is pertinent to consider which part of the cell surface is involved, because there are many data showing that contact between cells is more subtle than the random collision of homogeneous particles, and that only small areas of two opposing cells are involved in the contact or adhesive process. On the one hand, if the ionized groups at the surfaces of non-adhesive M cells are smeared out, then from the electrostatic viewpoint, one small area of their surface is the same as any other, and computations of interaction forces based on average, macroscopic electrokinetic data are expected to fit experimental observations, in showing that contact and adhesion are energetically improbable. On the other hand, if the ionized groups at the surfaces of the adhesive D cells have a zonal distribution, then from an energetic approach, contact is expected to involve surface regions offering less electrostatic resistance than can be overcome by the propulsive energy of low radius of curvature filopods [39]. In addition, the preceding discussion makes it clear that the electrokinetic surface of any cell should be regarded as a dynamic structure. Thus, in considering cell contact it is obligatory to ask not only *which* region of the surface of an individual cell is involved, but also *when*, and what the rest of the cell is doing at this time. It is presently impossible to provide clearcut answers to these questions.

It should be emphasized that although the role of electrostatic barriers to cell contact can be usefully examined in general terms in the light of DLVO-theory, the specific problems involving interactions over very short range $(H < 2/\kappa)$ can not.

References

[1] B.A.Pethica, Exptl. Cell. Res. Suppl. 8 (1961) 123.
[2] B.V.Derjaguin and L.Landau, Acta Physicochim. U.R.S.S. 14 (1941) 633.
[3] E.J.W.Verwey and J.Th.G.Overbeek, Theory of the Stability of Lyophobic Colloids (Elsevier, Amsterdam, 1948).
[4] L.Weiss and E.Mayhew, J. Cell Physiol. 68 (1966) 345.
[5] L.Weiss and E.Mayhew, J. Cell. Physiol. 69 (1967) 281.
[6] L.Weiss and E.Mayhew, Intern. J. Cancer 4 (1969) 626.
[7] L.Weiss, in: Biological Properties of the Mammalian Surface Membrane, ed. L.A. Manson (Wistar Inst. Sympos. Monogr. 8, 1968) 73.
[8] E.Barnard and W.D.Stein, J. Mol. Biol. 1 (1958) 339.
[9] A.M.Crestfield, W.H.Stein and S.Moore, J. Biol. Chem. 238 (1963) 2413.
[10] G.M.Glick, H.J.Gorney and E.A.Barnard, Biochem. J. 102 (1967) 7c.
[11] M.Bennett, E.Mayhew and L.Weiss, J. Cell Physiol. 74 (1969) 183.
[12] L.Warren, M.C.Glick and M.K.Nass, Specificity of Cell Surfaces, eds. B.D.Davis and L.Warren (Prentice Hall, New York, 1967) pp. 109–127.
[13] A.I.Lansing and T.B.Rosenthal, J. Cell. Comp. Physiol. 40 (1952) 337.

[14] E.Burka, W.Schreml and E.Kick, Biochem. Biophys. Res. Commun. 26 (1967) 334.
[15] J.Brachet, The Biological Role of Ribonucleic Acids (Elsevier, Amsterdam, 1960) p. 85.
[16] E.Mayhew, J. Gen. Physiol. 49 (1966) 717.
[17] E.Mayhew, J. Cellular Comp. Physiol. 69 (1967) 305.
[18] S.Eisenberg, S.Ben-or and F.Doljanski, Exptl. Cell Res. 26 (1962) 451.
[19] L.Weiss, J. Nat. Cancer Inst. 36 (1966) 837.
[20] L.Weiss and T.M.Ratcliffe, J. Natl. Cancer Inst. 41 (1968) 957.
[21] E.Mayhew and L.Weiss, Exptl. Cell Res. 50 (1968) 441.
[22] E.Mayhew and C.Levinson, J. Cellular Comp. Physiol. 72 (1968) 73.
[23] F.L.Bygrave, Nature 214 (1967) 667.
[24] M.Lubin, Nature 213 (1967) 1451.
[25] L.Weiss and C.Levinson, J. Cell Physiol. 73 (1969) 31.
[26] A.S.G.Curtis, The Cell Surface: Its Molecular Role in Morphogenesis (Logos/Academic Press, London and New York, 1967).
[27] L.Weiss and R.F.Woodbridge, Federation Proc. 26 (1967) 88.
[28] L.Weiss, The Cell Periphery, Metastasis, and Other Contact Phenomena (North-Holland, Amsterdam, 1967).
[29] L.Weiss, In Vitro 5 (1970) 48.
[30] A.D.Bangham and B.A.Pethica, Proc. Roy. Phys. Soc. 28 (1960) 43.
[31] L.Weiss, J. Cell Biol. 26 (1965) 735.
[32] L.Weiss, E.Mayhew and K.Ulrich, Lab. Invest. 15 (1966) 1304.
[33] L.Weiss, J. Cell Biol. 30 (1966) 39.
[34] L.Weiss, Exptl. Cell Res. 37 (1965) 540.
[35] L.Weiss, J. Theoret. Biol. 18 (1968) 9.
[36] L.Weiss, Exptl. Cell Res. 51 (1968) 609.
[37] L.Weiss, Exptl. Cell Res. 53 (1968) 603.
[38] L.Weiss, J. Gen. Microbiol. 32 (1963) 331.
[39] L.Weiss, J. Theoret. Biol. 6 (1964) 275.

GROWTH-REGULATING INTERACTIONS AMONG CULTURED ANIMAL CELLS*

H.RUBIN

Department of Molecular Biology and Virus Laboratory,
University of California, Berkeley, California 94720, USA

When skin is wounded, previously quiescent epidermal cells migrate into the wound and initiate multiplication which continues until the gap is filled [1]. Similar examples of wound healing are known for a variety of epithelial tissues in animals [2]. Disparate hypotheses have been proposed to explain the response to wounding. It has been variously proposed that (a) wounding releases a diffusible growth-promoting substance which stimulates multiplications - the so-called wound hormone hypothesis [3]; (b) wounding decreases the local concentration of a diffusible feedback inhibitor produced by the cells themselves, thus unleashing the full growth potential of the cells - the chalone hypothesis [1]; (c) the escape from contact with or enclosure by other cells is itself sufficient to initiate growth - the contact-inhibition hypothesis [4].

One thing all the hypotheses agree upon is that the relation between an animal cell and its neighbors has an important bearing on its growth rate. It is thus necessary to study growth-regulating effects of cells in populations of cells with well-defined geometrical relations to one another, and under highly reproducible conditions of numbers and milieu.

Tissue culture offers certain advantages for studying growth-regulating effects. The numbers and geometrical relationships can be varied at will. Manipulations are easily made, accurate measurements are available for many aspects of growth and metabolism, and the composition of the medium is subject to control, at least within certain limits. It has the disadvantage of course of requiring the disruption of the normal relationships between cells, tissues and organs and of changing the nutritional conditions. However, it seems a necessary compromise to advance our knowledge beyond the classical obser-

* This investigation was supported by U.S. Public Health Service Research Grants CA 04774 and CA 05619 from the National Cancer Institute.

vations of *in vivo* regulation. Since we must assume ignorance about the factors involved in regulation, the least we can do is try to maintain the normal genotype of the cells and some semblance of the normal relationships between cells.

Some recent experiments on growth regulation in tissue culture meet these minimal provisos. Chick embryos provide a constantly renewable source of cells, and we can minimize concern about the altered genotype of cells which is found in tissue culture lines by using only cells recently obtained from the embryo. Growing them in monolayers provides maximal opportunity for rapid and repeated manipulation, as well as precise quantitation while allowing cells to associate in groups.

Chick embryo cells grow in an exponential manner when the population density is low. If the medium is not changed, and the serum concentration is relatively low, the growth rate of the cells decreases when they become confluent. Emphasis is on "decreases", since the cells continue to grow, albeit at a reduced rate, as long as the medium is not depleted of nutrients. Either adenine or folic acid is needed in large amounts.

We now arrive at an apparent paradox which has plagued thinking in this field.

A non-depleted medium is defined as one which can support rapid multiplication of a low-density population of cells up to confluency at a rate equal to that of fresh medium. Medium removed from confluent cultures may be non-depleted in this sense, but is clearly altered since the addition of fresh medium to a *confluent* culture will initiate a burst of DNA synthesis and mitosis. The same fresh medium will not support any faster growth in non-confluent cultures than will the used medium removed from the confluent culture. So the used medium lacks material needed for maximal growth of confluent cells but not for maximal growth of non-confluent cells. The missing material can be provided by simply adding serum rather than by changing the medium. I use the word "material" because we have no indication that only a single factor in serum is responsible. It is apparent, however, that the material is either absorbed easily on cells, or is readily inactivated by them, because it quickly disappears from the medium when the population density of the cells is high.

It is evident that confluency or crowding slows down the growth rate of cells as long as we do not add fresh serum. It is also evident that mere contact among the cells is insufficient to slow the growth of the cells in our medium, since all the cells are in contact with one another, however limited that contact may be, when they have reached a population density only one-fourth as great as that of a confluent monolayer. Yet it is at this population density that the cells grow most rapidly. We have shown that the contacts are fully functional at the sub-confluent densities by measuring the electrical coupling between the cells (O'lague and Rubin, unpublished). The cells exhibit a high degree of coupling even when the areas of contact are small. The high degree of electrical coupling shows that ions move freely among the cells. In view of the sustained rapid growth of the cells after contact is first established, it seems inappropriate to refer to the growth-inhibiting effects of cellular inter-action as "contact inhibition" since the inhibition is expressed only after the cultures become confluent. A more neutral term, density-dependent inhibition, is more suitable at our current state of ignorance. (To complicate things a bit further, it should be remarked that it might be possible to find conditions, i.e., lowering the serum concentration or the use of selectively depleted media, which would unmask an effect of limited contact on growth rate.)

Chick embryo cells can be transformed to the malignant state by infection with Rous sarcoma virus (RSV). The definitive tissue culture characteristic of cells in this state is their escape from contact inhibition. They continue to grow at a maximal rate even after they have achieved confluency, as long as adequate nutrient is supplied. The transformed cells are less adhesive than normal cells to both cells and substratum, and tend to become rounded. Foci of transformed cells frequently have a cell-free "hole" in the center as a result of the detachment and retraction of the transformed cells under tension from the surrounding sheet of normal cells. Many of the transformed cells detach entirely from the dish, and float in the medium. In a culture containing many transformed cells, the entire sheet of cells including uninfected cells is readily detached. The morphological transformation itself can be suppressed among infected cells by incorporating relatively high concentrations of calf serum - and particularly of fetal bovine serum - in the medium [5].

This array of observations about the reduced adhesiveness of transformed cells, their effect on other cells and suppression of the transformation by serum, suggested that substances responsible for the transformation might be re-leased into the medium. Accordingly, we tested the medium of transformed cultures for its capacity to stimulate DNA synthesis and mitosis in crowded cultures of uninfected chick embryo cells.

Such activity can indeed be demonstrated in the medium, and it is not as-sociated with the virus particles. This "overgrowth stimulating factor", or OSF, is non-dialyzable and precipitated with 60% ammonium sulfate. It has no effect on the already rapid growth of sparse cultures of cells. A potent pre-paration of OSF can prolong confluent chick embryo cells in a rapid growth phase for at least 65 hr beyond the time that an untreated culture has slowed markedly in growth rate.

The activity of OSF is reduced by heating at $60°C$ for 30 min, but it is not abolished even at $90°C$, leading us to believe that more than one substance is involved. The action of OSF can be mimicked by adding small amounts of trypsin to the medium. Insulin and collagen also display some activity.

Our present guess is that the major component of OSF is a protease like trypsin, but with much more restricted substrate specificity. The most likely substrates would be those components of the cell surface responsible for the development of contacts with other cells and consequently for density dependent inhibition of cell growth. It is through this functional approach that we hope to learn more about the regulatory aspects of the social behavior of animal cells and ultimately about the nature of the cell surface and its plasma membrane.

References

[1] W.S.Bullough and E.Lawrence, Proc. Roy. Soc. (London) B151 (1960) 517.
[2] H.Florey, General pathology (Saunders and Co., London, 1962) 3rd ed., p. 559.
[3] M.Abercrombie, Symp. Soc. Exp. Biol. 11 (1957) 235.
[4] L.N.Castor, J. Cell Physiol. 72 (1969) 161–172.
[5] H.Rubin, Virology 12 (1960) 14–31.

CHANGES IN THE CHEMICAL ARCHITECTURE
OF TRANSFORMED CELL SURFACES*

Max M.BURGER
*Department of Biochemical Sciences, Princeton University,
Princeton, New Jersey 08540, USA*

1. Introduction

The cell surface is thought to be either a direct or indirect mediator for growth control. For this and other reasons, it is assumed that it is the surface membrane which is primarily involved in phenomena like invasive growth, loss of contact inhibition of growth as well as metastasizing properties of the neoplastic cell. Furthermore, many aberrations of biophysical phenomena can be ascribed to the cell periphery [1] and many histopathologic, i.e. morphologic aberrations can be seen in the cell periphery.

These changes, including the morphological ones, must be reflecting changes at the molecular or macromolecular level [2]. All efforts to find such chemical differences in the surface membrane, however, were only directed at possible differences in the analytical composition of normal versus malignant cytoplasmatic membranes [3–6]. In the upper half of fig. 1, I have summarized all different possibilities applying to such alterations in composition.

We have suggested a new type of change in the cell surface membrane [7] which is not compositional and which would not have been detected with analytical procedures. These are the configurational changes. Some of them are put together in the lower half of fig. 1. We are primarily thinking of configurational changes at the supramolecular level, i.e. at the level of whole macromolecular complexes or layers but we do not want to exclude rearrangements in the strict sense of conformational changes, i.e. within single macromolecules.

The detection of a change in the architecture of a cell membrane necessitates an approach entirely different from the analytical chemical approach. Such an attempt is summarized in the following.

* This investigation was supported by USPHS-grant CA-10151, Career award 1-K4-CA-16, 765 and grant P-450 from the American Cancer Society.

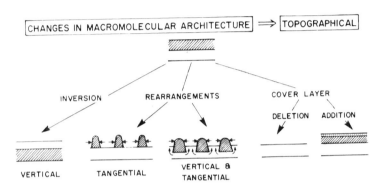

Fig. 1. Summary of possible membrane changes in the process of transformation from a normal to a malignant cell.

An agglutinin was found as an impurity of wheat germ lipase which reacted under similar conditions only with virally transformed cells but not with the untransformed mother cells indicating that the virally transformed cells had a component which was not present at the surface of the untransformed cell [8].

We purified this agglutinin initially by conventional procedures giving rise to two bands upon polyacrylamide disc gel electrophoresis [8]. A new procedure was developed [9] which yielded only one band [7]. The principle of this technique is outlined in fig. 2. Both procedures gave rise to a single symmetrical peak in the ultracentrifuge indicating further homogeneity for the final compound (fig. 3).

Agglutination was measured by two independent procedures. One consisted of counting the remaining amount of non-agglutinated single cells as well as the number of cells in the average aggregate. The other procedure consisted of measuring the adsorption of tritiated agglutinin to the cell surface [10]. It was found that the semi-quantitative procedure of counting with the microscope, which was chosen as a routine assay, was reliable and comparable to the adsorption procedure.

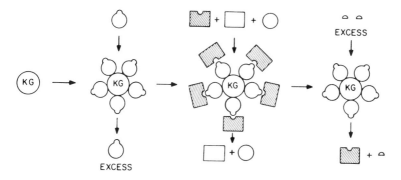

Fig. 2. Model for hapten elution purification technique. Ovomucoid molecules ⬠ which have a specific site interacting with agglutinin are attached to a column consisting of Kieselguhr beads KG . Crude wheat germ agglutinin is put over this column and only agglutinin molecules which have the specific interacting site for ovomucoid will stick to the columns. Everything else will come off the column. The hapten inhibitor (N-acetylglucosamine or chitobiose ⌒) which is added in excess and has the same type of site as ovomucoid will pull off specifically the agglutinin molecules and the small hapten can be removed by dialysis. Although the product was pure, very poor yields make this procedure less efficient than the one we have described earlier [8].

Using hapten inhibition, we found that N-acetylglucosamine must be part of the determinant site on the tumor cell surface but that the site must contain more than N-acetylglucosamine since chitobiose, i.e. the disaccharide of N-acetylglucosamine was even a better inhibitor per N-acetylglucosamine residue than the monosaccharide. Both the monosaccharide and the disaccharide also inhibit the uptake of ^{3}H-agglutinin [10] and both reverse the agglutination reaction, i.e. they dissociate aggregates. No other sugar had any effect on these processes. These findings are part of our evidence that transformed cell surfaces have an N-acetylglucosamine containing receptor on the surface which interacts directly with the agglutinin while the normal cell is lacking such a receptor at the surface. Recent work has confirmed [5] and refined [11] these conclusions.

2. Significance of this surface site

Does the acquisition of this agglutinin receptor site have anything to do with the neoplastic properties of the transformed cell? At the present time, we cannot give evidence for a causal relationship. All that can be said is that

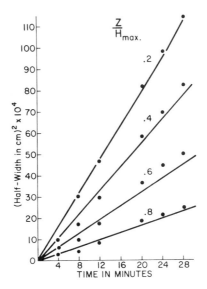

Fig. 3. Squared half widths of the ultracentrifugal peak at different times. The squared half widths were measured at different heights of the ultracentrifugal peak (20, 40, 60 and 80% of maximal height) at different time intervals during centrifugation. Linearity at different levels indicates that the peak is symmetrical and therefore that the material is homogeneous in the gravitational field. The results given are those from Goldberg [9] from material obtained by our earlier procedure. The same linear behavior was observed for the agglutinin purified by the hapten elution procedure described earlier [7].

there is a close correlation between the presence of this site on the cell surface and a property of the transformed cell which is thought to be closely related to malignancy in general, i.e. the loss of contact inhibition of growth.

(a) A comparison of different lines derived from the same mouse fibroblast line (3T3) revealed that agglutinability was in the order of their loss of contact inhibition of growth [12]. Dr. Pollack and I did not find any exception to this rule (fig. 4). If one could select cells which behave normally in tissue culture from a line of formerly transformed cells, the agglutinin site should also disappear if this site is closely related to the property of loss of contact inhibition of growth in the malignant cell. The results have corroborated this prediction precisely:

A cell line (F1^2-SV101) which was derived from the virally transformed SV101 line [13] and which had lost its neoplastic property of loss of contact inhibition did not agglutinate any more. This cell nevertheless still contained the tumor virus genome, made tumor-virus specific messenger RNA and tumor

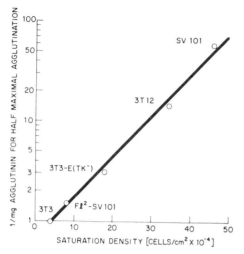

Fig. 4. Correlation between loss of contact inhibition of growth (= saturation density) and agglutinability. These results are given in non-graphical form in Pollack and Burger [12].

virus specific protein; i.e. T-antigen. We can, therefore, conclude from these results that the tumor virus genome may probably be necessary for initiating the surface changes to a tumor cell but it is certainly not sufficient to keep up the neoplastic characteristics.

(b) A comparison of the agglutinabilities of different cell lines from different animals (table 1) leads to the same conclusion. The saturation densities, i.e. the loss of contact inhibition of growth are not given but they would correlate in precisely the same order as is given in the table with increasing agglutinability.

It is becoming more and more evident that loss of contact inhibition of growth as measured *in vitro* seems to be correlated with the property of tumor identicity as measured *in vivo* [14] and we therefore would like to suggest that the expression of this agglutinin receptor site is closely related to changes in the cell surface which are sustaining or expressing malignant properties.

3. Mechanism of formation of the site

Whenever one found and whenever one will find differences in the future

Table 1
Half maximal agglutinability of different cell lines. Agglutinability was tested [8] on cells which were harvested with EDTA or occasionally mechanically (liver). Results are given in milligrams agglutinin per ml necessary for half maximal agglutination

Untransformed	mg/ml	Transformed lines	mg/ml
Rat liver cells	1.575	PY BHK	0.020
Chick embryo fibroblasts	1.200	PY 3T3	0.010
3T3 Subcultured before confluency	0.975	SV40 3T3	0.030
3T3 Selected for less contact inhibition by sub-culturing after confluency	0.660	AD 12 BHK	0.025
BHK 21	0.370		

between normal and tumor cells, immediately the question is asked how this particular change came about during the conversion from the normal to the tumor cell.

Whenever the histopathologist found morphological differences in tumor cells at the beginning of this century, he tried to explain cancer in morphological terms. Similarly, one tries nowadays to find molecular explanations for a newly discovered chemical change as soon as such a change is evident in the hope that it may become of more general validity later on.

I can think of three possible mechanisms for the conversion of the non-agglutinable to the agglutinable form (fig. 5).

(1) The host cell may be devoid of agglutinin receptors and the incoming virus which carries the information for the site in its DNA may start production of the agglutination sites.

(2) The host cell carries the information for the surface site and does not produce enough sites to allow agglutination to occur. The incoming virus induces or activates the formation of the surface site.

(3) The host cell may have virtually all agglutination sites in a cryptic form and the virus would convert the cell surface in such a fashion that the agglutination site would be exposed and become available to the agglutinin.

The first mechanism can be excluded since we have seen that some tissue

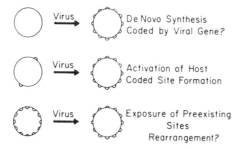

Fig. 5. Mechanism for the formation or exposure of the agglutinin receptor.

culture cells seem to have the agglutination site to a minor degree prior to viral transformation (BHK cells, table 1). Furthermore, this mechanism is unlikely since the many tumor viruses, some of them with very little DNA, would all have to carry the same gene coding for the formation of this particular surface site. It may be mentioned parenthetically that we have found various tumor cell lines which have been chemically transformed and which display this agglutination site as well.

The only way we can distinguish between mechanism 2 and mechanism 3 is by isolating and comparing the sites from the transformed and untransformed cells. We developed a procedure for isolating such surface sites [15] which consists of a hypotonic shock whereby surface particles are released (fig. 6). If the conditions which vary from cell to cell are chosen properly, only receptor sites-containing particles are released but no cells are disrupted, neither are the permeability barriers for cytoplasmatic macromolecules damaged. Measuring the total amount of receptor sites released with such a procedure, we could not find any significant difference between untransformed and transformed cells [16].

In view of the fact that untransformed cells do not agglutinate and do not absorb ^{3}H-agglutinin to N-acetylglucosamine containing receptor sites [10], we were left with only one interpretation of these results: the agglutination site is buried in the normal cell surface and this cryptic site becomes exposed during transformation.

Such reasoning is, however, based on indirect evidence and it would have been more convincing if we could have found direct proof that normal cells have the agglutinin site at all times and that agglutination can be directly demonstrated simply by exposing these sites.

The most obvious manipulation to expose this site was, of course, to digest the normal cell surface with enzymes. Lipases, glycosidases, mucopolysac-

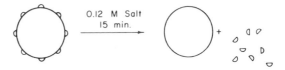

Fig. 6. Model for release of receptor site by hypotonic shock.

charide degrading enzymes, DNAse and RNAse did not expose the site.
Proteolytic enzymes, however, converted the normal cells into the agglutinable form [7]. Very low concentrations were active in a very short time
(0.007 mg/ml ficin in 2 min). All proteases we have tested so far were capable
of eliciting the conversion and all normal cells not agglutinating if harvested
from monolayers with EDTA became agglutinable after the short treatment
with proteases. The proteolytic activity is necessary since trypsin or pepsin,
inactivated by various means did not act [7]. Furthermore, the proteolytic
enzymes do not act just by binding to the surface and inducing a conformational change; neither do they act at the inside of the cell (or anywhere below
the surface) since the trypsin bound to a particle was as active as soluble trypsin. This particulate trypsin could be washed away from the cell surface after
only a 30-sec exposure of the cell surface to the enzymatic activity.

Criticism may be raised about the validity of comparing sites on virally
transformed cells with the protease exposed sites on the untransformed cells.
Although agglutination can be detected only after addition of agglutinin in
both cases, it could be that the two sites are qualitatively and quantitatively
different. Immunological identity in both the qualitative and the quantitative
sense was shown by the following findings:

Quantitatively: For both the trypsin treated untransformed as well as the
transformed cells, precisely the same agglutinability was eventually reached
by increasing protease concentrations or exposure time. Earlier, we have
shown results for hamster cells [7] identical to those in fig. 7 for mouse
fibroblasts (3T3). Sufficient trypsin treatment evokes precisely the same agglutinability in an asymptotical manner as is already present in virally transformed (Polyoma virus) cells, be they trypsin exposed or not.

Qualitatively: Exactly the same hapten inhibitors inhibit the agglutination
of trypsin treated normal cells as were found to inhibit the agglutination of
transformed cells. No other hapten inhibitors could be found, indicating that
the determinant group at the agglutination site is qualitatively identical in
trypsinized normal and transformed cell surfaces.

Further support for this notion comes from the following experiment:

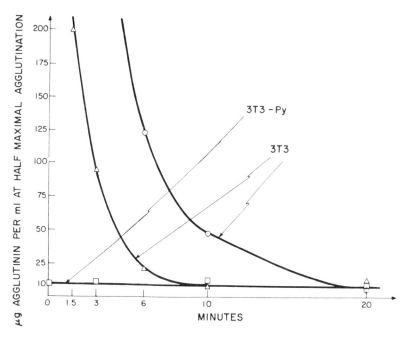

Fig. 7. Dependence of agglutinability of 3T3 mouse calls on duration of treatment with trypsin. For the time indicated, 4×10^6 cells per ml were treated with trypsin concentrations indicated below. The reaction was stopped with a five-fold excess of soybean trypsin inhibitor; the cells were pelleted, resuspended and tested for agglutinability. o—o 3T3 cells in 0.001% trypsin; △—△ 3T3 cells in 0.0025% trypsin. □—□ Polyoma virus transformed 3T3 cells in 0.0025% trypsin.

true hapten inhibitors should dissociate agglutinated cells based on mass law principles. Table 2 shows that the same compounds which were found to be inhibitors of the agglutination were also able to reverse agglutination of transformed cells. Reversal of agglutination of trypsinized untransformed cells occurred at the same concentrations as was found for transformed cells.

It could be argued that agglutination does not only reflect binding of the agglutinin molecule to its receptor site but the actual attachment of one cell to another which depends on many factors like zeta potential, etc. The difference brought about by trypsinization could then be interpreted not as a difference in exposure of the N-acetylglucosamine containing site but a difference in factors like the zeta potential. With the following finding, such arguments become very unlikely.

Table 2

Reversibility. The concentrations necessary for 50% reversibility of agglutination after 10 min are given. Where no results are given, no reversibility could be observed up to 0.1 M of the inhibitor. Cells harvested with EDTA were treated with 0.008% trypsin for 3 min and the enzyme stopped with soybean inhibitor

Compound	BHK Trypsinized	3T3 Trypsinized	Chick embryo fibroblast trypsinized	PY3T3 no trypsin	SV3T3 no trypsin
N-acetylglucosamine (M)	0.004	0.004	0.008	0.004	0.004
Chitobiose (M)	0.0006	0.0006	0.0012	0.006	0.006
Ovomucoid (mg/ml)	0.02	0.04	0.02	0.04	0.02
N-acetylgalactosamine (M)	–	–	>0.08	–	–
Glucosamine (M)	–	–	>0.05	–	–
Glucose (M)	–	–	–	–	–

Not only is agglutinability elicited by the treatment with proteolytic enzymes but the actual binding of ^{3}H-agglutinin to the surface receptor could also be brought up to precisely the same level as that of untreated transformed cell surfaces [10].

4. How do proteolytic enzymes expose the site?

Two different mechanisms can account for the proteolytic action. (1) The protease can release a protective cover layer from the surface. (2) The protease can cleave a few peptide linkages and without releasing any surface components expose the receptor site by rearranging the molecular or supramolecular architecture of the surface.

The following preliminary results tend to support the second mechanism by excluding the first: during brief treatment with the limiting doses of trypsin which expose the receptor site, none of the following procedures indicated a measurable release of any surface component above the release taking place in the control incubation without trypsin:

(a) no material was released absorbing at 280 mμ;

(b) no new bands could be observed in the incubation medium upon polyacrylamide disc gel electrophoresis;

(c) after labelling of the surface with fluorescein isothiocyanate at a physiologic pH, no fluorescent material came off. This is much more sensitive than the first procedure;

(d) after labelling of the surface with ^{3}H-leucine, no more label was released with the trypsin as compared to the control.

It might be added here that all procedures indicated a release of some material if significantly higher doses or significantly longer incubation periods were chosen, indicating that the negative results are valid.

Although we cannot exclude release of extremely minute amounts of surface components, we are thinking at the present time that the proteolytic enzymes are cleaving unspecifically a few peptide bonds on the surface. This then is followed by a rearrangement in the conformation or the molecular surface structure giving rise to the exposure of the same sites exposed by viral transformation.

The concept that conformational arrangements are important for agglutination to occur or not to occur is not so novel. I have suggested it earlier when we were forced to conclude that the role of the surface sialic acid in allowing agglutination to occur was to keep the N-acetylglucosamine containing receptor site in such a conformation that the agglutinin molecules could reach it [17].

5. The generality of the phenomenon: sites other than the wheat germ agglutinin sites that are exposed

After we found that viral transformation exposed this N-acetylglucosamine containing wheat germ agglutinating site, more and more evidence has been accumulating that other sites which are present but cryptic in normal cell membranes seem to be exposed upon transformation to the malignant state.

Screening through many plant agglutinins, we have so far found four of them which either agglutinate exclusively transformed cells or which show quantitative differences, indicating that the agglutinin receptor sites are less available in untransformed cells and become more available both after transformation as well as proteolytic treatment [10].

Most of the phyto-agglutinins react with determinant surface groups other than N-acetylglucosamine. For one of them (Concanavalin A) a recent elegant study showed that trypsin not only increases the agglutinability but also exposes further binding sites for labelled agglutinin [18]. Furthermore, as in the case of wheat germ agglutinin [12] again a good correlation could be found between agglutinability and loss of contact inhibition of growth (as measured by saturation densities) [19]. Together, we could establish that the determinant site for Concanavalin A is definitely a different one than that for wheat germ agglutinin.

Defendi is now gathering evidence that other antigenic sites which usually were assumed to be induced or even coded for by the tumor virus (SV40 - surface antigen) could be exposed with the same weak trypsin treatment on the surface of normal uninfected cells [20].

Based on our earlier work and conclusions as well as on confirming reports using similar exposures to proteolytic enzymes, we would like to reiterate the suggestion that multiple sites or whole layers buried within the surface of the normal cell membrane are being exposed during the process of transformation of a normal to a transformed cell. This very phenomenon can be imitated with a brief and light treatment of proteolytic enzymes.

6. Effect of proteolytic enzymes on cell growth

Transformed cells seem to contain surface sites which are not present on the normal untransformed cell. The presence of these sites seems to be linked to a loss of growth control under crowding conditions (loss of contact inhibition of growth). Proteolytic enzymes can expose exactly the same sites. Ergo:

(1) Transformation to malignant cells should: (a) increase or activate all or specific proteolytic enzymes; or (b) make the surface layers more available to the proteolytic enzymes during or after their biogenesis; or (c) change the biogenesis of the surface membrane so that the sites are exposed without the action of proteolytic enzymes.

We are currently working on these aspects without any conclusive results as yet.

(2) Proteolytic enzymes may change growth control mechanisms. We have been working on this problem for over one year with mixed success. Preliminary results have shown that mouse 3T3 cells can be brought to a higher saturation density by the exposure of the monolayer culture to low doses of trypsin. Not all cells respond, however, and the dosage range for different cells varies. The difficulties were mainly due to the fact that certain sera have specific trypsin inhibitors.

Nevertheless, the preliminary success with 3T3 cells makes us confident to suggest that the proteolytic effect on the cell surface may have some physiologic meaning insofar as it may stimulate the growth rate of contact inhibited, possibly also non-contact inhibited cells. This effect may be similar to that of serum [21], i.e. the serum factor itself could be proteolytic in nature.

References

[1] L.Weiss, The Cell Periphery, Metastasis and Other Contact Phenomena (North-Holland, Amsterdam, 1967).
[2] A.B.Pardee, Natl. Cancer Inst. Monograph 14 (1964) 7.
[3] N.Ohta, A.B.Pardee, B.R.McAuslan and M.M.Burger, Biochim. Biophys. Acta 158 (1968) 58.
[4] P.H.Black, H.Wu, E.Meezan, H.T.Robertson and P.W.Robbins, Fed. Proc. 28 (1969) 567.
[5] S.Hakamori and R.W.Jeanloz, J. Biol. Chem. 239 (1964) 3606; S.Hakamori and W.T.Murakami, Proc. Natl. Acad. Sci. U.S. 59 (1968) 254.
[6] C.Tal, Proc. Natl. Acad. Sci. U.S. 54 (1965) 1318.
[7] M.M.Burger, presented at the Gordon Conference on Cellular Contact and Interaction, Meriden, New Hampshire, June 1968, and Proc. Natl. Acad. Sci. U.S. 62 (1969) 994.
[8] M.M.Burger and A.R.Goldberg, Proc. Natl. Acad. Sci. U.S. 57 (1967) 359.
[9] A.R.Goldberg, Ph. D. Thesis, Princeton University (1967).
[10] M.M.Burger, unpublished.
[11] G.Uhlenbeck, H.Otten, W.Rehfeldt, U.Reifenberg and O.Prokop, Z. Immunitätsforsch. 134 (1968) 476.
[12] R.E.Pollack and M.M.Burger, Proc. Natl. Acad. Sci. U.S. 62 (1969) 1074.
[13] R.E.Pollack, H.Green and G.T.Todaro, Proc. Natl. Acad. Sci. U.S. 60 (1968) 126.
[14] S.A.Aaronson and G.T.Todaro, Science 162 (1968) 1024.
[15] M.M.Burger, Nature 219 (1968) 499.
[16] V.Jansons and M.M.Burger, unpublished observations.
[17] M.M.Burger, in: Biological Properties of the Mammalian Surface Membrane, Wistar Symp. Monogr., No. 8, ed. L.A.Manson (Philadelphia, Wistar Inst., 1968) p. 82.
[18] M.Inbar and L.Sachs, in press.
[19] M.Inbar, Z.Rabinowitz and L.Sachs, in press.
[20] V.Defendi and P.Hayry, in preparation.
[21] G.T.Todaro, Y.Matsuya, S.Bloom, A.Robbins and H.Green, Wistar Inst. Symp. Monogr. 7 (1967) 89; H.M.Temin, J. Cell Physiol. 69 (1967) 377; R.W.Holley and J.A.Kiernan, Proc. Natl. Acad. Sci. U.S. 60 (1968) 300.

A SPECIFIC ANTIGEN-ANTIBODY REACTION AFFECTING ION TRANSPORT IN SHEEP LK ERYTHROCYTES

J.C.ELLORY and E.M.TUCKER

A.R.C. Institute of Animal Physiology, Babraham, Cambridge, UK

1. Introduction

In 1937 Kerr showed that sheep erythrocytes had widely varying K^+ levels [1]. Reinvestigation of this phenomenon by Widdas [2] and Evans [3] in 1954 demonstrated two populations of animals with either high (HK) or low (LK) potassium levels in their red cells. Evans et al. [4] showed that the potassium type was controlled by a single gene pair, with LK dominant over HK. In 1966, Rasmusen and Hall [5,6] found that a specific blood group antibody, anti-M was identifying an antigen (M) on all HK and heterozygous LK cells. They proposed the scheme for genotypes shown in table 1. Tucker and Rasmusen, working independently, prepared an antibody which identified the complementary m factor, by immunizing HK sheep with LK cells [7,8]. Although this factor was first called m, Rasmusen and Tucker have since agreed that a more suitable nomenclature would be L. Since these two antigens appear to be very closely identified with the K^+ system in sheep red

Table 1
Potassium levels and genotypes in sheep erythrocytes

	LK	LK	HK
K^+ mM per 1 packed cells. $\pm$ S.E.M.	12.3 ± 0.8	15.1 ± 0.8	68.5 ± 0.9
Genotype	$Ka^L Ka^L$ LL (mm)	$Ka^L ka^h$ LM (mM)	$ka^h ka^h$ MM (MM)

cells, they may be intimately involved in the way in which K^+ gradients are maintained. Differences in the pump and leak fluxes of Na^+ and K^+ [9], and the Na^+-K^+ activated ATPase [10,11] between HK and LK cells have been demonstrated, and it seems that LK cells have 3–7 times less pump in their cell membranes than HK cells. This paper describes some effects of anti-M and anti-L on the pump in sheep red cells, in an attempt to investigate the involvement of the antigen with the pump.

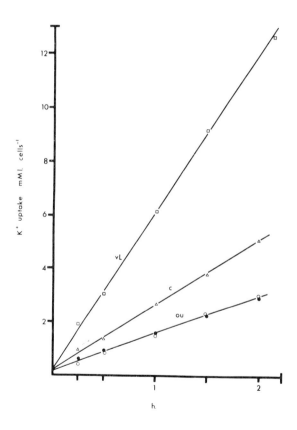

Fig. 1. Typical K^+ uptake for control (c) and anti-L-treated cells (vL). Control and sensitized cells were also incubated in the presence of 5×10^{-5} M ouabain. □–□ anti-L-sensitized cells; ○–○ anti-L-sensitized cells + ouabain; △–△ control; ●–● control + ouabain.

2. The action of anti-L and anti-M on the transport system

When LK sheep red cells, sensitized with anti-L, were incubated in a
^{42}KCl solution to measure the active potassium uptake, a surprising and
dramatic result was achieved: a fourfold stimulation of the ouabain-sensitive
K$^+$ uptake (fig. 1). Control experiments using various HK sera and other antibodies, and experiments with anti-M and anti-L on HK sheep red cells gave
no stimulation at all, and convinced us that the anti-L activation was a specific effect [8]. When other parameters of the transport system, such as the
Na$^+$-K$^+$ activated ATPase [8], or the ouabain-sensitive sodium efflux (fig. 2),
were studied, anti-L had the same stimulatory effect. Since the anti-L used in
the above experiments was a diluted absorbed serum, incubations with serial
dilutions were used to try to establish the maximum stimulatory effect of
anti-L. Fig. 3 shows the dose-response curve obtained in these experiments,

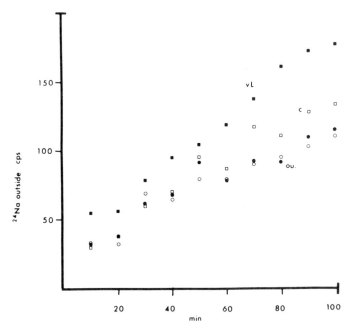

Fig. 2. Sodium loss from control (c) and anti-L-treated cells (vL). Treated and control
cells were also incubated with 5×10^{-5} M ouabain (ou). Cells were loaded with ^{24}Na
overnight. There is a large ouabain-insensitive component of sodium efflux, due to the
high (145 mM) external Na level. ■–■ anti-L-sensitized cells; □–□ control; ●–● anti-L-
sensitized cells + ouabain; ○–○ control cells + ouabain.

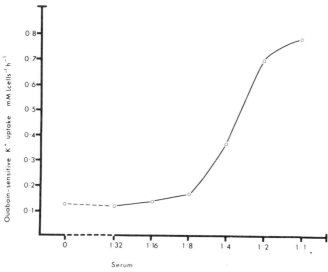

Fig. 3. Dose-response curve for anti-L-sensitization. Cells were incubated in the diluted serum for 1 hr at 32°C at a haematocrit of 0.02. After washing in isotonic buffer, the ouabain-sensitive K^+ uptake was measured over 2 hr.

and the maximum flux achieved with the antibody was 0.9–0.95 mmoles per litre packed cells per hour.

3. Specificity

If this effect is mediated by an antigen-antibody reaction on the LK cell surface, other membrane-bound enzyme activities may be affected. Table 2 shows acetyl-cholinesterase activity of sheep LK red cells before and after sensitization with antibody, measured by the method of Ellman et al. [12]. No change in enzyme activity was observed. Similarly, electrophoretic mobility measurements by the method of Bangham et al. [13] on control and sensitized cells, even after treatment with neuraminidase or at pH 3, showed no difference. It thus seems that the antibody is acting rather specifically at that part of the membrane associated with the potassium transport system.

Table 2
Sheep erythrocyte acetylcholinesterase activity. (Activity expressed in femtomoles per min per cell.)

Type	Control	vL
MM	0.011 ± 0.002	–
ML	0.012 ± 0.002	0.012 ± 0.002
LL	0.010 ± 0.002	0.014 ± 0.004
lamb LL	0.016 ± 0.002	0.019 ± 0.003

4. Development of the antigen L on lamb red cells

At birth all lamb red cells have a high internal K^+ level. In lambs which become LK adults (LL or ML) the red cell K^+ concentration progressively falls until adult levels are reached about 45 days after birth. In 1968 Tucker [14,15] followed the development of M antigen on lamb red cells. She showed that M antigen is only very weak or entirely absent from foetal red cells, and appeared gradually during the first 6 weeks after birth, at the same time that adult potassium levels were being established. This year experiments were carried out to follow the ouabain-sensitive K^+ uptake, and its stimulation by anti-L, in the red cells of three homozygous LK (LL) lambs. Simultaneously the L reaction was tested serologically, and the red cell K^+ recorded. The results [16] indicated the gradual appearance of the L-effect on the circulating cells, with a concomitant fall in both the cell K^+ level and active K^+ uptake. The data are consistent with new cells arriving in the circulation with a reduced pumping capacity and increased L activity.

This conclusion is supported by another experiment, in which red cells taken from lambs at 3 weeks of age, were treated with anti-L, followed by complement. The cells which remained unhaemolysed were recovered and analysed for K^+ by flame photometry, and haemoglobin type by starch gel electrophoresis. The results are shown in table 3. Potassium analysis data are expressed as the K^+/Hb ratio because the growing lamb presents a complex situation with populations of cells with different mean cell volumes, making it difficult to make comparisons on a litre packed cells basis. The recovered cells had a much higher K^+ concentration than the whole cell population, and contained nearly all foetal haemoglobin, indicating they were an older population of cells.

Table 3
Analysis of cells recovered after anti-L sensitization and complement lysis. Erythrocytes from 21- day-old lambs

Type	LL
K^+ meq per g Hb	
Control	0.255
Recovered	0.449
Haemoglobin	
Control	A, foetal, C
Recovered	foetal

5. The role of L substance in the active potassium transport system

There seems to be good evidence that the L factor is closely involved with the sodium pump in LK red cells. It is possible to suggest two hypotheses for its function in apparently modifying the pump:

(1) All lamb and sheep red cells have the same number of pump sites originally, which in LK adults are regulated by L substance to produce the final adult LK type with masked pump sites, and greatly reduced pumping activity.

(2) Sheep red cells always have different numbers of sites, the turnover or efficiency of which is regulated by L substance in LK cells.

If the first hypothesis were true, studies with radioactively-labelled cardiac glycosides should reveal an increased glycoside binding in anti-L-treated cells. In an elegant experiment, Dunham and Hoffman [17] showed 6–7 ouabain binding sites on LK sheep red cells, and 45 on HK sheep cells. We have so far failed to repeat their results, probably due to a higher non-specific binding component, but our experiments with labelled glycoside do show a significantly increased binding in anti-L-sensitized cells (table 4).

Table 4
Ouabain-binding in control and sensitized sheep erythrocytes. Cells exposed to 10^{-8} M ^{3}H-ouabain for 1 hr

	Molecules bound per cell $\pm$ S.E.M.		
No. of expts.	LK	LK vL	HK
5	37 ± 6	64 ± 6	71 ± 8

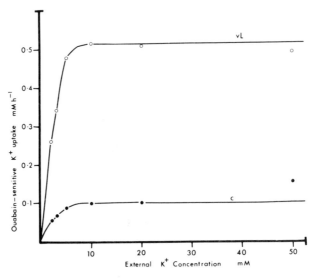

Fig. 4. Ouabain-sensitive potassium uptake in control and anti-L-treated cells at various external K^+ concentrations. ●—● control; ○—○ anti-L-sensitized.

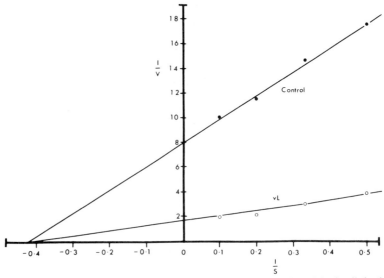

Fig. 5. Michaelis-Menten plot of the data in fig. 4. The control and sensitized cells both give the same K_m. ●—● control; ○—○ anti-L-sensitized.

The fractional increase in binding does not correspond with the larger fractional increase in ATPase activity and Na^+ and K^+ uptake, probably again due to non-specific binding.

If the second hypothesis were true, changes in the affinity of the transport complex might occur. In experiments measuring the active K^+ uptake at various external K^+ concentrations, both control and sensitized cells showed the same concentration dependence (fig. 4), and a Michaelis-Menten plot gave the same K_m for both samples (fig. 5), indicating no change in the affinity of the pump for K^+.

Although the first hypothesis is almost certainly a gross oversimplification, and there is already evidence for fundamental kinetic differences between HK and LK sheep red cells [11,18], it would seem that L substance is closely involved in the way the pumping capacity is regulated in LK red cells. Further studies, and attempts to isolate L substance itself may help to elucidate one of the mechanisms of cellular control of membrane function.

References

[1] S.E.Kerr, J. Biol. Chem. 117 (1937) 227.
[2] W.F.Widdas, J. Physiol. 125 (1954) 18P.
[3] J.V.Evans, Nature 174 (1954) 931.
[4] J.V.Evans, J.W.B.King, B.L.Cohen, H.Harris and F.L.Warren, Nature 178 (1956) 849.
[5] B.A.Rasmusen and J.G.Hall, Science 151 (1966) 1551.
[6] B.A.Rasmusen and J.G.Hall, in: Europ. Soc. for Animal Blood Group Res. Tenth Conf. Paris 453 (Institut National de la Recherche Agronomique, Institut Pasteur, 1966).
[7] B.A.Rasmusen, Genetics 61 (1970) 549.
[8] J.C.Ellory and E.M.Tucker, Nature 222 (1969) 477.
[9] D.C.Tosteson and J.F.Hoffman, J. Gen. Physiol. 44 (1961) 169.
[10] D.C.Tosteson, R.H.Moulton and M.Blaustein, Federation Proc. 19 (1960) 128.
[11] D.C.Tosteson, Federation Proc. 22 (1963) 19.
[12] G.L.Ellman, K.D.Courtney, V.Andres and R.M.Featherstone, Biochem. Pharmacol. 7 (1961) 88.
[13] A.D.Bangham, R.Flemans, D.H.Heard and G.V.F.Seaman, Nature 182 (1958) 642.
[14] E.M.Tucker, J. Physiol. 198 (1968) 33P.
[15] E.M.Tucker, in: Europ. Soc. for Animal Blood Group Res. Eleventh Conf., Warsaw (1968) in press.
[16] J.C.Ellory and E.M.Tucker, J. Physiol. 204 (1969) 101P.
[17] P.B.Dunham and J.F.Hoffman, Federation Proc. 28 (1969) 339.
[18] P.G.Hoffman and D.C.Tosteson, Federation Proc. 28 (1969) 339.

Part 3

CELL CONTACT PHENOMENA IN RELATION
TO IMMUNOLOGICAL AND PHAGOCYTIC PROCESSES

INTRODUCTION

The involvement of membrane-associated events in the initiation and regulation of immune-responses has been suspected for some time but has been supported by experimental evidence only quite recently. The third session of the Conference, entitled: 'Cell Contact Phenomena in relation to immunological and phagocytic processes' presents one of the first organized attempts to create a much needed synthesis between the data and interests of immunologists and of those who are more directly concerned with membrane events. Various aspects of cell interactions leading to immune-responses and of cell surface phenomena that play a role in immune-responses were cited and discussed.

Examples that were discussed include the recognition of the antigens by lymphoid cells; the capability of macrophages to concentrate antigens on their surfaces and the interaction between lymphocytes and tumor cells.

The interaction of macrophages with antigens, as known by many immunologists has a critical primary event in the initiation of immune-responses. The manner in which the molecular configuration and the changes of an antigen influence this interaction was discussed on the basis of recent studies with synthetic antigen. The fact that immune-responses are formed by membrane-associated events and cell to cell interaction was also supported by a report of the modification of the magnitude and quality of immune-responses by agents known to affect membranes.

ANTIGEN RECOGNITION BY LYMPHOID CELLS - A CELL SURFACE PHENOMENON

G.L. ADA

Department of Microbiology, John Curtin School of Medical Research, The Australian National University, Canberra, Australia

1. Introduction

There are many areas of biology where despite the great advances made in recent years, our knowledge of the basic mechanisms involved in biological reactions remains very incomplete. One such area is the relationship between cells - what are the factors which influence the reaction of a cell when it comes into contact with another cell, whether this be of the same or a different type. Of the many observed reactions, one of the most dramatic is between phagocytic cells of a given host animal and foreign (xenogeneic) red cells - the red cells are engulfed by the phagocytic cells. The same phagocytic cells presented with red cells from the same host (syngeneic) ignores them. Clearly, a recognition system is involved and it is most likely that the initial phase of this recognition is membrane mediated. However, it is not always easy to manipulate cell/cell systems so that the mechanisms of interactions can be elucidated. A rather more manageable system is to investigate the reaction of substances with cell surfaces, for the simple reason that the chemical and physical properties of a substance can be more easily studied than those of an intact cell.

The basic phenomenon in immunology is the recognition by a host that a substance, a cell or a collection of cells (tissue) is foreign to itself. This recognition of foreignness sets about a chain of reactions, the result of which is the destruction or removal of the foreign material. One of the ways this is accomplished is by the formation of specific protein molecules - antibodies - which combine with the foreign substance at the molecular level. It is one of the triumphs of molecular biology that in the last decade we have found out much about the structure of these antibody molecules and this in turn is telling us much about their origin and how they are formed. I wish to refer to this work in only a general way - only in so far as it bears on the main aspect of my talk.

Similarly, there has been quite an advance in our knowledge of the nature and structure of antigens - the foreign substances which upon introduction into a host may elicit an antibody response. The nature of antigens is considered elsewhere in the meeting and will not be dealt with here.

What I wish mainly to talk about is the question of recognition of foreign substances by cells and two of the mechanisms involved. My interest in this dates from about 1963 when G.J.V.Nossal and I started a programme to study what happened to antigen upon injection into an animal. In the intervening years, a lot has been found out about the distribution of antigen in lymphoid tissues in both our and a few other laboratories. In short, antigens show definite "localization" patterns in lymphoid tissues, because they become associated with particular cells which are present only in certain areas of the tissue. More recently, I and my co-workers have attempted to determine why antigens become associated with specific cells and what are the factors which influence this behaviour. As a result, we are now able to define some of the parameters of these reactions and it is two of our recent findings that I wish primarily to discuss. As a necessary introduction however, I would like to spend a little time in discussing antibody structure and cells.

2. The properties of antibody molecules

Antibodies are specialized molecules which are formed by the body in response to an antigenic stimulus. They are formed and secreted by specific cells and are present in the circulation. They are classified as globulins and from the point of view of this talk, they have several properties which we need to know about.

(1) Their reactions with antigen show a high degree of specificity, which is comparable in many cases with the specificity of most enzyme-substrate reactions.

(2) Those areas of the antibody molecule wherein lies this specificity - the combining sites for antigen - comprise only 2–3% of the molecule. Portion of the remainder of the molecule has other specific properties and this will be discussed later.

(3) In response to the injection of an antigenic (immunogenic) preparation - a purified "foreign" protein for example - the animal may make many different *types* of antibody molecules, perhaps as many as 10^5. The one feature which all these types of molecules have in common is the ability to react specifically with the antigen. Presumably this means that the amino acid sequences within the antigen-combining sites are the same in all these molecules but that variation occurs in other parts of the structure.

(4) The many different types of molecules can be grouped into at least 5 major classes which differ from each other in properties such as size, electrophoretic mobility, valency, the content of carbohydrate and the number of interchain disulphide bonds and the susceptibility of these bonds to sulphydryl reagents. In humans, these five main classes are called IgG, IgM, IgA, IgE and IgD (Ig denotes immunoglobulin, or antibody). Of these IgG is the most common and for purposes of simplicity and convenience, we will confine most of our future remarks to it.

(5) In electron micrographs [1] the IgG molecule appears to be shaped like the figure Y. It is known to consist of four polypeptide chains. Two of these are light chains (mol. wt. 22,000) and two are heavy chains (mol. wt. 50,000) and they are joined together by a total of four disulphide bonds. If we wed this information to the morphological appearance, a picture may be drawn as in fig. 1a. The four chains are joined as shown. The dashed part of the diagram indicates the region in which great variation in amino acid sequences has been shown or is postulated to occur. IgG has a valency of 2, i.e., one molecule may combine with two molecules of antigen, and electron micrographs show that the antigen binding sites are at the tips of the two upper arms of the Y, so that an antigen:antibody complex may be represented as in fig. 1b. Available evidence suggests that both L and H chains may contribute to the antigen binding site.

(6) IgG can be degraded in specific fashions to yield fragments which are

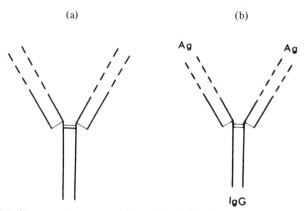

Fig. 1. (a) A diagrammatic representation of the IgG molecule. There are four peptide chains joined by 3 disulphide bonds. The dashed lines indicate regions of the peptide chains where considerable heterogeneity in amino acid sequence occurs.
(b) A diagrammatic representation of the IgG molecule, showing the regions where it is believed binding of antigen molecules (Ag) takes place.

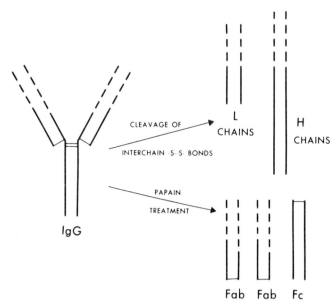

Fig. 2. A diagrammatic representation of the products of reaction if IgG is either treated so that the interchain disulphide bonds are cleavaged or treated with the enzyme papain. In the former case, each IgG molecule yields 2 light and 2 heavy chains whereas papain treatment results in the formation of three fragments, two of which (Fab) are similar, and will still react with antigen whereas the third (Fc) fragment will not react with antigen.

biologically active. Two main procedures are briefly and diagrammatically shown in fig. 2. The L and H peptide chains can be separated from each other if the molecule is treated with both a sulphydryl reagent and a dispersing reagent. No peptide bonds are broken by this procedure. In contrast, treatment of IgG with papain causes cleavage of the H chain at the "hinge" position so that three fragments of similar size but dissimilar properties are obtained. Two of these, the Fab portions, retain the ability to react with antigen but each is monovalent. The third piece, the Fc fragment, has no affinity for antigen but has other properties (see below).

(7) Thus, two arms of the molecule are concerned with the reaction with antigen. What is the purpose of the third arm, the Fc fragment? There is substantial evidence that complement binds to the Fc portion of the IgG molecule and that the Fc portion also confers on the intact molecule the ability to traverse the placenta. Some preparations of IgG bind to cells. The Fab

fragments, isolated from these preparations, do not bind to cells so it has
been inferred that the Fc portion of the IgG molecule is responsible for this
activity. Part of this article will be concerned with the demonstration that
the Fc portion of IgG will bind to particular cells.

3. Cells involved in the immune response

The structure of IgG is now known in some detail and current work supports the belief that antibody molecules are synthesized in a manner which
is consistent with the dogma that information flows from DNA-RNA protein.
Similarly, there is much information concerning the properties of antigens.
The area of great uncertainty is what happens in between the injection of an
antigen into an animal and the production of antibody by cells. Does antigen
only react with *one* type of cell causing it to form antibody? Is the co-operation of two or more types of cells needed for this purpose? The problem is
made more complicated (and far more interesting) by the knowledge that a
variety of effects may follow the introduction of antigen into a host - one is
the formation of antibody and this may result from the reaction of antigen,
possibly processed in some way after uptake by a macrophage, with either
"virgin" cells (primary response) or with primed cells, that is, a cell which
has previously come into contact with the same antigen (secondary response).
The other effect is the induction of tolerance, a specific reaction which is
manifested by the inability of the host to respond to a particular antigen
while still retaining the potential to respond to other antigens. It is currently
speculated that tolerance is the result of antigen reacting directly with "virgin"
cells so that they are inactivated and cannot respond by making sufficient
antibody to be recognised by standard techniques.
    Most evidence available supports the contention that the induction of
antibody formation requires the co-operation of at least two types of cells.
One cell is obviously the precursor cell of that which is stimulated to synthe-
size and secrete antibody. If we confine ourselves to a consideration of the
primary response, this cell is called a "virgin" cell, an immunologically competent cell or the progenitor cell. It is probably a small lymphocyte. The
identity of the other cell type(s) is in much greater doubt. In some systems,
macrophages may play an accessory role; in at least one other system, this
may not be the case.
    Nossal and I originated our research on the premiss that if we followed in
detail the fate of injected antigen, particularly in respect to the lymphoid
organs, we would be able to describe with some accuracy the behaviour of

the antigen, particularly regarding its distribution between various cell types in lymphoid tissues. This study has allowed two general statements to be made. (1) During an immune response, the cells in a lymph node which are actively secreting specific antibody contain few or no antigen molecules. (2) The injected antigen is trapped in two areas of the lymph node and two types of non-antibody forming cells are involved. (a) The first are phagocytic cells - macrophages - which engulf and degrade the antigen. (b) The second are reticular cells which occur in areas of the node called lymphoid follicles. It is about the reaction between antigen and reticular cells in lymphoid follicles I wish to speak.

The technique which has mainly been used in our studies is that of radio-autography. In brief, the antigen is labelled with the isotope ^{125}I. For *in vivo* work, the labelled antigen is injected into the animal and at various times thereafter, the lymph nodes draining the injection site are excised and their radioactivity measured. After the node is fixed, sections are cut, placed on slides and covered with photographic emulsion. After an appropriate exposure time, the emulsion is developed. Grains in the emulsion over the section indicate not only the areas in the tissue where antigen is present but also in many cases the cells in which the labelled antigen is present. Alternatively, a cell suspension prepared from lymphoid tissue may be mixed *in vitro* with labelled antigen. Those cells which react with antigen may be detected by making a "smear" of the cells on a glass slide and again carrying out radioautography. In this case, it is easy to detect individual cells which have reacted with the antigen.

In both the above procedures, examination is normally carried out at $100-1000 \times$ magnification and using ^{125}I, it is usually not possible to say where in a cell the isotope is present. Much higher resolution is obtainable by extending the technique to thinner sections covered with monomolecular layers of emulsion which may then be examined in the electron microscope.

4. The localization of antigen in follicles of lymph nodes

Portion of any antigen which is injected subcutaneously into an animal comes into contact with macrophages in the medullary area of the draining lymph nodes. The antigen is rapidly taken into the cells and is present mainly in vesicles which become associated with and fuse with lysosome-like bodies. Most of the antigen becomes degraded, but some persists. Very little remains at or near the plasma membrane [2] .

Some antigens may also become localized in the lymphoid follicles of the

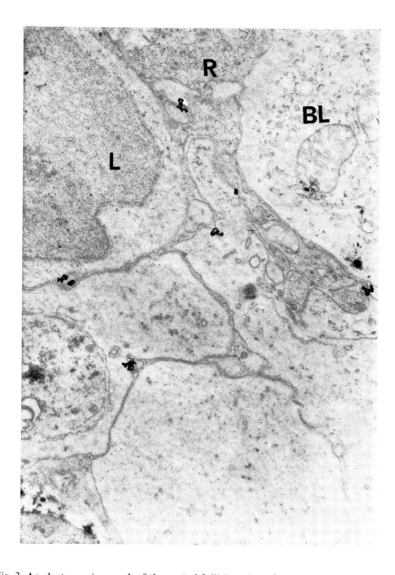

Fig. 3. An electron micrograph of the central follicle region of a rat lymph node, removed 24 hr after the injection of ^{125}I-labelled rat IgG. The grains in the radioautograph are located intercellularly. A reticular cell (R) is interposed between lymphocyte (L) and blast cell (BL). Magnification X 21,500. The author is indebted to his colleagues, Professor G.J.V.Nossal, Dr. Z.Herd, Mrs. J.Mitchell and Mr. A.Abbot for supplying this micrograph.

node. The follicles are collections of cells lying in the cortex of the node, and a few cell layers deep under the external capsule of the node. In lymph nodes that are not undergoing antigenic stimulation, the follicle consists primarily of a collection of lymphocytes which appear to be "held" in a three-dimensional random network of reticular cells. The reticular cells seem to be designed to have a high plasma membrane/cell volume ratio. This property is manifested by long cytoplasmic processes which interdigitate between the lymphoid cells. It is not hard to imagine in fact that this would be an ideal way for circulating cells - the lymphocytes - to have the maximum chance of contacting a fixed cell - the reticulum cell. And this is very close to what we believe is the purpose of this anatomical structure - to allow circulating cells to come into contact not so much with the reticular cell membrane but more importantly with material present on the outside surface of the membrane - with antigen in fact. For high resolution radioautographs indicate that antigen is held in lymphoid follicles on or near the plasma membrane of this reticulum cell (fig. 3). Experiments using ferritin as antigen (which can be seen in electron micrographs because of the iron core of the particle) are also consistent with this interpretation (Nossal and Abbot, personal communication). This then is a very different treatment of antigens compared to their fate in macrophages present in the medulla of the node.

Two important questions need to be asked and answered. (1) What is the *mechanism* of antigen localization in the lymphoid follicle? (2) What is the *purpose* of this phenomenon? We know more about the former than the latter.

There is now much evidence which supports the contention that the major cause of antigen localization in lymphoid follicles is the presence of antibody. (The evidence for this statement results from the work of several laboratories and will not be given in detail here.) The antibody may be in the form of the so-called natural antibody or may be specific antibody either given passively to the host or produced in the host during an immune response. The most dramatic effect can be seen when a labelled antigen, which if injected by itself does not localize in the follicle, is premixed with specific antibody before injection or injected into an animal previously immunized with this antigen. There may be a greater uptake of the antigen into the medullary macrophages compared to previously but there is also now a very heavy concentration of the antigen in the follicle. Three possible mechanisms to explain this localization in follicles come to mind. The first is that the follicle acts simply as a non-specific "filter" for the removal of large antigen-antibody complexes. This is very unlikely as particulate or flocculated antigens which might also be expected to be filtered off there because of their size do not lodge there [3].

G.L.ADA

The other two possibilities are either that antigen (and antigen-antibody complexes) might lodge in the follicles because of some affinity of the *antigen* for the reticular cell membrane or that globulin (antibody) or antigen-antibody complexes might lodge in the follicle because of some affinity of the antibody for the reticular cell membrane. The finding that labelled globulin (IgG or IgM: syngeneic or xenogeneic) injected alone became localized in the follicles seemed to favour the latter possibility but it could still be argued that a cross-reacting antigen, already present in the follicle, reacted with the injected globulin. A more definite answer was obtained by studying the behaviour of globulin fragments. These were prepared - L chains, H chains, the Fab and Fc fragments - from rabbit IgG, labelled and injected into rats. The answer was clear cut. Only those fragments containing the Fc portion of the molecule (i.e., the Fc fragment itself and H chains) localized in the follicles [4] . It seems most likely then that the molecular arrangement of antigen-antibody complexes in lymphoid follicles is like a sandwich in which the globulin is the filling and the antigen and cell wall are the slices of bread. We believe that the antigen is held by the Fab portions of the antibody and the Fc portion of the antibody anchors the antigen-antibody complex to the cell wall. It is then logical to ask - what is the mechanism of the reaction of the Fc fragment with the cell wall. Is there a configuration in the cell membrane which is in some way complementary to the Fc fragment? We have begun to look at this possibility. H chains from rabbit IgG were reacted with cyanogen bromide, a reagent which cleaves the peptide bond adjacent to a methionyl group. Three peptides (obtained through the courtesy of Dr. J. Cebra) were chosen, namely C3, C4 and C5. These peptides embraced most of the portion of the H chain which is present in the Fc fragment. Of these peptides, only one, C3, containing about 100 amino acid residues and a carbohydrate moiety, localized strongly in the lymphoid follicles. Work is in progress to see if smaller active peptides can be prepared.

What is the purpose of this phenomenon? As antigen present in follicles often persists there for some time (and frequently when antigen is no longer present in other areas of the node) the phenomenon may simply be a means of sequestering antigen so that it can no longer function as an inducer of an immune response; or, as we believe more likely, it is a means of retaining antigen (which would otherwise be rapidly phagocytosed) *extracellularly* so that contact with the appropriate cells can take place. An important facet of this second proposal is that, in terms of the amount of antigen required, this would be an extremely efficient method for bringing antigen into contact with many of the appropriate cells. If the antigen in the follicles was to play such a functional role, it would be expected that the other cells present in

the follicles - the lymphocytes - could be shown to circulate *through* the follicles and thus potentially be able to contact the antigen. Though there is
some evidence showing that this may occur [5] further work is needed. If
however we assume that contact between circulating lymphocytes and bound
antigen in the lymphoid follicle does occur, what is the biological effect?
There are at least three possibilities: (1) "Virgin" lymphocytes (progenitor
cells) are induced to differentiate and to proliferate, resulting in the formation and secretion of antibody. (2) Lymphocytes, already primed by prior exposure to the antigen, are triggered to undergo further differentiation; this
also results in the formation and secretion of antibody (a secondary response).
(3) The progenitor cells are inactivated and tolerance occurs. There is no
firm evidence that any of these possibilities happen as a result of follicular
localization of antigen. One interpretation of existing data on antigen localization patterns which occur during different types of immune responses [6,7]
suggests that the last two possibilities, but not the former, might occur as a
result of the follicular localization of antigen. The main advantage to be
gained from attempting such interpretations at present is the possibility of
logically planning further experiments.

5. A reaction between labelled antigens and lymphoid cells in vitro

We now turn to another aspect. Apart from the two cells - macrophage
and reticular cells - whose reaction with antigen we have described, are there
any other lymphoid cells with which antigen would be expected to react? In
the case of an animal producing antibody to a particular antigen which had
been injected earlier, one would expect the cell forming specific antibody to
react with the labelled antigen, because such cells would have specific antibody present at their surface. Such a reaction has in fact been shown to occur [8]. Furthermore, this reaction would be specific, in contrast to the reaction of macrophages with antigen [9]. But what about cells in an unim-
munized animal? Here again there was some reason to believe that cells
other than phagocytic or reticular cells would react. This was because of a
hypothesis originally proposed by Burnet. Based on a selective rather than an
instructive hypothesis Burnet [10] had proposed that in normal (unprimed)
animals there were "virgin" or progenitor cells (presumed to be lymphocytes)
present which could recognise a particular antigen. Such recognition might
occur because the cell, even *before* contact with a particular antigen, was
capable of producing specific antibody which would be present at the plasma
membrane. If, as considered by Burnet, a given progenitor cell had restricted

potential so that it could only produce antibody to one or a few antigenic determinants, perhaps only $\frac{1}{5,000} - \frac{1}{50,000}$ cells would be able to react with a particular antigen, depending partly on the number of different antigenic determinants possessed by the antigen.

After injection of labelled antigen into an animal, radioautographs of sections of the lymph nodes usually show much label over macrophages and reticular cells. The possibility of both detecting and identifying one or two labelled lymphocytes in such sections was poor. If they were present in the lymphoid tissues, a procedure more likely to be successful in their detection was to make cell suspensions from lymphoid tissues and to let the cells react *in vitro* with labelled antigens. This proved to be so. In 1967, Naor and Sulitzeanu [11] described a reaction between labelled bovine serum albumin (^{125}I-BSA) and mouse spleen cells. In their procedure, ^{125}I-BSA was mixed with a suspension of mouse spleen cells, held at $0°$ for 30 min and the unbound antigen removed by centrifugation. The washed cells were spread on a glass slide and radioautography carried out. The number of grains associated with about 10,000 cells was counted. They found that the many phagocytic cells present were lightly labelled but there were about $\frac{1}{5,000}$ cells which were relatively heavily labelled. Furthermore, these heavily labelled cells looked like small lymphocytes. When ^{125}I-BSA was injected into mice, a spleen cell suspension made and similarly examined, a small number of heavily labelled lymphocytes were also found. Naor and Sulitzeanu suggested that this finding was a confirmation of Burnet's hypothesis. The finding was indeed very encouraging and I and my colleagues have confirmed and extended their observations. In our studies, we have mainly used three antigens, soluble or polymerized flagellin, prepared from the flagella of different strains of *Salmonella* [12] and haemocyanin, prepared from the crayfish (*Jasus lalandii*). From the point of view of this article, similar results were obtained with each antigen so that the minor differences seen will not be commented upon further.

Antigen was labelled either with ^{125}I or ^{131}I and reacted at $0°$ with cell suspensions in 10% foetal calf serum for 30 min. After reaction, the cells were removed from free antigen by centrifugation through density gradients of foetal calf serum. A cell "smear" was made on gelatin-coated glass slides, subjected to radioautography and the cells stained.

Depending upon the tissue examined, many phagocytic cells and a few lymphocyte-like cells were labelled. The former but not the latter reaction was found to be inhibited by sodium azide.

Cell suspensions from mouse or rat spleen, thoracic duct lymph, peritoneal exudate and thymus were examined. Both spleen and thoracic duct lymph contained about $\frac{1}{5,000}$ lymphocyte-like cells which reacted with the antigen. Peritoneal exudate contained a significally larger number and thymus, very much fewer. Under the usual conditions of the experiment, the lymphocytes which had reacted were found to contain up to 40,000 molecules of the labelled antigen.

Several questions needed to be answered. Firstly, how could it be shown whether the reaction was specific, i.e., it was not due to "sticky" antigen or damaged cells? What was the mechanism of the reaction between labelled antigen and these cells? Where was the antigen located in the cells? Was this reactive cell one which was potentially capable of taking part in a specific antibody response?

Evidence for the specificity of the reaction was obtained by studying procedures which would inhibit the reaction. The most obvious one to try was pretreatment of cells with excess, unlabelled specific antigen. For example, if a given antigen but not other antigens inhibited a subsequent reaction with labelled specific antigen, it would not only be evidence in favour of the specificity of the reaction, but also would give some idea of the extent of the reaction between the cell and antigen. In fact, it was found that a 10,000-fold excess of unlabelled specific antigen was needed to inhibit by 90% the subsequent reaction between cell and labelled antigen. As 40,000 molecules of the antigen studied could occupy 0.1% of the cell surface, the necessity to use such an excess of unlabelled antigen to inhibit the reaction suggested that, if the reaction was a cell surface-mediated one, potentially all the cell surface could react with the antigen. Was the reaction taking place on or in the cell? My colleague, Dr. Tom Mandel, has examined spleen cells previously exposed to labelled antigen, using high resolution radioautography in the electron microscope. It is quite clear that cells with the morphological character of small lymphocytes react with labelled antigens and the reaction is confined under these circumstances to the cell plasma membrane. Furthermore, antigen becomes attached preferentially to some areas of the membrane.

What was the mechanism of the reaction? The likely possibility was that these cells, which came from mice not previously exposed to this antigen, were already making trace amounts of specific antibody. If this antibody was present at the plasma membrane and was the component of the membrane which reacted with the antigen, then masking of the antibody should interfere with the reaction. Pretreatment of the mouse spleen cells with specific anti-mouse globulin sera (supplied by Dr. Noel Warner) was found to inhibit the reaction. Thus, the mechanism of the reaction of cells with antigen was most likely to be mediated by antibody and suggested that performed antibody on the cell surface was the method by which antigen was recognised.

Finally, could we show that these reactive cells were those which normally took part in an antibody response? Pauline Byrt and I planned the following experiment in which we made use of a technique called adoptive immunity. In this procedure, animals are X-irradiated so that they can no longer undergo an antibody response if they are injected with antigen. Should however the irradiated animals be injected with spleen cells from a normal, unirradiated syngeneic host and then injected with antigen, an antibody response will ensue. The irradiated animals are "reconstituted" by the spleen cells. The great advantage of the technique is that the donor spleen cells can be manipulated *in vitro* before testing in the irradiated host. The rationale of our approach was that if cell suspensions were exposed to labelled antigen, those cells which took up the labelled antigen might be irretrievably damaged by the radiation from the isotopic label if such exposure was allowed to occur for a sufficient period of time. The cells should be "inactivated" and consequently unable to undergo an immune response. Furthermore, the specificity of the reaction between cell and labelled antigen could also be examined by testing the response of the reconstituted mice to both the same and to other antigens. Details of the procedure are given elsewhere [13] and are outlined in fig. 4. Polymerized flagellins from two different strains of *Salmonella* were used (SW 1338, H antigen, f, g; S.L. 871, H antigen, 1,2), which we will for convenience call strains A and B. Essentially, the physical properties of each antigen preparation were similar but they were serologically distinct. Spleen cells from the donor mouse were reacted at $0°C$ as usual with labelled polymer A. The cells were washed and allowed to stand at $0°C$ for 24 hr to give sufficient time for the radiation damage (^{125}I) to occur. The cells were then injected (10^7 cells/host mouse) into irradiated syngeneic mice and 24 hr later the host animals injected with both unlabelled polymer A and unlabelled polymer B. Eight days later the mice were bled and antibody titres to both polymer A and polymer B tested. The reverse experiment was also done in which labelled polymer B was used in the cell treatment. The results were clear cut. The antibody response of the host mice to polymer A but not to polymer B was abrogated if the injected spleen cell had been pretreated with *labelled* polymer A. If labelled polymer B was used, the subsequent response to polymer B, but not to polymer A, was eliminated. This inactivation was shown to be due to the ^{125}I-labelled antigen as pretreatment with unlabelled antigen or with antigen labelled with non-radioactive iodide did not result in a demonstrable inactivation of the cells.

Thus, these antigen reactive cells were cells which would normally take part in an antibody response. Antigen was recognised by the cells because of preformed antibody and this was a cell surface phenomenon. The results

SPECIFIC INACTIVATION OF ANTIGEN-REACTIVE CELLS

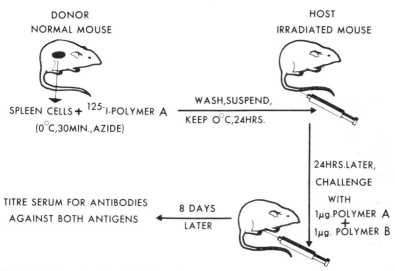

Fig. 4. A scheme showing the design of the experiments which demonstrate that cells which react with labelled antigen may be specifically inactivated by the radiation of the isotopic label.

were also consistent with Burnet's hypothesis that progenitor cells have a restricted potential. It should be stressed that much more work needs to be done before this second interpretation can be regarded as completely valid.

In conclusion, two reactions have been described which take place at the surfaces of two different types of cells. One, a fixed reticular cell, adsorbs antibody present in antigen-antibody complexes apparently because of a reaction between the cell membrane and part of the antibody molecule. In this way, antigen which would normally be phagocytosed and perhaps rapidly degraded inside a cell is held extracellularly. A likely reason for this is to allow the antigen to come into contact with other circulating cells. The other cell is present in the lymphoid tissues of normal rats or mice and morphologically looks like a small lymphocyte. A small proportion of these cells reacts specifically with a given antigen; this reaction occurs at the cell surface and is most likely mediated by specific antibody produced by that cell. These antigen reactive cells are an essential link in the chain of events which leads to antibody production and secretion.

Acknowledgements

Most work on the structure of antibody molecules reported in the early part of this paper is the work of many authors and is reported in greater detail elsewhere, (e.g. in The Antibodies, Cold Spring Harbor Laboratories, Vol. 32, 1967). The work described on the localization patterns of IgG fragments in lymph nodes and on the reaction of labelled antigens with lymphocytes was carried out in collaboration with Dr. Zana Herd and Mrs. Pauline Byrt respectively.

References

[1] R.C.Valentine and N.M.Green, J. Mol. Biol. 27 (1967) 615.
[2] G.J.V.Nossal, A.Abbot and J.Mitchell, J. Exptl. Med. 127 (1968) 263.
[3] P.G.Lang and G.L.Ada, Australian J. Exptl. Biol. Med. Sci. 45 (1967) 445.
[4] Z.L.Herd and G.L.Ada, Australian J. Exptl. Biol. Med. Sci. 47 (1969) 73.
[5] C.M.Austin, Australian J. Exptl. Biol. Med. Sci. 46 (1968) 581.
[6] G.L.Ada, P.G.Lang and G.Plymin, Immunology 14 (1968) 825.
[7] G.L.Ada and C.R.Parish, Proc. Natl. Acad. Sci. U.S. 61 (1968) 556.
[8] M.C.Berenbaum, Immunology 2 (1959) 71.
[9] J.M.Rhodes and J.Lind, Immunology 14 (1968) 511.
[10] F.M.Burnet, The clonal selection theory of immunity (Vanderbilt and Cambridge University Presses, 1969).
[11] D.Naor and D.Sulitzeanu, Nature 214 (1967) 687.
[12] G.L.Ada, G.J.V.Nossal, J.Pye and A.Abbot, Australian J. Exptl. Biol. Med. Sci. 42 (1964) 267.
[12] P.Byrt and G.L.Ada, Immunology 17 (1969) 503.

INTERACTIONS BETWEEN TUMOR TARGET CELLS AND LYMPHOCYTES *

Karl Erik HELLSTRÖM and Ingegerd HELLSTRÖM
*Departments of Pathology and Microbiology,
University of Washington Medical School, Seattle, Washington*

A main problem studied in our laboratory is the interaction between lymphocytes and tumor target cells. Two aspects of it will be considered here. First, to what extent can lymphocytes destroy cultivated tumor cells on the basis of immunological reactions to tumor specific antigens and, second, what is known about the mechanisms of such a destruction. We have recently discussed this topic in more detail elsewhere [1] and will, therefore, only give a summary of it.

1. Demonstration of cellular immunity to tumor antigens

Studies by Gross [2], Foley [3], Prehn and Main [4], Klein et al. [5,6], Sjögren [7], Habel [8], and others, have shown that experimentally induced animal tumors have specific antigens against which an immunity can be demonstrated with appropriate techniques. The most important of these antigens are the tumor specific transplantation antigens (TSTA), which are so called because they were first discovered by transplantation techniques: grafted tumor cells were found to be rejected by properly immunized syngeneic hosts but not by non-immune recipients or recipients immunized against antigens absent from the grafts [1–8]. The tumor specific transplantation antigens are localized at the cell surface [6,9,10], as can be demonstrated, for example, by immunofluorescence tests on living neoplastic cells.

Immunological reactions against TSTA have deserved much attention for at least two reasons. First, as already suggested by the way TSTA were

* The work of the authors described in this article has been supported by grants CA-10188 and CA-10189 from National Institutes of Health, U.S. Public Health Servive, and by grant T-453 from the American Cancer Society.

discovered, such reactions may lead to destruction of tumors and augmentation of them may therefore have a prophylactic and therapeutic value. Second, it has been suggested that TSTA of virus induced tumors are firmly associated with the neoplastic state, since non-antigenic cells can generally not be selected [7].

The immunological destruction of tumors with TSTA is primarily mediated by immune lymphocytes while cytotoxic antibodies seem to play a minor role [1,5,7]. The destructive effect of specifically immune lymphocytes can be demonstrated in several ways [1] : Immune cells can adoptively transfer immunity to non-immune recipients [8]. Admixture of specifically immune lymphocytes to neoplastic cells will inhibit tumor outgrowth upon transplantation to non-immune syngeneic hosts [5,7]. Specifically immune lymphocytes destroy or inhibit growth of cultivated tumors [11–13].

We have employed the colony inhibition (CI) assay [13] to study the inhibitory effect of immune lymphocytes on syngeneic and autochthonous tumor target cells. Dilute suspensions of tumor are seeded onto plastic Petri dishes. The following day, when the target cells have attached to the plastic surface, they are superseded with the lymphocyte suspensions to be tested. Tumor cells and lymphocytes are incubated together during 45 min with only a small amount of culture medium present, after which additional medium is added and the dishes are incubated for another 3–5 days before they are stained and the colonies counted. The colonies formed under these conditions are derived from the neoplastic cells, not from the lymphocytes. The percentage reduction of colony formation with specifically immune as compared to control lymphocytes (mostly immune to TSTA of some non-cross-reacting tumor) is calculated.

Colony inhibition tests have demonstrated cellular immunity to specific antigens of a variety of experimentally induced animal tumors [1,13–18] and to many human neoplasms as well [19,20]. The findings obtained have shown good correlation with tumor behaviour *in vivo* in that tumors whose antigens cross-react according to transplantation tests also do so according to CI assays. However, there is one discrepancy between the *in vivo* behaviour of neoplasms and the CI data in that lymphocytes from tumor-bearing animals are equally capable of inhibiting colony formation of plated neoplastic cells, as are lymphocytes from animals which have been immunized and are resistant to tumor grafts [15–17].

The finding of colony inhibition with lymphocytes from tumor-bearing individuals led to experiments aimed to clarify the interaction between tumor target cells, specifically immune lymphocytes and serum from tumor-bearing individuals. Colony inhibition tests were performed in which plated tumor cells were exposed to the sera to be tested, followed by lymphocytes specifically immune to their TSTA. It was found, first, that sera from animals with Moloney sarcomas protect tumors of that type from destruction by lymphocytes immune to their antigens [16] ; second, that sera from animals with persistent Shope papillomas protect Shope papilloma cells from destruction by immune lymphocytes [17]; third, that sera from animals with spontaneous mammary carcinomas block the inhibitory effect of lymphocytes immune to their antigens [18]; and fourth, that serum mediated protection of tumor target cells from inhibition by specifically immune lymphocytes can be detected with human neoplasm as well [21]. The blocking effect of the sera is specific so that serum protecting Moloney sarcomas does not protect mammary carcinomas or methylcholanthrene induced sarcomas and vice versa. Spontaneous mammary carcinomas of mice have both individually specific and common TSTA and sera from mice with such primary tumors contain antibodies which in each case protect cultivated autochthonous carcinoma cells from destruction by lymphocytes immune to their TSTA [18]. The blocking sera exert their effect on the target cells, not on the lymphocytes, since incubation of tumor cells (but not of lymphocytes) with serum abrogates target cell inhibition by immune lymphocytes [16]. The blocking molecules appear to be 7 s immunoglobulins and are, therefore, referred to as blocking antibodies. They have not yet been further characterized, however, and conclusions on the nature of the blocking molecules should await such a characterization.

It may be speculated that blocking antibodies present in the sera of tumor-bearing animals and human patients play a major role in facilitating the progressive growth of cancer cells in the presence of immune lymphocytes which would be otherwise capable of destroying them. It follows that elimination of the blocking antibodies may have a therapeutic value, if feasible.

It may be asked why an organism's ability to form blocking antibodies of the type described has been preserved by evolution when it increases its chances to die of cancer. We therefore tried to search for blocking antibodies under physiological conditions, and could recently show [22] that BALB/c mothers which are pregnant with C3H males contain both lymphocytes capable of destroying (BALB/c X C3H) F_1 embryonic cells *in vitro* and serum antibodies capable of specifically protecting the genetically foreign embryos from the lymphocyte effect. Both the cellular immunity and the blocking antibodies could be detected already after one pregnancy. The findings suggest that an animal's ability to form blocking antibodies may convey a selective advantage by helping to protect its embryos from destruction by such lymphocytes that have penetrated the placenta [23]. Since the blocking antibodies appear to be very efficient in protecting antigenic tissues from destruction by immune lymphocytes, the induction of such antibodies at will (if possible) may help facilitating the survival of allografts. It shall be pointed out that the demonstration of blocking antibodies both in tumor-bearing individuals and under physiological conditions offers one lead to further explore why cells with different surface structures can co-exist *in vivo*, e.g. in chimeras, without being eliminated by allogeneic inhibition [24]. It may also be worthwhile using the CI technique to study whether blocking antibodies play any role in the induction and maintenance of tolerance to allografts.

2. Discussion of the mechanisms of target cell destruction by immune lymphocytes

Two steps can be recognized in the reaction between specifically immune lymphocytes and their targets. First, the lymphocytes are attached to the target cells [25] and, second, they exert their cytotoxic effect. The attachment is generally believed to be mediated by antibodies present in minute amounts on the surface of the lymphocytes, although there is no definite proof of this. There are at least three possible mechanisms by which destruction of target cells can occur [1]. First, immune lymphocytes may carry minute amounts of cytotoxic antibodies [26] capable of killing their *in vitro* targets by binding to cell surface antigens together with complement present either in the lymphocytes, the target cells or the culture medium. Second, it may be hypothesized that the only specific part of the reaction is the lymphocytes' recognition of the foreign target cell antigens while the killing is mediated by non-specifically toxic substances released upon contact between the lymphocytes and the antigens [27,28]. According to the third hypothesis, the attachment is mediated by antibodies present on the lymphocytes and the killing caused by a close contact between the mutually different surfaces of lymphocytes and target cells [9], its mechanism being similar to that postulated to explain allogeneic inhibition [24].

Reasons favoring or disfavoring each one of the hypotheses can be easily cited but our knowledge of lymphocyte-target cell interactions is too limited to allow any meaningful conclusions at present. We want to point out, however, that independent of whether or not release of non-specifically toxic substances from immune lymphocytes confronted with specific antigens plays any role *in vivo*, such a release may form the basis for new, simpler *in vitro* assays of cellular immunity.

3. Summary

Tumor cells have specific antigens, absent from normal cells. These antigens are surface localized and can be recognized by lymphocytes which are capable of destroying the neoplastic cell *in vitro* and, under some conditions, also *in vivo*. The tumor cell destruction can be specifically blocked by "factors" (probably antibodies) present in the serum of tumor bearing animals. Its mechanism is still unknown.

References

[1] K.E.Hellström and I.Hellström, Advan. Cancer Res. 12 (1969) 167–223.
[2] L.Gross, Cancer Res. 3 (1943) 326–333.
[3] E.J.Foley, Cancer Res. 13 (1953) 835–837.
[4] R.T.Prehn and J.M.Main, J. Natl. Cancer Inst. 18 (1957) 769–778.
[5] G.Klein, H.O.Sjögren, E.Klein and K.E.Hellström, Cancer Res. 20 (1960) 1561–1572.
[6] G.Klein, E.Klein and G.Haughton, J. Natl. Cancer Inst. 36 (1966) 607–621.
[7] H.O.Sjögren, Progr. Exptl. Tumor Res. 6 (1965) 289–322.
[8] K.Habel, J. Exptl. Med. 115 (1962) 181–193.
[9] K.E.Hellström and G.Möller, Progr. Allergy 9 (1965) 158–245.
[10] G.Haughton, Science 147 (1965) 506–507.
[11] T.O.Yoshida and C.M.Southam, Japan J. Exptl. Med. 33 (1963) 369–383.
[12] W.Rosenau and D.Morton, J. Natl. Cancer Inst. 36 (1966) 825–835.
[13] I.Hellström, Intern. J. Cancer 2 (1967) 65–69.
[14] I.Hellström and H.O.Sjögren, J. Exptl. Med. 125 (1967) 1105–1118.
[15] I.Hellström, K.E.Hellström and G.Pierce, Intern. J. Cancer 3 (1968) 467–483.
[16] I.Hellström and K.E.Hellström, Intern. J. Cancer 4 (1969) 587–600.
[17] I.Hellström, C.A.Evans and K.E.Hellström, Intern. J. Cancer 4 (1969) 601–607.
[18] G.H.Heppner, Intern. J. Cancer 4 (1969) 608–615.
[19] I.Hellström, K.E.Hellström, G.E.Pierce and A.H.Bill, Proc. Natl. Acad. Sci. U.S. 60 (1968) 1231–1238.
[20] I.Hellström, K.E.Hellström, G.E.Pierce and J.P.S.Yang, Nature 220 (1968) 1352–1354.
[21] I.Hellström, K.E.Hellström, C.A.Evans, G.E.Pierce and J.P.S.Yang, Proc. Natl. Acad. Sci. U.S. 62 (1968) 362–369.
[22] K.E.Hellström, I.Hellström and J.Brawn, Nature 224 (1969) 914–915.
[23] M.Tuffrey, N.P.Bishun and R.D.Barnes, Nature 221 (1969) 1029–1031.
[24] K.E.Hellström and I.Hellström, Progr. Exptl. Tumor Res. 9 (1967) 40–76.
[25] W.Rosenau and H.D.Moon, J. Natl. Cancer Inst. 27 (1961) 471–478.
[26] F.Karush and H.N.Eisen, Science 136 (1962) 1032–1039.
[27] N.H.Ruddle and B.H.Waksman, Science 157 (1967) 1060–1063.
[28] G.A.Granger and W.P.Kolb, J. Immunol. 101 (1968) 111–120.

ANTIBODY SYNTHESIS AND ITS RELATIONSHIP TO MEMBRANE SYSTEMS OF THE CELL*

Mariano F.LA VIA and Albert E.VATTER

*Bowman Gray School of Medicine of Wake Forest University,
Winston-Salem, North Carolina, USA;
University of Colorado Medical Center and Webb-Waring Institute,
Denver, Colorado, USA*

The antibody response is primarily a defense mechanism characteristic of higher vertebrates. This process is initiated most often with the uptake of antigen by phagocytic cells. It appears that a stimulus is then transmitted to immuno-competent cells of the lymphoid series and these divide and differentiate to produce specific immunoglobulins. As in all cells a compartmentalization exists in these by subdivision into numerous organelles, either membrane bound or free within the cytoplasm or the nucleus. The synthetic activity takes place in relation to such compartments.

The early events occurring during antigen uptake and processing and the transmission of the antigenic stimulus have been discussed by Ada [1], Askonas [2] and Sela [3]. We would like to examine the role of some of the cellular membrane systems involved in the process of antibody synthesis, focusing our attention on the endoplasmic reticulum and on some modifications of cells occurring in the terminal stages of primary responses, the latter may be important in the genesis of memory cells.

The synthetic activity of ribosomes of immune systems has been examined by numerous authors [4–7]. Early studies indicated that two classes of polysome distribution existed in antibody forming cells. Some authors found polysomes compatible with the size of light and heavy chains of antibody [4,5] while others presented results that indicated shorter polysomes whose length was not compatible with either of these chains [5,7]. The experiments of Lennox [8] and Fleischman [9] elucidated new aspects of the kinetics of

* Supported in part by Grant T 290 C from the American Cancer Society and by Grant AI 9294-01 from the National Institute of Allergy and Infectious Diseases, NIH, USPHS

antibody synthesis and presented data which resolved this discrepancy. These authors have pointed out that synthesis for both light and heavy chains is carried out as a single piece, thus the polysomes must be of a length capable of supporting synthesis of a single polypeptide and not two separate pieces that would be joined together at a later stage.

Evidence to clarify the relative role of free and membrane bound polysomes in the synthesis of antibody have been presented by Leduc [10] who demonstrated that the first antibody appears in cisternae of the granular endoplasmic reticulum of large lymphocytoid cells (plasma cells). The morphology of these cells is the same as that of cells in either hemolytic plaques [11] or selected cells of the spleen during antibody production [12]. This information parallels our observation that there is an increase of cells with large amounts of granular endoplasmic reticulum and that the immune response is parallelled by a large increase in bound polysomes which can be isolated from the immunized rat spleen [14]. In addition several authors [18–20] have shown that antibody is made on these membrane-bound polysomes. We have confirmed these observations and extended them to show that the free polysomes from the immunized rat spleen are not involved in the synthesis of antibody [14].

I would like to turn our attention to a phenomenon which we have observed in rats during the late stages of primary response to *S. typhi* and RBC stimulation [15]. Recently this phenomenon has been observed in mice immunized with RBC. The first series of experiments carried out with rats [6] revealed the following sequence of events. About five days after antigen injection groups of plasma cells were seen in the red pulp of the spleen of the treated animals; on the sixth day we observed occasional "free" nuclei in a matrix of cytoplasmic contents. These nuclei were not surrounded by a plasmalemma. After the sixth day one observes the presence of large numbers of smaller lymphocyte-like cells in the spleen. These observations were interpreted by us to be one mechanism of formation of memory cells. This idea was strengthened by experiments of Gowans and Uhr [16], in which lymphocytes were identified as cells carrying immunologic memory.

A series of experiments was performed by us to clarify this phenomenon. We used the technique of Playfair et al. [17] as modified by Kind and Campbell [18]. This system permits the selection of portions of the spleen that contain antibody forming cells. Mice are exposed to a lethal dose of whole body X-radiation followed by an infusion of spleen cells from a donor isogenic mouse and immunization with RBC. The spleens of the recipient mice are taken at intervals, subdivided into small pieces which are arranged on a bed of agar containing RBC and incubated with complement. Positive pieces

containing antibody forming cells are hemolytic and can be separated from
the negative pieces and processed for electron microscopic observation. The
infusion of spleen cells from normal donors gives rise to two activities within
the recipient's spleen, one related to blood formation and the other related
to antibody production. These activities are quite distinct and can be visualized by electron microscopy.

In fig. 1 a hemopoietic region is illustrated. A reticulocyte containing
many polysomes is evident, and part of a mature erythrocyte is also seen.
The cell which occupies the largest portion of the illustration has several
characteristics which suggest that it may be a phagocytic cell (nucleus, many
profiles similar to lysosomes).

In fig. 2 a group of plasma cells are clustered in a typical configuration
which has been observed repeatedly on the fifth day after cell transfer and
immunization. The morphology and arrangement of these cells suggest that
they are antibody forming cells. Such cells always appear in clusters as illustrated. Fig. 3 shows the phenomenon observed on the sixth day. Two nuclei
are seen here enclosed by the nuclear envelope and with a well delineated
cisterna. We have termed these "free" nuclei since they are not separated
from each other by a cell membrane and appear to be immersed in a matrix
of organelles that fill the sinusoid. It is apparent from this illustration that
the nuclei are in intimate contact with each other, and that no plasmalemma
is present between them. The nucleus could be infolded producing this type
of image, however, such nuclei have not been observed in these situations.
We have never seen binucleated lymphocytes in normal or in antibody forming tissues. The lack of any plasmalemma delimiting the nuclei indicates that
they are not within a cell. This phenomenon was observed in preparations on
the sixth day after antigen injection. In some cases nuclei could be seen close
to and in intimate contact with the membrane of erythrocytes. On the
seventh day after antigen injection, in these experiments, we have observed
many small lymphocyte-like cells. These cells were not observed in large numbers previous to this time and are located in regions of the spleen that we
infer had previously been occupied by the groups of "free" nuclei on the
fifth day and sixth day after immunization.

These experiments are only morphological studies, however, the ability
to repeat the phenomenon makes us believe that these structures are not the
result of experimental artifact. Perfusion and dissection techniques have been
used to minimize trauma to the cells and the tissue during the preparatory
steps for electron microscopic observation [15].

This makes us confident that the cell disruption is related to some activity
which may be important in the sequence of cellular transformations that occurs

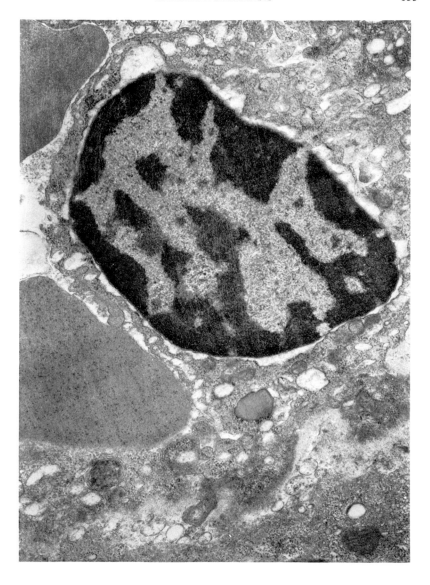

Fig. 1.

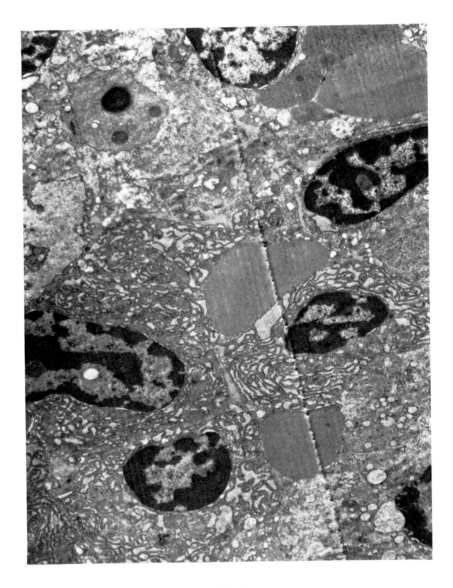

Fig. 2.

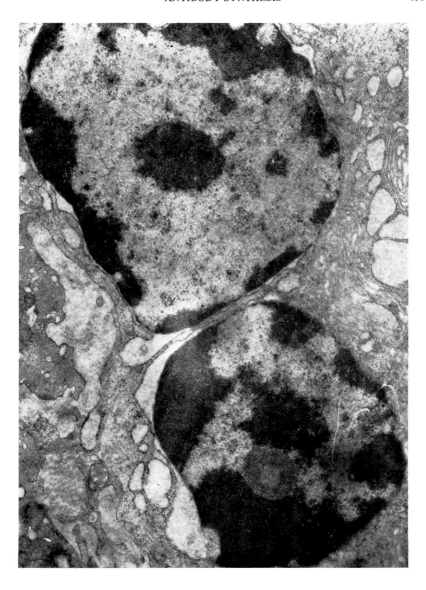

Fig. 3.

after the injection of antigen and leads to the production of antibodies. The current working hypothesis we hold is that this may be one of the ways in which antibody forming cells give rise to some memory cells that function in future immune responses. This function has recently been attributed to the small lymphocyte [16]. It is not necessary that all antibody forming cells terminate in the manner described in this paper since the data presented in the literature on cell kinetics during immune response indicate that if all antibody forming cells turned into memory cells one would be faced by a shortage of space to accommodate all these new cells within lymphoid organs. We believe that only certain antibody forming cells follow this route while the remaining undergo destruction. It is of interest, however, that in our studies we have never seen nuclear phagocytosis or an apparent increase in macrophages, a phenomenon that would be expected during an increase of cell destruction.

In blood collected from the spleen of immunized rats, on the sixth day after immunization one finds lymphocyte-like cells which contain antibody [19]. It has been shown that the large pyroninophilic cells which are present on the fourth and fifth day after immunization in the red pulp of the rat spleen are replaced during the subsequent 24 hours by cells which appear to be small lymphocytes under the light microscope [20]. The ultrastructural studies already reported [15] and those described in this paper have borne out some of these observations.

Cannon and Wisslér have recently published a series of experiments showing that the small lymphocyte-like cells found in the spleen in the terminal stages of primary immune response migrate to other lymphoid organs [21]. These lymphocytes could then be thought of as memory cells ready for a secondary response at a location different from their origination. Future studies should be directed to a clarification of the role of these lymphocytes in their new location in the hope of demonstrating that they are capable of antibody synthesis upon antigenic stimulation.

References

[1] G.L.Ada, This symposium.
[2] B.A.Askonas, This symposium.
[3] M.Sela, This symposium.
[4] M.D.Scharff and J.W.Uhr, Science 148 (1965) 646.
[5] W.L.Norton, D.Lewis and M.Ziff, Proc. Natl. Acad. Sci. U.S. 53 (1965) 851.
[6] A.R.Williamson and B.A.Askonas, J. Mol. Biol. 23 (1967) 201.

158   M.F.LA VIA and A.E.VATTER

[7] M.F.La Via, A.E.Vatter, W.S.Hammond and P.V.Northup, Proc. Natl. Acad. Sci. U.S. 57 (1967) 79.
[8] E.S.Lennox, P.M.Knopf, A.J.Munro and R.M.E.Parkhouse, Cold Spring Harbor Symp. Quant. Biol. 32 (1967) 249.
[9] J.B.Fleischman, Cold Spring Harbor Symp. Quant. Biol. 32 (1967) 233.
[10] E.H.Leduc, S.Avremeas and M.Bouteille, J. Exptl. Med. 127 (1968) 109.
[11] K.Hummeler, T.N.Harris, N.Tomassini, M.Hechtel and M.B.Farber, J. Exptl. Med. 124 (1966) 255.
[12] R.D.Moore, V.R.Mumaw and M.D.Schoenberg, Exptl. Mol. Path. 4 (1965) 370.
[13] M.F.La Via, A.E.Vatter and P.V.Northup, Submitted for publication.
[14] M.F.La Via, K.Ishizaka and P.V.Northup, Submitted for publication.
[15] M.F.La Via and A.E.Vatter, J. Reticuloendothelial Soc. 6 (1969) 221.
[16] J.L.Gowans and J.W.Uhr, J. Exptl. Med. 124 (1966) 1017.
[17] J.H.L.Playfair, B.W.Papermaster and L.J.Cole, Science 149 (1965) 998.
[18] P.D.Kind and P.A.Campbell, J. Immunol. 100 (1968) 55.
[19] C.H.Gunderson, D.Juras, M.F.La Via and R.W.Wissler, J. Am. Med. Assoc. 180 (1962) 1038.
[20] R.W.Wissler, F.W.Fitch, M.F.La Via and C.H.Gunderson, J. Comp. Cell Physiol. 50, Suppl. 1 (1957) 265.
[21] D.C.Cannon and R.W.Wissler, A.M.A. Arch. Path. 84 (1967) 109.

SILICA-INDUCED CYTOTOXICITY. POSSIBLE MEDIATION BY INTERACTION WITH THE LYMPHOCYTE MEMBRANE*

R.W.I.KESSEL

Department of Microbiology, University of Maryland, School of Medicine, Baltimore, Maryland

1. Introduction

The pathogenesis of silicosis has been hypothesized by Vigliani and Pernis to result from a primary destructive activity of silica upon cells of the reticuloendothelial system [1]. Saffiotti and his colleagues have demonstrated that the earliest observable pathological change is macrophage destruction [2], and Marks has demonstrated that such destruction can occur *in vitro* [3]. Kessel et al. have presented data suggesting that the action of crystalline silica is highly specific for the macrophage [4], and Allison et al. have demonstrated that this destruction is associated with the intracellular release of lysosomal enzymes [5]. This intracellular release of lysosomal enzymes has been confirmed by Kessel, who, however, has suggested that this may be a terminal rather than a primary event in the interaction between cells and silica [6]. Our present studies suggest that silica acts at the surface of cells, and that it may initiate pathological change by interaction with the lymphocyte which in turn liberates material capable of damaging macrophages. This could explain the apparent specificity of silica for "macrophages" because in the studies of Kessel et al. [4] these were in reality peritoneal exudate cell populations consisting of ca. 80% macrophages plus ca. 20% lymphocytes.
The present note will describe two types of experiment which have led us to the supposition that lymphocyte-silica interactions are capable of leading to the production of materials capable of exerting their activity on the macrophage. In the absence of evidence that lymphocytes are capable of ingest-

* This investigation was supported in part by Public Health Service Research Grant No. UI 00592 from the National Center for Urban and Industrial Health, and in part by Grant No. ES 00416 from the National Institute of Environmental Health Sciences.

ing particulate silica it is reasonable to suppose that the interaction between silica and the lymphocyte occurs at the latter's surface and involves the triggering of subcellular events as a result of changes brought about in the cell membrane.

2. Materials and methods

2.1. *Animals*. Male, Hartley, guinea pigs weighing 600 to 800 g were employed.

2.2. *Silica*. Preparations of trydimite and pumice were kindly supplied by Prof. E.Vigliani, Director, Clinica del Lavoro "Luigi Devoto", Milan, Italy.

2.3. *Silicosis*. Guinea pigs were rendered silicotic by the intracardial injection of 5 mg of trydimite 18 to 21 weeks previously.

2.4. *Macrophage migration*. The method of David et al. [7] was employed. Heated ($56°C$, 30 min) pooled, guinea pig serum, 10% in MEM was employed as the culture medium.

2.5. *Migration inhibiting factor (MIF) production*. Capillaries were packed as in 4. above such that a 1×3 mm column of cells contained 200 μg of silica. These were placed into culture dishes containing 1.5 ml of medium, the dishes were sealed and incubated for 48 hr at $37°C$. At this time the supernatant (MIF) was removed, diluted with an equal volume of fresh medium, and used to prepare capillaries of normal macrophages as in 4. above.

2.6. *Isolation of lymphocytes*. The method of Rabinowitz [8] was employed. Leukoplasma was obtained by mixing 1 part of 6% Dextran-250 (Pharmacia Fine Chemicals Inc.) in saline with 4 parts whole blood.

2.7. *Monolayer cultures*. Cultures of peritoneal exudate cells (PEC) were carried out as described by Kessel et al. [4]. Damage was assessed by the Trypan Blue exclusion test, 10 min after exposure at $37°C$ to 0.33% Trypan Blue.

3. Results

3.1. Effect of silica on the production of migration inhibiting factor (MIF)

Table 1 shows the result of one such experiment, the migration being expressed as the percentage of untreated controls. It may be seen that incubation of normal macrophages with supernatants from silica-medium mixtures resulted in no alteration of the migration pattern (lines 9 to 11). Similarly no migration inhibiting factor was produced by peritoneal cells from normal

Table 1
Effect of silica on migration inhibiting factor (MIF) production by guinea pig peritoneal exudate cells (GP PEC)

Source of MIF*	Migration index**
1. Normal GP PEC + Diluent	92
2. Normal GP PEC + Trydimite 56/63	71
3. Normal GP PEC + Trydimite 116	77
4. Normal GP PEC + Pumice 114	84
5. Silicotic GP PEC + Diluent	102
6. Silicotic GP PEC + Trydimite 56/63	60
7. Silicotic GP PEC + Trydimite 116	53
8. Silicotic GP PEC + Pumice 114	71
9. Trydimite 56/63 alone	110
10. Trydimite 116 alone	96
11. Pumice 114 alone	105

* See text.
** Migration of normal guinea pig peritoneal exudate cells in the presence of MIF, expressed as percentage of controls exposed to medium alone. Average of 3 replicates.

or silicotic guinea pigs in the absence of silica (lines 1 and 5). Inhibition of
migration was observed when supernatants from silica-treated peritoneal cells
were employed, and the migration of normal cells is perhaps less in the
presence of supernatants from silicotic (lines 6 to 8) than from normal (lines
2 to 4) animals.

3.2. Effect of silica on the production of lymphocyte "toxin"

Peripheral blood lymphocytes were suspended at a concentration of 5×10^6/ml in a medium consisting of 10% autologous plasma in Scherer's maintenance solution (SMS) with or without silica at 1 mg/ml. Controls also in-
cluded silica suspensions in the absence of lymphocytes. The mixtures were
incubated for 24 hr at 37°C.

Autologous peritoneal exudate cells (PEC) were harvested at the same
time as the lymphocytes, subdivided into aliquots, centrifuged, and the pel-
lets stored at 4°C for 24 hr. At this time the cells were resuspended using
supernatants from the lymphocyte-dust mixtures. 1-ml portions were distributed to Leighton tubes, and 24 hr later the viability of the peritoneal cell
monolayer was assessed by Trypan Blue exclusion.

Table 2 shows the results of such an experiment. Control cultures (lines 1
to 4) averaged 13 ± 4% Trypan Blue + ve. cells and did not differ significantly

Table 2
Toxicity of lymphocyte-silica supernatants for autologous normal guinea pig peritoneal exudate cells

	Source of supernatant*	% Trypan blue + ve. **
1.	Medium alone	12
2.	Lymphocytes alone	10
3.	Trydimite 56–63 alone	17
4.	Pumice 114 alone	15
5.	Trydimite 56–63 plus lymphocytes	39
6.	Pumice 114 plus lymphocytes	26
7.	Medium alone	7

* See text.
** Average of 3 replicates.

from the untreated controls (line 7). However, exposure of monolayers of normal peritoneal cells to the supernatants from lymphocytes plus either trydimite (line 5) or pumice (line 6) led to a significant increase in the proportion of "damaged" cells.

4. Discussion

The finding that exposure to silica can cause damage to cultures *in vitro* of peritoneal cells has been well documented [3–5]. This observation has been considered to be a demonstration of a specific cytotoxicity of silica for macrophages, as other cell types proved resistant, *in vitro*, to this dust [4]. While the macrophage containing silica does undergo lysosomal changes terminating in cell destruction [5], the present preliminary report indicates that such destruction may also be mediated indirectly via products released by the lymphocytes always present in peritoneal exudates, but not present in the other cell populations studied [4]. That an interaction between silica and purified populations of lymphocytes can occur is demonstrated by the production by such populations of both a migration inhibiting factor (table 1) and a cytotoxic factor (table 2). Parazzi et al. [9] have shown that silica can be cytotoxic for peritoneal cells in the absence of phagocytosis, and it would appear that the lymphocyte-silica interaction is another example of such a surface interaction. Thus silica may act in an analogous manner to phytohemagglutinin as a non-specific stimulator (activator) of lymphoid cells.

Studies are in progress, employing both silica and asbestos, aimed at determining whether other evidence (e.g. blast transformation) of interaction between these dusts and the surface of lymphocytes can be obtained.

Summary

Incubation of purified preparations of blood lymphocytes with silica leads to the production of a factor or factors cytotoxic for normal macrophages. This finding may explain the apparent specificity of silica's cytotoxicity for this cell type.

Migration inhibiting factor is likewise produced following the interaction of peritoneal exudate cells (presumably by their contained lymphocytes) and silica.

References

[1] E.C.Vigliani and B.Pernis, Adv. Tuberc. Res. 12 (1962) 230.
[2] U.Saffiotti, A.Tommasina-Degna and L.Mayer, Med. Lavoro 54 (1960) 161.
[3] J.Marks, M.A.Mason and G.Nagelschmidt, Brit. J. Ind. Med. 13 (1956) 181.
[4] R.W.I.Kessel, L.Monaco and M.A.Marchisio, Brit. J. Exptl. Pathol. 44 (1963) 351.
[5] A.C.Allison, J.S.Harington and M.Birbeck, J. Exptl. Med. 124 (1966) 141.
[6] R.W.I.Kessel, J. Reticuloendothelial Soc. 5 (1968) 7.
[7] J.R.David, S.Al-Askari, H.S.Lawrence and L.Thomas, J. Immunol. 93 (1964) 264.
[8] J.Rabinowitz, Blood 23 (1964) 811.
[9] E.Parazzi, G.C.Secchi, B.Pernis and E.C.Vigliani, Arch. Environ. Health 12 (1968) 850.

Part 4

SURFACE CHEMISTRY OF MONOLAYERS AND THIN FILMS

THE RELEVANCE OF STUDIES OF MONOLAYERS AT LIQUID INTERFACES TO BIOLOGICAL MEMBRANES

Craig M.JACKSON*

*Unilever Research Laboratory, Port Sunlight, Cheshire, UK***

1. Introduction

The classical models of biological membranes arising from the observations and proposals of Gorter and Grendel [1] and the subsequent proposals of Danielli and Davson [2] have led to the frequent view that a membrane lipid monolayer and associated protein could be regarded as one half a cell membrane. Contemporarily, however, it is probably acceptable to say only that: "Monolayers have a respectable position in membranology as half a bilayer, but they clearly have limitations as membrane analogues" [3]. The following discussion is an attempt to define the relevance of monolayers of polar lipids, proteins, and mixtures of lipids and proteins to biological membranes and more specifically, the contributions that can be made by studies of monolayers of membrane components to our understanding of the physical chemistry of membrane function. The underlying assumption of the ensuing discussion, that membrane phenomena are only a reflection of the physical and chemical properties of the components of the biological membrane system, will become obvious as this discussion is developed. Prior to considering monolayer studies specifically in studies of membranes it seems worthwhile to recall the fact that biological membranes are both functionally and compositionally diverse [4]. If the "simple" lipid protein interacting systems such as those involving enzymes which act on lipid substrates are included, as these or similar systems are probably involved in membrane structure and function, the diversity is even more obvious. For example myelin, a tissue with a relatively high ratio of lipid to protein [5] and an almost neg-

* Supported by a fellowship from the American Cancer Society (P.F. 442).
** Current address: Department of Biological Chemistry, Washington University School of Medicine, St.Louis, Mo. 63110, USA

ligible metabolic turnover of its chemical components, might well be expected to possess a very different membrane to subcellular organelles or erythrocytes. However, in spite of the functional diversity, which is probably predominantly enzyme-related, and the variety of specific lipid components, the major similarity in structure of the lipids found in membranes is perfectly obvious. It is the thesis of this presentation that monolayer techniques are particularly applicable to study of some of the physical properties of membrane components and that as a consequence of the knowledge of these physical properties, our opportunities for understanding membrane phenomena, that is describing and predicting membrane functional behavior, will be increased.

Firstly I should like to consider a number of correlations that have been found to exist between the activities of some surfactants and drugs in biological systems and the ability of these compounds to penetrate monolayers of lipids of biological origin.

Subsequently then I should like to consider the information potentially obtainable from the study of monolayers at liquid interfaces and the relevance of these studies to our understanding membrane function as it is determined by the structure and properties of its components.

2. Biological activity-monolayer property correlations

A number of investigators have demonstrated that the biological activity of many surfactants, drugs and anesthetic gases can be correlated with the effects of these substances on lipid monolayers.

Early work by Schulman and Rideal [6] demonstrated that hemolysis of erythrocytes by sodium cetyl sulfate could be nearly completely inhibited by including cholesterol in the hemolysing solution. Cetyl alcohol under similar conditions was not capable of inhibiting the hemolytic process. In both cases, however, monolayers of the alcohols were strongly penetrated by the sodium cetyl sulfate. It was also shown that the lytic properties of an equimolar mixture of cetyl sulfate and cetyl alcohol were nearly double those of the same amount of cetyl sulfate alone. A subsequent investigation by Schulman and Rideal [7] showed that twelve-carbon ionic surfactants when arranged in order of their hemolytic activity also gave exactly the same sequence in their ability to penetrate a cholesterol monolayer. Schulman and Armstrong [8] found that lysis of yeast cells by ω-diamidines was directly proportional to the number of methylene groups separating the two polar groups, whereas with the mono-amidines the series was not at all related to the hydrocarbon

chain length, i.e. $C_{14} > C_{16} > C_{12} > C_{18} > C_{10}$. Pethica and Schulman [9],
after further extensive investigation, proposed that the ability of detergents
to hemolyse erythrocytes could be related to the ability of the detergent to
produce a surface tension lowering equivalent to a surface pressure of 34
dyne/cm at the air/water interface. This proposal was based upon their observations that for nonionic detergents lysis appears at detergent concentrations capable of lowering the surface tension by 34 dyne/cm whereas for
ionic surfactants lysis occurs at surfactant concentrations at which they produce this pressure by penetration into a cholesterol monolayer.

The physical chemistry of hemolysis and bacteriolysis by surface-active
agents and antibiotics has been reviewed by Schulman et al. [10].

Skou [11] showed that the activity of tertiary amine local anesthetics
correlated with the ability of the amines to penetrate a monolayer of lipids
from peripheral nerve. In a subsequent investigation [12] these observations
were extended to both aliphatic and aromatic alcohols with similar correla-
tive results. The effects of organic solvent anesthetics on the permeability of
liposomes to cations have been investigated by Bangham et al. [13]. Again
relationships between the functional parameter, permeability and the surface
modifying properties of the narcotic agents were found. Seeman ([14] - this
Conference) has reported in detail the results of his extensive studies of the
effects of a large number of penetrants on red blood cells and red blood cell
ghosts.

Bangham et al. [15] in the light of the findings of Skou [11] investigated
the relationship between the ability of certain amphipathic substances to
prevent liver necrosis in rats poisoned by carbon tetrachloride and the surface activity of the protective compounds. They found that both the inhibition of the release of β-glucuronidase into serum and the prevention of necrosis as determined histologically correlated with the minimum concentration required to produce a lowering of the surface tension of water by 20
dyne/cm and the minimum concentration required to produce a rise in surface pressure from 20 to 35 dyne/cm by penetration of a lecithin-cholesterol
monolayer. In addition to these observations, however, these investigators
found that the sixteen carbon cationic amphipath was much more effective
than the sixteen carbon anionic compound investigated; in fact, the anionic
compound was hardly effective at all.

Bangham et al. [16] similarly found a relationship between the ability of
vitamin A_1 alcohol to hemolyse erythrocytes and the ability of the compound
to penetrate lipid films at the air/water interface. In contrast to earlier correlations between surfactant hemolysis and penetration of lipid monolayers,
vitamin A alcohol was found to interact more strongly with lecithin than
cholesterol.

The effects of various gaseous narcotic agents on monolayers of lipids and lipid-protein preparations have been investigated by Clements and Wilson [17]. From their results these workers concluded that "inert gases at partial pressures sufficient to bring about a standard effect in a biological system act on a lipoprotein-water interface to cause a standard decrease of 0.39 dyne/cm in the interfacial tension". It must be noted, however, that Felmeister et al. [18] obtained somewhat different results with nitrogen dioxide-olefin gas mixtures on lecithin films.

The system in which monolayer studies at the air/aqueous solution interface are probably most closely related to the actual biological membrane system itself is the lung surfactant system. The contribution of surface tension to the pressure-volume relationships for lung inflated with air versus lung inflated with a gum arabic solution was investigated and discussed by Von Neergaard [19]. Subsequent investigators [20,21] have extended and reinforced the evidence relating to this system. More recent studies [22–25] using partially fractionated preparations have added a number of details to our knowledge of this system.

In an extensive series of investigations Demel and co-workers studied the penetration of phospholipid-cholesterol monolayers by psychoactive drugs and polyene antibiotics. In the studies using psychoactive drugs [26] it was found that penetration of lipid films at surface pressure in excess of 18 dyne/cm depended upon the sign of the charge on the monolayer. Polyene antibiotic penetration of phospholipid-cholesterol films was found to correlate extremely well with the specificity shown by the antibiotic to microorganisms which differ in their relative phospholipid and cholesterol content [27,28].

Similar relationships between penetration of surface films of stearate and pharmacologic activity of veratrum alkaloids were shown to exist by Shanes and Gershfeld [29].

It has been established that definite qualitative and quantitative relationships exist between the biological activities of a variety of chemical substances and the ability of these compounds to interact with monolayers of membrane components. Furthermore, the selectivity demonstrated in the interaction of a number of these substances with the monolayers of biological compounds depends very much both on the chemical structure of the biological amphipath and the physical properties which are a consequence of the chemical structure.

In addition to the biological activity-monolayer interaction correlations cited above, recent investigations have demonstrated similarities in the physical behavior of phospholipid monolayers and the thermotropic properties

seen by calorimetric techniques with bulk systems. Surface pressure-area isotherms for phospholipid monolayers at the air/water interface published by
Chapman et al. [30], Cadenhead and Phillips [31], Vilallonga [32] and
Phillips and Chapman [33] show a monolayer phase transition comparable
to the chain melting transitions seen by differential thermal analysis of phospholipid dispersions [34]. Studies of phospholipid monolayers at the hep-
tane/water interface which have been carried out by Mingins and Taylor
[35] show similar phase transitions.

The question of the physical significance of cholesterol in biological membranes has been investigated using monolayer techniques by De Bernard [36].
He found that monolayers of egg lecithin at the air/water interface were
condensed by the addition of cholesterol, that is, the area/molecule at a
given surface pressure was less in the mixed film than would have been predicted from the average of the molecular areas of the individual components
at the particular composition. Subsequent experiments using synthetic phospholipids [36a], indicated that condensation of the phospholipid monolayer
was dependent upon the particular unsaturated fatty acids in the phospholipid. Further work by Demel et al. [37] and Standish and Pethica [38] demonstrated, however, that this simple explanation was inadequate and that the
condensation effect was dependent upon the temperature and thus physical
state of the phospholipid monolayer. Cadenhead [31] and Chapman et al.
[39] in detailed investigations of the condensing effect of cholesterol on a
variety of phospholipid monolayers and at different temperatures found that
expanded monolayers are condensed by cholesterol most dramatically when
the temperature of the experiment is above, but near the transition temperature for the change of state from a condensed to an expanded monolayer.
The relationship of this condensation phenomenon to the physical properties, rather than simply chemical structure, seems now almost trivial.

An alternative presentation of data from cholesterol-phospholipid mixed
mono-layer isotherms which compares the free energy of mixing of phospholipid-cholesterol mixtures with that predicted for thermodynamically ideal
mixing [40] has been made by Vilallonga et al. [41]. Demel and Joos [42]
from their comparison of the interaction of cholesterol and phospholipids at
the air/water and oil/water interfaces have concluded that the interaction is
of the Van der Waals-London sort, and not due to any more specific struc-
ture-related interactions.

The observations described earlier [27,28], that polyene antibiotics are
capable of penetrating phospholipid-cholesterol monolayers has been related
to the ability of these antibiotics to facilitate the release of marker substances
from liposomes. Experiments by Weissmann and Sessa [43], however, indi-

cated that cholesterol did not necessarily facilitate release of the marker molecules from liposomes. Further studies by Kinsky et al. [44] showed that cholesterol did indeed facilitate release, but that this was only apparent with lower concentrations of filipin or polyene antibiotic than used by Weissmann and Sessa [43] . The observation by Weissmann and Sessa [43] and confirmed by Kinsky et al. [44] that some of the potent antibiotics as determined by their 'penetration' of monolayers did not facilitate marker release from liposome remains to be explained. When explained, however, this discrepancy should lead to our further understanding membrane structure. Partial explanation may be related to the condensing effect of cholesterol on phospholipid monolayers discussed above. In a recent publication De Gier [45] demonstrated unequivocally that the effect of cholesterol incorporated into liposomes on the swelling rate of the liposomes in isotonic glycol and glycerol depended upon the chain length of the phospholipid fatty acids, and the temperature of the system. In fact, both reduction or enhancement of the permeability was found to occur depending upon the fatty acid chain length and temperature. Again, the physical properties as expressed by their dependence on temperature come to the fore.

3. Monolayer studies of proteins and lipid-protein interacting systems

Monolayer studies of proteins and lipid-protein interacting systems have provided considerably less information than studies of the type mentioned above or those carried out on single lipid species alone. With regard to the investigations of early workers the primary reason is probably as expressed by Bangham [46] "...by present day ideas their choice of proteins was irrelevant". In addition to the choice of proteins, inadequate attention to experimental technique has often provided uncertain data and not entirely obvious relationships between the monolayer systems investigated and biological membranes. The problems of experimental techniques as related to spread monolayers have been discussed in detail by Langmuir and Waugh [47] . The ambiguity due to differences in techniques used in studying proteins adsorbed onto lipid mono-layers has been demonstrated clearly by Colacicco et al. [48] in studies in which they compared the results obtainable by various previously used techniques.

The assumption that spread and adsorbed protein molecules unfold at interfaces to expose the peptide backbone has formed the basis for interpretation of a considerable amount of data on lipid monolayer-protein interactions, for example by Eley and Hedge [49] . This is however, called into doubt as a result of recent work by Malcolm [50,51] . Malcolm [51] has shown by a combination of deuterium exchange, infrared spectrophotometry and electron diffraction that poly-γ-benzyl-L-glutamate can exist in monolayers in the form of α-helices, rather than in the extended β-conformation. The results of Malcolm were confirmed by Loeb [52] using multiple internal reflection spectroscopy to investigate Langmuir-Blodgett film or poly-benzyl-L-glutamate. The re-evaluation of results obtained by monolayer techniques for proteins as a result of this recent work should lead to further development of this approach and additional understanding of proteins at interfaces. An excellent, detailed review of the surface chemistry of proteins and peptides is that by Loeb [52] ; Cheeseman and Davies [53] have reviewed the earlier work in depth.

The use of monolayer techniques for investigating the action of lipid hydrolytic enzymes, which was initiated by Hughes [54] , has provided considerable insight into the requirements of these enzymes for particular interfacial properties for their lipid substrates. Dawson [55] has reviewed these investigations, predominantly from his laboratory, which have demonstrated the requirements for a negatively charged interface for optimum activity of the snake venom phosphohydrolases. Monolayer techniques have been extensively applied to the investigation of lipid-protein interactions by Colacicco and co-workers, also [48,56–58] .

As these and earlier authors have recognised, the question of what surface pressure for the lipid film is most nearly like that of a membrane's lipid, is not known and is possibly not even a meaningful question. However, the performance of experiments in which proteins are either adsorbing to the surface of a lipid monolayer or penetrating it obligatorily begins by assuming that such a quantity exists and that a value can be chosen for it. If the lipid bilayer, that is black film, may be assumed to represent a membrane, then by analogy the monolayer surface pressure chosen to be like the "membrane value" would be in the vicinity of 30 dyne/cm or even considerably greater [59,60] . In the light of this, the use of initial surface pressures of 2 dyne/cm (for example, Eley and Hedge [49] , Colacicco [56]), is highly questionable. Further uncertainty in interpretation of monolayer experiments also exists as a result of many workers' failure to recognise the possible consequences of the monolayer phase transitions which have been shown to exist. Until considerably more data are available and the experimental techniques better developed, the potential contribution of monolayer studies to our understanding of lipid-protein interactions will probably remain a subject for debate.

4. Physicochemical data obtainable from monolayer investigations

Monolayer experiments, whether they are adsorption experiments in which the surface-active compound is present in one of the bulk phases, usually water or a hydrocarbon liquid, or experiments with spread monolayers in which the bulk phase concentration is assumed to be negligibly small, usually involve measurement of the surface tension or the surface pressure as a function of either concentration or area/molecule. The surface pressure, the change in the surface tension, ($\pi = \gamma_{\text{clean surface}} - \gamma_{\text{film-covered surface}}$) is the decrease in the free energy of formation of the surface or extension of the spread film [61−64]. From such measurements a π versus concentration or π versus area/molecule curve is constructed which describes the surface behavior of the surfactant compound under the particular conditions of the experiment. Detailed discussions of these measurements can be found in the above references and in Gaines [65] and Davies and Rideal [66].

The surface potential, that is the difference in the Volta potential in the absence and presence of a monolayer, is also frequently measured. This quantity, which is determined by the dipole moments of the monolayer-forming substance, the arrangement of the water molecules in the surface and the electrical double layer associated with a charged interface can provide information about the conformation of the monolayer-forming molecules. The relationship among these variables is complicated, however, and discussions by Cassie and Palmer [67], Parsons [68], Levine et al. [69,70] and Davies and Rideal [66], should be consulted for details.

Surface viscosity, a less frequently measured variable but possibly of extremely great significance, is reviewed in depth by Joly [71].

It is well established that polar lipids at air/water and oil/water interfaces are oriented specifically with their hydrophilic portions in the aqueous phase and their hydrocarbon portions in the air or non-polar oil [61,62,72,73]. The fact that this orientation is so definite has permitted investigations to be made of the physical effects of changes in the relatively independent portions of the oriented amphipathic molecule. By carrying out investigations at both air/water and oil/water interfaces the possibilities for separation of the contributions of the two distinct parts of the amphipathic molecule to the systems' interfacial properties can be extended considerably.

Although spread monolayers at the air/water interface have been investigated much more extensively than at oil/water interfaces, primarily due to early experimental difficulties, the hydrocarbon oil/water interface is probably much more like the interface which may be presented by a membrane than the air/water interface. As a result of recent developments in experimental technique, however, [74,75], it now is at least no more difficult to investigate monolayers at the oil/water interface than at the air/water interface.

Assuming acceptable experimental technique, a situation not always found in monolayer studies [65], what types of information specifically can monolayer investigations provide? The detailed information obtainable from monolayer investigations is probably most easily described by reference to a monolayer equation of state relating surface pressure to molecular area and based upon the analogy of a monolayer with a two-dimensional gas [66,76]. This equation considers the surface pressure π to be composed of contributions from: (1) the kinetic energy of the amphipathic molecules in the surface, π_{kT}, (2) cohesive forces which are due at the air/water interface predominantly to Van der Waals' interactions between hydrocarbon chains, $\pi_{cohesive}$ and (3) an electrical contribution resulting from the interactions between charged polar groups of the lipid and the electrical double layer associated with a charged interface, $\pi_{electrical}$.

At very large areas per molecule, the interaction between individual molecules becomes so small that the surface pressure is determined by the Brownian motion of the molecules alone and $\pi A = kT$. As the area per molecule is decreased both cohesive interactions between the hydrocarbon chains and electrostatic interactions, if the film-forming molecules are charged, become significant. Separation of these two effects is obtained by independent variation of the hydrocarbon chain length at constant electrolyte concentration in the subphase, and vice versa, and by comparison of the isotherms obtained from the same compound at the air/water and hydrocarbon liquid/water interfaces. The electrical properties of the charged interface are obtainable from both the surface pressure - area isotherms and the surface potential-area isotherms. (See, for example [70,77].) Obviously, variation in the ionic composition of the subphase permits evaluation of specific ionic interaction. For example, specific ion effects have been clearly shown for carboxylate and sulfate films. For carboxylate monolayers at high pH, the area per molecule at constant surface pressure depends upon the cation present in the subphase, with the film being expanded in the order $Cs^+ > Rb^+ > K^+ > Na^+ > Li^+$. This expansion series occurs in exactly the reverse order with monolayers of alkyl sulfates [78–81]. Surface potential measurements as a function of pH permit determination of the surface pK for ionisable groups [65].

Determination of the monolayer isotherms as a function of temperature provides the necessary data for determination of the thermodynamic parameters which characterise the film of oriented amphipathic molecules. The relevance of temperature and the monolayer state or phase to interaction of phospholipids and cholesterol was described earlier. The details of monolayer thermodynamics can be found in Harkins [62], Gaines [65] and Davies and Rideal [66]. Specific thermodynamic equations for use in evaluating data from penetration of monolayers by surfactants, the type of experiment which has provided the extensive correlations referred to earlier, were derived by Pethica [82] and Anderson and Pethica [83].

Although simple, but very useful, the description used above to divide the surface pressure into component contributions essentially ignores the role of the solvent in the properties of the monolayer. The thermodynamic treatment developed extensively by Fowkes [84] includes specifically the solvent in the formulation of the thermodynamic equations. This treatment, based upon the model of a monolayer which relates the surface pressure to the osmotic pressure of a region semipermeable to solvent, has not yet been used to evaluate data from studies of biological surfactants; however, in view of recent studies on water in biological systems, to continue to ignore the role of water in the properties of the interface would seem impossible.

The physical data obtained from studies of phospholipid monolayers and the experimental problems associated with the investigation of phospholipid monolayers have been critically reviewed by Pethica [3].

In conclusion, monolayer techniques can be seen to provide a wide variety of information about the physical and chemical properties of biological amphipaths in a definitely orientated state. The similarity of the observations on the effects of various compounds on monolayers, and other model systems used in investigating the physical chemistry of membrane components, and the correlations of many of the model system structure-activity sequences with biological activity argue strongly for use of this model system in membrane investigations. Monolayers, because of their relative simplicity and the particular variables measured in monolayer experiments, are a convenient model for membrane-related investigations, and thus are relevant to our understanding biological membranes.

Summary

The contribution of monolayer techniques to our understanding of biological membranes is reviewed and some brief comments are made about the information obtainable from monolayer studies of the constituents of biological membranes.

References

[1] E.Gorter and F.Grendel, J. Exptl. Med. 41 (1925) 439.

[2] J.F.Danielli and H.J.Davson, J. Cell. Comp. Physiol. 5 (1934) 495.

[3] B.A.Pethica, Structural and Functional Aspects of Lipoproteins in Living System, eds. E.Tria and A.Scanu (Academic Press, New York, 1969).

[4] J.S.O'Brien, J. Theoret. Biol. 15 (1967) 307.

[5] E.D.Korn, Fed. Proc. 29 (1969) 6.

[6] J.H.Schulman and E.K.Rideal, Proc. Roy. Soc. (London), Ser. B 122 (1927) 29, 46.

[7] J.H.Schulman and E.K.Rideal, Nature 144 (1939) 100.

[8] J.H.Schulman and W.Mc.D.Armstrong, Surface Chemistry, Research (Butterworth, London, 1949) p. 273.

[9] B.A.Pethica and J.H.Schulman, Biochem. J. 53 (1953) 177.

[10] J.H.Schulman, B.A.Pethica, A.V.Few and M.R.J.Salton, Progr. Biophys. Biophys. Chem. 5 (1955) 41;
D.F.Sears and J.H.Schulman, J. Phys. Chem. 68 (1964) 3529.

[11] J.C.Skou, Acta Pharmacol. Toxicol. 10 (1954) 325.

[12] J.C.Skou, Biochim. Biophys. Acta 30 (1958) 625.

[13] A.D.Bangham, M.M.Standish and N.Miller, Nature 208 (1965) 1295.

[14] P.Seeman, International Conference on Biological Membranes (NATO Advanced Study Institute, Stresa, Italy, June 1969).

[15] A.D.Bangham, K.R.Rees and V.Shotlander, Nature 193 (1962) 754.

[16] A.D.Bangham, J.T.Dingle and J.A.Lucy, Biochem. J. 90 (1964) 133.

[17] J.A.Clements and K.M.Wilson, Proc. Natl. Acad. Sci. U.S. 48 (1962) 1008.

[18] A.Felmeister, M.Amanat and N.D.Weiner, Environ. Sci. Tech. 2 (1968) 40.

[19] K.Von Neergaard, Z. Ges. Exptl. Med. 66 (1929) 373.

[20] E.S.Brown, R.P.Johnson and J.A.Clements, J. Appl. Physiol. 14 (1959) 717.

[21] R.E.Pattle, Nature 175 (1955) 1125.

[22] E.M.Scarpelli, J. Colloid Sci. 25 (1967) 90.

[23] M.Galdston and D.O.Shah, Biochim. Biophys. Acta 137 (1967) 255.

[24] M.Blank, A.B.Goldstein and B.B.Lee, J. Colloid Interface Sci. 29 (1969) 148.

[25] M.Galdston, D.O.Shah and G.Y.Shinowara, J. Colloid Interface Sci. 29 (1969) 319.

[26] R.A.Demel and L.L.M.Van Deenen, Chem. Phys. Lipids 1 (1966) 68.

[27] R.A.Demel, L.L.M.Van Deenen and S.C.Kinsky, J. Biol. Chem. 240 (1965) 2749.

[28] R.A.Demel, F.J.L.Crombag, L.L.M.Van Deenen and S.C.Kinsky, Biochim. Biophys. Acta 150 (1968) 1.

[29] A.M.Shanes and N.L.Gershfeld, J. Gen. Physiol. 44 (1960) 345.

[30] D.Chapman, N.F.Owens and D.A.Walker, Biochim. Biophys. Acta 120 (1966) 148.

[31] D.A.Cadenhead and M.C.Phillips, Adv. Chem. 84 (1968) 301.

[32] F.Vilallonga, Biochim. Biophys. Acta 163 (1968) 290.

[33] M.C.Phillips and D.Chapman, Biochim. Biophys. Acta 163 (1968) 301.

[34] D.Chapman, Biological Membranes, Physical Fact and Function, ed. D.Chapman (Academic Press, New York, 1968).

[35] J.Mingins and J.A.G.Taylor, Unpublished observations (Unilever Research Laboratory, Port Sunlight, Cheshire, England, 1968).

[36] L.De Bernard, Bull. Soc. Chim. Biol. 40 (1958) 161.

[36a] L.L.M.Van Deenen, U.M.T.Houtsmuller, G.H.De Haas and E.Mulder, J. Pharm. Pharmacol. 14 (1962) 429.

[37] R.A.Demel, L.L.M.Van Deenen and B.A.Pethica, Biochim. Biophys. Acta 135 (1967) 11.

[38] M.M.Standish and B.A.Pethica, Biochim. Biophys. Acta 144 (1967) 659.

[39] D.Chapman, N.F.Owens, M.C.Phillips and D.A.Walker, Biochim. Biophys. Acta 183 (1969) 458.

[40]| F.C.Goodrich, Proc. 2nd. Intern. Congr. Surface Activity, London, Vol. 1 (Butterworths, London, 1957) p. 85.

[41] F.Vilallonga, R.Altschul and M.S.Fernandez, Biochim. Biophys. Acta 135 (1967) 557.

[42] R.Demel and P.Joos, Chem. Phys. Lipids 2 (1968) 35.

[43] G.Weissmann and G.Sessa, J. Biol. Chem. 242 (1967) 616.

[44] S.C.Kinsky, J.Haxby, C.B.Kinsky, C.B.Demel and L.L.M.Van Deenen, Biochim. Biophys. Acta 152 (1968) 174.

[45] De Gier, J.G.Mandersloot and L.L.M.Van Deenen, Biochim. Biophys. Acta 173 (1969) 143.

[46] A.D.Bangham, Progr. Biophys. Mol. Biol. 18 (1968) 29.

[47] I.Langmuir and D.F.Waugh, J. Am. Chem. Soc. 62 (1940) 2771.

[48] G.Colaccico, M.M.Rapport and D.J.Shapiro, J. Colloid Interface Sci. 25 (1967) 5.

[49] D.D.Eley and D.G.Hedge, J. Colloid Sci. 11 (1956) 445.

[50] B.R.Malcolm, Surface Activity and the Microbial Cell, Soc. Chem. Ind. (London) Monograph 19 (1965).

[51] B.R.Malcolm, Nature 219 (1968) 929;
B.R.Malcolm, Proc. Roy. Soc. (London) Ser. A 305 (1968) 363.

[52] G.I.Loeb, U.S. Naval Res. Report 6381, Wash, D.C. (1965);
G.I.Loeb, J. Colloid Interface Sci. 26 (1968) 236.

[53] D.F.Cheesman and J.T.Davies, Advan. Protein Chem. 9 (1954) 439.

[54] A.Hughes, Biochem. J. 29 (1935) 437.

[55] R.M.C.Dawson, Biological Membranes, Physical Fact and Function, ed. D. Chapman (Academic Press, New York, 1968).

[56] G.Colacicco, J.Colloid Interface Sci. 29 (1969) 345;
G.Colacicco and M.M.Rapport, J. Lipid Res. 7 (1969) 258.

[57] G.Colacicco and M.M.Rapport, Advan. Chem. 84 (1968) 157.

[58] G.Camejo, G.Colacicco and M.M.Rapport, J. Lipid Res. 9 (1968) 562.

[59] D.A.Haydon and J.Taylor, J. Theoret. Biol. 4 (1963) 281.

[60] H.T.Tien and A.L.Diana, Chem. Phys. Lipids 2 (1968) 55.

[61] W.D.Harkins, Surface Chemistry AAAS No. 21 (Science Press Printing Co., Lancaster, 1941) p. 40.

[62] W.D.Harkins, The Physical Chemistry of Surface Films (Reinhold, New York, 1952).

[63] A.W.Adamson, Physical Chemistry of Surfaces, 2nd. ed. (Interscience, J.Wiley, New York, 1967).

[64] N.K.Adam, The Physics and Chemistry Surfaces, 3rd ed. (Oxford Univ. Press, Oxford, 1941).

[65] G.L.Gaines, Insoluble Monolayers at Liquid-Gas Interfaces (Interscience, J. Wiley, New York, 1966).

[66] J.T.Davies and E.K.Rideal, Interfacial Phenomena (Academic Press, New York, 1963).

[67] A.B.P.Cassie and R.C.Palmer, Trans. Faraday Soc. 37 (1941) 156.

[68] R.Parsons, Modern Aspects of Electrochemistry, eds. J.O'M.Bockris and B.E. Conway (Butterworth, London, 1954) p. 103.

[69] S.Levine, J.Mingins and G.M.Bell, J. Phys. Chem. 67 (1963) 2095.

[70] S.Levine, J.Mingins and G.M.Bell, J. Electroanal. Chem. 13 (1967) 280.

[71] M.Joly, Recent Progress in Surface Science, eds. J.F.Danilli, K.G.A.Pankhurst and A.C.Riddiford (Academic Press, New York, 1964) p. 1.

[72] I.Langmuir, Colloid Symp. Monograph III (1925) 48.

[73] A.E.Alexander, Trans. Faraday Soc. 37 (1941) 426.

[74] J.H.Brooks and B.A.Pethica, Trans. Faraday Soc. 60 (1964) 1.

[75] J.A.G.Taylor and J.Mingins, unpublished observations (Unilever Research Laboratory, Port Sunlight, Cheshire, England, 1968).

[76] J.T.Davies, Proc. Roy. Soc. (London) Ser. A 208 (1951) 224.

[77] J.Mingins, Thesis (University of Manchester Institute of Science and Technology, 1962).

[78] A.P.Christodoulou and H.L.Rosano, Advan. Chem. 84 (1968) 210.

[79] N.K.Adam and J.G.F.Miller, Proc. Roy. Soc. (London) Ser. A 142 (1933) 401.

[80] J.Rogers and J.H.Schulman, Proc. 2nd International Congr. Surface Activity, London, 1956, Vol. 3 (Butterworth, London, 1957) p. 243; H.L.Rosano, A.P.Christodoulou and M.E.Feinstein, J. Colloid Interface Sci. 29 (1969) 335.

[81] I.Weil, J. Phys. Chem. 70 (1966) 113.

[82] B.A.Pethica, Trans. Faraday Soc. 51 (1955) 1402.

[83] P.J.Anderson and B.A.Pethica, Trans. Faraday Soc. 52 (1956) 1982.

[84] F.M.Fowkes, J. Phys. Chem. 65 (1961) 355; F.M.Fowkes, J. Phys. Chem. 77 (1962a) 385; F.M.Fowkes, J. Phys. Chem. 66 (1962b) 1863; F.M.Fowkes, J. Phys. Chem. 67 (1963) 1982; F.M.Fowkes, J. Phys. Chem. 68 (1969) 3515.

TRANSPORT PROCESSES ACROSS LIQUID
INTERFACES AND MONOLAYERS*

Martin BLANK**
*Department of Physiology, College of Physicians and Surgeons,
Columbia University, 630 West 168 Street, New York, New York 10032*

1. Introduction

During the last few years, I have studied the properties of model systems in order to learn more about transport processes across natural membranes. In the first two sections of this paper I would like to review some of the results of studies on transport across monolayers and liquid/liquid interfaces, respectively. In the third section I shall describe, in brief, new experiments dealing with some properties of an enzyme at an interface. In all of these cases, the experiments have been chosen with specific biological problems in mind. The discussion on monolayers will aim at an understanding of the general characteristics (e.g. porosity, partition) of passive permeation through natural membranes. The section on interfaces will deal with aspects of the specific and accelerated ion fluxes in excitable membranes. The last section will explore some interfacial properties of an enzyme associated with active ion transport (the sodium pump) that relate to the ability to transfer charge across an interface.

2. Transport across monolayers

A number of years ago, Schroedinger [1] considered the validity of the statistical laws of physics in biological systems, specifically as applied to the problem of heredity. Systems must be relatively large in order to minimize

* The work described in this paper has been supported by Research Grants from the U.S. Public Health Service (GM-10101), the Office of Saline Water, U.S. Department of the Interior (14-01-0001-1797) and the National Science Foundation (GB-6846).
** Supported by Research Career Development Award (K3-GM-8158) of the U.S. Public Health Service.

the deviations (fluctuations) from statistical laws, and genes are apparently
too small to be reliable for the orderly transmission of information. Schroedinger suggested that in order to guarantee order, nature must utilize a mechanism that is not based on statistical laws. If we consider a membrane we see
that it is also too small in the statistical sense, and one can expect significant
fluctuations in the average values of its properties. The deviations from physical laws because of the size and structure of membranes may provide an important clue to an understanding of permeation mechanisms. It is from this
point of view that the study of transport processes across monolayers can
contribute to our understanding of transport in biological membranes.
Furthermore, since monolayers resemble membranes in composition and
structure (orientation) as well as in size, they appear to be particularly appropriate models.

In monolayer permeation the size of the permeant is comparable to the
thickness of the monolayers, and one cannot assume a multi-collision process
with consequent averaging, as with diffusion in macroscopic systems. Because of this fundamental difference there are notable differences between the
permeation of monolayers and of macroscopic phases. Since many monolayer systems have been studied under a variety of conditions, it is possible
to arrive at some generalizations regarding the process of monolayer permeation [2,3]. For example, the least permeable monolayers are of the close-
packed incompressible type, and the monolayers that are almost freely permeable form relatively open structures such as those of protein, cholesterol
or oleic acid films. In a homologous series, the permeability is related to the
length of the hydrocarbon chain, and in a series of compounds having the
same chain length, the permeability depends on the size of the polar group.
These effects correlate the permeability inversely with the compactness of
the film and directly with the amount of free space in it. In line with this
view, the differences between the permeabilities of a monolayer to different
gases are best explained by the effect of molecular size of the permeating
species. This last observation means that monolayers have functional pores,
without any reason to expect the presence of structural pores.

Monolayer permeation appears to resemble the process of diffusion in
macroscopic solid phases, where the permeability depends upon the size and
number of holes available in a lattice. Further support for this parallel comes
from experiments which show interference effects between a permeant and
another gaseous component of the system. (For example, studies of monolayer permeability to carbon dioxide [4,5] have indicated that water vapor is
operationally present in the monolayer as an additional resistance.) Two substances can usually interdiffuse independently in an inert bulk liquid phase,

but in a solid-like phase, if the holes normally available for diffusion are occupied, a lower permeation rate would be expected. The magnitudes of the
permeability and of the activation energy, although somewhat lower, are also
comparable to analogous values for solids. However, unlike the bulk process,
the monolayer process exhibits a variation of the activation energy with the
monolayer thickness that implies a one-step discontinuous permeation process. Additional evidence for this idea comes from the observation that there
are no interfacial partition equilibrium effects, i.e., interactions of the permeant with the monolayer, during permeation [2] . These results point to a
qualitatively different kind of process in monolayers.

    In summary, the monolayer can be thought of as a solid phase for the
purposes of understanding the permeation process, but one in which the number of events involved is not sufficient to allow for averaging. Thus the permeation of a monolayer involves a one-step jump across the layer, just as in
a solid lattice there is a jump of permeant to a hole. Theoretical descriptions
of this process have been in terms of an energy barrier at the surface, due to
the monolayer, which prevents the molecules at the lower end of the kinetic
energy distribution from passing through. The activation energy barrier to
the evaporation of water through monolayers [6,7] was first believed to be
equal to the energy to make a hole in a monolayer (by compression). More
recent work by LaMer and co-workers [8–10] considered the barrier equal
to the energy required to form a vacant site in a monolayer lattice (which they
related to the vaporization of the monolayer). The most recent approach to a
theory of monolayer permeation has been in terms of free spaces that become available for permeation as a result of the natural free area in a lattice
and from the equilibrium fluctuations in monolayer density at a (gas mole-
cule-monolayer) collision site [11–13] . The equations that arise from these
various approaches to the energy barrier have the same general form and can
account for the variation of the permeation rate with temperature and permeant size. However, the approach using fluctuations in monolayer density
gives rise to general expressions for the distribution and frequency of fluctuations, and has been used to derive the self diffusion coefficient, the viscosity
and the thermal conductivity of a monolayer in terms of properties that are
related to the surface isotherm [12] . The approach is also useful in considering the possible nature of carriers in a bilayer membrane [13] :

    The results of the studies on monolayer permeation have given an insight
into the factors that affect permeation in films about 24 Å in thickness.
They indicate the existence of functional pores, the absence of interactions
with the monolayer during permeation, interference effects between per-
meants, etc., effects that may be present in natural membranes which are

only a little thicker [2,3] . These effects are due primarily to the size of the
system, and they may account for many aspects of the passive permeation
properties of natural membranes, largely on the basis of their general size and
structure.

Recently it has been possible to make measurements of the permeability
of monolayers to ions [14] . These results have provided some information
about the effects of charge on the transport rate through very thin films, and
have pointed out some general characteristics of ion transport in these systems. At constant ionic strength the transport rate increases an order of magnitude for a change of about 4-5 dyne/cm in interfacial tension (which is related to monolayer packing). An increase in the ionic strength (at constant
interfacial tension) also causes a marked increase in the permeability. These
results suggest that similar effects occur in bilayers and natural membranes,
where changes in ionic strength are frequently introduced experimentally or
are brought about as a result of passing currents.

Before leaving the discussion of transport across monolayers I would also
like to mention other recent results that bear on membrane problems. These
relate to protein films [15] , which have been found to be at least an order of
magnitude more permeable to water than straight chain lipid monolayers. This
finding would imply that a relatively small section of membrane composed
only of protein would make the membrane almost freely permeable. Although
the structure of a protein monolayer at an interface may be different from
that of proteins extending through a membrane, permeability data appear to
restrict the range of models of the plasma membrane [3] .

3. Transport of ions across liquid/liquid interfaces

When a substance is transported between two liquid phases, the concentrations of the substance on the two sides of the interface are related, i.e.,
there is partition equilibrium. One must take this factor into account in considering the transport of charged as well as uncharged substances. However,
in the case of ions there is an additional complication during transference
that can lead to rather large changes in the interfacial concentration.

When an electric field is applied across an ionic solution, the cations move
toward the cathode, the anions toward the anode, and there are changes in
concentration in the vicinity of the electrodes. When current flows across a
liquid/liquid system, there can be concentration changes at the interface as
well as at the electrodes when an ion has different transport numbers in the

two solvents. The increase or decrease in the interfacial concentration depends upon the rate of flow of ions through the interface, and upon the rate of diffusion to or from the interface. The change of ionic concentration due to interfacial transference has been known for some time [16], and recent experiments have explored some of the interfacial changes due to these effects [17–20].

The changes in ion concentration due to transference should occur generally, i.e., in all cases where an ion moves across a region where there is a change in transport number. Most natural membranes are in this category, and one can expect changes in the ionic concentrations on the two sides of a membrane as a result of the flow of current from an external source. In considering the flow of current across an excitable membrane such as the squid axon, a cathodal stimulus (one in which the cathode is on the outside of the cell, and the anode is inside) should give rise to an increase in ionic concentration on the outer surface of the membrane. This effect could conceivably give rise to the sequence of events observed during excitation, by an ion exchange mechanism that has been described earlier [21,3].

The mechanism is based on the assumption that ions adsorb on the two surfaces of the membrane, sodium on the outside and potassium on the inside under normal resting conditions. The cathodal stimulus brings potassium ions into a region where sodium ions are bound and there is an adjustment of the ion binding equilibrium causing a release of sodium ions. Because of the enhanced gradient of sodium ions there is an increased inward flux, etc. This mechanism does not involve pores or carriers, but relies on the asymmetry of the system and the direction associated with the particular starting events. The selectivity changes during excitation result from the asymmetry (sodium bound on the outside and potassium on the inside). The proper phasing of the ion movements results from the sequential release of the ions and the buildup and depletion of the ionic gradients. (In principle the mechanism is reversible, but the asymmetry of the system limits the reversibility.) Because the two ionic fluxes are influenced by events on opposite sides of the membrane, one can account for the selective actions of certain chemicals on either of the ionic fluxes. Also, one can account for the functional separation of resting and action potentials on the basis of the different ion populations involved. There are many effects that can be discussed in qualitative terms with the aid of this model, and work is continuing on the quantitative aspects.

4. Transport of electrons across a liquid/liquid interface in the presence of Na-K activated ATPase particles

When considering the transport of charge across liquid/liquid interfaces there is a tendency to think in terms of ions, which are the current carriers in aqueous solutions. However, electrons are the current carriers in liquids such as mercury, and the mercury/water interface provides the contact between the two types of charge carriers. This type of interface is called an electrode, and it is the site where a redox reaction determines the equilibration between ions and electrons. As mentioned earlier [14], the mercury/ water interface has been used to study the permeability of a monolayer to ions, when the monolayer adsorbs at this interface and the transported ions engage in a redox reaction.

Because of the relative ease with which this interface can be used to study the transport of charge, it was decided to use this system to determine the properties of an enzyme associated with the transport of ions in natural membranes [22]. The experimental details and a full description of the results [23] will be published soon, but at this stage I would like to present a preliminary summary of this work.

The enzyme, the Na-K activated ATPase, is particulate, and it causes the appearance of current pulses when the particles collide with the interface. The direction of the currents varies with the charge on the interface, the mercury being a source of electrons when it is negative and a sink for electrons when positive. The voltage range in which there is a transfer of electrons between the particles and the interface is about 600 mV on either side of the zero point of charge. The average frequency of the currents and their median amplitude increase and then decrease to zero within that range.

The currents are completely dissociable from the ATPase activity of the suspension, since the currents can disappear in the presence of activity and the currents can persist in the absence of activity. The only relation between the two effects is that both can be made to disappear by the action of ouabain (which eliminates ATPase activity at a much lower concentration) and oligomycin (which eliminates the interfacial currents first).

The currents do appear to be related to elements of the electron transport and coupling mechanisms that are involved in oxidative phosphorylation. Uncouplers (dinitrophenol, dicoumarol, pentachlorophenol) and some inhibitors of electron transport (antimycin A, rotenone and thenoyltrifluoroacetone) eliminate the currents at relatively low concentrations. (Cyanide and azide have no effect.) The reversibility of electron transport at the interface fits in with the reversibility of mitochondrial electron transport, oxidative phosphorylation and the coupling mechanism that connects the two. In addition, the range in which the ATPase particles can absorb or release electrons, ± 600 mV, can allow effective coupling to the 1100 mV involved in mitochondrial electron transport. The potential range for interfacial electron transport and the action of some of the compounds discussed suggest that the ATPase particles may contain elements of complex III (as described in mitochondria) which includes the second phosphorylation site.

These experiments raise many questions about the redox reactions involved in interfacial electron transport and the modes of action of uncouplers, electron transport inhibitors, and compounds that inhibit phosphorylation or the ATPase reactions associated with ion transport. The conventional explanations do not always appear applicable to this interfacial system, and it may be that this experimental procedure may provide new ways of checking our concepts of electron transport mechanisms.

Since the random currents did not appear to relate to the ATPase activity, one may be tempted to rule out any relation to the problem of ion transport. However, if the chemi-osmotic theory [24] is correct, the ATPase may normally act by causing the establishment of a pH gradient across the membrane. If the mechanism causing the random currents can generate a pH gradient by absorbing energy directly at an electrode surface, then the random currents would not appear related to the ATPase activity. Preliminary experiments have indicated dependence of the random currents on pH, that is in line with this explanation.

References

[1] E.Schroedinger, What is Life? (Doubleday, New York, 1956).
[2] M.Blank, J. Phys. Chem. 66 (1962) 1911.
[3] M.Blank, J. Gen. Physiol. 52 (1968) 1918.
[4] M.Blank, in: Retardation of Evaporation by Monolayers, ed. V.K.LaMer (Academic Press, New York, 1962) p. 75.
[5] M.Blank, J. Phys. Chem. 65 (1961) 1698.
[6] I.Langmuir and D.B.Langmuir, J. Phys. Chem. 31 (1927) 1719.
[7] I.Langmuir and V.J.Schaefer, J. Franklin Inst. 235 (1943) 119.
[8] R.J.Archer and V.K.LaMer, J. Phys. Chem. 59 (1955) 200.
[9] M.Blank and V.K.LaMer, in: Retardation of Evaporation by Monolayers, ed. V.K. LaMer (Academic Press, New York, 1962) p. 59.
[10] H.L.Rosano and V.K.LaMer, J. Phys. Chem. 60 (1955) 348.
[11] M.Blank, J. Phys. Chem. 68 (1964) 2793.
[12] M.Blank and J.S.Britten, J. Colloid Sci. 20 (1965) 789.
[13] M.Blank and J.S.Britten, in: Conference on Physical Principles of Biological Membranes (Gordon and Breach, New York, 1970) p. 143.

[14] I.R.Miller and M.Blank, J. Colloid Interface Sci. 26 (1968) 34.
[15] M.Blank and P.R.Mussellwhite, J. Colloid Interface Sci. 27 (1968) 188.
[16] W.Nernst and E.H.Riesenfeld, Ann. Physik 8 (1902) 600.
[17] J.Guastalla, Mem. Serv. Chim. Etat (Paris) 41 (1956) 317.
[18] M.Blank and S.Feig, Science 141 (1963) 1173.
[19] M.Blank, in: Physics and Physical Chemistry of Surface Active Substances, ed. Overbeek, Vol. II (Gordon and Breach, Belfast, 1967) p. 233.
[20] M.Blank, J. Colloid Interface Sci. 22 (1966) 51.
[21] M.Blank, J. Colloid Sci. 20 (1965) 933.
[22] J.C.Skou, Physiol. Rev. 45 (1965) 596.
[23] M.Blank and J.S.Britten, J. Membrane Biol. 2 (1970) 1.
[24] R.N.Robertson, Protons, Electrons, Phosphorylation and Active Transport (Cambridge, 1968).

A CRITIQUE OF THE BLACK LIPID
FILM AS A MEMBRANE MODEL

D.A.HAYDON

Laboratory of Biophysical Chemistry and Colloid Science,
University of Cambridge, Free School Lane, Cambridge

1. Some general considerations

A membrane model should facilitate our understanding of one or more of
the many structural aspects or functions of biological membranes. It is self-
evident that, at present at least, to try to construct, or to expect to find, one
model which covers all the diverse aspects of membrane structure and function is quite unreasonable. Many different types of model are likely to be
needed and, furthermore, it is quite likely that models may be needed to
understand models, and so on until one reaches the plastic molecule construc-
tion kit.

The primary model would in most cases resemble closely one of the structures present in a biological membrane. There is, of course, no question of
finding a black lipid film in a biological membrane and from this point of
view it is not obvious in what way the black film may be a useful model.
There is, however, some evidence that a bimolecular lipid leaflet, or something very similar, is present to some extent in many biological membranes.
The question of the utility of a black lipid film as a membrane model breaks
down therefore into two questions: (1) Is the bimolecular lipid leaflet a useful
model for a biological membrane? (2) Is the black lipid film a useful model of
a bimolecular lipid leaflet?

The first question has been discussed on countless occasions and in this
paper it is not intended to offer any further evidence or to review the arguments. It seems incontrovertible that there is a barrier to the exchange of substances across biological membranes and that for small water soluble molecules and ions, at least, this barrier consists largely of closely packed hydrocarbon groups. It is also fairly clear that the hydrocarbon barrier must be of
the order of 50 Å in thickness. It is perhaps debatable to what extent this
barrier exists in various membranes and it is also debatable to what extent

185

the hydrocarbon groups which make up the barrier originate from lipid or protein molecules. If, however, the lipid contributes substantially to the barrier, a bimolecular lipid leaflet is likely to be a good model in the sense that it has a continuous hydrocarbon core of the right order of thickness and it has an independent existence in aqueous media. Unfortunately, although vesicles bounded by single lipid leaflets have been prepared [1], the range of physical measurements that can be made on them is severely limited and for this reason the bimolecular lipid leaflet is not a very convenient model. The black lipid film, on the other hand, is very convenient for some of the important physical measurements but is essentially a model of a model. The second question given above inevitably arises, therefore, and the remainder of this article is concerned with a comparison of the bimolecular lipid leaflet with the black film.

2. The known properties of the bimolecular lipid leaflet in relation to those of the black lipid film

There are few properties which are known precisely for both the black film and the lipid leaflet. The composition and the thickness are, however, both known with reasonable accuracy.

Composition. As the black film is formed from a solution of lipid in hydrocarbon and remains in contact with such a solution it is inevitable from thermodynamic considerations that there must be some hydrocarbon in the film. A determination of the amount of *n*-decane in a black film containing *n*-decane and egg yolk phosphatidyl choline [2] yielded the result shown in table 1. The proportion of hydrocarbon present is quite large and although much of it can evidently be displaced by cholesterol [2] its presence is likely in either case to endow the black film with properties quite different from those of the pure lipid leaflet.

The foregoing remarks apply strictly to the equilibrium black film. Such a structure may be formed only after an inconveniently long time (several hours) and it is usually necessary to make measurements on films after relatively short times from their formation. In such circumstances it is common to find numerous small lenses of hydrocarbon trapped in the film [3,4]. For many purposes, for example, permeability measurement, the presence of these lenses is unimportant as they occupy only a very small fraction of the total film area. Optical properties of the films may, however, be drastically affected, as the lenses reflect and scatter far more light than the black film itself. In this respect therefore the presence of the solvent hydrocarbon makes the black film a poor model for the bimolecular lipid leaflet.

Table 1
Comparison of egg yolk lecithin leaflet and black film

	Lipid leaflet	Black film
Composition	Polar lipid only	Polar lipid + 33% (vol) hydrocarbon solvent
Thickness of hydrocarbon region	33 Å *	47 Å
Area per polar group	70 Å^2 *	60 Å^2
State of hydrocarbon	Liquid	Liquid

* Data of Small and Bourgès [5].

Thickness. The effective thickness of the bimolecular lipid leaflet can only be inferred from X-ray studies of a mesomorphic phase in equilibrium with excess aqueous phase. Under these conditions interaction between leaflets is a perturbing factor and it is probable that only the thickness of the hydrocarbon part of the leaflet, as estimated by Small and Bourgès [5], is useful for present purposes. For egg yolk phosphatidyl choline this thickness is ca. 33 Å [5] and in the author's opinion this is likely to be a good indication of the corresponding thickness of an isolated leaflet in aqueous media. The thickness of the hydrocarbon region of a black film stabilized by egg yolk phosphatidyl choline is somewhat larger. With *n*-decane as the solvent this thickness, as indicated by capacitance measurement [6,7] is ca. 47 Å.

According to Small and Bourgès the number of phospholipid molecules in 1 cm^2 of lipid leaflet is 2.8 X 10^{14} while for a black film the corresponding number is 3.2 X 10^{14} [2]. It is doubtful whether the difference between these two numbers is significant. If this is so, it follows that in the conversion of a lipid leaflet into a back film by the addition of hydrocarbon, the hydrocarbon has been accommodated entirely through an increase in thickness of the structure.

State. Although nothing quantitative can be said concerning this property, both the black film and the lipid leaflet (or at least their hydrocarbon parts) appear to be in a liquid state. The evidence for the black film lies in the mobility of objects in the film and in its quickly reversible deformability. The evidence for the lipid leaflet has been given by several authors [8–10] and rests mainly on the results of X-ray and other spectroscopic experiments. It seems reasonable to expect that the density of hydrocarbon in both the black film and the lipid leaflet will be closely similar.

Apart from the difference in composition, the black film is thus closely

similar to the lipid leaflet in that both structures are sheets of liquid hydrocarbon bounded by roughly equal densities of polar groups. For the same
polar lipid (e.g. egg yolk, phosphatidyl choline) the thicknesses differ, but
may in principle be equalized by the use in the black film of a shorter chain
lipid [11]. The rheological properties of the two structures must be assumed
to differ significantly.

3. Some predicted properties of the bimolecular lipid leaflet in relation to
those of the black lipid film

    The black lipid film, in contrast to the lipid leaflet, has the great merit that
many of its important properties are accessible to measurement. The results
of such measurements have made it possible to predict certain properties of
the lipid leaflet with some confidence.
    Capacitance and resistance. For a black film it has been established that
the capacitance is effectively determined by the thickness and dielectric constant of the hydrocarbon interior of the film. If, as seems almost certain, the
same principles hold for the leaflet as for the black film the capacitance of a
leaflet of egg yolk phosphatidyl choline in aqueous media should be ca.
$0.56 \mu F/cm^2$. The value for the corresponding black film is $0.38 \mu F/cm^2$.
    The resistance of the black film is similarly determined by the hydrocarbon
interior of the film. Although the resistances are variable and difficult to
measure with precision it is clear from the black film result that the lipid
leaflet resistance should be of the order of $10^9 \Omega/cm^2$.
    Compressibility in electric fields. On application of an electric field nor-
mal to its surface, the capacitance of a black film increases (fig. 1). This result
is attributable to a decrease in the film thickness [12] and it can be calculated
that for a film of glycerol mono-oleate and n-decane the compressibility for
systems at equilibrium is ca. $10^{-6} cm^2 dyne^{-1}$. For films of egg yolk phosphatidyl choline and n-decane no accurate data have been obtained but the
compressibility appears to be smaller by a factor of two or three.
    The thinning of the black film in the applied field occurs primarily through
the loss of hydrocarbon solvent. Thus, the field has the effect of changing the
chemical potentials of the constituents of the film, and as the film must remain in equilibrium with the adjacent bulk meniscus, its composition changes.
The rate of the equilibration may, however, be quite slow in some systems and
require several hours for completion.
    In contrast to the black film, the lipid leaflet cannot thin by changing its
composition, so excluding preferentially one of its components. The lipid

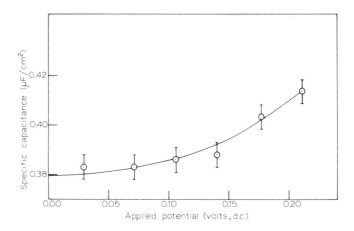

Fig. 1. The increase in specific capacitance with applied potential for a black film of glycerol mono-oleate + n-decane is 0.1 N NaCl. The calculated compressibility for this system is 0.4×10^{-6} cm^2 dyne^{-1}.

leaflet is composed of only one substance and it can become thinner only if either its density changes or its area increases. In fact both processes must occur although the magnitude of the density change is likely to be negligible. An increase in area must result in an increase in hydrocarbon/water contacts at the surface of the leaflet. If all the work of the field in compressing the leaflet is done in creating hydrocarbon/water interface the compressibility of the leaflet would be ca. 5×10^{-9} cm^2 dyne^{-1}, i.e. two hundred times less than the black film. This estimate is obviously crude as there may well be other important contributions to the free energy of the leaflet which depend appreciably on its area. Nevertheless it should be clear that the equilibrium compressibility of the lipid leaflet is likely to be quite different from that of the black film.

A *non-equilibrium* compressibility of the black film could, however, be much closer to that of the leaflet. If, for example, the compressibility of the black film could be measured before its composition had time to change, the factors governing the thinning would be very similar to those for the leaflet and the result much more comparable to that of a leaflet. Such experimental data as is at present available tends to confirm the deduction in the previous paragraph that the compressibility of the bimolecular lipid leaflet is small.

Adsorption from the aqueous phase. The interaction of substances in the aqueous phases with a membrane of molecular dimensions is essentially an adsorption. The fact that the membrane has two interfaces rather than one tends to complicate the treatment of the adsorption at a molecular or statistical level, although the thermodynamics are scarcely affected. Indeed for a symmetrical two-sided structure the application of the Gibbs adsorption equation is somewhat simpler than for a single interface [13,2]. A knowledge of the adsorption of molecules and ions on to a membrane is essential in order to understand not only the membrane composition and structure, but also its permeability to the species in question.

From the differences between the lipid leaflet and black film which have been emphasized in earlier sections it may seem that their interactions with other substances should be quite different. The following simple thermodynamic analysis enables the adsorption on to the two types of structure to be semi-quantitatively compared.

At adsorption equilibrium the chemical potentials of a species in bulk (l) and membrane (m) must be equal,

$$\mu_i^l = \mu_i^m . \tag{1}$$

For simplicity of argument it will be assumed that the adsorbing species forms a perfect solution in both bulk and membrane phases, in which instance (14)

$$\mu_i^l = \mu_i^{o,l} + RT \ln x_i^l \tag{2}$$

and

$$\mu_i^m = \mu_i^{o,m} + RT \ln x_i^m - \sigma a_i . \tag{3}$$

$\mu_i^{o,l}$ and $\mu_i^{o,m}$ are standard chemical potentials in the bulk and membrane phases respectively, x_i^l and x_i^m are the mole fractions in the two regions, a_i is the partial molar area of i in the membrane, and σ is the tension of the membrane. From (1), (2) and (3)

$$x_i^\sigma = x_i^l \exp \left[\frac{-\Delta\mu^o + \sigma a_i}{RT} \right], \tag{4}$$

where $\Delta\mu^o = \mu_i^{o,m} - \mu_i^{o,l}$. Eq. (4) is obviously an adsorption isotherm which relates the mole fractions of the adsorbing species in bulk and membrane through a free energy term. The difference in adsorption of a substance to a leaflet and a black film is thus determined by the difference in the free energy term for the two structures. $\Delta\mu^o$ arises only from the difference in chemical environments of the substance in bulk and membrane. If, for example, the adsorbing molecules pass wholly into the hydrocarbon interior of the membrane, $\Delta\mu^0$ is likely to be much the same for a leaflet and a black film. The difference in adsorption for the two types of membrane can then arise only from the tension term. For a black film this term may be estimated, as the tension of the film is measurable. For a lipid leaflet the tension is not known, but must evidently be lower than that for a black film owing to the absence of hydrocarbon solvent. There are no records of a black film with a tension of more than ca. 10 dyne/cm and hence the difference between black film and leaflet tensions must be less than this value. For reasonable values of a_i, therefore, exp $(\sigma a_i/RT) \lesssim 3$. The adsorption into the leaflet and black film under these conditions should consequently differ by less than a factor of three. Even if the adsorbing species interacts with the polar groups of the membrane, there is no reason to suppose that $\Delta\mu^0$ would necessarily be very different for the two structures since, as indicated in table 1, the number of polar groups per unit area of membrane may be similar for both lipid leaflet and black film.

The above discussion applies strictly only when the adsorption is so low that the original tension of the membrane is scarcely affected. The adsorption (or desorption) of a substance is, however, bound to change the tension of the membrane and the term exp $(\sigma a_i/RT)$ must change as the adsorption procedes. Should the surface excess of the substance in the membrane be negative and the membrane tension rise, the similarity of the adsorptive properties of the leaflet and black film would probably hold, in principle at least, to an unlimited extent. When the surface excess of the adsorbing substance is appreciably positive, however, a difficulty arises over the use of the black film as a model for a thin hydrocarbon membrane.

The great advantage of a black film as a model is its stability in the form of large planar sheets of known area. Once the planarity is lost a large part of the advantage is lost, and if the film becomes unstable and breaks up into small units the remainder of the advantage disappears. Both these processes tend to occur if the tension of the film is decreased. Indeed the mere removal of the hydrocarbon solvent from the film decreases the tension and converts it into a leaflet which has the very disadvantages that it wished to avoid. The tension may, however, also be reduced by adsorption. When the tension lowering becomes more than a few dynes/cm at most i.e. the film tension approaches zero, the black film will deform and rupture and, as a model, becomes useless.

The black film is therefore a good model for the lipid leaflet provided the adsorption is small. Fortunately many important systems fall into this cate-

gory, e.g. water, most inorganic ions, non-surface active organic molecules
such as glycol, glycerol, urea, hexoses etc., small polymeric molecules such
as monactins, valinomycins and other antibiotics and some water soluble
proteins. All these substances may reasonably be expected to interact similarly with a lipid leaflet and a black film. At sufficiently low concentrations
the same may be said for strongly adsorbing substances such as long chain
surfactants and other highly surface active substances. Structural protein
may well be in this class. At higher concentrations, however, the black film
disintegrates and the comparison with the leaflet is no longer of interest.

   Insomuch as any permeating ion or molecule must adsorb on to the membrane the similarity between lipid leaflet and black film outlined above indicates that the latter is, for permeability studies, a good model for the former.
There is, however, one possibly important reason for supposing that under
some circumstances the adsorption into the leaflet and black film may very
greatly differ. This situation may arise when the thickness of the two structures is different.

   In the discussion of adsorption given above it was supposed that the ad-

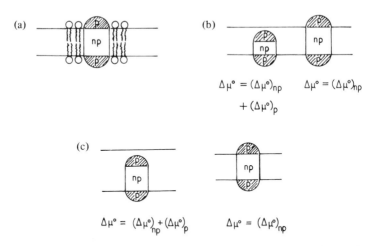

Fig. 2. (a) A molecule which interacts simultaneously with both sides of a membrane.
The regions marked 'p' and 'np' are supposed to be polar and non-polar respectively.
(b) The influence of the size of the molecule. In the example on the left $(\Delta\mu^{\text{o}})_{\text{np}}$ will
be strongly negative and $(\Delta\mu^{\text{o}})_{\text{p}}$ strongly positive, and hence $\Delta\mu^{\text{o}}$ is likely to be small.
In the example on the right, however, $\Delta\mu^{\text{o}}$ would be strongly negative. (c) The influence
of the thickness of the membrane. The energetics of the system are similar to (b). The
adsorption would be very much stronger in the thin than in the thick membrane.

sorbing molecule either passed completely into the hydrocarbon interior of the membrane and did not interact specifically with either surface, or it interacted with one surface only. As the size of the adsorbing molecule increases, however, it becomes more likely that it will interact simultaneously with both sides of the membrane (fig. 2). If this occurs it can make a very large difference to the strength of the interaction and the extent of the adsorption. This point is illustrated in fig. 2b. It is supposed that the adsorbing molecule has two polar regions separated by a non-polar region. It is also supposed for simplicity that unless the polar regions transfer to the hydrocarbon region of the membrane they do not contribute to the standard free energy of adsorption. Thus, when the polar regions are simultaneously on both sides of the membrane the free energy of adsorption is entirely due to transfer of the non-polar region from water to the membrane hydrocarbon, and is strongly negative. If, however, the molecule is too small for both polar groups to be on the outsides of the membrane, and one is in the hydrocarbon, the standard free energy of adsorption will be much less negative and may even be positive. The same type of situation obviously arises when the size of the molecule is constant but the membrane thickness varies as it does for an egg yolk phosphatidyl choline leaflet and black film (table 1; fig. 2c). It must be concluded, therefore, that where an adsorbing molecule may interact with both sides of a membrane, the adsorption into a lipid leaflet and a black film could differ by several orders of magnitude entirely owing to the thickness difference. Thus, where no adsorption or interaction is found for the black film, it may not be safe to conclude that no adsorption or interaction occurs with the leaflet.

References

[1] W.D.Seufert and W.Stockenius, Abstracts of papers presented at I.U.P.A.B. Symposium on Biophysical Aspects of Permeability, Jerusalem (1968) 58.
[2] G.M.W.Cook, W.R.Redwood, A.R.Taylor and D.A.Haydon, Kolloid-Z 227 (1968) 28.
[3] D.M.Andrews and D.A.Haydon, J. Mol. Biol. 32 (1968) 149.
[4] F.A.Henn, G.L.Decker, J.W.Greenawalt and T.E.Thompson, J. Mol. Biol. 24 (1967) 51.
[5] D.M.Small and M.Bourgès, Molecular Crystals 1 (1966) 541.
[6] T.Hanai, D.A.Haydon and J.Taylor, Proc. Roy. Soc. Ser. A 281 (1964) 377.
[7] D.A.Haydon, Proc. Duke University Membrane Symposium (1968, to be published); D.A.Haydon, in: The molecular basis of membrane function, ed. D.C.Tosteson, The Society of General Physiologists (Prentice Hall, New York, 1969) p. 111.
[8] F.O.Schmitt, J. Cellular Comp. Physiol. 18 (1941) 31.
[9] D.Chapman, J. Chem. Soc. (1958) 784.

[10] C.Luzzati, H.Mustacchi, A.Skoulios and F.Husson, Acta Cryst. 13 (1960) 660.
[11] J.Taylor and D.A.Haydon, Discussions Faraday Soc. 42 (1966) 51.
[12] D.M.Andrews, Ph. D. Dissertation, Cambridge (1970).
[13] B.V.Derjaguin, G.A.Martynov and Yu.V.Gutop, Kolloidn. Zh. 27 (1965) 298.
[14] R.Defay, I.Prigogine, A.Bellemans and D.H.Everett, Surface Tension and Adsorption (Longmans, Green and Co. Ltd., London, 1966) Ch. XII.

THE LIPOSOME AS A MEMBRANE MODEL

A.D.BANGHAM

A.R.C. Institute of Animal Physiology, Babraham, Cambridge

With minor alterations and appropriate up-dating of references, I am quite
content to repeat verbatim, the opening remarks delivered to this same meeting held exactly four years ago. It read as follows: "The recognition that bio-
logicall cells exploit the surface-active properties of lipids to define anatomical membranes has, in recent years, encouraged many workers to develop and
study model systems based upon the orientation of lipids at interfaces [1]. A
considerable advance was made when Mueller et al. [2] and Taylor [3] reported a technique for the preparation of isolated bimolecular lipid membranes separating two aqueous compartments. Such preparations (now variously called 'black lipid membranes' or BLM's, 'thin films' or simply 'bilayers'),
although somewhat fickle, have enabled a variety of physical parameters to
be measured. The technique lends itself pre-eminently to electrical studies of
a.c. and d.c. resistance and of capacitance (Haydon, this volume). The major
criticism of the technique, however, is that the precise composition of the
'black' (bimolecular) membrane is in some doubt, since it has not been found
possible to spread the membranes in the absence of a relatively large mole
fraction of a 'filler' hydrocarbon and of water-insoluble solvents. Indeed, according to Clements and Wilson [4], if as little as 1% of the lipid mass in a
membrane contains non-polar compounds, e.g. chloroform, the membrane
may be considered to be in a fully anaesthetized state. A further difficulty is
encountered when lipid mixtures analogous to those present in biological
membranes fail to produce useful membranes".

The liquid crystal (smectic mesophase or liposome) is a preferred phase
structure of many biological lipids in the presence of water or salt solutions.
It may be ascribed to the nature and heterogeneity of the hydrocarbon moieties and to the possession by the lipids of either polar, ionogenic or both
types of head groups. The precise geometry of the structures depends upon
the relative concentration of the two principal components (lipid and water),
the temperature, the composition of the lipid and the salt concentration of
the aqueous phase (for review: Bangham [1]). Over a wide range of such vari-

ables, however, the commonest phase structure appears to be that of a layer-lattice giving rise to spherulites and myelins, both being composite structures consisting of many concentric bimolecular layers of lipid each separated by an aqueous compartment. For thermodynamic reasons, it is probable that at equilibrium each and every lipid bilayer forms an unbroken membrane - there being no exposed hydrocarbon/water interface - from which it follows that every aqueous compartment would be discreet and iso-lated from its neighbour, including a complete separation of the outermost aqueous compartment of the whole structure from the continuous aqueous phase in which it is suspended. Since these 'liposomes' form spontaneously when dry lipids are allowed to swell in aqueous salt solutions, it seemed reasonable to test for the integrity of unbroken membranes by measuring the amount of electrolyte solution trapped in the aqueous spaces and also to test the rate of any subsequent leakage of ions into the bulk aqueous phase [5].

In summarizing the properties of the liposomes at that time (1965) it was concluded that:

1. The model membrane systems may be formed from egg lecithin with or without cholesterol, long chain anions or cations, as well as from whole lipid extracts from RBC's, etc.

2. Solvent molecules are not required and are not present.

3. They are permeable to water.

4. Positively charged membranes are impermeable to cations. Negatively charged membranes are relatively permeable to Li^+, Na^+, K^+, Rb^+, Cs^+ (50% exchange diffusion time - 100 hr at 22°C). The kinetics are probably not Fickean, but are linear for the first 24 hr. E = 15 kcal/mole. Cation permeabil-ity increases steeply with increasing surface charge density. There is no selec-tivity between K^+ and Na^+, but preliminary results suggest that the incorpo-ration of certain cyclic polypeptides enables the membranes to distinguish be-tween Li^+ or Na^+ and K^+ or Rb^+.

5. They are osmotically sensitive.

6. The membranes appear to be about 10^2 times more permeable to anions than to cations. Positive, negative and pure lecithin (net uncharged) mem-branes exhibit rapid anion diffusion rates. The membranes are selectively per-meable to anions, those with the smallest hydrated ion radius diffusing most rapidly.

7. Steroids which cause lysis of lysosomes increase the diffusion rates of ca-tions. Steroids that protect lysosomes against various physical or chemical insults reduce the cation diffusion rates.

8. The membranes respond to alcohol, chloroform and ether by increasing the cation diffusion rates in a manner related to their thermodynamic activity. The effects are measurable at narcotic concentrations.

9. The membranes respond to local anaesthetics by showing a reduction in the cation diffusion rate. At high concentration this trend is reversed, even though the zeta potentials continue to become more positive.

During the past four years many of these properties have been confirmed, some refined, yet others extended and a few questioned.

Inevitably the model system has been used by individuals or groups of workers within the context of their pre-existing interest or speciality. Thus for example, Weissmann and his group have persevered in using liposomes as analogues to lysosomes; judging by their results (for review: Sessa and Weissmann [6]) they have little cause for complaint! A charming experiment, unmatched by any of the BLM exponents, was to prepare 'male' and 'female' reacting liposomes by 'doping' them with characteristic male or female steroids. Mimicking a total-animal response i.e. a differential response following the injection of etiocholanolone into human males and/or females, the liposomes containing 17 oestradiol did not show the very significant increase in permeability to marker ions, exhibited by the control or testosterone-doped liposomes. Weissmann was quick to exploit the advantage of the liposome model in his studies with polyene antibiotics. These compounds, known to be effective only against cells whose membranes contain sterol, were soon tested against liposomes with and without cholesterol [7,8]. Kinsky et al. [9] rounded off this problem and showed some convincing negatively-stained preparations of liposomes damaged with filipin. Weissmann's tenth paper on the effect of drugs (tumor promoting agents) affecting lysosomes [10] is also the first in which liposomes have behaved in a significantly different manner from biological organelles. As with the inexplicable (at the time) failure of all-trans retinal to increase the permeability of phosphatidyl choline liposomes [11] an explanation may be forthcoming which will have further ramifications.

Van Deenen and his group in Utrecht have, for many years, emphasized the relationship between the detailed composition of cell membranes (e.g. type of phospholipid, species of head group and nature of the hydrocarbon moiety) to their characteristic physical behaviour. For this reason a number of communications in which liposomes of varying chemical composition have been used, have appeared during the past four years. Using the principles and experimental methods for following osmotically driven water into and out of liposomes [12], De Gier and colleagues have systematically measured the permeability of liposomes prepared from phospholipids having varying chain lengths and degree of chain saturation, with and without cholesterol, to non-electrolytes e.g. glycol, glycerol [13–15]. Interestingly, cholesterol was shown to reduce the permeability of liposomes prepared from unsaturated

chain phospholipids, but, by greatly reducing the temperature dependence
for saturated chain phospholipids, a paradoxical reversal of effect relative to
the cholesterol-free system was observed. Their data might yield some interesting conclusions were it analysed according to the Eyring absolute rate
theory (see for example Johnson and Bangham [16], and Sweet and Zull
[17]).

Sweet and Zull [17] have recently used liposomes in a study of protein/
lipid interaction. Their criterion of reactivity of the protein to lipid was
judged by an increase of some 4-fold of the permeability of the liposomes to
glucose. Significantly, they only observed an increased permeability when
the protein (serum albumin) was below its isoelectric point and the liposomes
were negatively charged. The reversed situation viz., a protein above its isoelectric point and a positively charged liposome surface exhibited control
permeability characteristics. Such specificity for electrostatic interactions of
protein to variously charged liposomal surfaces has been reviewed and reported upon some years ago by the present author [18,19] and by Dawson
[20]. More surprising perhaps, was Sweet and Zull's [17] finding that the
serum albumin increased the permeability of the liposomes to glucose with
the same enthalpy (ΔH^*) of activation - a result (fig. 4) which we have recently reported for 'anaesthetized' and valinomycin treated liposomes with
respect to their permeability to univalent cations [21]. We also have some
evidence that general anaesthetics do not increase the permeability of liposomes to glucose as significantly as they do to small cations.

As has already been mentioned, Bonting and Bangham [11] were discon-
certed to find that all-trans retinal had remarkably little effect on liposomes
prepared from egg phosphatidyl choline, knowing it to be an extremely lytic
agent for erythrocytes [22,23]. However, when it was realized that all-trans
retinal (vitamin A aldehyde) could react to form a Schiff-base with amino-
containing phospholipids e.g. phosphatidyl ethanolamine, a novel mechanism
of membrane physical-chemistry was conceived. The consequence of the
Schiff-base reaction was tantamount to the addition of a long chain acid -
namely, the acquisition of a foreign long chain molecule and the gain of a net
negative charge. Bonting and his group in Nijmegen have justifiably suggested
this mechanism as being a relevant one in the visual process [24,25].

One of the tentative claims made four years ago [26] at this meeting was
that selective permeability towards monovalent cations was conferred by the
then almost unknown compound valinomycin. I recollect reporting the results which were subsequently confirmed and presented by Chappell to a biochemical symposium on Mitochondrial Function [27]. Since then Chappell and

his group have brilliantly exploited the liposome model system by running
it parallel to their studies on mitochondrial and erythrocyte membranes [28].
Summarising their results simply by quoting the summary of their paper: (1)
They studied the action of the antibiotics enniatin A, valinomycin, the actin1
homologues, gramicidin, nigericin and dianemycin on mitochondria, erythrocytes and smectic mesophases of lecithin-dicetyl hydrogen phosphate. (2)
These antibiotics induced permeability to alkali-metal cations on all three
membrane systems. (3) The ion specificity on each membrane system was the
same. (4) Enniatin A, valinomycin and the actins did not induce permeability
to protons, whereas nigericin and dianemycin rendered all three membrane
systems freely permeable to protons. (5) Several differences were noted between permeability induced by nigericin and that induced by gramicidin. (6)
The action of all these antibiotics on mitochondrial respiration could be accounted for by changes in passive ion permeability of the mitochondrial
membrane similar to those induced in erythrocytes and phospholipid membranes, if it is assumed that a membrane potential is present in respiring mitochondria.

Our own efforts have been directed towards improving the reproducibility
and increasing the simplicity of the system. As Johnson and Bangham [16]
point out, the earlier models suffered at least three serious defects. Firstly
the results could not be expressed as true permeabilities or fluxes since the
surface area of the dispersions was not measured. This fault was remedied
by developing a technique for measuring the surface area of a liposomal preparation [12]. In principle this method uses a monolayer of the liposome-
type phospholipid as an UO_2^{++} electrode. UO_2^{++} ions have a very high affinity
for phosphate groups and form ion pairs at low concentration (10^{-6} M),
even in the presence of 0.145 M univalent cation. The concentration, therefore, of UO_2^{++} can be monitored by measuring the change in the surface potential of a saturated phospholipid monolayer at the air/water interface
(fig. 1a). If a large, but unknown, area of liposomes are now introduced into
the bulk aqueous phase beneath the monolayer, the UO_2^{++} will redistribute
themselves between the insignificantly small monolayer and the liposomes
(fig. 1b). From the Gouy equation,

$$\sinh \frac{\Delta\Delta V_{obs}}{50.86} = \frac{134 \times 6023}{A\sqrt{0.16}} S \qquad \text{at } 22°\text{C} ,$$

so that by plotting $\sinh (\Delta\Delta V_{obs}/50.86)$ against S, the moles of UO_2^{++} added,
the surface area in cm^2, A can be calculated from the gradient of the graph.

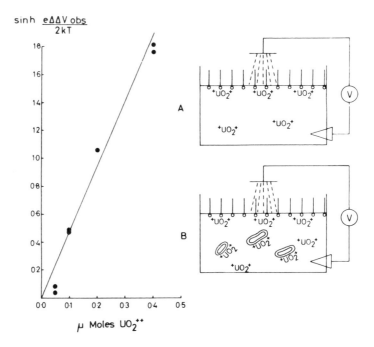

Fig. 1. Principles of the method and titration curve of a dispersion of liposomes.

0.16 is the univalent salt concentration (KCl). Fig. 1. illustrates the principles of the method and shows a titration curve.

As might be expected upon consideration of their structure, the maximum liposomal surface area per μmole of phospholipid (vesicles bounded by a single bilayer) is given by:

$$\frac{\text{Avogadro's number} \times 70}{10^6 \times 2 \times 10^{16}} = 2000 \text{ cm}^2 \text{ approx.},$$

where 70 is the area in Å^2 per phospholipid molecule when packed in a smectic mesophase [29]. Thus, measurements of surface area not only permit permeability coefficients to be computed, but day by day or batch to batch variation in flux can be corrected for; for example over a period of about a year the K^+ permeability coefficient for weekly preparations varied between 3.0 and 8.0×10^{-13} cm sec^{-1} at 20°C.

A second defect is the rather complicated exchange kinetics of multiple, concentric compartments. Although Bangham et al. [12] were probably justified in accepting the *initial rate* of swelling or shrinking of large liposomes as a valid measure of water permeability of one membrane, their analysis of the complete swelling curve illustrates the complexity of the problem.

A third complication which has been apparent for some time is the effect of decomposition (presumably by oxidation) during the process of sonication (see also Papahadjopoulos [30]). Unless oxygen is carefully excluded, a progressive chemical reaction takes place from the moment sonication starts (fig. 2) and continues at a steady rate for at least 5 hr [31]. The nature of the decomposition is uncertain but the spectrographic and chromatographic data obtained by Klein [31] leave no doubt that it takes place (fig. 3). As can be seen in fig. 3, sonication in the presence of N_2 prevents these reactions from taking place.

Johnson and Bangham [16] have, to a large extent, overcome these defects and can now reasonably claim that reliable methods are available that give essentially two-compartment kinetics and which measure surface areas. Combined, such methods allow measurement of permeability coefficients over some four orders of magnitude ($10^{-13} - 10^{-9}$ cm sec^{-1}). For the moment, high permeability coefficients ($10^{-4} - 10^{-3}$ cm sec^{-1}) can only be measured indirectly by following light-scattering changes following the osmotic movement of water and solute [12].

Using such improved methods, Johnson and Bangham [21] have recently investigated in detail the energy barriers to diffusion of small cations and the

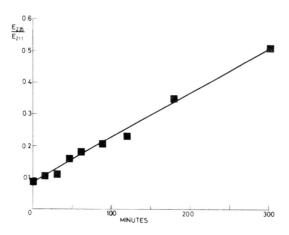

Fig. 2. Liposomes sonicated under air. From Klein [31].

A.D.BANGHAM

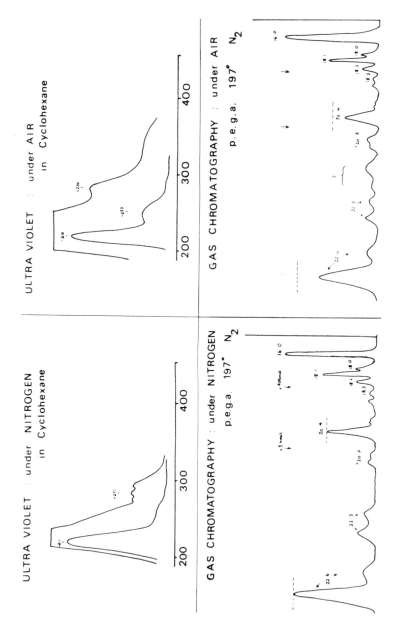

Fig. 3. Liposomes sonicated under air or nitrogen. From Klein [31].

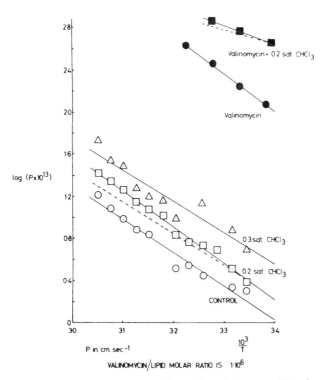

Fig. 4. Liposome permeability with chloroform. From Johnson and Bangham [21].

Table 1

Anaesthetic	Partial molar volume (cm³)	† A_{nar} liposome K^+ permeability $\times 10^2$	A_{nar} axon block $\times 10^2$	A_{nar} synapse block $\times 10^2$
n-butanol	98	4.4	4.6	4.6
chloroform	81	27.2	19.0	6.3
diethyl ether	105	12.0	12.0	4.2

From Johnson and Bangham [21].
† A_{nar} is the thermodynamic activity of a compound producing narcosis.

effect upon them of general anaesthetics and of the specific K^+ ionophore, valinomycin. A typical result is shown in fig. 4 where values of $\log P$ are plotted against $1/T$ for untreated preparations of egg lecithin liposomes, the same preparation in the presence of two different concentrations of chloroform and finally with valinomycin pre-incorporated at a mole ratio of 1 : 10^6. When corrections (not significant for chloroform) for the ether and butanol partition coefficients at various temperatures are applied to such Arrhenius plots, it was found that the enthalpy of activation (ΔH^* = 15.4 ± 1.1 kcal/ mole) was the same whether the anaesthetics were there or not; to account for the increase in permeability a small increase in the entropy of activation (ΔS^* = 1.5 cal/deg) was suggested. For the three general anaesthetics studied, ΔS^* seemed to be proportional to the quantity of anaesthetic in the membrane and ΔS^* could therefore be calculated from the relation:

$$\frac{\Delta S^*}{2.303R} = \log P_{\text{anaesthetic}} - \log P_{\text{control}} \cdot$$

Table 1 shows the values of A_{nar} for the three anaesthetics calculated to produce a ΔS^* of 1.74 cal/mole/deg. They are to be compared with the values for A_{nar} which produce a 50% reduction in the axon potentials of synaptic and non-synaptic or axonal conduction in the perfused stellate ganglion of the cat [32]. It will be seen that there is a good correlation between the A_{nar} required for the biological end-point of axonal block and a thermodynamic end-point in liposomes of ΔS^* = 1.7 cal/mole/deg. Broadly interpreting such results it might be suggested that anaesthetic molecules act by increasing the disorder of the lipid components of a membrane.

In many ways a more unexpected result is also shown in fig. 4 namely, that the enthalpy of the activated state (ΔH^*) when valinomycin was present, is no different from that of the control despite the fact the K^+ permeability is some $\times 10^2$ greater. In a closely argued discussion Johnson and Bangham [21] conclude that an increase in ΔS^* of 35 cal/deg could account for this discrepancy but that the rate limiting step must be when the K^+ leaves the membrane. Further work on this system is envisaged and should be helpful towards our understanding of trans-membrane ion movement.

Finally one recalls a series of papers by Papahadjopoulos and co-authors, during and after his time as a National Heart Institute Fellow at Babraham. The most comprehensive review appears in his 1968 paper [30] whose title summarises much of his work with phospholipids and liposomes: "Surface

Properties of Acidic Phospholipids: (The) Interaction of Monolayers and Hydrated Liquid Crystals with Uni and Bi valent Metal Ions". Chronologically his other papers dealing with liposomes prepared from the less accessible (but more interesting) phospholipids are listed as follows: Bangham and Papahadjopoulos [33], Papahadjopoulos and Bangham [34], Papahadjopoulos and Miller [35], Papahadjopoulos and Watkins [36].

By way of a postscript another type of thin-walled phospholipid vesicle has recently been described [37]. Their manner of formation is subtly different but the end result could well be a practical improvement on the liposome, the great advantage being that the volume trapped to lipid ratio is vastly increased. However, unless it can be shown that a constant (preferably one) number of membranes constitute the permeability boundary their use for membrane kinetics may be limited.

References

[1] A.D.Bangham, Progr. Biophys. Molec. Biol. 18 (1968) 31.
[2] P.Mueller, S.O.Rudin, H.Ti.Tien and W.C.Wescott, Circulation 26 (1962) 1167.
[3] J.Taylor, Ph. D. Thesis, University of Cambridge (1963).
[4] J.A.Clements and K.M.Wilson, Proc. Natl. Acad. Sci. U.S. 48 (1962) 1008.
[5] A.D.Bangham, M.M.Standish and J.C.Watkins, J. Mol. Biol. 13 (1965) 238.
[6] G.Sessa and G.Weissmann, Biochim. Biophys. Acta 150 (1968) 173;
    G.Sessa and G.Weissmann, J. Lipid Res. 9 (1968) 310.
[7] G.Weissmann and G.Sessa, J. Biol. Chem. 242 (1967) 616.
[8] G.Sessa and G.Weissmann, Biochim. Biophys. Acta 135 (1967) 416.
[9] S.C.Kinsky, S.A.Luse, D.Zopf, L.L.M.Van Deenen and J.Haxby, Biochim. Biophys. Acta 135 (1967) 844.
[10] G.Weissmann, W.Troll, B.L.Van Duuren and G.Sessa, Biochem. Pharmacol. 17 (1968) 2421.
[11] S.L.Bonting and A.D.Bangham, Exptl. Eye Res. 6 (1967) 400.
[12] A.D.Bangham, J.De Gier and G.D.Greville, Chem. Phys. Lipids 1 (1967) 225.
[13] J.De Gier, J.G.Mandersloot and L.L.M.Van Deenen, Biochim. Biophys. Acta 150 (1968) 666.
[14] R.A.Demel, S.C.Kinsky, C.B.Kinsky and L.L.M.Van Deenen, Biochim. Biophys. Acta 150 (1968) 655.
[15] J.De Gier, J.G.Mandersloot and L.L.M.Van Deenen, Biochim. Biophys. Acta 173 (1969) 143.
[16] S.M.Johnson and A.D.Bangham, Biochim. Biophys. Acta 193 (1969) 82.
[17] C.Sweet and J.E.Zull, Biochim. Biophys. Acta 173 (1969) 94.
[18] A.D.Bangham, Advan. Lipid Res. 1 (1963) 65.
[19] A.D.Bangham and R.M.C.Dawson, Biochim. Biophys. Acta 59 (1962) 103.
[20] R.M.C.Dawson, in: Biological Membranes, ed. D.Chapman (Academic Press, New York, 1968).

206 A.D.BANGHAM

[21] S.M.Johnson and A.D.Bangham, Biochim. Biophys. Acta 193 (1969) 92.

[22] J.T.Dingle and J.A.Lucy, Biochem. J. 84 (1962) 611.

[23] A.D.Bangham, J.T.Dingle and J.A.Lucy, Biochem. J. 90 (1964) 133.

[24] F.J.M.Daemen and S.L.Bonting, Biochim. Biophys. Acta. 163 (1968) 212.

[25] F.J.M.Daemen and S.L.Bonting, Nature 222 (1969) 879.

[26] A.D.Bangham, M.M.Standish, J.C.Watkins and G.Weissmann, Protoplasma 63 (1967) 183.

[27] J.B.Chappell and K.N.Haarhoff, in: Biochemistry of Mitochondria, eds. E.C. Slater, Z. Kaninga and L.Wojtczak (Academic Press, New York, 1967).

[28] P.J.R.Henderson, J.D.McGivan and J.B.Chappell, Biochem. J. 111 (1969) 1.

[29] D.M.Small, J. Lipid Res. 8 (1967) 551.

[30] D.Papahadjopoulos, Biochim. Biophys. Acta 163 (1968) 240.

[31] R.Klein, Chemical changes of sonicated liposomes (1970, to be published).

[32] F.Brink and J.M.Posternak, J. Cellular Comp. Physiol. 32 (1948) 211.

[33] A.D.Bangham and D.Papahadjopoulos, Biochim. Biophys. Acta 126 (1966) 181.

[34] D.Papahadjopoulos and A.D.Bangham, Biochim. Biophys. Acta 126 (1966) 185.

[35] D.Papahadjopoulos and N.Miller, Biochem. J. 135 (1967) 624.

[36] D.Papahadjopoulos and J.C.Watkins, Biochem. J. 135 (1967) 639.

[37] J.P.Reeves and R.M.Dowben, J. Cellular Comp. Physiol. 73 (1969) 49.

THE THERMODYNAMICS OF MEMBRANE TRANSPORT

Patrick MEARES

Chemistry Department, The University, Old Aberdeen, Scotland

1. Introduction and general considerations

Recent developments in the physical and chemical methods of examining biological membranes have made possible some spectacular advances in the understanding of membrane structure. These achievements have led to a concentration of effort on structural researches and some lessening of interest in the mechanism of membrane function. Previously membranes were characterized primarily by studying their functionality. A thorough quantitative description of a membrane's transport properties, and their comparison with the properties of synthetic model systems, seemed to offer the best hope of deducing something about its structure. Unfortunately this hope was largely unfulfilled because the fundamental theory of membrane transport was insufficiently advanced to undertake so difficult a task. Improvements in the theory of transport processes have now prepared the way for a more detailed and rewarding interpretation of the results of experiments on membranes. The intention of this article is to encourage the collection of transport data in a form suitable for use with these newer theories.

Systematic attempts at applying thermodynamics to membrane transport date from the skillful combination by Teorell [1,2] and Meyer and Sievers [3,4] (in future denoted by TMS) of the Nernst-Planck flux equation and the Gibbs-Donnan expression for thermodynamic equilibrium between phases containing constrained ions.

The Nernst-Planck equation has a kinetic origin. It treats diffusion down a concentration gradient as a consequence of the random molecular Brownian motion and hence makes use of the familiar Nernst-Einstein relation between the diffusion constant D and the absolute mobility u

$$D = uRT . \tag{1}$$

Furthermore ionic transport resulting from a gradient of electric potential is treated as an independent process superimposed upon the diffusion flow. Hence Fick's and Kohlrausch's equations may be added together to give the flux density ϕ_i of ions i when subjected simultaneously to a concentration gradient dc_i/dx and a potential gradient $d\psi/dx$:

$$\phi_i = -D_i dc_i/dx - z_i F u_i c_i d\psi/dx , \tag{2}$$

where z_i is the valency (including sign) of i and F is Faraday's number. Equation (2) is essentially the Nernst-Planck equation and by virtue of equation (1) it can be rewritten as

$$\phi_i = u_i c_i [-d(RT \ln c_i + z_i F\psi)/dx] . \tag{3}$$

Equation (3) is in the important form

$$\text{flux} = \text{mobility} \times \text{concentration} \times \text{force} , \tag{4}$$

where the term in square brackets is the force.

Equation (3) is a local equation. That is to say it relates the flux at a plane represented by the distance x with the concentration and the gradients at x. The steady flow ϕ_i is independent of x and u_i may be independent of x (although usually it is not) whereas c_i and ψ are functions of x. Thus to describe the results of a macroscopic experiment equation (3) requires to be integrated between known limits and subjected also to certain restrictions such as the requirement of local electrical neutrality. This is

$$\sum_{\substack{\text{all mobile} \\ \text{ions}}} z_i c_i + \omega X = 0 , \qquad \text{at all } x , \tag{5}$$

where X is the concentration and ω the valency of any ions chemically or physically bound to the membrane. There must also be correspondence of the net charge flux due to the ions with the electric current density i: i.e.

$$i = F \sum_{\substack{\text{all mobile} \\ \text{ions}}} z_i \phi_i . \tag{6}$$

The limits of the integration of equation (3) are usually taken as the concentrations and distances in the membrane at the two interfaces between it and the surrounding solutions. However the concentrations which may be determined experimentally are those in the external solutions. The TMS theory invokes the Gibbs-Donnan membrane equilibrium to interrelate the concentrations just inside and just outside the membrane at the interfaces so as to evaluate the limits of the integration from observable concentrations.

The use of the Gibbs-Donnan equation in this context introduces the postulate that the intensive variables of classical equilibrium thermodynamics, in particular the electrochemical potential of an ionic species, have a real meaning and obey the well-established equilibrium equations when applied in a local sense in a non-equilibrium system i.e. one in which net fluxes are occurring. It is important to understand that this is a postulate which can only be verified by experiment, that it can only hold rigorously in the limit of infinitesimal departures from equilibrium and that its range of validity in any particular case must depend on the nature of the membrane and solutions considered. One may expect that the breadth of the concentration interval across which this postulate of local equilibrium holds would be roughly proportional to the membrane thickness because the local gradients are a measure of the departure from equilibrium. The postulate will therefore be a more serious limitation with thin biological membranes than with thick synthetic ones. At present there is but little quantitative information on this problem in thin membranes but the postulate appears to be widely valid for passive transport in thick membranes.

In practical circumstances the integration of equation (3) when combined with (5) and (6) and the Gibbs-Donnan principle, still requires an assumption to be made and various authors have used different assumptions [5–7]. The resulting equations can give at best a semi-quantitative account of the ion fluxes across a membrane.

2. Extensions of TMS theory

Many attempts have been made to refine this treatment of membrane processes along two main lines [5,8,9]. It will be seen that the force in equation (3) derives from the gradient of $(RT \ln c_i + z_i F \psi)$ which is the isothermally and isopiestically variable part of the electrochemical potential of i if the membrane phase may be treated as an ideal mixture of components. If the notion of chemical potential has meaning at the interfaces in order to apply the Gibbs-Donnan equation to the non-equilibrium system then the same should apply inside the membrane and instead of $(RT \ln c_i + z_i F \psi)$ the gradient of the electrochemical potential μ_i should be used as the force. Thus the term for the gradient of activity coefficient is required but is usually not determinable and is probably quite small. The restriction of constant pressure may be removed at the same time by including in the chemical potential a term $p\overline{V}_i$ where p is pressure and $\overline{V}_i$ the partial molar volume. This term also is usually small and the above refinement of the TMS theory is not of great assistance except that it introduces the notion of gradients of thermodynamic variables as driving forces.

The other line of refinement may be appreciated by considering first the flux of solvent. There is nothing in the Nernst-Planck equation which restricts its use to ionic components. Provided $z_i = 0$ is used for non-ionic substances, the equation reduces to Fick's equation and should be valid generally. Thus the flux of a non-ionic substance in the absence of a concentration gradient should be zero. The phenomenon of electro-osmotic flow of solvent is however well known and contradicts the above conclusion. Moreover it has often been observed that the osmotic flow of solvent is far larger than can be accounted for by simple diffusion flow calculated by using a diffusion coefficient determined with an isotopic tracer [10].

These solvent fluxes can be accounted for only if the direct transfer of momentum between flowing particles is taken into account. In the case of electro-osmosis the transfer is from ions to solvent molecules whereas in osmosis the transfer is from one solvent molecule to another. The effect is greater the higher the concentration of solvent in the permeable regions of the membrane. The transfer of momentum sets up a convective streaming in the membrane which carries the components along more or less indiscriminately while the thermodynamic gradients generate fluxes of the individual components relative to the local centre of volume.

Attempts have therefore been made to introduce the effect of this convective streaming into the flux equation by writing in place of equation (3)

$$\phi_i = u_i c_i [-\mathrm{d}(RT \ln c_i + z_i F\psi)/\mathrm{d}x] + c_i v , \qquad (7)$$

where v is the velocity of the local centre of volume. Equation (7) is more difficult to integrate and v has usually to be measured experimentally. However equation (7) forms the basis of a good quantitative representation of the fluxes in homogeneous membranes [5,8,11].

3. Coupling of flows and non-equilibrium thermodynamics

Although the addition of a convective term to the TMS equations permits a much better fit between theory and experiment it does not take into account in any detail the way in and extent to which momentum is transferred between flowing components. This phenomenon is generally spoken of as coupling between the fluxes of different components.

It is not possible to introduce specific coupling phenomena into the TMS theory without greatly changing its basic character and simplicity. However the thermodynamic theory of irreversible processes [12] seems ideally suited for the inclusion in a formal way of coupling phenomena into a general theory of membrane processes [13].

The most detailed development of the non-equilibrium thermodynamics of membranes has been limited to the so-called linear region in which flux is given by a sum of terms each of which is proportional to one of the forces acting on the system [14]. These linear flux expressions are valid only close to equilibrium and this may be a serious restriction on the usefulness of the theory. It may be noted that the integrated TMS equations are in general not in a linear form.

It is clear that many important membrane phenomena, especially in biology, are non-linear and attention is being increasingly devoted to developing the theory of the non-equilibrium thermodynamics of such phenomena [15,16] but the mathematical difficulties are severe.

To date the principal achievements of the thermodynamics of irreversible processes in membrane studies have been semi-quantitative and somewhat philosophical. It has been demonstrated, for example, how substances may be transported against their thermodynamic gradients without violating the second law of thermodynamics, how metabolic reactions and transport processes may interact in isotropic and in anisotropic media and how some types of oscillatory phenomena can occur. Important rules have been discovered also which regulate the rates of simultaneous processes in steady states.

Little progress has been made towards interpreting the data from even quite simple transport experiments in terms of those properties of a membrane which may be expected to be closely related to its structure. Efforts along these lines must, in the first instance, be limited to the region of linear behaviour because of the experimental as well as the theoretical difficulties.

The basic problem is that in a system of n mobile components in which only passive transport is taking place $\frac{1}{2}n(n+1)$ independent coefficients have to be considered. Of these n are so-called straight coefficients, which loosely correspond with the n mobilities required to characterize the system in the TMS theory. The remaining $\frac{1}{2}n(n-1)$ are coupling coefficients. Since almost nothing is known quantitatively about these coupling coefficients none of them should be heedlessly neglected or approximated. As a result chemically very simple systems have to be carefully investigated first.

If the irreversible thermodynamic theory cannot be quantitatively applied in such cases then its prospects as a means of relating membrane structure and transport properties in a detailed way must be considerably diminished. Some relatively minor modifications of common experimental methods are discussed here which facilitate the quantitative application of linear non-equilibrium thermodynamics to membranes.

4. Linear theory of salt and water transport

Attention is restricted to a simple system of wide general interest namely the passive flows of water and a single salt dissociating into two kinds of ions. The isothermal steady state is considered. Provided there is an external circuit so that a net electric current can flow through the membrane there are three independent fluxes and forces in such a system. These fluxes and forces are interconnected by six phenomenological coefficients which can be determined only by performing at least six independent transport experiments. The problem of evaluating the coefficients from the experimental data is greatly simplified if the measurements are made under conditions in which some of the fluxes and forces are held at zero.

For the purposes of unravelling the transport mechanisms in the membrane the independent fluxes are most suitably chosen as the fluxes of water, cations and anions. With this choice, the appropriate forces are the differences in the electro-chemical potentials of these species between the two sides of the membrane. The constraints required to hold some of these fluxes and forces at zero are experimentally inconvenient.

There is considerable freedom in the choice of the fluxes and forces provided they are correctly conjugated, that is provided the sum of their products gives the rate of dissipation of free energy by the flows in the system. Whatever choice is made the number of independent fluxes and forces remains fixed and they are interconnected by six coefficients (provided the Onsager reciprocal relations hold [17]).

A very useful set of fluxes for practical use has been suggested by Staverman [13] and Kedem and Katchalsky [14]. They are the flux density of the cations ϕ_1, the defined volume flux density ϕ_v given by

$$\phi_v = \overline{V}_s \phi_1/v_1 + \overline{V}_w \phi_w , \qquad (8)$$

where $\overline{V}_s$ and $\overline{V}_w$ are the partial molar volumes of salt and water in the external solution into which ϕ_v is measured, v_1 the number of cations per mole of salt and ϕ_w the flux density of water, and the electric current density i given by

$$i = F(z_1\phi_1 + z_2\phi_2) \ . \tag{9}$$

The force which conjugates with ϕ_1 is the reduced osmotic force $\pi/v_1\bar{c}_s$, where π is the difference in the osmotic pressure between the external solutions and $\bar{c}_s$ is a mean concentration exactly defined by

$$\bar{c}_s = \pi/RT\Delta \ln a_s \ , \tag{10}$$

and $\Delta \ln a_s$ is the difference between the logarithms of the salt activities in the external solutions. ϕ_v conjugates with $(p-\pi)$, where p is the pressure difference across the membrane, and i with the potential difference E registered by electrodes reversible to the anions.

Provided the forces are sufficiently small the linear theory postulates a set of equations interconnecting the fluxes and forces in which the conductance coefficients $L_{\alpha\beta}$ are independent of the sizes of the fluxes and forces. These equations are:

$$\phi_1 = L_\pi(\pi/v_1\bar{c}_s) + L_{\pi p}(p-\pi) + L_{\pi E}E \ , \tag{11}$$

$$\phi_v = L_{p\pi}(\pi/v_1\bar{c}_s) + L_p(p-\pi) + L_{pE}E \ , \tag{12}$$

$$i = L_{E\pi}(\pi/v_1\bar{c}_s) + L_{Ep}(p-\pi) + L_E E \ . \tag{13}$$

The $L_{\alpha\beta}$ coefficients with a single subscript in equations (11–13) are called straight coefficients and must be positive. The others are coupling coefficients and normally obey the reciprocal equality

$$L_{\alpha\beta} = L_{\beta\alpha} \ . \tag{14}$$

This formulation, in which differences rather than gradients are chosen as forces, is called the discontinuous representation and is needed here because observations can be made only in the solutions outside the membrane.

5. Limits of linear behaviour

A major problem in using these equations lies in defining the range over which linear behaviour can be expected to hold for each force. The limitations are not too serious in the cases of the electric potential and pressure gradients provided these are not so great as to appreciably orient molecular dipoles or modify the molecular Brownian motions. Such effects would change the permeability of the membrane material.

The difficulty lies in the osmotic force π. This can be varied only by altering the concentrations in the external phases and hence, to some extent, the concentrations in the membrane. The $L_{\alpha\beta}$ coefficients are functions of the concentrations in the membrane and hence appear to be functions of π. This destroys the overall linearity of the behaviour.

Thus it is not unusual to find that, although the linear flux equations hold locally in any volume element when the local gradients are varied at constant local composition, they do not hold globally, i.e. across the membrane as a whole. This is true because varying the gradients at one plane changes the concentration profiles in the membrane and the observed $L_{\alpha\beta}$ coefficients are averages along the whole concentration profile in the membrane. An experimental programme should include tests to ensure that linearity of behaviour holds and, whenever possible, methods of obtaining the local or concentration dependent values of the $L_{\alpha\beta}$ coefficients [18].

6. Determination of transport coefficients

The easiest set of experimental conditions is to keep $\pi = 0$ and $p = 0$. In this way two forces are made zero and constant composition holds across the membrane. With only one force to consider the flux equations (11–13) are greatly simplified to

$$\phi_1 = L_{\pi E} E , \tag{15}$$

$$\phi_v = L_{pE} E , \tag{16}$$

$$i = L_E E . \tag{17}$$

Hence three of the six $L_{\alpha\beta}$ coefficients may be obtained from well known electrical measurements of the electrical conductance κ, cation transport number t_1 and electro-osmotic permeability W since

$$L_E = (i/E)_{\pi,p=0} = \kappa , \tag{18}$$

$$L_{\pi E}/L_E = (\phi_1/i)_{\pi,p=0} = t_1/z_1 F \, , \tag{19}$$

$$L_{pE}/L_E = (\phi_v/i)_{\pi,p=0} = W \, . \tag{20}$$

Another straightforward experiment is to measure the osmotic flows of water and solute under short circuit ($p = 0, E = 0$) and open circuit ($p = 0$, $i = 0$), in each case with $\pi \neq 0$. The flux equations under short circuit can be rearranged to

$$(i/\pi)_{p,E=0} = L_{E\pi}/v_1\bar{c}_s - L_{Ep} \, , \tag{21}$$

$$(\phi_v/\pi)_{p,E=0} = L_{p\pi}/v_1\bar{c}_s - L_p \, , \tag{22}$$

$$(\phi_1/\pi)_{p,E=0} = L_{\pi}/v_1\bar{c}_s - L_{\pi p} \, . \tag{23}$$

Under open circuit the equivalent expressions are

$$(E/\pi)_{p=0}^{i=0} = (L_{Ep}-L_{E\pi}/v_1\bar{c}_s)/L_E \, , \tag{24}$$

$$(\phi_v/\pi)_{p=0}^{i=0} = (L_{Ep}-L_{E\pi}/v_1\bar{c}_s)(L_{pE}/L_E) + L_{p\pi}/v_1\bar{c}_s - L_p \, , \tag{25}$$

$$(\phi_1/\pi)_{p=0}^{i=0} = (L_{Ep}-L_{E\pi}/v_1\bar{c}_s)(L_{\pi E}/L_E) + L_{\pi}/v_1\bar{c}_s - L_{\pi p} \, . \tag{26}$$

These equations are not all independent. If they were the problem of determining the six $L_{\alpha\beta}$ would be easily solved. From equations (21-26) it can be derived that

$$\left(\frac{\phi_1}{\pi}\right)_{p,E=0} - \left(\frac{\phi_1}{\pi}\right)_{p=0}^{i=0} = v_1\bar{c}_s\left[\left(\frac{\phi_v}{\pi}\right)_{p,E=0} - \left(\frac{\phi_v}{\pi}\right)_{p=0}^{i=0} - \left(\frac{E}{\pi}\right)_{p=0}^{i=0}\left(\frac{i}{\pi}\right)_{p,E=0}\right] \tag{27}$$

should hold. Equation (27) can be tested experimentally by measuring the membrane potential, short circuit current and the changes in the cation and volume fluxes on switching from open to short circuit conditions. This provides a test of whether the linear equations are obeyed over the range of π and E being examined and of whether changing from $i = 0$ to $E = 0$ changes the concentration profiles in the membrane enough to affect the values of the $L_{\alpha\beta}$ significantly. If equation (27) is found not to hold the work must be repeated at a lower value of π and in this way the range of linear behaviour with respect to changes in π may be explored.

7. Differential transport coefficients

If measurements could be made with only an infinitesimal concentration difference across the membrane, say between c_s and $(c_s + dc_s)$ the $L_{\alpha\beta}$ coefficients would be characteristics of the membrane in equilibrium with a solution of a definite concentration c_s. Such coefficients may be called the differential phenomenological coefficients of the discontinuous system of membrane and solutions. They will be denoted by $\mathcal{L}_{\alpha\beta}$.

In the event that the part of the membrane which is effective in controlling the fluxes is homogeneous and uniform in its properties then the $\mathcal{L}_{\alpha\beta}$ may be determined as functions of c_s from a set of fluxes measured across finite concentration intervals. Consider, for example, the osmotic permeability $(\phi_v/\pi)_{p=0}^{i=0}$. If the concentration on one side of the membrane $c_s(1)$ is held constant and that on the other side $c_s(2)$ is varied, so as to measure a series of values of ϕ_v at different $c_s(2)$, then a plot can be made of ϕ_v versus $c_s(2)$.

The slope of this plot at any chosen concentration c_s may be written $(\partial\phi_v/\partial c_s)_{p=0,c_s(1)}^{i=0}$ and it may be shown [18] that under the restrictions stated above this slope is independent of $c_s(1)$ and is a function only of c_s.

The osmotic pressure difference π between the pair of concentrations $c_s(1)$ and $c_s(2)$ is a definite quantity and hence the plot of ϕ_v versus $c_s(2)$ may easily be converted into a plot of ϕ_v versus π at constant $c_s(1)$. The slope of this plot $(\partial\phi_v/\partial\pi)_{p=0}^{i=0}$ at a particular chosen π is a function only of the value of c_s which corresponds with the chosen π. Hence the differential value of the osmotic permeability may be obtained as a function of c_s by drawing a series of tangents to the ϕ_v versus π plot.

Similar principles apply to the treatment of data on other fluxes and forces. This procedure and an additivity rule derived from it for evaluating fluxes over wide concentration ranges has been found to hold well in practice [18,19]. The additivity rule states that if $\phi(c_s(1) \rightarrow c_s(2))$ is the flux between concentrations $c_s(1)$ and $c_s(2)$ and $\phi(c_s(2) \rightarrow c_s(3))$ is the flux between $c_s(2)$ and $c_s(3)$ then

$$\phi(c_s(1) \rightarrow c_s(3)) = \phi(c_s(1) \rightarrow c_s(2)) + \phi(c_s(2) \rightarrow c_s(3)) \tag{28}$$

should hold provided the membrane is uniform and homogeneous and measurements are made in the linear range. An experimental test of equation (28) is therefore a test that the latter conditions hold.

The notion of using differential flux/force coefficients was discussed earlier by Kedem and Michaeli [20]. Since the coefficients can be determined as functions of concentration by the method just described, the flux/force equations (21–26) can be rewritten in terms of them as follows

$$(\partial i/\partial \pi)_{p,E=0} = \mathcal{L}_{E\pi}/\upsilon_1 c_{\rm s} - \mathcal{L}_{Ep} \, , \tag{29}$$

$$(\partial \phi_{\rm v}/\partial \pi)_{p,E=0} = \mathcal{L}_{p\pi}/\upsilon_1 c_{\rm s} - \mathcal{L}_p \, , \tag{30}$$

$$(\partial \phi_1/\partial \pi)_{p,E=0} = \mathcal{L}_{\pi}/\upsilon_1 c_{\rm s} - \mathcal{L}_{\pi p} \, , \tag{31}$$

$$(\partial E/\partial \pi)_{p=0}^{i=0} = (\mathcal{L}_{Ep} - \mathcal{L}_{E\pi}/\upsilon_1 c_{\rm s})/\mathcal{L}_E \, , \tag{32}$$

$$(\partial \phi_{\rm v}/\partial \pi)_{p=0}^{i=0} = (\mathcal{L}_{Ep} - \mathcal{L}_{E\pi}/\upsilon_1 c_{\rm s}) (\mathcal{L}_{pE}/\mathcal{L}_E) + \mathcal{L}_{p\pi}/\upsilon_1 c_{\rm s} - \mathcal{L}_p \, , \tag{33}$$

$$(\partial \phi_1/\partial \pi)_{p=0}^{i=0} = (\mathcal{L}_{Ep} - \mathcal{L}_{E\pi}/\upsilon_1 c_{\rm s}) (\mathcal{L}_{\pi E}/\mathcal{L}_E) + \mathcal{L}_{\pi}/\upsilon_1 c_{\rm s} - \mathcal{L}_{\pi p} \, , \tag{34}$$

where the symbols $\mathcal{L}_{\alpha\beta}$ indicate the differential values of the coefficients all at the chosen value of the concentration $c_{\rm s}$.

8. Evaluation of the differential coefficients

Four experimentally accessible quantities A, B, C and D may be defined by

$$A \equiv (\partial E/\partial \pi)_{p=0}^{i=0} \, , \tag{35}$$

$$B \equiv (\partial i/\partial \pi)_{p,E=0} \, , \tag{36}$$

$$C \equiv (\partial \phi_1/\partial \pi)_{p=0}^{i=0} - (\partial \phi_1/\partial \pi)_{p,E=0} \, , \tag{37}$$

$$D \equiv (\partial \phi_{\rm v}/\partial \pi)_{p=0}^{i=0} - (\partial \phi_{\rm v}/\partial \pi)_{p,E=0} \, . \tag{38}$$

When these are compared with equations (29–34) it is easily shown that

$$\mathcal{L}_E = -B/A , \tag{39}$$

$$\mathcal{L}_{pE} = D/A , \tag{40}$$

$$\mathcal{L}_{\pi E} = C/A . \tag{41}$$

Provided the measurements have all been made within the range of linear behaviour, the values of $\mathcal{L}_E$, $\mathcal{L}_{pE}$ and $\mathcal{L}_{\pi E}$ should in a homogeneous membrane agree with L_E, L_{pE} and $L_{\pi E}$ evaluated at the same c_s from equations (18–20), which refer to experiments with no concentration gradient. It may also be shown that

$$C = -c_s(D+AB) \tag{42}$$

should hold provided the linear equations are obeyed on the local scale.

The differential procedure makes it possible to determine $\mathcal{L}_E$, $\mathcal{L}_{pE}$ and $\mathcal{L}_{\pi E}$ or the electrical coefficients κ ($= \mathcal{L}_E$), W ($= -D/B$) and t_1 ($= -z_1 F v_1 c_s (D/B+A)$) as functions of c_s when the concentrations on opposite sides of the membrane cannot be made equal and when only one can be varied provided the other can be held fixed.

Only five independent measurements can be carried out by varying π and E at constant p. In order to extract the individual values of $\mathcal{L}_p$, $\mathcal{L}_\pi$ and $\mathcal{L}_{p\pi}$ an additional measurement is needed in which $p \neq 0$. This poses severe experimental difficulties because pressure is a very weak thermodynamic force when compared with concentration and potential difference. These difficulties may be lessened if a truly non-permeating solute can be introduced into one of the solutions without upsetting the thermodynamic relationships of the other components. The osmotic pressure π_i of this non-permeating solute may then be regarded as thermodynamically equivalent to an applied pressure equal to $-\pi_i$ without the mechanical side effects of a real pressure.

The mathematically attractive conditions $p \neq 0$, $\pi = 0$ are experimentally impracticable and one has to use $p \neq 0$, $\pi \neq 0$. Open circuit $i = 0$ is easier to achieve than $E = 0$. Whenever $\pi \neq 0$ it is necessary to perform a series of experiments at varying π and to differentiate the curves obtained in order to obtain the concentration dependent $\mathcal{L}_{\alpha\beta}$ coefficients.

9. Measurements with a pressure difference

Two experimental situations are convenient for study. The reflection coefficient σ is given by

$$\sigma = (p/\pi)^{\phi_v, i=0} .\tag{43}$$

By measuring p at zero volume flow as a function of π at constant $c_s(1)$ with varying $c_s(2)$ the differential values of the reflection coefficients $(\partial p/\partial \pi)^{\phi_v, i=0}$ may be evaluated. Simple algebra [18] then shows that $\mathcal{L}_p$ is given by

$$\mathcal{L}_p = W^2 \kappa - \left(\frac{\partial \phi_v}{\partial \pi}\right)^{i=0}_{p=0} \Big/ \left(\frac{\partial p}{\partial \pi}\right)^{\phi_v, i=0} .\tag{44}$$

Once $\mathcal{L}_p$ has been found $\mathcal{L}_{p\pi}$ follows from equation (33) and, since

$$\mathcal{L}_{p\pi} = \mathcal{L}_{\pi p}$$

$\mathcal{L}_\pi$ is obtained from equation (34).

The alternative to measuring the reflection coefficient is an experiment which resembles reverse osmosis and is valuable when the osmotic pseudo-equilibrium cannot be clearly established. In this method pressure is applied to the solution in a large stirred reservoir in contact with the membrane and in which the concentration remains effectively constant. A steady flow is soon set up and the rate of efflux and concentration of the effluent are determined. These data give π and also the cation flux ϕ_1. By using a range of pressures and a differential analysis of the data $(\partial \pi/\partial p)^{i=0}$, $(\partial \phi_v/\partial p)^{i=0}$ and $(\partial \phi_1/\partial p)^{i=0}$ may be found. $\mathcal{L}_p$ and $\mathcal{L}_{\pi p}$ then follow from

$$\mathcal{L}_p = W^2 \kappa + (\partial \phi_v/\partial p)^{i=0} - (\partial \phi_v/\partial \pi)^{i=0}_{p=0}(\partial \pi/\partial p)^{i=0} ,\tag{45}$$

$$\mathcal{L}_{\pi p} = W t_i \kappa/z_1 F + (\partial \phi_1/\partial p)^{i=0} - (\partial \phi_1/\partial \pi)^{i=0}_{p=0}(\partial \pi/\partial p)^{i=0}\tag{46}$$

and $\mathcal{L}_\pi$ from equation (34).

10. Conclusion

It has thus been shown that by making a combination of osmotic flow
and pressure determinations and measurements of ion flux under open and
short circuit conditions the full set of phenomenological coefficients required
to characterize the three flows in a membrane may be determined while including all possible coupling processes in a general way. Once these coefficients are determined straightforward calculations [18,19] are sufficient to
convert them to the coefficients relative to the molecular fluxes and to resistance and friction coefficients which may be discussed in terms of molecular
flow mechanisms and membrane models.

It is to be hoped that measurements along these lines in a variety of membranes will soon be performed. Unless the thermodynamics of irreversible
processes is applied to membrane transport in this rigorous way then it appears that structural information is unlikely to be derived from the more
subtle flux interactions, although such interactions are a potential source of
information about the relative dispositions of particles and pathways in the
membrane. The alternative is to remain content with the crude general in-
ferences about the relations between transport and structure which have for
a long time been based on ill-characterized permeability and mobility measurements.

References

[1] T.Teorell, Proc. Soc. Exptl. Biol. Med. 33 (1935) 282.
[2] T.Teorell, Trans. Faraday Soc. 33 (1937) 1053.
[3] K.H.Meyer and J.-F.Sievers, Helv. Chim. Acta 19 (1936) 649, 948.
[4] K.H.Meyer and J.-F.Sievers, Helv. Chim. Acta 20 (1937) 634.
[5] R.Schlögl, Stofftransport durch Membranen (Steinkopff-Verlag, Darmstadt, 1964).
[6] F.Helferrich, Ion Exchange (McGraw-Hill, New York, 1962).
[7] D.E.Goldman, J. Gen. Physiol. 27 (1943) 37.
[8] R.Schlögl and U.Schödel, Z. Physik Chem. (Frankfurt) 5 (1955) 372.
[9] J.S.Mackie and P.Meares, Proc. Roy. Soc. (London), Ser. A 232 (1955) 498.
[10] J.R.Pappenheimer, Physiol. Rev. 33 (1953) 387;
     H.H.Ussing, Advan. Enzymol. 13 (1952) 21;
     P.M.Ray, Plant Physiol. 35 (1960) 783.
[11] J.S.Mackie and P.Meares, Proc. Roy. Soc. (London), Ser. A 232 (1955) 510.
[12] S.R.De Groot and P.Mazur, Non-equilibrium Thermodynamics (North-Holland,
     Amsterdam, 1962).
[13] A.J.Staverman, Trans. Faraday Soc. 48 (1952) 176.
[14] O.Kedem and A.Katchalsky, Trans. Faraday Soc. 59 (1963) 1918.

[15] I.Prigogine, Introduction to Thermodynamics of Irreversible Processes (Inter-science, New York, 3rd ed., 1967).

[16] A.Katchalsky and R.Spangler, Biophys. Rev. 1 (1968) 128.

[17] L.Onsager, Phys. Rev. 37 (1931) 405.

[18] H.Krämer and P.Meares, Biophys. J. 9 (1969) 1006.

[19] P.Meares, J.F.Thain and D.G.Dawson, in: Membranes - A series of advances, ed. G.Eisenman (Marcel-Dekker, New York, in press).

[20] I.Michaeli and O.Kedem, Trans. Faraday Soc. 57 (1961) 1185.

CRITERIA FOR MEMBRANE STRUCTURE
USING PROBE MOLECULES

J.C.METCALFE

*M.R.C. Molecular Pharmacology Unit,
Department of Pharmacology, Cambridge*

1. Introduction

A membrane structure is conventionally regarded as intact if it retains its appropriate functional capacities. These may be biochemical functions such as enzymic activities associated with the membrane, or they may be physiological functions dependent for example on the excitable membranes in nerve and muscle. On the other hand, there are few structural criteria for an intact membrane. Gross morphological changes may be detected by electron microscopy, but more subtle changes at the molecular level are generally beyond the scope of the technique. It is known that the components of a number of membranes possess an inherent order from their low angle X-ray diffraction patterns, but as yet this has not provided a definitive description of the organisation of the membrane components. This information is essential if the function of membranes is to be described in terms of the structure at a molecular level.

In the first part of this paper, it is shown that the interaction of extraneous probe molecules with the membrane is precisely determined by the membrane structure. In other words, in its interactions with probe molecules the membrane does not behave simply as the sum of its separated structural components, but its interactions are modified and restricted by the organization of the components within the membrane. The three independent parameters of interaction which are described provide a stringent set of criteria for an intact membrane structure.

The insertion of probe molecules into the membrane causes perturbations of the structure, and by using probes with suitable physical properties, information about the nature of the induced perturbations may be obtained. In particular the two magnetic resonance techniques which are described here provide information about changes in molecular motion within the membrane.

Although the techniques depend on quite distinct magnetic resonance phenomena, they provide consistent descriptions of membrane perturbations.

The usefulness of probe molecules would be greatly extended if the perturbations which they sense could also be used to give direct information about the organization of the membrane components with which they interact, and the last part of the paper discusses some methods for using probes as structural determinants.

2. Interaction parameters

For all three interaction parameters the local anaesthetic benzyl alcohol (($\bigcirc$)CH_2OH) is a convenient probe molecule.

2.1. Partition coefficients

The simplest example of the way in which interaction depends on the structure of the membrane is the amount of probe molecule which is bound. The partition coefficient (P.C.) of benzyl alcohol in human erythrocyte membranes at 25°C is shown in fig. 1. Up to 80 mM the P.C. is constant at 3.05, but at higher concentrations there is a marked increase. The P.C. in the separated membrane lipids in vesicle suspension is constant at 4.25 up to 150 mM, and the value for membrane protein prepared in a soluble form by the method of Maddy [1] is 8.15 over the same concentration range. Both components therefore have higher P.C.'s than the intact membrane, and the mean lipid and protein value appropriate to the composition of the intact membrane is close to 6.15 (fig. 1). If the intact membranes are treated with benzyl alcohol at concentrations up to 80 mM, which is then removed by dialysis, the P.C. is unaltered by the pretreatment. However, pretreatment at 300 mM results in an increased P.C. of 5.35 over the whole concentration range, which is quite close to the mean value for the separated components (fig. 1). Pretreatment at concentrations between 80 and 300 mM results in correspondingly smaller increases in the P.C. Over this concentration range in which the effects of pretreatment are irreversible, benzyl alcohol also causes lysis of intact erythrocytes. Fig. 2 shows that at concentrations up to 80 mM, benzyl alcohol stabilizes the erythrocyte membrane against hypotonic haemolysis, but higher concentrations cause lysis at all ionic strengths.

From these simple experiments, it seems clear that in the lytic concentration range the membrane progressively tends to interact with benzyl alcohol as the sum of its separate components, and there is direct evidence of the

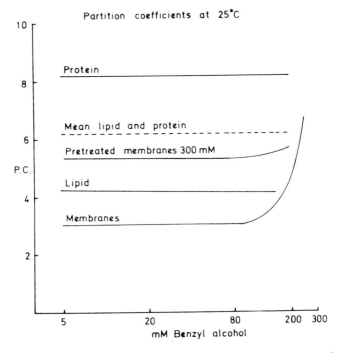

Fig. 1. The partition coefficients of benzyl alcohol in human erythrocyte membranes and various membrane preparations at 25°C.

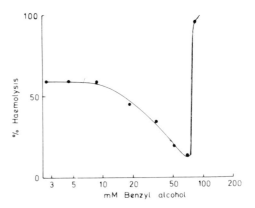

Fig. 2. The effect of benzyl alcohol on the hypotonic haemolysis of human erythrocytes.

physical degradation of the membrane structure. In the prelytic concentration range, the interaction of benzyl alcohol with the membrane is restricted
by the structure of the membrane to be less than the sum of the interactions
with the separated components. Any membrane perturbations induced by
benzyl alcohol appear to be reversible in the prelytic concentration range as
judged by the partition coefficient. It is also clear that the increased P.C. in
the lytic concentration range is dominated by the exposure of new protein
binding sites which were inaccessible or protected in the prelytic concentration range. This structural change is not reversible on removing benzyl alcohol.

The exposure of the new protein binding sites provides a marker for those
interactions within the membrane which hold the structure in a form in which
it interacts reversibly with benzyl alcohol. Disruption of these interactions
marks the onset of irreversible structural perturbation of the membrane.

2.2. Nuclear magnetic relaxation

When benzyl alcohol molecules are partitioned into the ordered structure
of the membrane, their molecular motion is likely to be restricted whether
they are inserted into the lipid part of the membrane or are bound to the
membrane protein. This motional restriction results in a broadening of the
resonance adsorption signals from benzyl alcohol (both the aromatic and the
methylene proton signals). From the resonance broadening it is possible to
calculate the proton relaxation rates $(1/T_2)_{\text{bound}}$ of the alcohol molecules
bound in the membrane (see Metcalfe et al. [2]). In the present experiments,
$(T_2)_{\text{bound}}$ is directly proportional to the rate of rotation of the alchol mole-

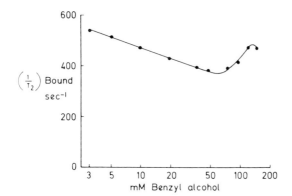

Fig. 3. The relaxation rate $(1/T_2)_{\text{bound}}$ of the aromatic protons of benzyl alcohol bound
to erythrocyte membranes at 25°C.

cules in the membrane. The curve for $(1/T_2)_\text{bound}$ for benzyl alcohol in erythrocyte membranes is biphasic (fig. 3) The decreasing relaxation rate with increasing alcohol concentration in the prelytic range implies that the molecules find themselves in an increasingly fluid environment within the membrane.

The upswing in the relaxation rate occurs over the lytic concentration range, and its origin was revealed by experiments with the separated mem-

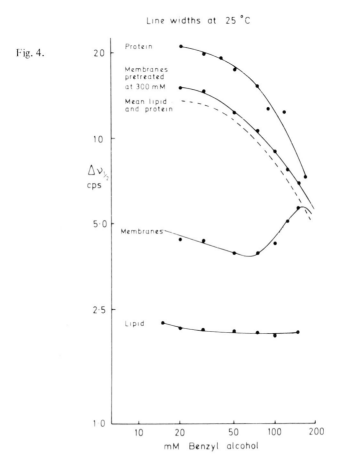

Fig. 4. The effect of erythrocyte membranes and various membrane preparations on the line width ($\Delta\nu_{1/2}$) of the aromatic protons of benzyl alcohol at 25°C. All preparations are 1.0% by weight. The dashed curve is the mean line width of the separated lipid and protein components corresponding to the composition of the membrane.

brane components and pretreated membranes. The data for these membrane preparations are most easily compared from their effect on the line widths ($\Delta\nu_{1/2}$) of the benzyl alcohol resonances. The line width curve for the erythrocyte membranes (fig. 4) has a similar biphasic form to the relaxation curve in fig. 3, which is calculated from the line width measurements and the P.C. data. The corresponding line width curves for the separated membrane lipids and protein are both monotonic, and the mean curve calculated from the separated components as before, is quite distinct from the membrane curve. The line width changes are reversible after pretreating membranes with up to 80 mM benzyl alcohol but for membranes pretreated at 300 mM the line width curve lies close to the mean curve for the separated components. This mean curve is dominated by the contribution from the membrane protein, and the upswing in the membrane curve in the lytic concentration range results from a progressive increase in the contribution of the membrane protein. This parallels the conclusions from the P.C. data and confirms that in the lytic range the membrane tends to interact as the sum of its components.

In these experiments it is the upswing in the relaxation curve which coincides with the onset of irreversible structural changes in the membrane and provides a second marker for the critical membrane interactions.

2.3. Electron spin resonance (ESR)

The third criterion for an intact erythrocyte membrane makes use of its interactions with nitroxide spin labels. This technique was first applied to membranes by Hubbell and McConnell [3] and an excellent introduction to nitroxide spectra and spin labelling is given by Hamilton and McConnell [4]. Briefly, the membrane is labelled with a molecule containing the nitroxide group ($> N - O$), which has a simple three line ESR spectrum which is sensitive to the rotational rate of the spin label. The spin label is used at a sufficiently low concentration to cause a negligible perturbation of the membrane, and changes in membrane structure induced by chemical agents such as local anaesthetics, are detected from changes in the ESR spectrum of the spin label.

We have examined the effects of perturbing agents on a range of spin labels in erythrocyte membranes and found that steroid spin labels were especially useful in providing a clear indication of the irreversible structural changes produced by lytic concentrations of benzyl alcohol [5]. The steroid nitroxide derivative I (synthesized by Dr. Wayne Hubbell) shows an intermediate immobilized spectrum in erythrocyte membranes, corresponding to rotational rates of the spin label of the order of $10^8 \ sec^{-1}$ (fig. 5).

Prelytic concentrations of benzyl alcohol cause a sharpening of the spec-

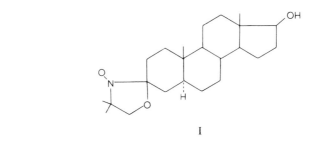

I

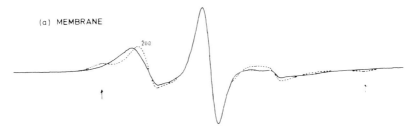

(a) MEMBRANE

Fig. 5. The ESR spectrum of the steroid spin label I (1.0×10^{-4} M) in the presence of 1.0% erythrocyte membranes at 25°C. (————) no benzyl alcohol; (--------) with 200 mM benzyl alcohol. The arrows indicate the strongly immobilized component of the spectrum which only appears in the lytic concentration range.

trum corresponding to a fluidizing effect of the alcohol on the environment of the spin label in the membrane. This effect was observed with all the spin labels examined. In the lytic concentration range an entirely new component is observed in the spectrum (fig. 5), which arises from a fraction of the spin labels which are now highly immobilized at their binding sites. This component is not observed in the spectrum of spin label I in separated membrane lipid vesicles. On the other hand in separated membrane protein, highly immobilized binding sites form a major component of the spectrum. We conclude that the new spin label binding sites detected in the membrane in the lytic concentration range are located on the membrane protein, and are exposed simultaneously with the new protein binding sites for benzyl alcohol detected in the lytic range by P.C. and NMR measurements. We take these highly immobilized spin label binding sites as a third marker of irreversible structural changes in the membrane.

3. Structural information from probe techniques

3.1. Structural criteria

These three types of experiment using benzyl alcohol as a perturbing agent provide a sensitive test of whether the erythrocyte membrane is structurally intact. The intact membrane must have the correct partition coefficient, the biphasic NMR curve, and the appropriate ESR spectral changes induced by benzyl alcohol. It is the interactions in the prelytic concentration range which are characteristic of the intact membrane; in the lytic range the membrane tends to interact as the sum of its separated components. Thus in each kind of experiment a characteristic change is observed in the lytic concentration range.

All the membrane modifications which have been examined have resulted in changes in one or more parameters. As an example, we may use the biphasic NMR curve as a test to determine whether reaggregated structures of membrane protein and lipid are reconstructed in the same way as in the native membrane. In the Proceedings of the previous conference, Zahler [6] described some recombinants of erythrocyte membranes. Erythrocyte membranes were dissolved in methyl cellosolve ($CH_3OCH_2CH_2OH$) and then dialysed against a 5 mM tris buffer solution at pH 7.4. It was found that extensive interactions between lipid and protein had occurred, although full antigenic and enzyme activities were not recovered. It was concluded that the reaggregated structures might be useful for studying interactions between membrane components, in spite of the incomplete recovery of functional properties. Fig. 6 shows the NMR curve (plotted as direct line width measurements) for a recombinant prepared by Zahler's procedure, together with the same data for membranes pretreated with 300 mM benzyl alcohol. It is immediately apparent that the two curves are coincident and that the critical membrane interactions have not been re-established. For a properly reconstituted membrane structure we would expect a biphasic curve similar to that in fig. 4. It should be emphasized that it is not claimed from these preliminary experiments that reconstitution cannot be achieved by this method. However there is no doubt that in this instance the attempt was unsuccessful and that NMR measurements provide a simple test procedure. It is significant that whatever structures are formed in the recombinant, they do not result in any significant restriction on the interaction of benzyl alcohol with the membrane components.

3.2. Structural perturbations

The two magnetic resonance techniques give a consistent description of

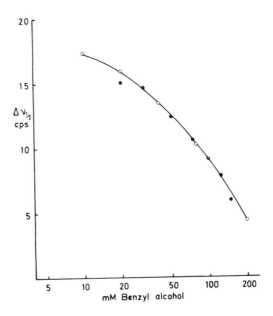

Fig. 6. The line width of the aromatic protons of benzyl alcohol in the presence of 1.0% by weight erythrocyte membranes pretreated with 300 mM benzyl alcohol (○) and a membrane recombinant prepared by Zahler's procedure (●); see text.

structural perturbations in the membrane. Both indicate a progressive fluidising effect on the membrane components in the prelytic concentration range of benzyl alcohol. Eventually the membrane is so perturbed that new protein binding sites are exposed which are predominantly located on the membrane protein. This is demonstrated most directly by the P.C. data and is confirmed by the magnetic resonance experiments. This effect may be regarded as a critical structural perturbation because it is not directly reversible, and it is suggested that it is due to the disruption of essential interactions, most probably between membrane lipids and protein.

It is worth noting here the limitations on the information content of probe technique applied to an unknown structure. It is assumed that the motional freedom of the probes reflects the motional freedom of the membrane components. This is a reasonable inference where a range of different probes have provided consistent evidence for the kind of perturbations produced in the membrane. On the other hand, only simultaneous observation of the actual membrane components would constitute proof of the structural changes which occur. An experiment of this kind in a model system is described later.

A second limitation is that it is only in the lytic concentration range where the membrane interacts with probes approximately as the sum of its components, that the effects observed can be attributed to a particular membrane component. Thus it is quite clear that the new protein binding sites provide the major interaction of benzyl alcohol with the membrane in the lytic range. In the prelytic range, where the distribution of the probe between lipid and protein components is not readily determined, the information obtained is less precise. The overall environment of the probe molecules becomes more fluid, but we cannot immediately distinguish perturbations occurring in the lipid and protein components. Generally the qualitative response of the separated membrane components to perturbation is similar. For example the NMR curves for benzyl alcohol bound to membrane lipids and protein have a similar monotonic form, although quantitatively they are quite distinct. Spin labels bound to separated lipid and protein also respond in a qualitatively similar way to perturbing agents [5]. Underlying this similarity is the similar nature of the chemical forces involved in interactions between both components and extraneous molecules. To distinguish the interactions it is therefore necessary to estimate them quantitatively.

In the prelytic concentration range it has been possible to estimate the distribution of benzyl alcohol between lipid and protein in the intact membrane in two independent ways. The first estimate was based on an analysis of the temperature dependence of the partition coefficient data, and the second value was obtained from the NMR line width data [7]. Both estimates can only be regarded as approximate, but are consistent in indicating that the membrane protein is the major binding component for benzyl alcohol in the prelytic concentration range.

3.3. Structural organization

The identification of the critical structural interactions responsible for holding the membrane in its integral state provides a convenient starting point in attempting to use probe molecules to determine structural organization. The interactions are marked by the appearance of the 'abnormal' binding sites for benzyl alcohol and the steroid spin label on the membrane protein, in the lytic concentration range. Using acrylamide gel electrophoresis as a means of separating the 15–20 distinct protein components of the membrane, it is already clear that some fractions carry the abnormal binding sites whereas others do not. It should now prove possible to identify these abnormal binding sites and hopefully to establish the conditions under which a membrane protein can be restored to its conformation in the intact membrane, in which the abnormal sites are inaccessible. The steroid spin label is particularly useful as a means of following this conformational change.

This suggests the next logical step of reconstituting the whole membrane in its native form, using the set of interaction parameters to determine whether structural reconstitution has occurred, in the way already described. If reconstitution is technically feasible, then the usefulness of probe molecules as structural determinants will be greatly enhanced. It should be possible to covalently spin label individual membrane components and determine their average distances of separation from other membrane components in the reconstituted structure. A prototype of this kind of experiment is readily demonstrated in lecithin vesicles. The high resolution NMR spectrum at 220 Mc of egg lecithin vesicles in D_2O suspension is shown in fig. 7. The resonances are assigned after Chapman and Penkett [8]. Spin label II is an

II   III

amphiphilic molecule which is expected to orient itself in a vesicle with the quaternary charge and the nitroxide group at the aqueous interface. This is confirmed by the selective broadening of the choline methyl protons $(-N^+(CH_3)_3)$ compared with the alkyl chain signals from lecithin vesicles containing the spin label. The broadening is due to paramagnetic relaxation induced by the proximity of the nitroxide group to the methyl protons, and depends on the inverse sixth power of the distance. Conversely, spin label III causes a selective broadening of the alkyl chain signals indicating that it is buried in the hydrophobic interior of the vesicle. In appropriate membrane systems similar experiments with labelled membrane components appear to be feasible.

Similar information about the localization of benzyl alcohol in lecithin vesicles may be obtained from the effects of the alcohol on the NMR spectrum of the vesicles. One effect is an upfield shift in the position of the choline methyl resonance, which increases with increasing concentrations of benzyl alcohol (fig. 8). This shift results from the apposition of the choline methyls to the faces of the aromatic ring of benzyl alcohol. It is caused by

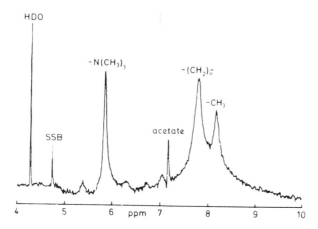

Fig. 7. The NMR spectrum at 220 Mc of sonicated lecithin vesicles at 5.0% by weight in D_2O buffer solution ($I = 0.01$; pH 7.4). The acetate is added to provide an internal reference. Temperature 13°C.

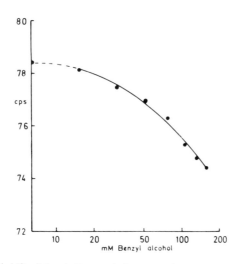

Fig. 8. The upfield shift of the choline methyl groups of sonicated lecithin vesicles in the presence of benzyl alcohol at 25°C. The shifts are measured at 60 Mc in cps downfield from the internal acetate reference.

the induced magnetic field perpendicular to the plane of the ring which arises from the delocalized ring current; it is not observed with non-aromatic perturbing agents. Benzyl alcohol has no significant effect on the position of the lecithin alkyl chain resonances, suggesting that the aromatic ring is located for relatively little time in the hydrophobic interior of the vesicles, compared with the time spent in the polar head group region of the choline methyl groups. It is therefore likely that the alcohol molecules are preferentially distributed at the vesicle interface, probably by the influence of the hydrophilic hydroxyl group.

If we examine the homologous series $\langle\text{O}\rangle\text{-(CH}_2)_n\text{-OH}$ in which the distance between the hydroxyl group and the aromatic ring is progressively increased by the methylene groups, there is a systematic decrease in the upfield shift of the choline methyl resonance. This may be attributed to increasing penetration of the aromatic ring into the hydrophobic interior of vesicle, away from the choline methyl groups. The orientation proposed for benzyl alcohol is supported by X-ray diffraction experiments on oriented lecithin layers, with Levine and Wilkins (unpublished data).

Benzyl alcohol also causes a progressive narrowing of the choline methyl resonance with increasing concentration, which is paralleled by a simultaneous narrowing in the aromatic resonance of the alcohol itself. This indicates a simultaneous increase in rotational freedom of both the lecithin and the alcohol molecules, suggesting that it is reasonable to infer increasing fluidity of membrane components from the behaviour of the perturbing agent.

These experiments represent some preliminary attempts to extend the use of probe molecules and perturbation techniques to provide direct information about membrane structural interactions.

References

[1] A.H.Maddy, Biochim. Biophys. Acta 117 (1966) 193.
[2] J.C.Metcalfe, P.M.Seeman and A.S.V.Burgen, Mol. Pharmacol. 4 (1968) 87.
[3] W.L.Hubbell and H.M.McConnell, Proc. Natl. Acad. Sci. U.S. 61 (1968) 12.
[4] C.L.Hamilton and H.M.McConnell, in: Structural Chemistry and Molecular Biology, eds. A.Rich and N.Davidson (W.H.Freeman and Co., Folkestone, 1968) p. 115.
[5] W.L.Hubbell, J.C.Metcalfe and H.M.McConnell, (1969, in preparation).
[6] P.Zahler, in: Membrane Models and the Formation of Biological Membranes, eds. L.Bolis and B.A.Pethica (North-Holland, Amsterdam, 1968) p. 181.
[7] J.C.Metcalfe and A.S.V.Burgen, (1969, in preparation).
[8] D.Chapman and S.A.Penkett, Nature 211 (1966) 1304.

PROTEIN PHOSPHOLIPID INTERACTION
STUDIED BY ELECTRO-OSMOSIS

L.BOLIS, P.LULY, W.DORST, M.MARCHETTI and C.BOTRÈ

Istituto di Fisiologia Generale, Universita di Roma, Rome, Italy
Laboratoire d'Anatomie et Physiologie Comparées, Université de Genève,
Geneva, Switzerland
Laboratorium voor Medische Chemie, Rijksuniversiteit, Leiden, The Netherlands
Istituto Chimico Farmaceutico, Università di Roma, Rome, Italy

1. Introduction

It has been found [1–3] by various methods that lipoids and proteins or lipoproteins form complexes of a definite stoichiometric ratio. Thus far, little is known about the structural changes concomitant with such a complex formation. The present work deals with interaction between gelatin and several lipoid substances, including the steroid hormone derivative sodium-hydrocortisone succinate. The results show that inclusion of the steroid hormone in the gelatin membranes markedly changes their electro-osmotic properties. These changes may be associated with water structural changes in the gel, but other explanations are not excluded.

2. Experiments and results

It is probable that the water structure in a membrane strongly affects solvent electro-osmosis. We have measured the electro-osmotic flow in both directions through the following membrane array:

Cathode/KCl ref. sol./M_1/M_2/KCl sol. anode

where the potassium chloride reference solution was 0.05 N, or 0.02 N. The transport cell consisted of two lucite chambers, each of 60 ml capacity. The cathode and anode were of silver gauze coated with AgCl. M_1 was a commercial cation exchange membrane (thickness 0.03 cm); membrane M_2 (thick-

235

ness 0.3 cm) was constructed as follows: 0.2 g of gelatin (iso-electric point 5.0) was dissolved in 5 ml of the KCl reference solution; 0.1 g of sodium-dodecylsulphate was then added and dissolved. The solution was then allowed to gel. In the separate experiments with sodium hydrocortisonesuccinate (the hydrocortisoneacetate is insoluble in water) 80 mg of this substance was in 5 ml of the gel mixture with a slight equivalent excess of dodecyl sulphate so that a new membrane M_2 could be built up. Since the capillaries attached to the cell for measuring water flow had an internal diameter of 0.2 mm, temperature control by means of a thermostate proved unnecessary.

The room temperature was $22 \pm 0.5°C$. Stabilization of the water transport occurred almost instantaneously. Stirring was provided by rotating magnetic rods; the current density was $1mA/cm^2$. The water flow results are given in tables 1 and 2.

The water flow through M_1 is only 20 eq/Faraday [4]. Obviously the ar-rangement M_1/M_2 "amplifies" differences in water flow through M_2 as can be predicted from recent theories [5]. The asymmetry between M_1 and M_2 also explains the strong polarity, appearing in table 1.

Electro-osmotic measurements on single membrane M_2 were made by supporting the gels in a perspex grid, which was clamped between the anode and cathode compartment. The solutions were KCl 0.04 N. The membranes differed only in their added constituents; the total number of equivalent added charges was kept constant to 0.02 N. Table 2 gives the results.

The "potassium soaps" were obtained in the gels by exchanging the cor-responding sodium soaps with the KCl bathing solution. In the case of the

Table 1
Electro-osmotic water flow

Water transport number (eq/Faraday)	Membrane conditions	Solution concentration
100	M_1/M_2	
300	M_1/M_2 (hormone added)	
0	M_2/M_1 (hormone added)	0.05 N
50	M_2/M_1	
170	M_1/M_2	
500	M_1/M_2 (hormone added)	
10	M_2/M_1 (hormone added)	0.02 N
80	M_2/M_1	

Table 2
Electro-osmosis in single gels

Composition of M_2	Solution concentration	Water transport number (eq/Faraday)
Potassiumheptadecyl-sulphate	0.03 N KCl	55
Potassiumdodecyl-sulphate	0.03 N KCl	50
Dodecylpyridinium-thiocyanate	0.03 N KCNS	− 52
Potassiumdodecyl-sulphate + potassiumhydrocortisonesuccinate (1 : 1)	0.03 N KCl	70

positive soap, AgCNS electrodes were used. When M_2 contains only gelatin, the solvent flow is about 60 eq/Faraday.

3. Discussion

Using the formalism of nonequilibrium thermodynamics we may write the following equation for electro-osmotic solvent flow [4]

$$r_{1W}J_1 + r_{2W}J_2 - R_{WW}J_W = 0 . \tag{1}$$

Relation (1) applies to our membrane system, in which the force on the water, $R_{WW}J_W$, is counterbalanced by that on the ions 1 and 2 given by the first two terms in (1). The forces are represented by products of flows (J) and friction coefficients (R,r). When the co-ion flow is negligible, equation (1) gives

$$\frac{1}{t_W} = \frac{c_1}{c_W} + \frac{f_{WM}}{f_{1W}} , \tag{2}$$

where $f_{WM} = r_{WM}c_{WM}$ and $f_{1W} = r_{1W}c_W$. In eq. (2), index M refers to the membrane matrix, whereas c_i denotes concentration of species i. The number of water moles transported through the membrane by one Faraday of

238   L.BOLIS et al.

electricity is represented by t_W. In the given case, $1/t_W$ varies between 10^{-1} and 10^{-2}, whereas c_1/c_W is about 4×10^{-4}. Thus eq. (2) reduces to

$$t_W = \frac{f_{1W}}{f_{WM}}. \tag{3}$$

If any change in the membrane matrix occurs, it will be accompanied by different water structure along the pore walls, i.e. a different value of f_{WM}. Since for our loose membrane f_{1W} may be put equal to its corresponding value in the bathing solution, the numerator of eq. (3) may be regarded as a constant.

Accordingly, a change in f_{WM} can be detected by measurement of t_W. In this connection, it is interesting to note that for the first three membrane compositions represented in table 2 f_{WM} remains constant, since the membrane charge determines the direction of flow. However, when the steroid is introduced, electro-osmotic flow increases. Subject to further experiments on the tightness of the binding of the hormone in the gel, and possible electro-dialysis effects, it seems likely that the steroid causes significant changes in the properties of water in the membrane.

References

[1] A.Scanu, J. Biol. Chem. 4 (1967) 711.
[2] L.Bolis, C.Botrè, S.Borghi and M.Marchetti, in: Membrane Models and the Formation of Biological Membranes, eds. L.Bolis and B.A.Pethica (North-Holland, Amsterdam, 1968).
[3] H.L.Booij and H.G.Bungenberg de Jong, in: Biocolloids and their Interactions, Protoplasmatologia Bd. 1/2 (Springer Verlag, Wien, 1956).
[4] W.Dorst, A.J.Staverman and R.Caramazza, Rec. Trav. Chim. 83 (1964) 1329.
[5] O.Kedem and A.Katchalsky, Trans. Faraday Soc. 59 (1963) 1918.

ON THE QUATERNARY STRUCTURE OF THE PROTEIN SUBUNITS IN A SOLUBLE LIPOPROTEIN*

A.SCANU**

Departments of Medicine and Biochemistry, The University of Chicago, and Argonne Cancer Research Hospital***, Chicago, Illinois 60637

The studies about which I wish to report were carried out in collaboration with Mr. Pollard, a graduate student in the Department of Biochemistry, and Dr. E.W.Taylor, from the Department of Biophysics of the University of Chicago.

Studies on the structure of serum low density lipoprotein, LDL, are relevant because this macromolecule is (a) among the better known naturally-occurring lipoproteins; (b) plays an important role in fat transport; (c) is probably implicated in atherosclerosis; and (d) serves as a useful model for investigating the possible general nature of protein-lipid interactions [1].

In the current investigation, LDL (d = 1.019–1.063) from human serum and apo-LDL, its lipid-free derivative, were prepared as described previously [2]. The immunologically pure LDL contained: 22% protein, 22% phospholipid, 37% cholesterol esters, 8% free cholesterol and 10% triglycerides. By sedimentation equilibrium analysis (method of Yphantis) the mol.wt. of LDL was $2.2 - 2.3 \times 10^6$. On the other hand apo-LDL, which was completely free of lipids, had a minimum mol.wt. of $2.5 - 2.7 \times 10^5$. From these data, the number of protein subunits in LDL was computed as $18 - 22$.

By electron microscopy (negative staining technique) LDL was homogeneous with spherical particles of an average diameter of 193 Å and a mol.wt. (assuming d = 1.040) compatible with the ultracentrifugal results. Each particle had a sub-structure with subunits (assuming sphericity and d = 1.37) of

---

* Supported in part by grants from the U.S. Public Health Service (HE-08727), Life Insurance Medical Research Fund (G68-27) and Chicago and Illinois Heart Association (RM 68-12).
** Recipient of Career Development Award HE-24,867 from the U.S. Public Health Service.
*** Operated by the University of Chicago for the United States Atomic Energy Commission.

5-fold axis   2-fold axis   3-fold axis

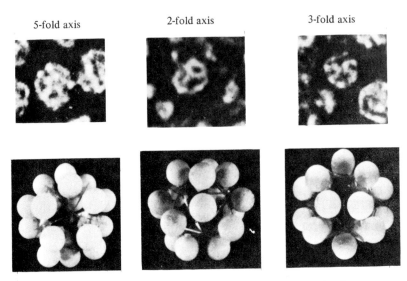

Fig. 1. Views along the principal rotation axes of LDL particles seen in the electron microscope (top row) and of a scale dodecahedral model (bottom row). (From H. Pollard et al. [3].)

$2.6 - 2.9 \times 10^5$ mol.wt. Spherical particles of the size of LDL were not seen in apo-LDL. Instead, the subunits were arranged predominantly as beaded strings up to 500 Å in length.

An analysis of enlarged electron micrographs of LDL suggested that the protein subunits may occupy the vertices of a dodecahedron giving 2-, 3- and 5-fold rotation axes characteristic of an icosahedral symmetry. Similar photographs were obtained with a scale model of LDL made of a transparent plastic icosahedral armature having a spherical styrofoam ball, 2.5 cm diameter, on each face (see fig. 1). From measurements made on such a model it was deduced that phospholipids (and probably free cholesterol) together with proteins are at the surface of the molecule, whereas the neutral lipids (cholesterol esters and glycerides) would be in the interior. Support for the surface localization of phospholipids was obtained from studies with phospholipase A and C carried out with highly purified enzymic preparations. In both instances, hydrolysis was complete and followed first-order kinetics. Some suggestion for the inner localization of neutral lipids came from solubility studies, but the results were not considered conclusive.

The present studies, whose detailed description has recently appeared [3], do not resolve the problem as to whether the general organization of LDL is directed by protein-protein or protein-lipid interactions, or both. Although LDL is similar to spherical viruses in possessing 'icosahedral symmetry', there are only 20 protein subunits which must then be placed at the center of a face of the icosahedron. Consequently, to preserve strict icosahedral symmetry each subunit must lie in a three-fold rotation axis. This symmetry requirement might be satisfied by the structure of the protein subunit itself or by the spatial distribution of regions of the protein surface which interact with lipids. It is hoped that X-ray diffraction analysis of LDL and apo-LDL will provide some answers to these relevant structural problems.

References

[1] A.Scanu, Adv. Lipid Res. 3 (1965) 63.
[2] A.Scanu, H.Pollard, H.Hirz and K.Kothary, Proc. Natl. Acad. Sci. U.S. 62 (1969) 171.
[3] H.Pollard, A.Scanu and E.W.Taylor, Proc. Natl. Acad. Sci. U.S. 164 (1969) 304.

CONCERNING THE INTERPRETATION OF OPTICAL ROTATION DATA ON MEMBRANOUS (OR PARTICULATE) SYSTEMS

D.W.URRY

Institute for Biomedical Research, Education and Research Foundation, American Medical Association, 535 North Dearborn Street, Chicago, Illinois 60610

1. Introduction

Optical rotation patterns of biological membranes resemble those of the α-helix but they are of low amplitude and red shifted [1–7]. (This general description correctly pertains to both optical rotatory dispersion and circular dichroism as the two types of data are related by mathematical transformations.) Attempts to interpret data on membranes have led to suggestions that lipids have optically active transitions which could distort the patterns in this manner, that the low amplitude may result from cancelling of β structure and random coil patterns, that the red shift and broadening is due to lipid helix interactions, and that the red shift derives from interaction of associating helices.

More recently we have proposed that the low amplitude and red shifted optical rotation patterns of membranes derive in varying degree from absorption flattening and light scattering distortions [8,9]. We have adopted the Duysens treatment of absorption flattening [10], have derived expressions for calculating the dispersion distortions (the light scattering artifact), and have shown that these effects distort the optical rotation patterns in the required manner. We are now well advanced in the process of working out a satisfactory means of correcting the distorted membrane spectra.

Once the spectra are corrected we are brought again to the possibility of interpretation in terms of structural aspects within the membrane. In general, the corrections increase the magnitude of optical rotation and render the patterns more nearly characteristic of the α-helix. *If* the patterns may be interpreted as reflecting α-helix, this means that approximations of α-helical contents for the membrane protein will result in calculated values larger than previously reported. The direct, but perhaps too naive, approach would be to so interpret the data. However, caution is required for two reasons: firstly it has now been demonstrated that peptide systems which are not α-helical can exhibit optical rotation patterns markedly resembling those of the α-helix [11,12], and secondly there are many other optically active transitions within a membrane in addition to those of the peptide moiety.

In what follows we will briefly discuss the problem of the uniqueness of protein and polypeptide optical rotation patterns, demonstrate the nature of the optical rotation spectral distortions by presenting data on poly-L-glutamic acid suspensions in water and on poly-L-alanine films. A table for calculated and experimental values will be included to show that the distorted curves may be calculated satisfactorily.

2. The problem of the uniqueness of protein and polypeptide optical rotation patterns

The optical rotation data discussed and presented here will be circular dichroism data reported in terms of ellipticity. It should be remembered that mathematical transformations relate ellipticity and optical rotatory dispersion such that what is observed in one measurement is reflected in the other. These and other general aspects of optical rotation of biomolecular systems are treated in a recent review [13]. Circular dichroism is more readily analyzed as it is a difference absorption measurement with spectrally localized bands. Optical rotatory dispersion is a measurement of the difference in index of refraction of the circularly polarized beams. As its name implies, the latter is a dispersion function where the observable at a given wavelength has contributions from all the electronic transitions in the molecule.

2.1. The α-helix type circular dichroism pattern
Very excellent work, largely from the Doty [14,15] and Blout [16] laboratories, has established that a variety of α-helix containing proteins and α-helical polypeptide homo- and copolymers exhibit similar optical rotation patterns and that the shape and magnitude of the optical rotation pattern is proportional to the α-helical content. This significant work has demonstrated in many cases that one can meaningfully calculate α-helical contents. The question of concern here is whether such an extrapolation is always unambiguous and to what extent caution is required.

Fig. 1 contains the circular dichroism patterns for several proteins and polypeptides which have been shown by other methods to contain α-helices.

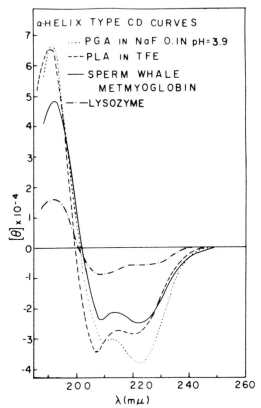

Fig. 1. Circular dichroism patterns for α-helical containing proteins and polypeptides.
From Quadrifoglio and Urry [31].

The patterns is one of two negative bands followed by a larger positive band
at shorter wavelengths. Even in those systems which are completely helical,
substantial variations in magnitude and position of bands do occur. This is
evidenced in fig. 1 for the cases of poly-L-alanine (PLA) and poly-L-glutamic
acid (PGA).

2.2. The β-pleated sheet circular dichroism pattern

Work, principally in the Doty [17], Yang [18] and Fasman [19] laboratories, has shown that the β-pleated sheet conformation in proteins and polypeptides exhibits a circular dichroism pattern of one negative band and a
single positive band. Both bands are found with lower ellipticity than in the

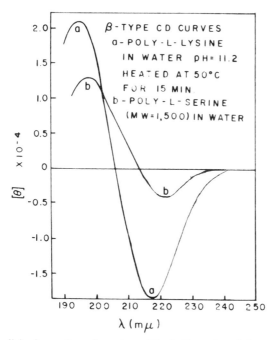

Fig. 2. Circular dichroism patterns for polypeptides in the β-pleated sheet conformation.

case of the α-helix. The circular dichroism patterns of two polypeptides which occur in the β-conformation are given in fig. 2. The circular dichroism pattern for the β-conformation exhibits more variation in relative magnitudes and position of bands than do characteristic α-helical systems. Part of this variability may be related to the difficulty of solubilizing the β-conformation. One often must work with turbid solutions and films. It is perhaps worth noting, with regard to the nature of the light scattering artifacts, that an α-helix CD pattern may be distorted to give the appearance of a β-type pattern with a red shifted initial negative extremum (see below).

2.3. α-Helix type circular dichroism pattern exhibited by non-helical systems
From the standpoint of analysis of optical rotation data the simplest optically active peptide chromophore is found in L-5-methyl pyrrolid-2-one. The structure of 5-substituted pyrrolidones is given in fig. 3. In water and other more polar solvents this molecule gives a circular dichroism pattern which resembles that of the β-type [11,20]. In cyclohexane a CD pattern is

L-PYRROLID-2-ONE

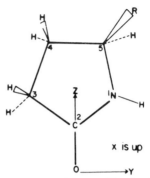

Fig. 3. Structure of 5-subsituted L-pyrrolid-2-ones. The circular dichroism pattern when R is methyl resembles the β-type in water solutions and the α-helix type in cyclohexane solutions.

obtained which markedly resembles that of the α-helix [11]. As may be seen by referring to fig. 4 the second negative band and the positive band are blue shifted by a few mμ. (This variation could be explained by the low refractive index of the medium.) The essential point is that the pattern is similar to that of the α-helix, perhaps even more so than the uncorrected membrane patterns.

Gramicidin S is a second molecular system which gives an α-helix type CD pattern but which is most reasonably not in that conformation. The solution circular dichroism curve of this cyclic decapeptide antibiotic is included in fig. 5 (see curve a). Hydrogenation of the two phenyl moieties in gramicidin S results in a molecule in which the only chromophoric moieties down to 185 mμ are the peptides. The CD curve of the hydrogenated molecule is even more characteristically that of the α-helix, as the positive band shifts to 190 mμ [12]. Calculations of α-helical content in gramicidin S, using the negative CD bands or the Moffitt and Yang treatment [21,14] of the ORD data, result in values near 100%. As the molecule is cyclic, this cannot be the case. The structure arrived at by nuclear magnetic resonance studies [22,23] and one of several possibilities considered from the X-ray data [24] is given in fig. 6. This structure was also early proposed by Schwyzer [25]. The essential point to be made here is that molecular structures which are not α-helical can give optical rotation patterns which closely resemble those of the α-helix. These findings do not vitiate the many correct correlations which have been experimentally demonstrated but they do make tenuous attempts to unambiguously

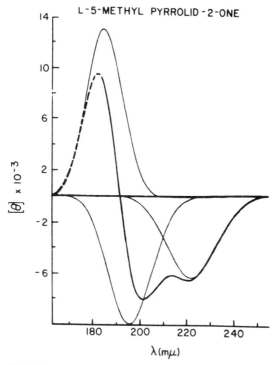

Fig. 4. Circular dichroism curve (bold faced) for L-5-methyl pyrrolid-2-one in cyclohex-ane.

conclude the presence of α-helix and particularly to estimate helical contents when ellipticity values are low.

3. Dispersion and absorption flattening distortions in the circular dichroism patterns of suspensions and films

That distortions in the optical rotation patterns of suspensions exist is easily demonstrated. One example is seen in fig. 5. Gramicidin S, which is a very stable molecule, precipitates at high pH on deprotonation of the ornithyl residues. Resuspension of the precipitate results in the CD pattern seen as curve b in fig. 5. Depending on the size of the particles one can progress in regular manner from curve a to curve b. An interesting feature about curve b

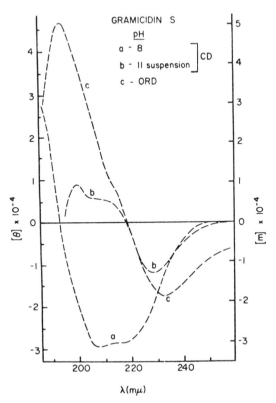

Fig. 5. Circular dichroism curves (a and b) and optical rotatory dispersion curve (c) for gramicidin S. Note that the circular dichroism curve of the suspension more closely simulates that of the solution optical rotatory dispersion curve. From Urry [13].

is that this circular dichroism pattern looks more like the optical rotatory dispersion pattern, curve c, for the molecularly dispersed system. Accordingly, there is a differential scatter of the left and right circularly polarized beams which is dependent on the difference in refractive index of the particle to left and right circularly polarized light. It is for this reason that the grossly distorted curve resembles an optical rotatory dispersion curve which, of course, is a measurement of the difference in refractive indices.

3.1. *Circular dichroism of aqueous suspension of poly-L-glutamic acid*
There are two variables attending the poly-L-glutamate system in the low

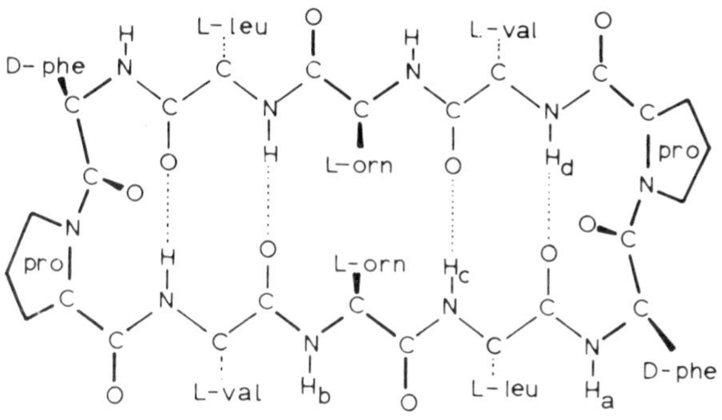

Fig. 6. Conformation of gramicidin S.

pH range prior to the pH elicited helix-coil transition; one is the degree of
ionization of the side chain whereas the other is the aggregation of helical
rods [26]. In an effort to separate the two effects and to study the effect of
particle formation we have taken as our reference state poly-L-glutamic acid
in doubly distilled water at pH 3.9. At this pH the degree of ionization is less
than 5% [27,20] and the extent of association as judged from the data of
Tomimatsu et al. [28] would be less than ten helical rods. The pH is then
lowered to 2.4 where sonication is used to achieve the desired turbidity and
therefore to control the size of the aggregates. Fig. 7 gives the resulting set of
circular dichroism data. Curve a is at pH 3.9 where the solution is transparent.
Curves b, c, d and e are in order of increasing turbidity as measured by increases in apparent absorption at 300 mμ (well outside the absorption region
of the polypeptide). A progressive red shift of the initial negative extremum
from 222.5 mμ and dampening is observed. There is proportionately greater
dampening of the 210 mμ and 190 mμ bands. This data remarkably resembles
that of mitochondria and mitochondrial fragments and correlates with variations observed when differential centrifugation of mitochondrial fragments
is used to grossly separate according to particle size [9,29].

   Calculation of curves b, c, d and e of fig. 7 from curve a provides a test of
the interpretation for the source of the variations and for the form of the corrections required to obtain more meaningful data on particulate systems.
Table 1 contains in column 2 the values for the molecularly dispersed systems,
in column 3 the calculated values for distorted curve e and in column 4 the
experimental values for curve 3. Reference [13] contains the details of the
calculation.

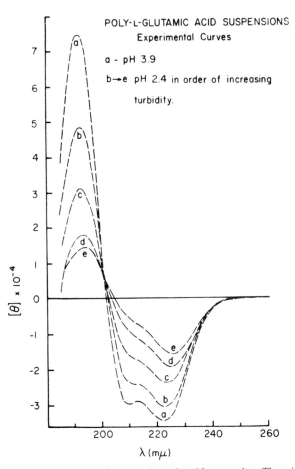

Fig. 7. Circular dichroism curves of poly-L-glutamic acid suspension. There is a regular relation between turbidity and deviation from curve a. From Urry [13].

3.2. Poly-L-alanine films

Many systems which one wishes to study, e.g. coacervates, are too optically dense to examine in the usual manner. Often, however, they may be studied as films. This has recently been done with solubilized elastin to show that it undergoes a dramatic conformational change on coacervation [30]. When molecularly dispersed, solubilized elastin exhibits a CD pattern characteristic

Table 1
Calculation of theta with absorption flattening and dispersion distortion. Suspensions of
poly-L-glutamic acid curve e of fig. 7

	Theta (pH 3.9) $\times 10^{-4}$	Theta calcd. $\times 10^{-4}$	Theta exptl. (suspension) $\times 10^{-4}$
240	− 0.31	− 0.31	− 0.26
238	− 0.49	− 0.44	− 0.44
236	− 0.82	− 0.67	− 0.67
234	− 1.22	− 0.91	− 0.85
232	− 1.71	− 1.14	− 1.10
230	− 2.32	− 1.42	− 1.34
228	− 2.72	− 1.53	− 1.51
226	− 3.17	− 1.58	− 1.59
225	− 3.36	− 1.60	− 1.60
224	− 3.42	− 1.54	− 1.54
223	− 3.45	− 1.47	− 1.50
222	− 3.48	− 1.41	− 1.39
220	− 3.42	− 1.26	− 1.28
218	− 3.20	− 1.09	− 1.10
216	− 3.11	− 1.03	− 0.98
214	− 2.99	− 0.93	− 0.84
212	− 2.93	− 0.79	− 0.67
210	− 2.96	− 0.74	− 0.61
208	− 2.93	− 0.34	− 0.48
206	− 2.44	− 0.14	− 0.24
204	− 1.59	0	0.04
203	− 0.98	0.10	0.31
202	− 0.36	0.21	0.43
201	0.49	0.39	0.58
200	1.22	0.53	0.67
198	3.66	0.98	1.06
196	5.49	1.13	1.25
194	6.83	1.34	1.37
193	7.32	1.41	1.40
192	7.45	1.38	1.37
190	7.32	1.30	1.24
188	6.10	0.78	1.01

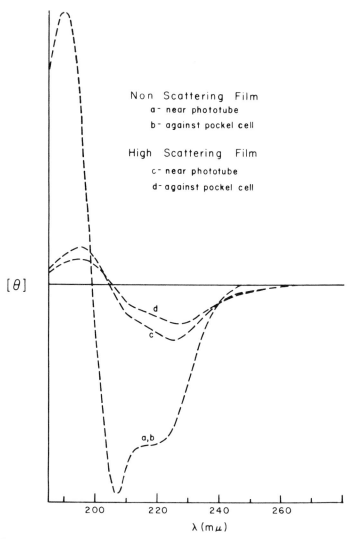

Fig. 8. Circular dichroism curves of poly-L-alanine films cast on quartz windows. Extent of scattering by film correlates with distorted curve. (Hinners and Urry, unpublished data.)

of disordered proteins. As the coacervate, it exhibits a CD pattern characteristic of the α-helix with ellipticity values corresponding to systems which are approximately 50% helical.

In order to understand the optical distortions produced by films we have been studying films of poly-L-alanine. Circular dichroism data on two PLA films are seen in fig. 8. By infrared both films are α-helical. While the non-scattering film is rather typical of solution spectra (see fig. 1), the high scattering film is much distorted exhibiting a curve characteristic of biological membrane suspensions. By placing the film near the phototube, where a greater portion of the forward scattered light is captured, less distortion is observed.

There are many details in both the PGA and PLA work which deserve much discussion. We have only attempted to demonstrate that distortions exist and that it is possible to understand them and correct for them. Work is in progress to correct the optical rotation patterns of a series of different biological membranes.

References

[1] B.Ke, in: The Chlorophylls, eds. L.P.Vernon and G.R.Seely (Academic Press, New York, 1966) p. 427.
[2] D.F.H.Wallach and P.H.Zahler, Proc. Natl. Acad. Sci. U.S. 56 (1966) 1552.
[3] J.Lenard and S.J.Singer, Proc. Natl. Acad. Sci. U.S. 56 (1966) 1828.
[4] D.W.Urry, M.Mednieks and E.Bejnarowicz, Proc. Natl. Acad. Sci. U.S. 57 (1967) 1043.
[5] J.M.Stein and S.Fleischer, Proc. Natl. Acad. Sci. U.S. 58 (1968) 1292.
[6] J.Lenard and S.J.Singer, Science 159 (1968) 739.
[7] D.F.H.Wallach and A.S.Gordon, in: Regulatory Functions of Biological Membranes, ed. J.Jarhnfelt, B.B.A.Library 11 (1968) 87.
[8] D.W.Urry and T.Ji, Arch. Biochem. Biophys. 128 (1968) 802.
[9] T.H.Ji and D.W.Urry, Biochem. Biophys. Res. Commun. 34 (1969) 404.
[10] L.N.M.Duysens, Biochim. Biophys. Acta 19 (1956) 1.
[11] D.W.Urry, J. Phys. Chem. 72 (1968) 3035.
[12] D.W.Urry, A.L.Ruiter, B.C.Starcher and T.A.Hinners, Antimicrobial Agents and Chemotherapy (1968) p. 87.
[13] D.W.Urry, in: Spectroscopic Approaches to Biomolecular Conformation (Amer. Med. Assoc. Press, Chicago (1970) p. 34.
[14] P.Urnes and P.Doty, Advan. Protein Chem. 16 (1961) 401.
[15] G.Holzwarth and P.Doty, J. Am. Chem. Soc. 87 (1965) 218.
[16] J.P.Carver, E.Schechter and E.R.Blout, J. Am. Chem. Soc. 88 (1966) 2550, and preceding papers in the series.
[17] P.K.Sarkar and P.Doty, Proc. Natl. Acad. Sci. U.S. 55 (1966) 981.
[18] E.Iizuka and J.T.Yang, Proc. Natl. Acad. Sci. U.S. 55 (1966) 1175.

D.W.URRY

[19] G.D.Fasman and J.Potter, Biochem. Biophys. Res. Commun. 27 (1967) 209.
[20] D.W.Urry, Ann. Rev. Phys. Chem. 19 (1968) 477.
[21] W.Moffitt and J.T.Yang, Proc. Natl. Acad. Sci. U.S. 42 (1956) 596.
[22] A.Stern, W.Gibbons and L.C.Craig, Proc. Natl. Acad. Sci. U.S. 61 (1968) 734.
[23] M.Ohnishi and D.W.Urry, Biochem. Biophys. Res. Commun. 36 (1969) 194.
[24] D.C.Hodgkin and B.M.Oughton, Biochem. J. 65 (1957) 752.
[25] R.Schwyzer, P.Sieber and B.Gorup, Chimia 53 (1958).
[26] J.Y.Cassim and J.T.Yang, Biochem. Biophys. Res. Commun. 26 (1967) 58.
[27] F.Quadrifoglio, D.W.Urry and A.L.Ruiter, Abstracts of the 153rd Meeting of the American Chemical Society, R015 (1967).
[28] Y.Tomimatsu, L.Vitello and W.Gaffield, Biopolymers 4 (1966) 653.
[29] J.M.Wrigglesworth and L.Packer, Arch. Biochem. Biophys. 128 (1968) 790.
[30] D.W.Urry, B.Starcher and S.M.Partridge, Nature 222 (1969) 795.
[31] F.Quadrifoglio and D.W.Urry, J. Am. Chem. Soc. 90 (1968) 2755.

Part 5

STRUCTURE OF EXCITABLE MEMBRANES

RECENT STUDIES OF PHOSPHOLIPID/ALAMETHICIN INTERACTIONS

D.CHAPMAN

Molecular Biophysics Unit, Unilever Research Laboratory Colworth/Welwyn, The Frythe, Welwyn, Herts, England

1. Introduction

The molecule alamethicin, a cyclic polypeptide antibiotic produced by *Trichoderma viride* [1,2] has been shown recently by Mueller and Rudin [3] to induce 'action potentials' when added to bimolecular lipid films (black films) and by Pressman [4] to induce ion movements and energy-linked K^+ accumulation in mitochondria. An understanding of these properties may be relevant to the problems of membrane function in general, to the mechanism of ion transport, nerve impulses and to the mode of antibiotic action in particular.

In our laboratory we have been studying phospholipid/alamethicin interactions in simple systems and also using black film methods. Here I shall summarise some of our recent work. A more detailed account is given elsewhere [5].

2. Structure

Alamethicin is a cyclic polypeptide (molecular weight 1771) which contains the following amino acids $(GluN)_2$, $(Glu)_1$, $(Pro)_2$, $(Gly)_1$, $(Ala)_2$, (2-methyl Ala)$_7$, $(Val)_2$, $(Leu)_1$. The amino acid sequence has now been determined by Hartley and Payne [6]. The average molecular diameter in the plane of the ring is approximately 25 Å, while normal to the plane of the ring it is about 4.5 Å. A model can be arranged in a conformation in which the molecule becomes amphipathic with the exterior of the ring, or one side of it essentially hydrophobic, that is with the three polar groups located in the interior or to one side of the ring*.

*A molecular model shows that $(GluN)_{18}$ group in the molecule is very flexible and can bridge the ring. Its α-carboxy and γ-amide groups can align with another $(GluN)_6$ group to provide a chelating site blocking the centre of the ring [6].

Alamethicin forms a lipid-soluble complex with alkali metal ions over a wide pH range. This suggests that, as in such complexes with other macrocyclic compounds, the ion is held in the interior of the ring by ion-dipole interactions [4] . (From a model it can be deduced that a number of conformers with differences in internal ring dimensions are possible which may explain the observed absence of sodium/potassium selectivity.) The glutamic acid residue in the structure contains an ionisable carboxyl group which imparts a negative electrophoretic mobility to the particles in a paraffin emulsion or egg yolk lecithin dispersion. The mobility increases as the pH is raised from 5 to 10 due to greater dissociation of the carboxyl group and is reduced by addition of sodium ions at constant pH.

3. Physical properties

In common with other cyclic antibiotics, the amphipathic nature of the molecule and the proportion of hydrophobic (methyl Ala) residues ensures that alamethicin is extremely surface-active and therefore aggregates in solution. Ultra-centrifugal analysis of alamethicin in various organic solvents and aqueous solutions show that in ethanol the alamethicin is a monomer, whilst in a saturated solution ($\sim 0.4\%$) in phosphate buffer at pH 8, alamethicin forms clusters of about 8 molecules in equilibrium with monomers. From determinations of the interfacial tension of aqueous alamethicin solutions against n-decane, the critical micelle concentration in pH 8 sodium hydroxide solution is 2.4 μM, and the interfacial tension is reduced by approximately 33 dyne/cm.

Alamethicin forms insoluble monolayers at the air-water interface. When spread from hexane/ethanol on either H_2O or 0.1 M NaCl (pH 5.5) at 22°C, an initial rise in surface pressure occurs at about 320 Å^2/molecule. This is close to the theoretical minimum area of the condensed planar configuration. The film can be compressed to a pressure of 30 dyne/cm at which point the film is unstable and each alamethicin molecule occupies about 200 Å^2. Adsorption of alamethicin from solution leads to a maximum decrease of 30 dyne/cm in the surface tension of water which suggests that the conformation of spread and adsorbed molecules is the same. Molecular models suggest that a fully extended alamethicin molecule oriented with the plane of the peptide ring in the interface would occupy about 600 Å^2. Alamethicin is therefore tilted or takes up some folded conformation at the interface.

Addition of alamethicin in nanomolar concentrations to phosphate buffer does not significantly affect the surface tension. However, if the same concentration of alamethicin is added to the same substrate below a lipid monolayer, the peptide readily penetrates the monolayer. Penetration occurs as long as the film pressure of the lipid is below 30 dyne/cm (i.e., area/lipid molecule 60 − 110 $Å^2$) and continues until the pressure eventually increases to the collapse pressure of alamethicin. The lipid solubility of alamethicin enables it readily to form mixed monolayers with lipids.

X-ray studies of the effect of adding alamethicin to 3% dispersions of lipid in water show that the intensity of the lamellar diffraction lines decreases with increasing amounts of alamethicin until at a 15/1 molar ratio of phospholipid/polypeptide the sharp diffraction lines completely disappear. This is consistent with a gradual breakdown of the multilamellar phase. At a molar ratio of 7/1 a broad diffuse peak centred at a Bragg spacing equivalent to ~ 58 Å is present. The structure most simply related to the original dispersion and which can give rise to this type of X-ray scattering is a modified single bilayer vesicle. However the large size of the lipid/peptide particles compared with a sonicated lecithin dispersion makes this structure unlikely and a more drastically modified lipid/peptide structure is envisaged as occurring. (Lipid dispersions at concentrations of 50% lipid to water show some differences from this behaviour [5].)

High resolution MNR spectra of sonicated 1% dispersions of bovine brain phosphatidylserine (monosodium salt) and egg yolk lecithin in D_2O containing alamethicin show that the addition of very small amounts of alamethicin has large effects upon the peak integral (referenced to an external standard of 10% C_6H_6 in CCl_4) of the signal associated with the lipid alkyl chain $(CH_2)_n$ group. When the molar ratio of phosphatidylserine to alamethicin is 3000/1, there are about 1.6 times more protons contributing to the signal than is observed with the pure lipid dispersion (where only about half of the protons give rise to a high resolution signal). It is probable that alamethicin, through its surfactant properties, is improving the efficiency of the sonication process breaking the lipid particles into smaller units. A further increase in the peptide concentration to a molar ratio of 500/1 causes the peak integral to fall to a minimum value (see fig. 1). More alamethicin is required with egg yolk lecithin to achieve the same result. The $N(CH_3)_3$ signal in the lecithin spectrum is broadened, although to a lesser extent than the $(CH_2)_n$ signal.

Calculations of the tumbling rates of the particles in these systems show that the observed loss of the $(CH_2)_n$ signal cannot be due to an increase in particle weight alone. Addition of alamethicin must also reduce the internal motion of the egg yolk lecithin and phosphatidylserine molecules probably reducing the conformational freedom of the lipid chains*.

Hence addition of alamethicin to phospholipid causes reaggregation of

*E.s.r. spin label studies support this conclusion.

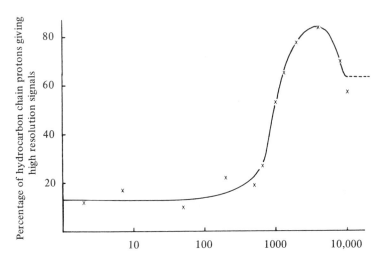

Fig. 1. Variation of peak integral with molar ratio of phosphatidylserine/alamethicin
(dispersions 1% in phosphatidylserine).

phospholipid molecules with formation of tightly bound lipid-polypeptide
structures in which some sort of cooperative hydrophobic interactions must
play a role. (Valinomycin behaves similarly when added to egg-yolk lecithin
liposomes [8].)

4. Experimental bilayers (black films)

Working with bilayers formed from a 1% solution of egg lecithin in decane,
we have [5] reproduced in our laboratory most of the effects reported by
Mueller and Rudin [3]. Adding alamethicin in concentrations as low as 10^{-7}
M to one side of a film in 0.1 M KCl develops a cationic conductance in the
bilayer which becomes strongly voltage dependent as the applied voltage is
increased. When both protamine and alamethicin are added to the aqueous
phase, a negative resistance region occurs in the current-voltage characteristic
and bistability is observed in the presence of an ion gradient.

The mechanism by which the applied voltage controls the conductance of
the bilayer is an important factor. According to Mueller and Rudin the low
conductance observed at low voltage is simply the intrinsic conductance of
the bilayer. They suggest that the effect of the voltage is to drive monomers
of the alamethicin-cation complex into the bilayer where they aggregate as

hexamers. The hexamers are able to conduct ions, possibly by forming 'pores' in the bilayer, while the monomers are non-conducting. As we have seen, alamethicin however can readily penetrate into a lipid bilayer without the assistance of an applied voltage. When conductance-voltage curves are plotted for two alamethicin concentrations in the aqueous phase the results show that at low voltage there is a region in which the conductance is independent of voltage. The conductance in this region is, therefore, not the intrinsic conductance of the bilayer. We consider that this low voltage conductance is due to the monomeric form of the alamethicin-cation complex, and that it may be essentially similar to the voltage independent conductances induced by other macrocyclic molecules [7]. At higher applied voltages the conductance varies exponentially with the voltage. The latter effect probably involves aggregation of alamethicin molecules. The asymmetry of the conductance-voltage curves is probably due to different alamethicin concentrations in the water on either side of the bilayer.

The alamethicin in the aqueous phase is below its critical micelle concentration and must be present in the bulk solution mainly as the monomer. These monomers will adsorb initially to the polar group region of the bilayer.

5. Conclusions

a. Alamethicin is highly surface active and aggregates in aqueous systems when present in very low concentrations.

b. The peptide readily penetrates lipid monolayers.

c. When alamethicin is added to 3% dispersions of egg yolk lecithin in water a large structural reorganisation of the lipid occurs with a concomitant reduction in motions of the lipid alkyl chains. As with other macrocyclic compounds, like valinomycin, this may be relevant both to its ion transport properties and also to its antibiotic action.

d. With a small applied voltage alamethicin appears to transport ions across lipid bilayers (black films) by a simple carrier mechanism whereas, at higher applied fields, the conductance becomes voltage dependent related to some aggregation effect. It may be that localised structural changes of the phospholipid similar to those found in the dispersed lipid systems are involved in the observed conductance changes.

e. It may be that in natural membranes segments of protein can rearrange into an appropriate cyclic conformation simulating some of the properties of molecules like valinomycin and alamethicin.

References

[1] C.E.Meyer and F.Reusser, Experientia 23 (1967) 85.
[2] F.Reusser, J. Biol. Chem. 242 (1967) 243.
[3] P.Mueller and D.O.Rudin, Nature 217 (1968) 713.
[4] B.C.Pressman, Federation Proc. 27 (1968) 1283.
[5] D.Chapman, R.J.Cherry, E.G.Finer, H.Hauser, M.C.Phillips, G.G.Shipley and A.I. McMullen, Nature (1969).
[6] B.S.Hartley and J.Payne, personal communication, to be published.
[7] P.Mueller and D.O.Rudin, Biochem. Biophys. Res. Commun. 26 (1967) 398.
[8] E.C.Finer, H.Hauser and D.Chapman, Chem. Phys. Lipids 3 (1969) 356.

THE IONIC PERMEABILITY OF NERVE MEMBRANES

H.MEVES

Physiologisches Institut der Universität Kiel, Kiel, Germany

Hodgkin and Katz [1] studied the effect of sodium ions on the electrical activity of the giant axon of the squid. They showed that sodium ions in the external medium are essential for the production of action potentials. The action potential is rapidly abolished if sodium chloride is replaced by dextrose. The membrane currents underlying the action potential were analyzed by Hodgkin and Huxley [2], and Cole and Moore [3] with the voltage clamp technique. A typical voltage clamp run is illustrated in fig. 1. Depolarization of the membrane to − 44 or − 14 mV leads to an initial inward current which is followed by a delayed outward current. Hodgkin and Huxley were able to show that the early current is carried by sodium ions whereas the delayed current is due to an outward movement of potassium ions, both sodium and potassium ions moving down their respective electrochemical potential gradients. With increasing depolarization the sodium inward current reaches a maximum, decreases again, becomes zero at a potential which is close to the sodium equilibrium potential and is outward for large depolarizations (fig. 1).

An important question is whether other ions can substitute for sodium in carrying the early current which underlies the rising phase of the action potential. An answer to this question would probably throw some light on the nature of the early permeability change.

Quantitative information about the ability of the nerve membrane to discriminate between the various alkali metal ions was obtained by experiments on intracellularly perfused squid axons. Methods for intracellular perfusion of squid giant nerve fibres were developed by Baker et al. [4], Oikawa et al. [5], and Tasaki [6]. They consist in removing the bulk of the axoplasm and perfusing the interior of the fibre with artificial salt solutions. Fig. 2 shows voltage clamp records from an axon perfused with 300 mM KCl. The records are rather similar to those obtained from intact axons. For small depolarizations there is a brief capacity current, an early transient inward current and a delayed outward current. The early inward current disappears for pulses which shift the membrane potential to + 60 or + 70 mV. At larger depolarizations

261

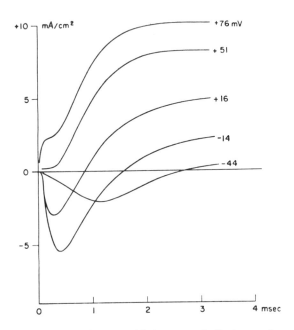

Fig. 1. Voltage clamp records from a squid giant axon. Ordinate: membrane current density; outward current upward. Abscissa: time after change of membrane potential. Five records superimposed. Membrane potential during voltage clamp pulse given at the right-hand side of each curve. The membrane was held at − 70 mV between pulses. Temperature 10°C. From Moore and Cole [3a].

an early outward current is obtained which is clearly separated from the delayed outward current. The appearance of an early outward current in the absence of internal Na^+ strongly suggests that the internal K^+ can partially substitute for Na^+ in the early permeability change. Replacing the internal KCl by either RbCl, CsCl, or sucrose substantially reduces the early outward current. It is therefore concluded that the early outward current associated with large voltage pulses in a KCl perfused axon is carried by potassium.

Further experiments provided fairly conclusive evidence that the potassium ions which flow through the membrane during the early outward current are moving through the same channels which are normally used by sodium ions. Chandler and Meves [7] showed that the time course of the early outward current corresponds closely to the time course of the sodium permeability measured by repolarizing the membrane to the resting potential at different times after the beginning of the large depolarizing pulse. They also found

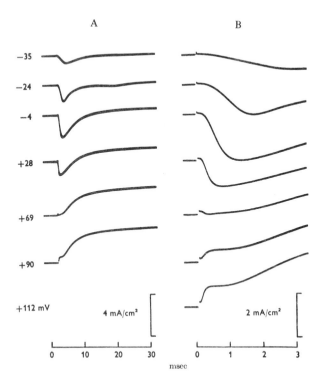

Fig. 2. Voltage clamp records from an internally perfused squid axon. The perfusion fluid was 300 mM KCl, isotonicity maintained with sucrose. The external solution was K-free artificial sea water. Membrane potential during voltage clamp pulse given at the left-hand side. Membrane hyperpolarized to − 108 mV for 18 msec preceding each pulse. Note higher current gain and higher sweep speed in B. Temperature 1 °C. From Chandler and Meves [7].

that the steady state inactivation of the early outward current resembles the steady state inactivation of the sodium inward current. Finally, the early outward current can be completely abolished by adding to the external fluid a small amount of the puffer fish poison tetrodotoxin which selectively blocks the sodium current, but has little if any effect on the delayed current. An experiment of this kind on a fibre perfused with 300 mM KF is illustrated in fig. 3. Again, the early current is inward for small depolarizations and outward for large depolarizations (see records 97 mV and 130 mV in fig. 3 A, lower half); it is followed by the delayed outward current. Tetrodotoxin in a

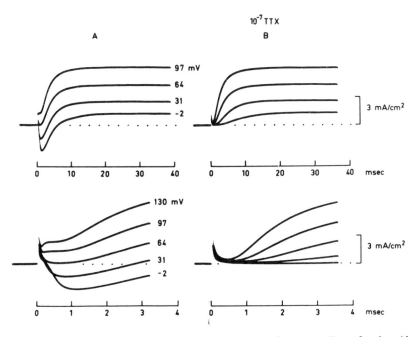

Fig. 3. Effect of tetrodotoxin on the membrane currents of an internally perfused squid axon. Internal solution: 300 mM KF, isotonicity maintained with sucrose. External solution: K-free artificial sea water (A), K-free artificial sea water + 10^{-7} g/ml tetrodotoxin (B). Membrane potential during voltage clamp pulse given at the right-hand side of each curve. Note ten times higher sweep speed in lower row. Temperature 2°C. From Chandler and Meves (unpublished experiments).

concentration of 10^{-7} g/ml or 0.3 μM in the external fluid (records in fig. 3 B) completely blocks the early current, both the inward component (carried by external Na^+ ions) and the outward component (carried by internal K^+ ions); it does not affect the delayed outward current. We conclude from this experiment that the K^+ ions which carry the early outward current are moving through the tetrodotoxin-sensitive channel normally used by sodium ions.

Very similar results were obtained by Rojas and Atwater [8] in voltage clamp experiments on the giant axon of the large Chilean squid *Dosidicus gigas* (fig. 4). Records A in fig. 4 clearly demonstrate the early outward current associated with large voltage pulses in an axon perfused with a potassium salt solution. A small amount of tetrodotoxin in the external fluid completely abolishes the early inward and outward currents whereas capacitive current,

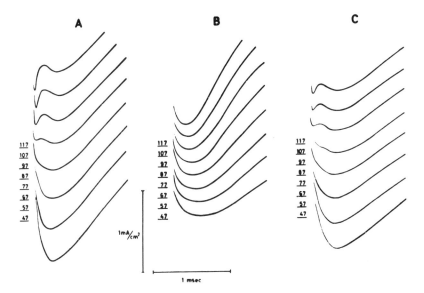

Fig. 4. Voltage clamp currents from an internally perfused giant axon of the Chilean squid *Dosidicus gigas*. Internal solution: 500 mM KF + 50 mM KCl. External solution: K-free artificial sea water (A), K-free artificial sea water + 10⁻⁸ M tetrodotoxin (B), K-free artificial sea water without tetrodotoxin (C). The numbers and the underlines give the clamped membrane potential in mV and the base line, respectively. Temperature 8.5°C. From Rojas and Atwater [8].

leakage current and delayed current remain unchanged (records in fig. 4 B). Run C, taken after a 17 min washout, reveals partial recovery of the early inward and outward currents. Rojas and Atwater [8] also showed that tetraethylammonium, the blocking agent for the delayed channel, applied internally in a concentration of 1 mM, reversibly inhibits the delayed potassium outward current, but does not interfere with the early outward current carried by potassium ions.

A quantitative estimate of the relative permeability of the early channel for Na^+ and K^+ can be obtained from the equation

$$V_e = \frac{RT}{F} \ln \frac{P_{Na}}{P_K} \frac{[Na]_o}{[K]_i},$$

where V_e is the equilibrium potential at which the early current changes its sign. The equation is valid for K-free sea water and Na-free internal solution.

$[Na]_o$ and $[K]_i$ are the activities of external sodium and internal potassium, P_{Na} and P_K are the Na and K permeabilities of the active membrane, and R, T and F have their usual meaning. The average equilibrium potential V_e in the experiments of Chandler and Meves [7] was + 67.8 mV at 0°C, corresponding to an average P_{Na}/P_K = 12. Thus the early tetrodotoxin-sensitive channel is twelve times more permeable to Na^+ than to K^+.

Further voltage clamp experiments were carried out to determine the relative permeability of the sodium channel to Li^+, Rb^+ and Cs^+. This was done by replacing the external NaCl with LiCl or the internal KCl with RbCl or CsCl and determining the equilibrium potential V_e for the early current. On the assumption that only monovalent cations go through the sodium channel the relative permeabilities of Li:Na:K:Rb:Cs were $1.1:1:1:\frac{1}{12}:\frac{1}{40}:\frac{1}{61}$. The finding that P_{Li} is nearly equal to P_{Na} is consistent with the old observation that Li^+ ions can fully replace Na^+ ions in the action potential mechanism. The permeabilities for K^+, Rb^+ and Cs^+ are much smaller than for Na^+. The sequence of the permeabilities coincides with the sequence of the crystal ionic radii.

In the past three years the results of Chandler and Meves [7] were confirmed and extended by new experiments. Moore and coworkers [9] working on intact squid axons found the permeability ratio Li:Na close to 1. The experiments of Rojas and Atwater [8] on perfused giant axons of the Chilean squid *Dosidicus gigas* gave an average permeability ratio P_{Na}/P_K of 25 instead of 12; in a more recent experiment [10] P_{Na}/P_K equal to 10 was found. A similar value, 9.1, was obtained by Binstock and Lecar [11] for internally perfused axons of *Loligo pealii*. Pickard and coworkers [12] concluded from measurements on intact axons in Cs-rich sea water that Cs^+ ions are completely unable to pass through the early or the delayed channel. However, a new experiment of Chandler and Meves (unpublished) on an axon internally perfused with a caesium salt solution gave a permeability ratio P_{Na}/P_{Cs} = 58 which is in excellent agreement with the earlier value.

Experiments were also extended to include organic cations. It is known since the work of Lorente de Nó and coworkers [13] that the organic cations guanidinium, hydrazinium, hydroxylammonium or ammonium can partially substitute for Na^+ in the action potential mechanism of frog nerve. The same is true for squid giant axons as shown by Tasaki and Singer [14], and Watanabe et al. [15]; the action potentials obtained with these organic cations are abolished by tetrodotoxin as is the normal sodium action potential. Recently, Binstock and Lecar [11] studied in detail the ability of NH_4^+ ions to move through the early and the delayed channel. Fig. 5 compares the sodium action potential and the ammonium action potential of a squid axon.

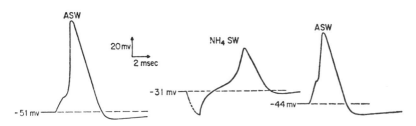

Fig. 5. Action potentials of a squid axon in artificial sea water with 430 mM NaCl (ASW), in artificial sea water with 430 mM NH₄Cl (NH₄SW) and after returning to artificial sea water with 430 mM NaCl (ASW). The axon was stimulated by means of an internal electrode. Temperature 9°C. From Binstock and Lecar [11].

The resting potential is markedly reduced after replacing the external NaCl by NH₄Cl. This is due to the fact that NH_4^+ ions are able to move through the delayed channel normally used by K^+ ions, thus external NH_4^+ depolarizes like external K^+. Depolarization causes inactivation of the sodium channel which can be removed by an anodal pulse. Upon the break of the anodal pulse an ammonium action potential is elicited (fig. 5, record NH₄SW). The permeability ratio P_{Na}/P_{NH_4} for the early tetrodotoxin-sensitive channel was determined in voltage clamp experiments on intact axons in artificial sea water with 430 mM NH₄Cl and on axons perfused with 500 mM NH₄F as internal solution. The average P_{Na}/P_{NH_4} was 3.7, i.e. the early channel is more permeable to NH_4^+ than to K^+. A similar figure, 4, was obtained by Chandler and Meves (unpublished experiments) for the permeability ratio Na:guanidinium in voltage clamp experiments with artificial sea water containing guanidine hydrochloride instead of NaCl. There is also an indication from the work of Tasaki and Singer [14] and Binstock and Lecar [11] that tetraethylammonium, the specific blocking substance for the delayed channel, is sufficiently permeable in the early channel to give measurable inward currents and concomitant active responses which are blocked by tetrodotoxin.

Finally, it can be concluded from the experiments of Tasaki and coworkers [15–18] that divalent cations (Ca^{++}, Ba^{++}, Sr^{++}), at least under extreme conditions, are able to move through the early tetrodotoxin-sensitive channel. The basic observation is illustrated by fig. 6. The normal sodium spike of an intact squid giant axon immersed in artificial sea water with 300 mM NaCl and 100 mM CaCl₂ is shown in record A. The fibre becomes inexcitable when the external NaCl is replaced by glycerol (record B). Excitability is, however, regained when internal perfusion with an isotonic perfusion fluid containing

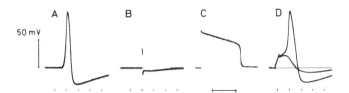

Fig. 6. Action potentials of a squid axon in artificial sea water containing 300 mM NaCl, 100 mM $CaCl_2$ and glycerol (A and D) or only 100 mM $CaCl_2$ and glycerol (B and C). Records A and B before initiation of internal perfusion; record C 12 min after the onset of internal perfusion with an isotonic solution of 10 mM sodium phosphate and glycerol; record D with 400 mM KF as perfusion fluid. The stimulus duration was 0.1 msec for A and B, 100 msec for C and about 0.3 msec for D. Time marks in A, B and D are 1 msec apart; horizontal bar in C represents 10 sec. Temperature 21°C. From Watanabe et al. [17].

glycerol and a small amount (10 – 25 mM) of a phosphate or fluoride salt is started. Under these conditions, i.e., with 100 mM $CaCl_2$ and no sodium in the external medium and with a solution of low ionic strength containing a 'favourable' anion (see page 270) as internal fluid, an action potential of more than 10 sec duration can be elicited by a long lasting stimulus (record C in fig. 6). The usual type of action potential is restored after switching to 400 mM KF as perfusion fluid and returning to artificial sea water with 300 mM NaCl and 100 mM $CaCl_2$ on the outside (record D). The most likely explanation is that the long-lasting action potential shown in record C is a calcium spike, i.e., due to an influx of calcium ions. Hodgkin and Keynes [19] found a small but significant extra calcium influx on stimulation of 0.08 pMol/cm^2 per impulse for an intact axon in artificial sea water with 392 mM NaCl and 112 mM $CaCl_2$. Although this value is two orders of magnitude less than the corresponding flux of sodium ions, it might play a role in impulse propagation when sodium is removed from the external solution. To account for the action potential in record C of fig. 5, a calcium influx at least four times as large would be needed. Action potentials of the type illustrated by fig. 5C are abolished by tetrodotoxin; it was therefore suggested by Hille [20] that calcium ions under these conditions are probably moving through the early channel normally used by sodium ions.

Table 1 summarizes the quantitative information, obtained by various authors in the past years, about the ionic selectivity of the sodium system of the active nerve membrane. The crystal radii of the ions are quoted from Robinson and Stokes [21] except the value for guanidinium which was calculated by Hille [20]. In general the permeabilities follow the sequence of

Table 1

	Li	:	Na	:	NH_4	:	Guanidinium	:	K	:	Rb	:	Cs
Relative permeability	1.1	:	1	:	$\frac{1}{3.7}$	:	$\frac{1}{4}$	:	$\frac{1}{12}$	:	$\frac{1}{40}$	:	$\frac{1}{61}$
Ionic radius	0.60		0.95		1.48		2.70		1.33		1.48		1.69 Å

the ionic radii with the exception of the two organic cations. These quantitative results enable us to draw two conclusions:

(1) The sodium channel of the active nerve membrane is not exclusively permeable for sodium ions; other ions can also move through the channel. The permeability for Na^+ and Li^+ is, however, many times (at least four times) larger than for any other cation thus far studied. Thus the active nerve membrane is primarily permeable to Na^+ and Li^+. With a normal ionic composition of the external fluid the rising phase of the squid axon action potential is therefore entirely due to an inward current of Na^+ ions.

Additional experimental evidence for the 'sodium hypothesis' was obtained in the recent work of Atwater et al. [10] on giant axons of the Chilean squid *Dosidicus gigas*. Using the voltage clamp technique on perfused axons in sea water with radioactive ^{22}Na, they applied depolarizing pulses of varying amplitude and measured (a) the influx of ^{22}Na by determining the radioactivity in samples of the perfusion fluid; and (b) the ionic flux during the early permeability change by integrating the early current. As illustrated in fig. 7 the two sets of measurements gave almost identical results. In 17 measurements on 6 different axons the average ratio tracer flux:electrical flux was 0.92. This shows that the early inward current can be completely accounted for by the sodium influx.

(2) The permeability sequence for the five alkali metal ions can be compared with the sequences found in various other (living or non-living) systems (see review of Diamond and Wright [22]). Although the five alkali metals can be arranged in 5! = 120 possible permutations only 11 are observed in living or non-living systems. One of these 11 sequences is the sequence Li > Na > K > Rb > Cs which is found for the sodium channel of the active nerve membrane. The 11 sequences are predicted by the theory of selectivity developed by Eisenman [23]. According to this theory the sequence Li > Na > K > Rb > Cs is characteristic for interaction of the alkali ions with anion sites of high electric field strength. The smallest cation (Li^+) will have its center of charge nearest the site and will experience the largest attractive force.

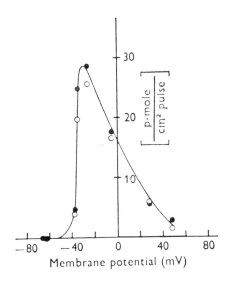

270 H.MEVES

Fig. 7. Tracer sodium influx (○) and electrically measured ionic flux during the early
transient current (●) in a perfused axon of *Dosidicus gigas*. Ordinate: flux in pMol/cm^2
per depolarizing voltage clamp pulse. Abscissa: membrane potential in mV during voltage
clamp pulse. External solution: artificial sea water with ^{22}Na. Internal solution: 550 mM
KF. Temperature 17°C. From Atwater et al. [10].

The theory of Eisenman has also been applied to the anion selectivity of
membranes. Out of 24 possible permutations of the four halide anions 7
selectivity sequences are predicted by the theory and are found in living and
non-living systems (see Diamond and Wright [22]). One of these 7 sequences
is I > Br > Cl > F with the smallest anion (F$^-$) on one end and the largest anion (I$^-$) on the other end. It could serve to explain the observation of Tasaki
et al. [24] that for internal perfusion of squid axons solutions with F$^-$ as the
anion are most favourable as judged from the survival time of the axon. The
'favourability' increases in the direction from I$^-$ to F$^-$, perhaps due to decreasing permeability.

The favourable effect of F$^-$ as the internal anion as described by Tasaki
[24] has been confirmed by other authors. Fluoride solutions are now being
widely used for intracellular perfusion. Due to the low permeability of the
membrane to F$^-$ it is possible to maintain a high resting potential without intracellular K$^+$. This enables one to study action potentials and membrane
currents in the absence of internal (and external) potassium. A fibre with

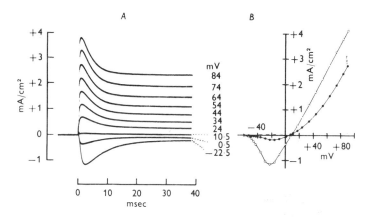

Fig. 8. Voltage clamp currents from a squid axon internally perfused with 300 mM NaF. A: superimposed membrane currents associated with step depolarizations of varying amplitude. Membrane potential during voltage clamp pulse given at the right-hand side. B: peak current (○) and current at 39 msec (●) as a function of membrane potential during the pulse. Dashed line indicates leakage current. Internal solution: 300 mM NaF + sucrose (K-free). External solution: K-free artificial sea water with 470 mM NaCl. Temperature 0°C. From Chandler and Meves [27].

300 mM NaF as internal fluid and K-free artificial sea water with 470 mM NaCl as external medium gives an action potential which lasts more than 5 sec and on its peak reaches the sodium equilibrium potential [25] . The membrane currents underlying these long lasting action potentials were analyzed by Adelman and Senft [26] , and Chandler and Meves [27] (fig. 8). The currents which are inward for small depolarizations and outward for large depolarizations decay to sustained levels (fig. 8A). Both the early and the residual components appear to be carried by sodium ions moving through the sodium channel, since they reverse direction at the sodium equilibrium potential V_{Na} = 10.5 mV (fig. 8A and B) and are completely blocked by external tetrodotoxin, 10^{-7} g/ml. The simplest interpretation is that the sodium conductance is only partially inactivated by a short depolarizing pulse. The incomplete inactivation of the sodium conductance is probably responsible for the long duration of the action potentials. As shown in fig. 8B the amount of inactivation depends on voltage, being less complete at large depolarizations. A detailed analysis of the inactivation process in NaF-perfused fibres is being done at the moment (Chandler and Meves, to be published).

Acknowledgements

I am indebted to Dr. W.K.Chandler and Dr. W.Ulbricht for reading the manuscript and for much helpful criticism.

References

[1] A.L.Hodgkin and B.Katz, J. Physiol. (London) 108 (1949) 37–77.
[2] A.L.Hodgkin and A.F.Huxley, J. Physiol. (London) 117 (1952) 500–544.
[3] K.S.Cole and J.W.Moore, J. Gen. Physiol. 44 (1960) 123–167.
[3a] J.W.Moore and K.S.Cole, in: Physical Techniques in Biological Research, Vol. VI (Academic Press, New York, 1963).
[4] P.F.Baker, A.L.Hodgkin and T.I.Shaw, Nature 190 (1961) 885–887.
[5] T.Oikawa, C.S.Spyropoulos, I.Tasaki and T.Teorell, Acta Physiol. Scand. 52 (1961) 195–196.
[6] I.Tasaki, J. Gen. Physiol. 46 (1963) 755–772.
[7] W.K.Chandler and H.Meves, J. Physiol. (London) 180 (1965) 788–820.
[8] E.Rojas and I.Atwater, Proc. Natl. Acad. Sci. U.S. 57 (1967) 1350–1355.
[9] J.W.Moore, N.Anderson, M.Blaustein, M.Takata, J.Y.Lettvin, W.F.Pickard, T. Bernstein and J.Pooler, Ann. N.Y. Acad. Sci. U.S. 137 (1966) 818–829.
[10] I.Atwater, F.Bezanilla and E.Rojas, J. Physiol. (London) 201 (1969) 657–664.
[11] L.Binstock and H.Lecar, J. Gen. Physiol. 53 (1969) 342–361.
[12] W.F.Pickard, J.Y.Lettvin, J.W.Moore, M.Takata, J.Pooler and T.Bernstein, Proc. Natl. Acad. Sci. U.S. 52 (1964) 1177–1183.
[13] R.Lorente de Nó, F.Vidal and L.M.H.Larramendi, Nature 179 (1957) 737–738.
[14] I.Tasaki and I.Singer, Ann. N.Y. Acad. Sci. 137 (1966) 792–806.
[15] A.Watanabe, I.Tasaki, I.Singer and L.Lerman, Science 155 (1967) 95–97.
[16] I.Tasaki, A.Watanabe and L.Lerman, Am. J. Physiol. 213 (1967) 1465–1474.
[17] A.Watanabe, I.Tasaki and L.Lerman, Proc. Natl. Acad. Sci. U.S. 58 (1967) 2246–2252.
[18] I.Tasaki, L.Lerman and A.Watanabe, Am. J. Physiol. 216 (1969) 130–138.
[19] A.L.Hodgkin and R.D.Keynes, J. Physiol. (London) 138 (1957) 253–281.
[20] B.Hille, Ph. D. Thesis, Rockefeller University, New York (1967).
[21] R.A.Robinson and R.H.Stokes, Electrolyte Solutions, 2nd rev. edition (Butterworths, London, 1965).
[22] J.M.Diamond and E.M.Wright, Ann. Rev. Physiol. 31 (1969) 581–646.
[23] G.Eisenman, Biophys. J. 2 part 2 (1962) 259–323.
[24] I.Tasaki, I.Singer and T.Takenaka, J. Gen. Physiol. 48 (1965) 1095–1123.
[25] W.K.Chandler and A.L.Hodgkin, J. Physiol. (London) 181 (1965) 594–611.
[26] W.J.Adelman and J.P.Senft, Nature 212 (1966) 614–616.
[27] W.K.Chandler and H.Meves, J. Physiol. (London) 186 (1966) 121–122 P.

FIXED CHARGE STRUCTURE OF THE
SQUID AXON MEMBRANE

E.ROJAS, I.ATWATER and F.BEZANILLA
Laboratory of Cellular Physiology, Faculty of Sciences,
University of Chile, Santiago, Chile

1. Introduction

This paper is a modest attempt to discuss the experimental evidences of fixed charges in the axon membrane within the framework of the problem of molecular organization of the cell membrane and to utilize the general results of membrane models. We propose a fictitious scheme of membrane fixed charges and challenge the theoreticians to propose a conclusive experiment.

2. Results and discussion

2.1. Experiments on axons in sea water

In general, membranes with a molecular structure that have ionizable charges have properties which depend on the ionic strength of the surrounding solutions. At high ionic strength these charges are 'shielded' by the counter ions and, consequently, their effects are noticeable only by lowering the ionic strength. The degree of ionization of these charges is often controlled by pH or the presence of divalent ions in the solutions. Unfortunately, studies of excitability on squid giant axons must be carried out in sea water for which the ionic strength is about 700 mM. The neutralizing effects of calcium and magnesium ions are present even if the ionic strength is lowered by replacing the sodium chloride from the sea water with sucrose.

Intracellular perfusion has made it possible for the first time to expose the inner side of the axon membrane to solutions deprived of divalent cations and of much lower ionic strength (sucrose being used to maintain the tonicity of the internal solutions equal to that of the external solution).

The first studies of the effects of low internal ionic strength showed that

273

for 6 mM K^+ the resting potential (usually of the order of -60 mV, negative inside the fiber, with 550 mM K^+) was near zero and that action potentials of long duration but full size (about 100 mV) could be elicited [1,2,3]. The observed changes in resting potential with internal potassium dilution are reasonably well accounted for by the constant field equation [3]. The increase in duration of the action potential is explained as being due to the reduction of the internal potassium concentration which in turn induces a decrease in the outward potassium ionic movement responsible for the recovery phase of the action potential. However, the fact that the sodium permeability change (inward sodium movement responsible for the rising phase of the action potential) could be initiated from such a low resting potential suggested that the voltage dependence of the sodium permeability change in these axons was different from that of axons internally perfused with 550 mM K^+. Voltage clamp experiments on axons internally perfused with solutions of low ionic strength revealed a displacement along the voltage axis of the voltage dependence of the sodium permeability change in the direction of a more positive internal potential [4,5]. That this effect was due to low ionic strength and not due to the low internal potassium concentration was shown by lowering the internal potassium concentration while maintaining the ionic strength with other ions; there was no displacement of the voltage dependence of the sodium permeability change [5]. This effect of lowering the internal ionic strength could not be explained with the available formal expressions for describing the voltage dependence of the sodium permeability change [6].

We have investigated the effects of low internal ionic strength upon several membrane electrical characteristics and focused our attention to the reversal potential of the early transient sodium currents (that potential at which the early current during an applied pulse changes from inward to outward) [7].

As a general procedure, giant axon fibers from the squid *Dosidicus gigas* were bathed in potassium-free artificial sea water (430 mM NaCl, 50 mM $MgCl_2$, 10 mM $CaCl_2$, 5 mM Tris-Cl at pH 7.5) and internally perfused with potassium fluoride solution (550 mM KF, 5 mM Tris-Cl at pH 7.3). The axons were subjected to several voltage clamp experiments during which the internal potassium was diluted. Fig. 1A shows the effects of lowering the ionic strength of the internal potassium fluoride solution from 550 to 100 mM upon the action potential. It can be seen that after a few minutes of internal perfusion with 100 mM KF, both the height and the duration of the action potential increase. Changes in resting potential are not apparent in this figure because these are tracings of records of action potentials recorded with the internal platinum-platinum black plated electrode. Fig. 1B shows the current-voltage relationships (I–V curves) at two different internal ionic

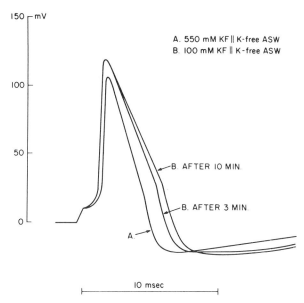

Fig. 1A. Effect of internal ionic strength on the action potential. (Temp. about 10°C.)

strengths: 550 mM and 50 mM. The following is apparent from this figure:

(i) The slope of the steady state I—V curve obtained with an internal concentration equal to 550 mM is 6 times the slope of the steady state I—V curve obtained with 50 mM. This factor is very close to the ratio of potassium activities in both solutions, namely 355/41.

(ii) There is a displacement of the I—V curve corresponding to the maximum early sodium currents along the voltage axis in the direction of a more positive internal potential. The magnitude of the maximum inward sodium currents was quite independent of the internal ionic strength provided that the membrane potential was clamped near −60 mV.

(ii) The membrane potential at which the early current changes from inward to outward (indicated in this figure by an arrow) is also shifted in the same direction along the voltage axis.

Table 1 summarizes some of the relevant data obtained in a systematic investigation of the effects of lowering the ionic strength of the internal solution upon: (a) resting potential, (b) membrane action potential height, (c) reversal potential for the early currents, (d) maximum sodium conductance defined as the slope of the current-voltage curve corresponding to the maximum inward currents for large depolarizations, and (e) maximum potassium

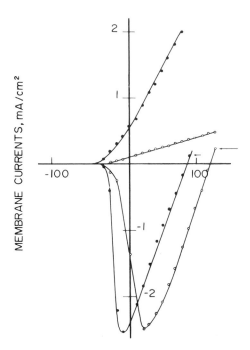

ABSOLUTE MEMBRANE POTENTIAL, mV

Fig. 1B. Effect of internal ionic strength on the current-voltage curves measured under voltage clamp. This figure shows the I–V curves obtained from two different axons bathed in K-free ASW and internally perfused with ● ● 550 mM KF and ○ ○ 50 mM KF + 1000 mM sucrose. In both experiments the resting potential was held at −60 mV. Arrows indicate the reversal potential. (Temp. about 10°C for both experiments.)

conductance defined as the slope of the current-voltage curve corresponding to the maximum outward currents for large depolarizations.

The constant field equation [8,9] for an axon internally perfused with only potassium fluoride and externally perfused with K-free ASW, the reversal potential, V_{Na}, is equal to the following expression:

$$V_{Na} = \frac{RT}{F} \ln \frac{P_{Na} a_{Na}^{o}}{P_{K} a_{K}^{i}}, \tag{1}$$

where R, T and F have their usual meanings; P_{Na}, P_{K} are the permeabilities to Na^{+} and K^{+} respectively, and a_{Na}^{o}, a_{K}^{i} are the chemical activities of Na^{+}

Table 1
Some membrane parameters for axons bathed in K-free sea water and internally perfused with potassium fluoride solutions of different ionic strengths

Ionic strength		a	b	c	d	e	$\frac{1}{\kappa}$
mM			mV		mmho/cm^2		Å
550	(28)	-55 ± 2	117 ± 6	83 ± 8	22 ± 4	12.6 ± 3	4.3
275	(4)	-52 ± 2	104 ± 5	92 ± 4	22 ± 2	13.0 ± 3	5.3
100	(2)	-50	115	105	19	4	10
50	(8)	-18 ± 13	90 ± 24	124 ± 8	24	2 ± 0.8	14

Data given as average ± S.E. (Numbers in parenthesis represent number of experiments
averaged.) (a) Resting potential, measured with two Ag-AgCl electrodes in contact with
the internal and external solutions through KCl bridges of low impedance. (b) Action
potential height. (c) Reversal potential for the early currents. (d) Maximum sodium conductance. (e) Maximum potassium conductance. $(1/\kappa)$ The 'thickness' of the ionic atmosphere. The temperature ranged from $5°C$ to $15°C$.

and K^+ respectively. It can be seen that $V_{Na}F/RT$ is linearly dependent on
$\ln a_{Na}^o/a_K^i$. We have found that the observed changes of reversal potential
with internal dilution are not equal to the expected changes according to eq.
(1). The existence of a surface layer of negative charges has been postulated
to explain these results [5,7]. We would like to illustrate how.

A surface layer of fixed charges in the membrane gives rise to a diffuse
layer of counter ions extending into the solution. These two layers of
charges of opposite sign constitute the ionic double layer. As theoretical
treatments of these static double layers have been critically reviewed and extensively discussed elsewhere [10,11], we write here only the basic equations
of Boltzmann and Poisson for the simplest treatment, that of the diffuse
double layer, together with the most important assumptions to illustrate how
these equations may be used to explain the effects of lowering the internal
ionic strength upon the reversal potential for the early currents.

The concentration of ions at a distance x from the surface of fixed charges
is related to the potential at that point Ψ_x by a Boltzmann equation:

$$C_x = C_b \exp \left[- \Psi_x \frac{F}{RT} \right], \tag{2}$$

where C_b is the concentration in the bulk of the solution. The Poisson equation relates the electrical potential Ψ_x to the charge density in the solution.

Utilizing the Boltzmann equation to calculate Ψ_x, assuming that the dielectric parameter D is a constant and that the absolute value of the potential Ψ_x is smaller than 0.03 volts [10], this relation takes the form:

$$\frac{d^2\Psi_x}{dx^2} = \kappa^2 \Psi_x ,$$
(3)

where

$$\kappa = \left[\frac{8\pi F^2 C}{DRT}\right]^{\frac{1}{2}} .$$
(4)

C is the concentration of uni-univalent electrolyte and D is the dielectric constant of the water. Integration of equation (3) gives:

$$\Psi_x = \Psi_0 \exp\left[-\kappa x\right] .$$
(5)

The 'thickness' of the diffuse ionic layer next to the plane of fixed charges is $1/\kappa$. The relationship between density of charges in the surface of the membrane, σ_0, and the surface potential is given by:

$$\sigma_0 = \frac{D\kappa}{4\pi} \Psi_0 .$$
(6)

Let us consider again the effects of lowering the internal ionic strength upon the reversal potential for the sodium currents. In the experiments summarized in table 1 only the activity of the internal potassium was changed. Assuming that the dilution of the internal potassium concentration does not affect the selectivity ratio, P_{Na}/P_K, then V_{Na} according to eq. (1) is linearly dependent on $\ln(a_{Na}^0/a_K^i)$. Fig. 2 shows the predicted curve according to eq. (1) and the experimentally measured values. There is a clear difference between them and this difference increases as the internal ionic strength is lowered. Regardless of any possible variations of the selectivity ratio with ionic strength [5], we would like to point out that activities in eq. (1) should most correctly be surface activities. Utilizing eq. (2) we define a separation factor, ρ, as the ratio of the activity at the inner surface of the axon membrane, $a_{K,s}$, to the activity in the bulk of the solution, $a_{K,b}$:

$$\rho = \frac{a_{K,s}^i}{a_{K,b}^i} .$$
(7)

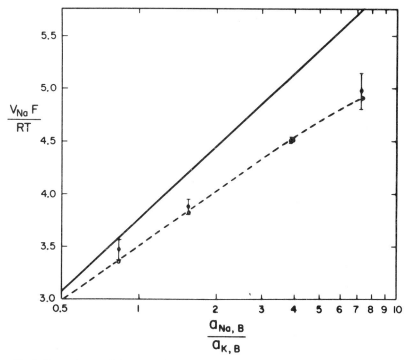

Fig. 2. Dependence of the reversal potential of the early currents on ionic strength of the internal solution. The solid line represents $V_{Na}(F/RT)$ as predicted by eq. (1) as a function of the ratio a^o_{Na}/a^i_{Na}. The dashed curve (drawn through the open circles) represents $V_{Na}(F/RT)$ calculated utilizing eq. (9). Filled circles are the values of $V_{Na}(F/RT)$ obtained from the experimentally measured reversal potentials. Vertical bars represent two times the S.D.

This separation factor can be computed measuring the difference between the ordinates in fig. 2 at different $a_{Na}/a_{K,b}$ ratios. Thus,

$$V_{Na,eq.} - V_{Na,meas.}$$

$$= \frac{RT}{F} \ln \frac{P_{Na}a^o_{Na}}{P_K a^i_{K,b}} - \frac{RT}{F} \ln \frac{P_{Na}a^o_{Na}}{P_K a^i_{K,s}} = \frac{RT}{F} \ln \frac{a^i_{K,s}}{a^i_{K,b}}. \qquad (8)$$

This factor is greater than one for all the experimental points shown in fig. 2, indicating that the surface activities are greater than the bulk activities. The natural interpretation for this result is the existence of a surface charge [7] . We have computed from fig. 2 $V_{Na,eq.} - V_{Na,meas.}$ and with the known bulk potassium activity, we have computed a surface potassium activity, $a_{K,s}^i$. The surface potential, ψ_0, at each given internal potassium activity, $a_{K,b}^i$, can be calculated with eq. (2) (or directly with eq. (8)). Using the relationship between surface potential, charge density and κ as given by eq. (6), we have constructed a diagram of the surface potential as a function of bulk potassium activity for different densities of charges at the surface. The points calculated with eq. (8) fell precisely on the theoretical curve for $\sigma_0 = 1 \ \mu C/cm^2$ (or $1 \ e^-/1600 \ Å^2$). Eq. (1) can now be modified to take into account the effects of the internal layer of charges.

$$V_{Na} = \frac{RT}{F} \ln \frac{P_{Na} a_{Na}^o}{P_K a_{K,b}^i} + \frac{4\pi}{D} \frac{\sigma_o}{\kappa} . \tag{9}$$

Fig. 2. shows the predicted dependence of the reversal potential V_{Na} on the internal potassium activities calculated with eq. (9) (dashed curve). The predicted variation accounts for the measured variation.

We have estimated the charge density which affects the reversal potential of the sodium currents to be nearly one negative charge every $1600 \ Å^2$. A uniform rectangular arrangement of these charges gives a separation of $40 \ Å$ between them. Fig. 3 represents a possible distribution of these charges with respect to the opening of the sodium channel at the inner surface. It also illustrates the 'thickness' of the ionic atmosphere around each charge for three different internal ionic strengths, 550, 40 and 25 mM.

There are some basic differences between the sodium and potassium systems as revealed by the effects of internal ionic strength upon sodium and potassium conductances. It is clear that the electrical resistance from the opening of the channels to the solutions in each side sets an upper limit to the resistance in the channel irrespective of the shape or the permeation mechanism. This resistance is proportional to the solution resistivity. Therefore, the resistance of the channels should change if the resistivity of the bathing solution is changed. For example, the resistance of the sodium channels should increase six times when changing the internal solution from 550 mM (resistivity equal to about 20 ohmcm) to 50 mM (resistivity equal to about 120 ohmcm). The total membrane conductance, which is equal to the summation of all these unit conductances in parallel, should also be decreased by a factor of six. However, we have seen that the sodium conductance is independent of the internal potassium concentration. The postulated charges

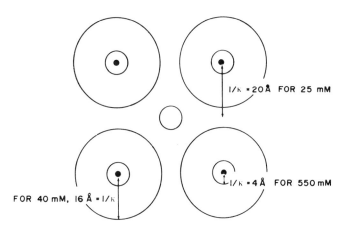

I/ĸ ＝20Å FOR 25 mM

I/ĸ ＝4Å FOR 550 mM

FOR 40 mM, 16 Å ＝I/ĸ

Fig. 3. Distribution of negative charges around the internal opening of a 'sodium channel', assumed to be located in the center of a rectangular array of charges. The separation between the charges is 40 Å.

around the internal opening of the sodium channel would locally control the concentration and therefore, the resistance from the opening of the sodium channel to the solution will be independent of internal dilution. Supporting this interpretation are the results of external sodium dilution with sucrose (maintaining the concentration of calcium and magnesium unchanged) [12]. It was found that concomitantly with the increase in resistivity of the external solution there was a proportional decrease in the maximum potassium conductance. This observation is another example of the differences between the potassium and sodium systems. We interpret these results to indicate that the opening of the potassium system to the external solution is located in a patch of membrane deprived of negative charges and conclude, therefore, that both the inner and the outer membrane surface around the potassium channels are uncharged.

2.2. Experiments on axons in potassium chloride solutions

In order to use the theoretical analysis developed for artificial membranes [13–16], we have simplified the experimental conditions by working with only one cation species on both sides of the axon membrane and have temporarily overlooked the time-dependent phenomena to consider steady state conditions [7,17]. In designing experiments to determine the presence of

E.ROJAS, I.ATWATER and F.BEZANILLA

Table 2
Effects of H^+ and Mg^{++} on the resting influx of Cl^- in axons bathing in KCl solutions

Experiment	a	b	c	d	Temp.
	mV	pH	pMole/cm^2sec	mV	°C
6 A–R	96	8.1	30	110	17
8 A–R	112	8.1	24	120	16.5
14 A–R	98	7.5	31	102	20.5
11 A–R	96	6.8	24	88	21.5
16 A–R	120	4.0	40	116	18
9 A–R	118	7.7			
		+ 50 mM $MgCl_2$	29	115	17.5
12 A–R	105	7.7			
		+ 50 mM $MgCl_2$	11	104	19.5
17 A–R	116	7.7			
		+ 50 mM $MgCl_2$	25	108	18

(a) Action potential height recorded before the experiment. (b) Experimental condition, in the external KCl solution. (c) Resting influx of chloride ions. (d) Action potential height after replacement of K-free ASW. Both internal and external solutions were buffered with 5 mM Tris-Cl. Area of the axons bathing in KCl solution about 0.5 cm^2.

charges, we have been hindered by the lack of a single definite test to distinguish the charged from the uncharged membrane. Our general approach to the study of the axolema as a fixed-charged membrane has been firstly to determine the sign of the net charge by showing selective ion permeability and, secondly, to determine a possible charge density. Thirdly we have tried to characterize the possible charge-contributing groups by modifying the degree of ionization of the fixed charges. Each group of experiments should be considered within the framework of the entire section.

The axons were internally and externally perfused with solutions containing potassium as the only cation species, a condition which can be maintained for at least 30 min without permanent loss of the excitability [7,17]. All the experiments described here were completed on axons which were exposed to sea water before and after the treatment with potassium solutions and showed the electrical behaviour of an excitable axon (resting potential, action potential, voltage clamp currents).

2.2.1. Sign of the net fixed charge during rest
2.2.1.1. *^{36}Cl influx measurements.* The axons were suspended in artificial sea water and internally perfused with a solution of 550 mM KF; the membrane action potential was recorded. Then the sea water was replaced by

550 mM KCl solution in order to rinse the axon and remove the divalent cations. After 3 or 4 min the KCl solution was replaced by one of the same composition but with ^{36}Cl. The ^{36}Cl inflow was measured by collecting the internal solution, which was flowing through the axon at a rate of about 0.15 cm^3/min. Samples of the perfusate were collected every 48–80 sec and their radioactivity was measured. The resting chloride influx was calculated using the area of the axon membrane bathing in the potassium solution, the specific activity of the external solution and the sampling time. Table 2 shows the data obtained in these experiments. Column a gives the height of the action potential before removing the K-free ASW, b gives the experimental condition in the external 550 mM KCl solution, c the resting chloride influx and, d the height of the action potential after the experiment when the K-free ASW was replaced. The average resting influx of chloride ions is about 25 pMole/cm^{2}sec. It is interesting to mention here that the resting chloride permeability in these axons exposed to potassium solutions is very similar to the resting chloride permeability of axons in sea water [18].

In a separate group of experiments not reported here we have studied the resting permeability of rubidium ions for an axon membrane exposed to 550 mM RbCl solution. Using ^{86}Rb as a tracer, the resting rubidium influx in five experiments was about 200 pMole/cm^{2}sec, eight times greater than the influx of chloride ions under the same experimental conditions (pH about 7.5). This indicates that the axolema exposed to solutions without divalent cations and at rest is cation selective.

2.2.1.2. K^+-concentration dependent resting potential. The selectivity of the axon membrane towards cations was tested by a second group of experiments in which the resting potential was measured and its dependence upon potassium concentration differences studied. Potassium solutions were diluted to various concentrations by addition of 1 M sucrose or mannitol. To avoid longitudinal spreading of the potentials in the non-perfused region of the axon, in which the ionic concentration cannot be controlled, the axons were perfused internally along the same length as was bathed externally (25 mm). Fig. 4 shows a diagram of the technique used and gives the recorded resting potential along the perfused region of the fiber. The resting potential sensing electrodes are outlined (the current platinum electrodes are shown in black). Both the external and internal electrodes were slowly moved along the 25 mm of the perfused axon, stopping about every 2 mm to record the resting potential, in order to detect possible longitudinal variations and any end-effects. In fig. 4, the resting potential (given on the vertical axis in mV) is shown as it was recorded along the fiber. Concentrations of the internal and external

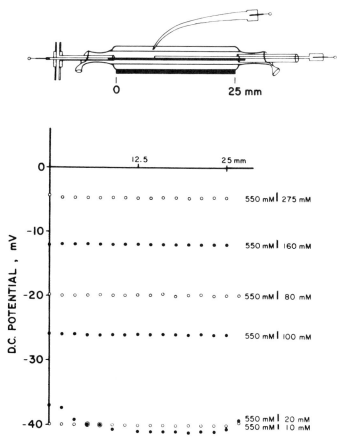

Fig. 4. Longitudinal uniformity of the resting potential. The upper part of this figure shows diagramatically the perfusion of a squid axon, the black platinum plated current electrodes and the movable potential recording electrodes. Internal solution was always 550 mM KF. External solution was either ● ● KF or o o KCl.

solutions for each set of measurements are given as:

internal KF//external K$^+$.

Open circles are used when the external solution was KCl and filled circles when the external solution was KF. As can be seen, the potentials measured along the axon were constant (with the exception of a variation of a few mV

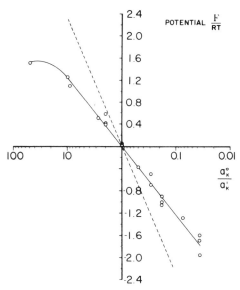

Fig. 5. K-concentration dependent resting potential. Vertical axis represents the resting potential V_0 multiplied by F/RT. Horizontal axis represents the ratio 'potassium activity in the external solution/potassium activity in the internal solution' in a logarithmic scale. Each open circle represents one measurement as described in fig. 4. The solid curve is drawn through the experimental points and is a straight line from $(a_K^o/a_K^i) = 10$ to 0.03. Its slope is half the slope of the straight dashed line which represents predicted Nernst potentials.

at the ends when the solution junction was 550 mM KF//20 mM KF). Thus, this resting membrane is under conditions of zero net current.

Resting potentials were similarly measured for ionic dilutions of the internal solution and for various combinations with both external and internal solutions at lowered ionic strengths. Fig. 5 shows a graph of the experimental resting potentials (multiplied by F/RT) as a function of the ratio 'potassium activity in the external solution/potassium activity in the internal solution' on a semi-logarithmic scale. The solid line has been drawn through the experimental points and is straight except for the deviation at $a_K^o/a_K^i = 55$ (solution junction: internal, 10 mM//external, 550 mM KCl). We have no explanation for this deviation, except possibly the lack of experimental points at that extreme. The dashed line represents the predicted potassium diffusion potential (multiplied by F/RT) as given by the Nernst equation. The slope of the solid line is half the slope of the dashed line.

Ionic diffusion through membranes can be formally represented by an electrical equivalent circuit [19]. This equivalent circuit evolves from the integration of the basic flux equation across the membrane. The simplest treatment using this equivalent circuit assumes a homogeneous uncharged membrane in which the mobilities of all the ions are constant during steady state conditions [19]. For the experimental conditions, indicated above, namely potassium fluoride on both sides of the axon membrane, the flux equation can be integrated to give the ionic currents,

$$F\Phi_K \int_o^i \frac{dx}{F^2 u_K C_K} = -\frac{RT}{F} \ln \frac{C_K^o}{C_K^i} + V_o , \qquad (10a)$$

$$F\Phi_F \int_o^i \frac{dx}{F^2 u_F C_F} = \frac{RT}{F} \ln \frac{C_F^o}{C_F^i} + V_o , \qquad (10b)$$

where Φ_K, Φ_F are net ionic fluxes, u_K, u_F are molar mobilities (or mobility divided by the Faraday number) within the membrane and C is the concentration of K or F at any point, x, in the membrane. C^o, C^i are concentrations of K and F in the external and internal solutions respectively and V_o is the membrane potential.

To write the equation for the equivalent circuit let:

$$\Phi_K F = I_K$$

$$\Phi_F F = I_F$$

and the integral resistance to be:

$$\int_o^i \frac{dx}{F^2 u_K C_K} = R_K , \qquad (11a)$$

$$\int_o^i \frac{dx}{F^2 u_F C_F} = R_F . \qquad (11b)$$

The Nernst potentials in eqs. (10a) and (10b) are represented as V_K and V_F. Introducing these terms into eqs. (10a) and (10b), the total current gives the equation for the equivalent circuit as:

$$I = I_K + I_F = G_K(V_o - V_K) + G_F(V_o - V_F) ,$$ (12)

which is illustrated in fig. 6. The free diffusion potential can be calculated to be

$$V_o = \frac{RT}{F} \frac{u_K - u_F}{u_K + u_F} \ln \frac{C^i}{C^o} .$$ (13)

We can use this last expression to analyze the data shown in fig. 5. The ratio 'slope of the theoretical straight line/slope of the experimental straight line' is 0.5. Therefore, from eq. (13), $(U_K - U_F)/(U_K + U_F) = 0.5$, which is satisfied when $U_K/U_F = 3$. Since the value of the potential V_o is only slightly sensitive to changes in external anions (chloride and fluoride), also $U_K/U_{Cl} = 3$.

In summary, we can account for the electrical potential difference measured in axons internally and externally perfused with potassium solutions assuming a homogeneous uncharged membrane selective to potassium. There are evidences presented later on in this section which indicate the presence of a small density of negative sites under conditions of external and internal potassium bathing solutions. Thus, we feel that this treatment does not exclude the possibility of cation selectivity due to the presence of fixed negative charges.

2.2.2. Sign of the charges during current clamp

To study the ionic selectivity of the axon membrane during applied rec-

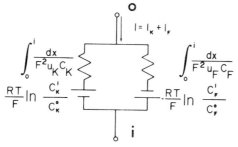

Fig. 6. Equivalent circuit (modified from ref. [19]). o = outside, i = inside.

Table 3
Transport numbers across the axon membrane with potassium as the only internal and external cation

Exp.	a	b	c	d	e	f	$\dfrac{e}{f}$	$1 - \dfrac{e}{f}$
		mV		$\dfrac{\text{pMole}}{\text{cm}^2\text{sec}}$	$\dfrac{\text{pMole}}{\text{cm}^2\text{pulse}}$	t_{Cl^-}	t_{K^+}
TN−6	−58.5	108	+ 9.0	22.6	0.21	2.87	0.07	0.93
	−52.0	90						
TN−9	−60.0	105	+ 8.5	28.8	0.03	0.53	0.06	0.94
	−62.5	108						
TN−17	−58.0	118	+ 11.5	30.8	0.04	2.42	0.02	0.98
	−57.0	90						
TN−18	−60.0	110	+ 9.0	19.6	0.08	2.58	0.03	0.97
	−59.0	108						

(a) Resting potential before (top number) and after (second number) the experiment in external KCl solution. (b) Action potential height before and after experiment in KCl. (c) Resting potential in 550 mM KCl solution. (d) Resting chloride influx. (e) Extra influx of chloride during the current clamp. (f) Integral of the current record divided by the Faraday number. (e/f) Transport number for Cl^- and (1−e/f) Transport number for K^+. The experiments were performed at room temperature of about 17°C.

tangular pulses of current, we measured transport numbers for axons bathing in the 550 mM KCl solution. The experimental procedure is essentially very similar to that outlined above. After measuring a steady state resting influx, current pulses (of different magnitude and duration in different experiments) were applied repetitively over a period of 10 min, enough time to establish a new steady state level of chloride influx, and the extra-influx due to a single pulse of membrane current was calculated and compared to the net ionic flux measured from the current record. In table 3, these transport numbers are given for several axons; it can be seen that chloride is not carrying more than 7% of the current. This indicates that the membrane currents recorded under current clamp conditions are mainly carried by potassium ions and that the membrane is cation selective. The resting flux was measured again after the period under clamp as a control to check the condition of the membrane. Then the external solution was replaced by artificial sea water and resting and action potentials and voltage clamp currents were measured. During the current pulse the membrane potential was positive inside the fiber.

We have seen that both the data on diffusion potentials and on transport numbers indicate that the axon membrane exhibits a significant selectivity towards potassium ions. These results may indicate the presence of negative charges and a selectivity to cations in general.

2.2.3. The charge density

With potassium as the only internal and external cation, membrane currents recorded under voltage clamp conditions are time dependent, both for depolarizations (positive inside the fiber during the pulse) and for hyperpolarizations (negative inside the fiber during the pulse) [7,17]. However, only steady state currents for rectangular pulses of depolarizing and hyperpolarizing voltage are considered here. Fig. 7A shows a comparison between the steady state current-voltage curves measured in K-free ASW and those measured in KCl. The slope of the I−V curve obtained in 550 mM KCl is about 7 mmho/cm^2 for large depolarizations. The slope of the steady state I−V curve obtained in K-free ASW is about 19 mmho/cm^2.

When the internal and external potassium solutions were diluted with isotonic sucrose solution, the conductance for large depolarizations diminished from 7.4 mmho/cm^2, average value measured in 550 mM, to 1.3 mmho/cm^2 average value measured in 10 mM. Our determinations were performed with current electrodes immersed in the potassium solutions on both sides of the

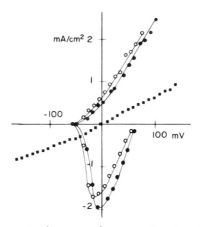

Fig. 7A. Steady state current-voltage curve from axons in external KCl solution in contrast to the I−V curves measured in sea water. (The axon was internally perfused with 550 mM KF solution.) ○ ○ I−V curves in sea water, ■ ■ I−V curve in 550 mM KCl solution, ● ● I−V curves in sea water after the experimental run in KCl solution.

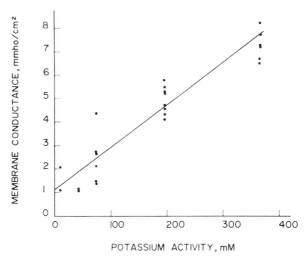

POTASSIUM ACTIVITY, mM

Fig. 7B. Dependence of the steady state membrane conductance on ionic strength with potassium as the only internal and external cation. Each point represents one experiment, externally and internally perfusing with solutions of the same K concentration. Vertical axis represents the membrane steady state conductance (obtained after correcting for the series resistance as described in the text). The ionic strength was lowered in the internal and external K solutions by adding 1 M sucrose solution. Horizontal axis represents the potassium activity in the internal KF solution. The activity values were measured with a potassium electrode and were found to be insensitive to osmotic pressure. The equation of the regression line ($y = ax+b$) drawn is: $G_M = (0.018 \pm 0.001)a_K$ + (1.15 ± 0.31) mmho/cm^2 where the first parenthesis represents average $a \pm$ S.E.$_a$ and the second parenthesis represents average $b \pm$ S.E.$_b$.

axonal membrane (internal, platinum-platinum black plated wire; external, platinum-platinum black plated current electrodes). From these measurements one can only determine total resistance, R_T, of the system. The membrane resistance is the difference $R_T - R_S$, where R_S is the series resistance, or the resistance of the solution between the internal voltage electrode and the axon membrane plus the resistance of the solution between the axon membrane and the external voltage electrode including the Schwann cell layer. The accuracy of the determination of the membrane resistance and therefore membrane conductance as a function of ionic strength hinges on the exact determination of this series resistance. R_S was estimated by either measuring the slope resistance of V–I curves obtained when voltage clamping the solutions without an axon but maintaining the geometry of the system or by measuring the conductivity of the solutions. A detailed description of these methods can be found in previous publications [7].

Fig. 7B shows the membrane conductance (that is to say, conductance of the membrane corrected for the series resistance) as a function of the activity of the potassium ions in the internal KF solution. It can be seen that the membrane conductance decreases linearly with the potassium dilution. The scattering of the data is quite large, perhaps due to differences among axons; however, the effect was also seen in individual axons, which were always tested for various concentrations. This figure also shows the least squares regression straight line:

$$G_M = (0.018 \pm 0.001)a_K + (1.15 \pm 0.31),$$

where the first parenthesis represents average slope $\pm$ S.E. and the second parenthesis represents the intercept $\pm$ S.E. It can be seen that the limiting membrane conductance when the potassium activity tends to zero is 1.15 mmho/cm^2. A simple interpretation of these results is as follows. Fig. 6 illustrates the equivalent circuit for the experimental conditions as two conductances in parallel. One is the potassium conductance and is linearly dependent on potassium activity,

$$G_K = 0.018\,a_K \text{ mmho/cm}^2.$$

The other conductance, called leakage but also carried by potassium, is independent of the external potassium activity,

$$G_L = 1.15 \text{ mmho/cm}^2.$$

The total conductance is the addition of these two conductances in parallel. This interpretation of the experimental results leads to the following conclusions: (i) the potassium conductance system is uncharged, (ii) the leakage conductance system is charged. Assuming a membrane with cylindrical potassium and leakage pores (volume = $\pi r^2 1 \cong 3 \cdot 4$ Å$^2 \cdot 100$ Å $\cong 5000$ Å^3), a proportion of seven uncharged pores to one charged pore (1 e$^-$/5000 Å^3) would account for the conductance results, as one charge per pore makes G_L constant up to 333 mM in the bathing solutions.

2.2.4. Characterization of membrane charges
2.2.4.1. *Effects of magnesium or calcium upon membrane currents and conductance.* The effects of magnesium and calcium upon membrane currents

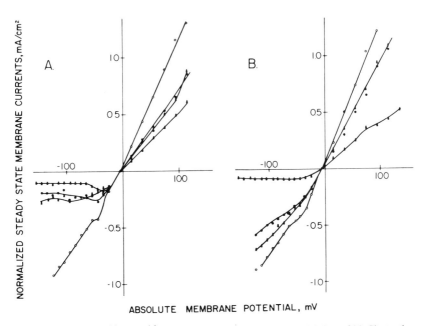

Fig. 8. Effects of Mg^{++} or Ca^{++} upon membrane currents: (A) addition of MgCl$_2$ to the external KCl solution, (B) addition of CaCl$_2$ to the KCl external solution. ○ 10 mM; △ 25 mM; ● 40 mM; ▲ 50 mM.

and conductance were analysed in a previous publication [20]. From this analysis, it was concluded that although the steady state membrane currents are greatly reduced by addition of magnesium or calcium to the external solution, the magnitude of the time dependent component was not changed. It was also suggested that the steady state inward currents are mostly leakage currents.

Control experiments with potassium as the only internal and external cation gave conductances for depolarizing steps ranging from 5.0 to 10.2 mmho/cm^2 (average in 8 experiments ± S.D. was 7.2 mmho/cm^2 ± 1.2). We have normalized the data of experiments with magnesium and calcium to this average slope-conductance. In this way the effects of adding increasing amounts of either calcium or magnesium could be adequately compared. Normalized data of the effects of adding magnesium (A) or calcium (B) are shown in fig. 8. Clearly the net effect is to decrease both depolarizing and hyperpolarizing steady state membrane currents. A possible interpretation of these effects, more pronounced for the inward currents than for the outward currents, is that the divalent cations are adsorbed by negatively charged groups present in the axonal membrane, resulting in neutralization of these charges. Consequently, the number of mobile counter-ions within the membrane is reduced and the steady state conductance decreased.

2.2.4.2. Effects of external pH upon membrane currents and conductance. Ion-exchange membranes are often characterized by studies of the effects of pH on ion-sorption equilibrium [21]. Comparable ion exchange studies on axon membranes are virtually impossible. Some of the relevant information is obtained, however, from an alternative experiment which can be performed on giant axons.

Axons internally and externally bathed in 550 mM K^+ solutions can be exposed to pH changes in the external solutions over a rather large range (at least pH 3.0–8.7). This treatment causes no irreversible changes in the electrophysiological properties of the membrane [7]. The inner side of the axon membrane is rather sensitive to pH changes; internal solutions were maintained at pH 7.2 for all experiments.

Using the voltage clamp procedure, one can impregnate the axon membrane with counter ions (in this case K^+ and H^+) in a few milliseconds by forcing ionic current through it. Ion-exchange equilibrium is achieved when the currents reach a steady state condition. Fig. 9A shows the effect of external pH on steady state I–V curves in axons being perfused internally and externally with 550 mM K^+ solutions. Hyperpolarizing currents are driving counter-ions from the external solution into the membrane, and depolarizing currents are driving counter-ions from the internal solution into the membrane. Three I–V curves are shown in this figure: a control I–V curve for which the pH of the external solution was 7.2 and two experimental I–V curves, in which the external pH was lowered to 3.7 or raised to 8.2. Attention is called to the effects of external pH on steady state currents for hyperpolarizations.

I–V curves were obtained with different axons over a pH range of 3.0 to 8.7. The steady state conductance was measured for hyperpolarizing currents. Fig. 9B represents these conductances as a function of external pH. The conductance versus pH curve, or 'titration curve', shows two sharp inflections, one at pH = 4.5 and the other at pH = 7.5. These inflections suggest that the chemical groups contributing to the fixed charge in the leakage channel are carboxyl and phosphoric groups [22].

294   E.ROJAS, I.ATWATER and F.BEZANILLA

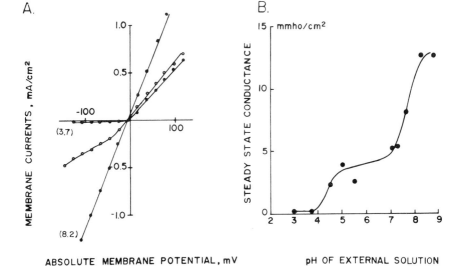

ABSOLUTE MEMBRANE POTENTIAL, mV   pH OF EXTERNAL SOLUTION

Fig. 9. A 'titration curve' of perfused axons in KCl solutions. (A) Effect of external pH
on steady state I–V curves. ○ ○ control I–V curve in KCl measured at pH = 7.2, ● ●
I–V curves in KCl varying the external pH from 7.2 to 3.7 or 8.2. (B) Steady state conductance for hyperpolarizations (corresponding to the currents shown in the lower-left
quadrant of fig. 9A). Each point represents one experiment. Experiments were controlled in sea water before and after exposure to 550 mM KCl solution (measuring resting
and action potentials and membrane currents) and in KCl at pH 7.2 before altering the
external pH (to standardize the data and compare experiments in different axons).

3. Concluding remarks

In summary, our results have led us to a tentative proposal of a fixed
charge structure of the axon membrane. We differentiate three regions of the
membrane, corresponding to the Na and K systems as proposed by Hodgkin
and Huxley [6] and a cation selective leakage system.
   (a) The sodium system is a 'channel' which opens to the internal side of
the membrane in a region with surface negative charges, the density of charges
being about 1 e⁻ every 1600 square Å. A rectangular distribution of the
charges gives a separation of 40 Å; the opening of the 'Na channel' is in the
center of the rectangular array. We think that the outer surface of the region
around the 'Na channel' has no effective charges because calcium and mag-

nesium neutralize any potentially available charges; and in the absence of Ca, the 'Na channel' is inoperative [23].

(b) We propose that the K system is uncharged.

(c) There is a cation selective leakage system, operative at rest as well as during activity, which carries 20 to 30% of the outward current. For a system composed of cylindrical channels of 5000 $Å^3$ volume, we propose 1 e^- per channel.

(a) Chandler et al. [24] studied the dependence of voltage clamp membrane currents on internal ionic strength. They calculated a charge density σ_o of every 700 square Å. Cole [26] has discussed the implications of a uniform versus discrete distribution of surface charges on calculations of ψ_o utilizing the diffuse double layer treatment. He concludes that σ_o evaluated from ψ_o measurements on the assumption of a uniform charge is "about as accurate as is useful at the present time".

Adelman and Taylor [12] lowered the external ionic strength of the sea water and measured the early inward currents. From their data, we find no indication of external fixed charges around the 'Na channel'. Segal [25], by measuring the electrophoretic mobility of axons bathed in sea water, estimated an external charge density of 1 e^- every 80,000 square Å. This very low charge density indicates that the high external divalent cation concentration is neutralizing any potentially available charges.

(b) Adelman and Taylor [12] showed with voltage clamp experiments that the outward potassium currents decreased when the external concentration of sodium was diluted ten times with sucrose. As they were working with intact axons, the internal potassium concentration was presumably unmodified by this treatment. They explained the effect as due to an increase in the sea water resistivity. The increase in convergence resistance at the external opening of the 'K channel' explains the linear decrease in K conductance observed by us as well.

(c) Hodgkin and Huxley [6] defined leakage currents operationally as the time-independent components of the membrane currents. Recently, we have separated and analyzed the leakage and potassium currents for perfused axons bathing in potassium chloride solutions [20]. From that study, we concluded that only the leakage currents were altered by magnesium and calcium added to the external solution and that there was no effect on the time dependent potassium currents (different results, however, were obtained by Gilbert and Ehrenstein [27] on intact axons in KCl solutions).

We think that the leakage currents are carried by both cations and anions. Since we have found that the resting chloride permeability in axons exposed to potassium solutions is almost the same as that in axons in sea water [18] and, since the chloride permeability did not change in the presence of external magnesium or when the external pH was altered, we think that the chloride permeates an uncharged region of the membrane.

Vargas [28] has estimated a fixed charge density of 10 mEq within the membrane by measuring streaming potentials and streaming currents in perfused axons with internal and external potassium solutions. (Considering the potassium and leakage systems together, our data [7] gives a similar value, 40 mEq, for the net negative charge density.) Vargas used the approach developed by Schmid and Schwarz [13,14] which assumes a system of charged pores in the membrane. He explained the low density of charges as possibly due to a heterogeneous pore system. Our proposal of two potassium systems, charged (leakage) and uncharged, is a heterogeneous system which can explain his and our results.

References

[1] P.F.Baker, A.L.Hodgkin and H.Meves, J. Physiol. 164 (1962) 355.
[2] T.Narahashi, J. Physiol. 169 (1963) 91.
[3] P.F.Baker, A.L.Hodgkin and H.Meves, J. Physiol. 170 (1964) 541.
[4] J.W.Moore, T.Narahashi and W.Ulbricht, J. Physiol. 172 (1964) 163.
[5] W.K.Chandler, A.L.Hodgkin and H.Meves, J. Physiol. 180 (1965) 821.
[6] A.L.Hodgkin and A.F.Huxley, J. Physiol. 116 (1952) 473.
[7] E.Rojas and I.Atwater, J. Gen. Physiol. 51 (1968) 131s.
[8] D.Goldman, J. Gen. Physiol. 27 (1943) 37.
[9] A.L.Hodgkin and G.Katz, J. Physiol. 108 (1949) 32.
[10] J.T.G.Overbeek and J.Lijklema, in: Electrophoresis, Theory, Methods and Applications, ed. M.Bier (Academic Press, New York, 1959).
[11] D.A.Haydon, in: Recent Progress in Surface Science, eds. J.F.Danielli, K.G.A. Pankhurst and A.C.Riddiford (Academic Press, New York, 1959) vol. 1.
[12] W.J.Adelman and R.E.Taylor, Biophys. J. 4 (1964) 451.
[13] G.Schmid and H.Schwarz, Z. Elektrochem. 55 (1951) 295.
[14] G.Schmid and H.Schwarz, Z. Elektrochem. 56 (1952) 35.
[15] T.Teorell, Z. Elektrochem. 55 (1951) 460.
[16] R.Schlögl, Z. Physik. Chem. 1 (1954) 305.
[17] E.Rojas and G.Ehrenstein, J. Cellular Comp. Physiol. 66 (1965) 71.
[18] R.D.Keynes, J. Physiol. 169 (1963) 690.
[19] A.Finkelstein and A.Mauro, Biophys. J. 3 (1963) 215.
[20] E.Rojas, R.E.Taylor, I.Atwater and F.Bezanilla, J. Gen. Physiol. 53 (1969) 532.
[21] F.Helfferich, Ion Exchange (McGraw-Hill, New York, 1962).
[22] E.Rojas and J.M.Tobias, Biochim. Biophys. Acta 94 (1965) 394.
[23] B.Frankenhaeuser and A.L.Hodgkin, J. Physiol. 137 (1957) 218.
[24] W.K.Chandler, A.L.Hodgkin and H.Meves, J. Physiol. 180 (1965) 821.
[25] J.R.Segal, Biophys. J. 8 (1968) 470.

[26] K.Cole, Biophys. J. 9 (1969) 465.
[27] D.L.Gilbert and G.Ehrenstein, Biophys. J. 9 (1969) 447.
[28] F.Vargas, J. Gen. Physiol. 51 (1968) 1235.

ENTROPY CHANGES IN NERVE MEMBRANES

J.M.RITCHIE

Department of Pharmacology, Yale University School of Medicine,
New Haven, Connecticut

The earliest attempts to measure the heat production associated with the passage of a single impulse in nerve [1] were unsuccessful because of the lack of sufficiently sensitive recording instruments. However, it became clear during the decade after 1925 (see Feng [2]) that soon after the passage of a single nerve impulse in crustacean nerve there was a rise in nerve temperature of about $2\mu°C$, which was followed by slower evolution of recovery heat. Further experiments by Abbott et al. [3] revealed that the initial rise was really much greater: there was in fact a rise in temperature of $10\mu°C$, which was followed almost immediately by a phase of reabsorption of heat. The rise of $2\mu°C$ observed in the earlier experiments was thus the net temperature rise produced by two opposing phases of initial heat production. Subsequent work on the non-myelinated fibres of the rabbit cervical vagus nerve [4,5] has shown that the initial positive heat is associated with the depolarizing phase of the action potential while the initial negative heat is associated with the phase of repolarization. The reason for the continuing interest in nerve heat production has been the hope that measurement of such thermal changes might throw some light on the molecular basis of the nerve impulse. For example, any gross conformational change associated with the spike might well be associated with thermal changes.

One major factor limiting knowledge of the thermal events in nerve lies in the smallness of the temperature changes that occur; for after a single stimulus to rabbit nerve the temperature rises by less than $5\mu°C$. The thermopiles currently available have sensitivities of about 5000 μV per °C. This means that the output resulting from the passage of a single action potential along a nerve laid on top of a thermopile is about 50×10^{-9} V, which is several orders of magnitude smaller than can be recorded on conventional amplifiers. Signals of this size can, however, be recorded by the use of a galvanometer/ photocell amplifier (see Hill [6]). But such an instrument is necessarily slow; and the thermal events in nerve can be recorded reliably only if they are slowed

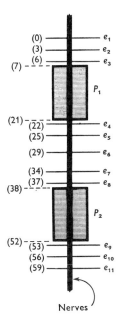

Fig. 1. Diagram of thermopile. The numbers in brackets indicate the distance in mm of
the various electrodes from e_1.

down to match the slowness of this system, by cooling the preparation. The
thermopile used most recently to record the temperature changes in the non-
myelinated fibres of the rabbit cervical vagus nerve is shown diagrammatically
in fig. 1. It consisted of two recording elements each 14 mm long. Eight desheathed cervical vagus nerves, each of which was 70–80 mm long, were
mounted along the mid-line of the thermopile. Electrodes e_2, e_5, e_7 and e_{10}
were usually used as stimulating cathodes.

When a train of impulses (20 impulses, 2.5/sec) is applied to the nerve, a
long-lasting rise in the temperature of the nerve occurs (fig. 2N). This rise in
temperature reaches a maximum soon after stimulation and returns to its
original value over the next few minutes. A small part of this heat is stimulus
artifact; for the electric currents used to stimulate the nerve produce heat,
which gradually diffuses along the nerve to the thermopile. The contribution
of this artifact to the records can be gauged by applying the same stimulating
procedure to a preparation rendered inexcitable by isotonic potassium chloride (fig. 2, KCl). The total heat production, after allowance for the stimulus
heat, is largely the heat associated with the recovery processes in the nerve.

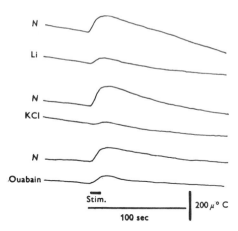

Fig. 2. The total heat production (initial heat plus recovery heat) in the non-myelinated fibres of a rabbit desheathed cervical vagus nerve at 21°C after 20 shocks at intervals of 400 msec. The records labeled *N* were taken in ordinary Locke solution. Interpolated between these records are the responses obtained after the nerve had been equilibrated in: a solution in which all the sodium chloride had been replaced by lithium chloride (Li); a Locke solution in which all the sodium chloride had been replaced by potassium chloride (KCl); and a Locke solution containing 1 mM ouabain.

Thus, it is reduced or abolished when the sodium of the Locke solution has been replaced by lithium (fig. 2, Li) or when the nerve has been exposed to 1 mm ouabain (fig. 2, ouabain).

The total heat production associated with a single stimulus is about 100 μcal/g i.e. about 420 μjoule/g [5,7]. Measurement of the extra oxygen consumption associated with an impulse in these same nerves is about 900 pmole/g·impulse [8], which would correspond with a value of about 420 μjoule/g·impulse if the utilization of each litre of oxygen were associated with the evolution of 20,900 joule (i.e. 5000 cal). Furthermore, the time course of decay of the total heat production is roughly the same as the time course of decay of the extra oxygen consumption with stimulation [8,9] and as the time course of decay of the post-tetanic hyperpolarization [10], which reflects the activity of the electrogenic sodium pump in these fibres. It is clear, therefore, that the total heat production largely represents the recovery heat production in these nerves.

The changes in temperature that *immediately* follow a single impulse are much smaller than the recovery heat changes just described. Indeed, the deflexion in the experimental records produced by these initial heat changes is barely detectable above the random noise in the recording system. How-

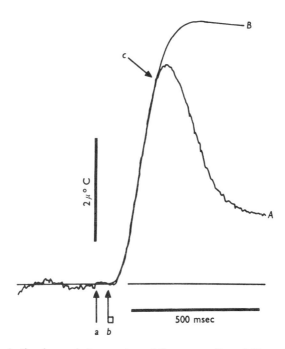

Fig. 3. Curve A: the changes in temperature of the non-myelinated fibres of a rabbit
desheathed vagus nerve at 4.2°C in response to a single maximal shock 2 msec in duration applied at a. The record is the result of averaging twenty records electronically.
Curve B: The rise in temperature of the same nerve, after it had been rendered inexcitable by isotonic potassium chloride, in response to a block of heat (twenty-one 200
μsec pulses of current applied between the two ends of the nerve at 1 msec intervals)
beginning at b. The amplification for B was adjusted to make the early part of the rising
phase of B coincide with the early part of curve A.

ever, by suitable averaging techniques (using a CAT computer) 20–40 single
records can be averaged with a consequent improvement in the signal/noise
ratio. Such experiments show that soon after a single stimulus is applied to a
desheathed rabbit vagus nerve (a, fig. 3) the temperature of the nerve rises to a
maximum and then declines (curve A). That this decline in nerve temperature
really corresponds with an absorption of heat, and is not due to the passive
characteristics of the recording system, is shown by the following experiment:
the preparation was rendered inexcitable by exposing it to isotonic potassium
chloride. It was then briefly heated, for the period indicated by the flag at b
(fig. 3), by passing twenty-one 200 μsec pulses of current at 1 msec intervals

between the two ends of the nerve. Because of the electrical heating, the nerve temperature quickly rose to a maximum, from which it slowly declined as the heat was conducted away to the sides of the thermopile (curve B). Had the active nerve only produced positive heat, the record that would have been obtained should have followed a similar time course. The fact that the record from the active nerve (curve A) eventually fell markedly below the heating control (curve B) means that heat re-absorption must have taken place. Furthermore, the point at which the two curves deviated, which is marked by the arrow, c, in fig. 3, must have corresponded with the time of onset of the negative heat. The arrow b indicates the time of the positive heat.

The heating control (curve B) gives the record that would have been obtained in response to a 20 msec block of heat applied at b. The true time course of the heat production in the nerve that gave rise to curve A can be obtained using this heating control to perform a 'heat block' analysis. Such an analysis can either be performed manually, using the method described by Hill [11], or by a computer [5]. The results obtained with the different methods of analysis are in close agreement with each other (fig. 4): at about 5°C there is a mean positive initial heat of 30 μjoule/g·impulse of which 20 μjoule/g·impulse is soon re-absorbed.

The first clear suggestion that the two phases of initial heat might be related temporally to the depolarizing and repolarizing phases of the action potential came from experiments in which the shape of the action potential was altered by various pharmacological procedures. The extreme left-hand record in fig. 5 shows the shape of the compound action potential in the non-myelinated fibres of the rabbit vagus nerve bathed in normal Locke solution at 6°C. The middle record shows the shape of the compound action potential of the same preparation shortly after it had been soaked in a Locke solution from which the potassium had been removed. Finally, the extreme right-hand record shows the action potential obtained from another nerve (whose action potential was originally similar to that of the right-hand record) after it had soaked in a Locke solution in which 92.4 mM sodium chloride had been replaced by 70.2 mM barium chloride. Clearly, in the potassium-free solution there is a marked positive after-potential (see Ritchie [12]), whereas in the barium solution both the size and duration of the compound action potential are markedly prolonged [13]. A potassium-free solution thus enhances the phase of repolarization, whereas the barium solution greatly slows it. If the two phases of initial heat really correspond closely with the two phases of the action potential, the compound thermal response in these two solutions ought to resemble the form of the compound action potential. Figs. 6 and 7 show that this is indeed the case. When the response of a preparation in po-

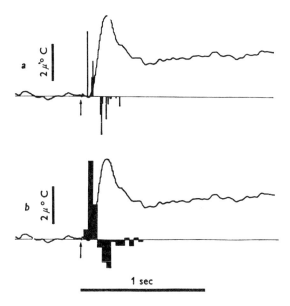

Fig. 4. Analysis of the initial heat production of the non-myelinated fibres of a rabbit desheathed vagus nerve at 5.3°C in response to a single shock applied at the arrow. Superimposed on the experimental record are: a, the result of a conventional heat block analysis using an analysis time of 10 msec (upper record); b, the result of a computer analysis and an analysis time of 40 msec (see Howarth et al. [5]).

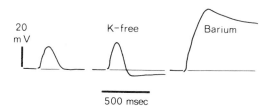

Fig. 5. Records of compound action potentials of the non-myelinated fibres of a rabbit desheathed vagus nerve. The left-hand record was taken before, and the middle record after, the preparation had soaked in potassium-free Locke solution. The right-hand record was taken from another preparation, whose action potential was initially similar to that of the extreme left-hand record, after it had soaked in a solution in which 70.2 mM barium chloride had replaced 92.4 mM sodium chloride. The temperature was about 6°C.

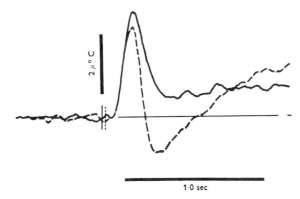

Fig. 6. The effect of removing external potassium on the initial heat production of the non-myelinated fibres of a rabbit desheathed vagus nerve at 5.1°C in response to a single shock applied at the short vertical bar. The response in a potassium-free Locke solution (interrupted line) has been superimposed on the response in ordinary Locke solution.

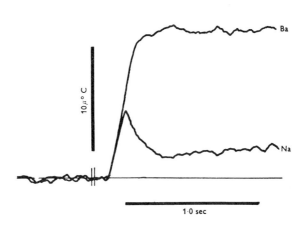

Fig. 7. The effect of barium on the initial heat production of the non-myelinated fibres of a rabbit desheathed vagus nerve 6°C in response to a single shock applied at the short vertical bar. A response in a modified Locke solution in which 70.2 mM barium chloride replaced 92.4 mM sodium chloride (Ba) has been superimposed on the control response in ordinary Locke solution (Na) taken shortly beforehand.

tassium-free solution (broken line, fig. 6) is super-imposed on the response in ordinary Locke solution (solid line, fig. 6) it is clear that there is little difference in the initial positive heat but that the initial negative heat is greatly enhanced. Indeed, this latter phase may be so enhanced that the preparation actually becomes *cooler* than its initial temperature. Fig. 7 shows the effect of barium on the initial heat production of the mammalian non-myelinated fibres in response to single shocks. Clearly, the rate of positive heat production is initially unaffected by this procedure; for the rising phases of the temperature records from both the normal and the barium treated nerves are the same and almost exactly super-imposed. The temperature record in the barium treated nerve, however, continues to rise to a rather flat plateau; and the phase of negative heat production seems to be largely abolished.

The close correspondence between the thermal and electrical records in these experiments thus strongly supports the hypothesis that the initial heat is closely linked temporally to the action potential. Further evidence for this hypothesis comes from experiments in which the form of the compound thermal response has been synthesized on the basis of the electrical records and compared with the experimentally obtained thermal responses [5]. The procedure, which is more fully described by Howarth et al. [5], suggests that after a latent period of 33 msec for nerves at about 5°C positive heat production would begin and would continue for about 80 msec. There would then be a silent period, during which no further heat change occurs; this period would end about 130 msec after the stimulus when a period of heat re-absorption lasting about 170 msec would begin. These predicted values, both for the onset of the two phases of initial heat and for their duration, were found to agree excellently with the values obtained by direct analysis of the thermal records [5].

When such a comparison between the synthetic and the actual experimental thermal responses is carried out at a series of different temperatures, the agreement is again good. For example, the solid line in fig. 8 shows the relationship between temperature and the time of onset of the negative heat in rabbit C fibres that would be predicted from the electrical experiments. The experimental points obtained in a series of different preparations at different temperatures (i.e. corresponding with *c* in fig. 3) are given by the closed circles. Clearly, the correspondence between prediction and theory is close over the whole range of temperature examined (0–15°C).

Because the thermal response is measured over a length of nerve on the thermopile rather than at a single point, and because of temporal dispersion, there is a considerable degree of cancelling out of the positive and negative heats in the different fibres. Indeed, the synthesis of the thermal response

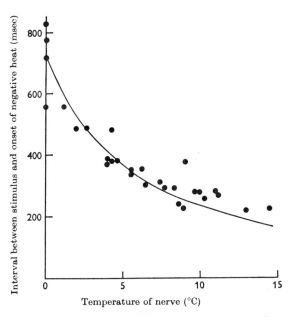

Fig. 8. The relationship between temperature and the measured time of onset of the negative heat in the non-myelinated nerve fibres of a rabbit desheathed vagus nerve. The continuous line is the corresponding relationship predicted from electrical measurements on the basis of the condenser theory.

from the electrical record suggests that at 5°C the overlap effect reduces the peak temperature rise by a factor of 3.4 [5]. This means that at 5°C the true value of the positive initial heat is about 102 μjoule/g·impulse; the negative initial heat, which is 10 μjoule/g·impulse less, is thus 92 μjoule/g·impulse.

What is the origin of these heats? One possibility that was discussed by Abbott et al. [3] is that the initial heat is generated by the interchange of ions between the external bathing solution and the axoplasm. In mammalian non-myelinated fibres the ionic interchange during a single impulse is about 12.2×10^{-9} moles/g [5]. Thus, a positive heat of 102 μjoule/g is equivalent to about 8000 joule/mole. This seems to exclude the heat of ionic mixing as a possible explanation of the observed temperature changes; for the heat of mixing of NaCl, KCl or LiCl with each other in pairs never amounts to more than a few joules per mole [5, table 11].

Probably the simplest explanation for the origin of the positive and nega-tive initial heats is the condenser theory first considered by Hill in 1932. According to this theory the positive heat represents the Joule heat liberated in the nerve by the electric currents that discharge the membrane capacity during the depolarization phase of the action potential, while the negative heat results from storage of the same quantity of energy in the capacity during repolarization at the expense of some of the thermal energy of the ions in the external solution. In the earlier experiments on crab nerve [3] there was an awkward discrepancy in the timing of the negative heat, which seemed to occur rather too late to fit in with the down-stroke of the action potential. However, this may have been caused by the nature of the electrical recordings in these experiments, which could have given a misleading impression of the contribution to the heat made by the smallest and most slowly conducting fibres. Certainly, in the later experiments on rabbit nerve described above this discrepancy disappeared, so that the critical question that remains is whether or not the condenser theory can account for the *size* of the heat.

It is difficult to calculate exactly the free energy stored in the membrane capacity (which would be available for Joule heating on discharge) because the values for the membrane capacity and voltage are not known for certain. However, calculation based on a value of 0.9 $\mu F/cm^2$ given by Straub [14] for the membrane capacity and on a value of 6000 cm^2 for the area of membrane in a gram of vagus nerve [15], gives a value for the positive heat released by discharging the membrane of $(27 \times 10^{-4})V^2$ μjoule/g, where V is the size of the resting potential in millivolts. The resting potential in this preparation is unlikely to be greater than the potassium equilibrium potential, which was estimated by Keynes and Ritchie [15] to be 82 mV at 20°C; this yields a positive heat of 18 μjoule/g. Another approach is to assume that the extra leakage of potassium ions out of the fibres during stimulation can be equated with the charge in the membrane capacity. At 5°C the potassium movement is 12.2×10^{-9} moles/g·impulse [5], so that the corresponding heat for a resting potential of 82 mV is 48 μjoule/g. Both these values, which give *upper* limits to the free energy released when the membrane capacity is discharged, are considerably less than the amount of heat obtained experimentally, which was 102 μjoule/g.

This discrepancy between the calculated and observed heats, however, does not mean that the condenser theory has to be rejected. The main objection to the condenser theory in the crude form originally discussed (e.g. Abbott et al. [3]) is that no account was taken of the entropy changes that must occur in the dielectric of the condenser during the charging and discharging processes. It has been pointed out by Gurney [16] that such entropy changes may be far from negligible in comparison with the free energy changes involved. Thus, the change in enthalpy (ΔH) on discharging a con-

denser of capacity C at a temperature T may differ considerably from the
free energy change (ΔF) of $\frac{1}{2}CV^2$ by an amount $T\Delta S$, which is equal to
$\Delta F(T/C)(\mathrm{d}C/\mathrm{d}T)$.

A particular good discussion of this point is that of Gurney [16] who has
shown that when a condenser with a dielectric constant ϵ is discharged the
heat that is released is increased above, or decreased below, the amount de-
rived from the change in free energy by an amount $\Delta F(T/\epsilon)(\mathrm{d}\epsilon/\mathrm{d}T)$ depending on whether $\mathrm{d}\epsilon/\mathrm{d}T$ is positive or negative. For many liquids $\mathrm{d}\epsilon/\mathrm{d}T$ is negative, so that the total heat released is less than that predicted from the energy
change; for example, water at 20°C has a value of 80 for ϵ and a temperature
coefficient $\mathrm{d}\epsilon/\mathrm{d}T$ of -0.37. This means that $T\Delta S = 1.36\ \Delta F$; and when a condenser with water as its dielectric is discharged, a quantity of heat equal to
1.36 times the free energy released is absorbed by the dielectric giving rise to
an appreciable net cooling. However, $\mathrm{d}\epsilon/\mathrm{d}T$ need not necessarily be negative.
Indeed, it can be negative, zero, or positive depending on the temperature
at which it is measured. Fig. 9, which is taken from Fröhlich [17], shows that
in general $\mathrm{d}\epsilon/\mathrm{d}T$ is zero near the absolute zero of temperature; and that as the
temperature increases from zero it is first positive, and then becomes negative
at temperatures above a certain critical temperature. Below this critical temperature electrical polarization of the dielectric increases its entropy (S, fig. 9);
above this temperature, polarization decreases the entropy. Water at room
temperature is operating on the right-hand side of fig. 9, $\mathrm{d}\epsilon/\mathrm{d}T$ being negative.
However, oriented films of lipid in biological membranes seem to differ in this
respect from water. For films of glycerol mono-oleate plus n-decane have a
positive temperature coefficient for the dielectric constant (see Howarth et al.
[5]) and these films thus behave like crystalline materials in general, which
operate on the left-hand side of fig. 9.

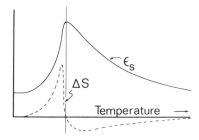

Fig. 9. The variation of dielectric constant, ϵ, with temperature. The broken line shows
the increase in entropy (S) associated with electrical polarization of the dielectric (modi-
field from Fröhlich [17]).

In general, and whatever the cause of the dependence of the membrane capacity on temperature, extra heat equal to $\Delta F(T/C)(dC/dT)$ is produced when a capacity C is discharged if dC/dT is positive. What is the situation in nerve? In squid giant axons there is evidence [18] that the temperature coefficient for the dielectric constant is indeed positive. Thus, defining the complex capacity of the membrane C, by $Z_c = (jC)^{-1}$ where $C = C_1 - jC_2$, it was found that, between 4 and 22°C and over the frequency range 10–70 kc/s, $C_1 = 0.62\ (1 + 0.0073\ T)$ and $C_2 = 0.145\ (1 + 0.023\ T)$. For C_1, which is probably the more important component of the capacity for the present argument, the ratio $T\Delta S/\Delta F$ at 5°C is therefore +2.0. If the membrane capacity in rabbit vagal nerve fibres has a similar temperature dependence, it would be predicted that the total warming on discharge would be about three times the energy stored in the condenser. It is interesting, therefore, that the actual heat observed, 102 μjoule/g, is indeed nearly three times the mean value of the two estimates of the free energy released when the membrane capacity is discharged, which is about 33 μjoule/g.

But although the total heat produced is much larger than the free energy change, the entropy change responsible is still comparatively small. Thus, taking the area occupied by each phospholipid molecule in the membrane to be about 50×10^{-16} cm^2, one can calculate that the number of phospholipid molecules in 1 g of nerve (containing 6000 cm^2 of membrane) is about 2×10^{-6} grammolecules. A positive heat of 102 μjoules/g therefore corresponds to about 50 joule/mole phospholipid. With a resting potential of 40 mV, the electric field across a structure less than 10^{-6} cm in thickness is over 40,000 V/cm; when such a large field collapses, so small an entropy change can hardly be regarded as improbable.

What is the absolute size of the decrease in entropy that occurs on discharge of the membrane capacity? At 5°C a lower limit to the extent of this decrease per impulse, obtained using the upper limit of 48 μjoule/g·impulse for the free energy change, is (102–48)/278 i.e. 0.20 μjoule/g·degree: the upper limit, obtained by taking the free energy change to be zero, is 102/278 i.e. 0.37 μjoule/g·degree. These changes are small even when related to the weight of the nerve membrane rather than to the weight of the whole nerve. For the average cross-sectional area of a non-myelinated fibre in the rabbit vagus nerve is 0.292×10^{-8} cm^2 [15, p. 355] and the average length of the perimeter is 2.36×10^{-4} cm [15, p. 354]. Allowing for the fact that only one quarter of the nerve is occupied by non-myelinated fibres [15, p. 354–355], and taking the thickness of the membrane to be 10^{-6} cm, one can calculate that the fraction of the whole nerve occupied by C fibre membrane is $\frac{1}{4} \times (2.36 \times 10^{-4} \times 10^{-6})/(0.292 \times 10^{-8})$ i.e. 0.02. Thus at 5°C the entropy

change per gram of *membrane* per impulse is between 10 and 18.5 μjoule/
degree. At a higher temperature, although the information is less complete,
the above calculation can still be made. At about $15°C$ the observed positive
heat is reduced by a factor of about 2 [5, fig. 7] and the overlap factor is
about the same as at the lower temperature [5, table 10]; the true positive
heat (per gram of nerve) is thus about 51 μjoule/impulse. The ionic flux required to discharge the capacity may also have been reduced, to about 0.6 of
its value at $5°C$ [5, p. 771]. The upper limit for the free energy change is
thus about 29 μjoule/g·impulse; the lower limit is, of course, zero. This means
that there is still an entropy decrease; but it is smaller than at the lower temperature, lying between 0.079 and 0.184 μjoule/g·degree. Thus at $15°C$ the
entropy change per impulse per gram of *membrane* amounts to between 4.0
and 9.2 μjoule/degree.

The large size of the initial heat is thus postulated to be a direct consequence of an appropriate change during the action potential. The order
of magnitude of this change, and its direction, have been determined in the
preceding paragraphs on the basis of the discrepancy between the observed
heat changes (the enthalpy) and the calculated free energy changes. That the
entropy of the membrane does in fact increase on its being polarized, as is
required by the hypothesis, might seemingly have been more simply established by another, more general, argument than that used above. For the entropy increase ΔS on polarizing the membrane capacity is equal to minus
$d(\Delta F)/dT$. Thus one could have predicted an entropy decrease on discharging the membrane capacity, and a consequent evolution of extra heat, if the
temperature coefficient of the free energy change could be shown to be negative. However, the critical question concerning the variation of the free energy with temperature, although simple to formulate, is difficult to answer. If
the *upper* limits to this free energy that were calculated above, did in fact
represent the actual free energy changes, the average value of $d(\Delta F)/dT$ in
the range $5-15°C$ would be $(29-48)/10$ μjoule/degree i.e. -1.9 μjoule/degree.
The coefficient is thus negative and a decrease in entropy on discharge is
indicated. Thus, at $10°C$ (the mid-point of the range temperatures) there
would be an extra warming on discharge of 1.9×283 μjoule/g·impulse, very
much greater than that derived from the free energy change, which would be
about 40 μjoule/g·impulse. But this argument is insecure because the upper
limits used in the calculation are certainly different from the actual changes.
Thus some of the potassium that leaves the fibres on stimulation, particularly
at the lower temperature when the duration of the action potential is large,
may exchange with sodium (or move with an anion) and so does not contribute to the current discharging the membrane; and, furthermore, the mem-

brane potential may be as little as half the potassium equilibrium potential [5]. The simplicity of the second approach is thus tempered by the patent unreliability of the calculation. For this reason the more restricted argument used earlier, which is based on the temperature dependence of the membrane capacity, still provides the best framework for discussing the entropy changes in nerve membrane.

References

[1] H.Helmholtz, Arch. Anat. Physiol. (1848) 144−164.
[2] T.P.Feng, Ergeb. Physiol. Biol. Chem. Exptl. Pharmakol. 38 (1936) 73−132.
[3] B.C.Abbott, A.V.Hill and J.V.Howard, Proc. Roy. Soc. (London) Ser. B 148 (1958) 149−187.
[4] R.D.Keynes and J.M.Ritchie, in: Nerve as a Tissue (Harper and Row, New York, 1965).
[5] J.V.Howarth, R.D.Keynes and J.M.Ritchie, J. Physiol. 194 (1968) 745−793.
[6] A.V.Hill, J. Sci. Instr. 25 (1948) 225−229.
[7] J.V.Howarth, R.D.Keynes and J.M.Ritchie, J. Physiol. 186 (1966) 40−42P.
[8] J.M.Ritchie, J. Physiol. 188 (1967) 309−329.
[9] H.P.Rang and J.M.Ritchie, J. Physiol. 196 (1968) 163−181.
[10] H.P.Rang and J.M.Ritchie, J. Physiol. 196 (1968) 183−221.
[11] A.V.Hill, Trails and Trials in Physiology (Edward Arnold, London, 1965).
[12] J.M.Ritchie, in: Biophysics of Physiological and Pharmacological Actions (American Association for the Advancement of Science, Washington, D.C., 1961) pp. 165−182.
[13] C.J.Armett and J.M.Ritchie, J. Physiol. 165 (1963) 130−140.
[14] R.W.Straub, Pflügers Arch. ges. Physiol. 278 (1963) 108−109.
[15] R.D.Keynes and J.M.Ritchie, J. Physiol. 179 (1965) 333-367.
[16] R.W.Gurney, Ionic Processes in Solution (Dover, New York, 1962).
[17] H.Fröhlich, Theory of dielectrics (Oxford University Press, London, 1958).
[18] R.E.Taylor and W.K.Chandler, Biophys. Soc. Abstracts (1962) TD1.

BIREFRINGENCE CHANGES IN
ACTIVE CELL MEMBRANES

Bertil HILLE

*Department of Physiology and Biophysics, School of Medicine,
University of Washington, Seattle, Washington, USA*

1. Introduction

Recently electronic signal averaging computers have been used to detect
small changes in the optical properties of nerves and electroplates concurrent
with electrical activity. Changes in the birefringence and light scattering of the
tissue and changes in the fluorescence of bound dyes have been recorded
[3–6,21,22]. Of these the birefringence may be the easiest to interpret as it
relates most simply to the organization of the tissue.

2. Method

The tissue lies between crossed polarizers in an intense beam of light and
is oriented at 45° with respect to the plane of polarization of the light. Because of its birefringence, the axon appears bright against the dark back-
ground (fig. 1). The light from the axon is averaged over enough stimuli to
give a clear picture of any signal. Errors in the birefringence signal introduced
by changes in the light absorption or linear dichroism of the tissue or by electrical and mechanical artifacts are controlled for by optical tests with birefringent plates. True birefringence signals reverse completely when the resting
birefringence of the tissue is overcompensated by the plate. Other signals are
discarded.

3. The characteristics of the signal

The results with nerves from walking legs of crabs, with squid giant axons,
and with electroplates of the electric eel are similar. During the depolarizing

0.5 mm

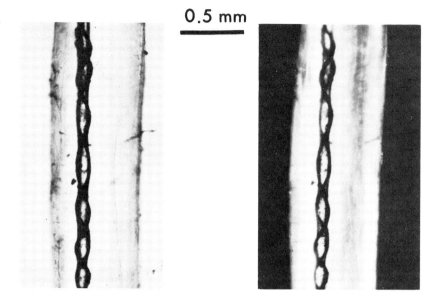

Fig. 1. A squid giant axon with axial wire electrode in polarized light. On the left the analyzer is parallel to the polarizer. On the right it is rotated 90° to show the birefringence of the axon.

phase of the action potential, the net birefringence of squid axons and crab nerves decreases and that of electroplates increases (fig. 2a). The time course of the optical changes always resembles the time course of the membrane potential changes whether these are due to propagating action potentials, locally stimulated action potentials, hyperpolarizing current pulses, or voltage clamp steps [3,6,22]. In the squid giant axon under voltage clamp, the optical signal is unaltered when all the external sodium ion is replaced by choline or when the axon is anesthetized with procaine or butanol [4].

The large size of the squid axon permits analysis of the light gathered from different parts of the axon in the field of the microscope. The edge of the fiber gives the largest optical change and the center gives none at all. Furthermore, replacing most of the axoplasm with a salt solution does not interfere with the birefringence change [6]. These tests demonstrate that the change is a birefringence increase with a radial optic axis that arises somewhere in the region of the axon membrane or the sheath. The very close correspondence between the membrane potential and the optical signal in three tissues and the absence of a sheath in electroplates virtually assures that the birefringence change arises at the excitable membrane.

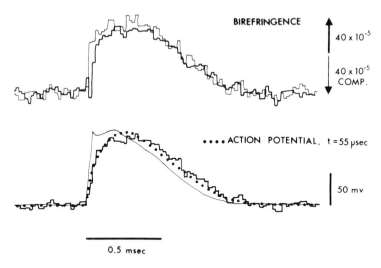

Fig. 2. Birefringence changes during the action potential in the main electric organ of
Electrophorus electricus. Top: The time course of the light intensity without (thick line)
and with (thin line) an overcompensating birefringent plate. The compensated record is
inverted for comparison. Bottom: The action potential before (smooth line) and after
(dots) delaying it with a 55 μsec exponential time constant compared with the averaged
light intensity (stepped line). The light measuring circuit had a time constant of 18 μsec.
Temperature 26°C [3].

The optical signal always lags behind the voltage changes more than can
be explained by instrumental time constants. The extra delay is equivalent to
an exponential time constant of 37 μsec in an electric organ at 26°C (fig. 2b)
[3]. The equivalent time constant with a squid axon is about 40 μsec at 6°C
and less than 10 μsec at 21°C. In the squid giant axon the relationship between membrane potential and birefringence is also nonlinear. The birefringence varies approximately as the square of the potential but with the minimum of the curve lying at +100 mV (absolute) [4].

Two agents, tetrodotoxin and saxitoxin, strongly affect the birefringence
changes of squid axons. At 100 mM concentration they more than double the
amplitude of the optical response to steps of voltage, and they lengthen the
time constant to more than 1 msec. These dramatic effects develop only some
minutes after the specific reduction of sodium permeability caused by the
toxins, and although the sodium permeability returns when the toxin solution
is washed away, the optical responses remain modified [4,6].

4. The mechanism of the change

The birefringence change seems to arise from an effect of the electric field on the membrane. Whereas the birefringence (difference between the principal refractive indices) of the membranes of red blood cells and of myelin is about 10^{-2} [15,19], the change during the action potential in a squid axon is only 10^{-5} to 10^{-4} (referred to a membrane 35 Å thick) [6]. Hence a very small change of the membrane structure could account for the observed effects. Two explanations can be suggested. The electric field may align anisotropic molecules as in Kerr electric birefringence, or the mutually attracting ionic double layers may compress the membrane altering its intrinsic and form birefringence.

4.1. Kerr effect

The physics of the Kerr effect is relatively well understood [2,14]. Electric birefringence develops as rapidly as molecules can rotate and varies with the square of the electric field up to the saturation point where the orientation becomes complete. The effect is larger for more anisotropic molecules and increases as the square of the dipole moment of the molecules. The field needed for saturation varies inversely as the dipole moment.

The Kerr effect could explain the voltage dependence of the birefringence of the membrane, if it is also assumed that the membrane is asymmetrical or internally biased by some local potentials. Were the membrane made of water, changing the potential from -100 mV to 0 mV would give a radial birefringence decrease of 0.5×10^{-4} in much less than a nanosecond. The effect would not saturate in fields less than 10^6 V/cm. The magnitude fits well, but, of course, the membrane is not made of water and the time constant and sign are wrong. The ineffectiveness of procaine and butanol suggests that molecular reorientation within the lipid regions may contribute little to the birefringence changes. Furthermore nonpolar molecules have very small Kerr effects. However, some protein molecules exhibit Kerr effects so large [23] that even a small amount of protein at the inner or outer surface of the membrane could suffice to explain the observations.

The Kerr effect in liquid water develops over 10^5 times faster than the changes in the membrane. The relaxation of bound water and of protein side chains takes only a few nanoseconds, and the rotation of small proteins in solution occurs in tens of nanoseconds [9,12,20]. Theoretically a sphere 500 Å in diameter could reorient with a time constant of 40 μsec in water [8]. The Kerr effect of hemocyanin aggregates has time constants in this range [17]. However, such structures seem too large to be part of the membrane. Thus free rotation in an aqueous environment probably does not explain the observations. We are left with the possibility that there are smaller proteins rotating in an extremely viscous environment or that there is a conformational change rather than a rotation. Conformational changes in ribonuclease have time constants near 100 μsec at 25°C and a large temperature coefficient [10].

4.2. Compression of the membrane

Charging a membrane of 1 μF/cm^2 capacity to 100 mV would lower the surface energy by 5×10^{-3} erg/cm^2 and generate a pressure of 0.1 atmosphere on the membrane. The pressure is proportional to the square of the voltage. Black lipid films may serve as a model. Step pulses of 100 mV rapidly increase the area [13] and the specific capacitance of black films [1,18,24]. The first effect arises from the lowered surface tension and the second from the compression of the membrane. After a long pulse the thickness probably decreases by 1–5% (cf. Haydon in this volume).

There have been no studies of the mechanical effects of voltage on biological membranes, except for Cole and Curtis's [7] search for capacity changes during activity in squid giant axons. The 2% decrease which they found at the peak of the action potential was almost indistinguishable from no change in their system. If it is real, it could represent a release of the compression of the same type as has been found in black lipid films. A repetition of the experiment with newer methods would be useful. Naively one could suppose that a thickening of the membrane leads to the 1% increase in its birefringence (radial axis) needed to explain the observed net decrease in birefringence (longitudinal axis) of the axon at the peak of the action potential. If the membrane had the mechano-thermal properties of rubber, expansion and recompression would also generate positive and negative heats seen during the action potential (cf. Ritchie in this volume).

The optical effects of saxitoxin and tetrodotoxin are much slower to develop and reverse than their effects on membrane permeability, suggesting some second step in the actions of these toxins. It is remarkable that so few molecules per μm^2 of membrane [16] have such a large influence. Perhaps the toxins induce a cooperative change in the membrane.

5. Conclusion

The birefringence of the membranes of excitable cells is voltage dependent. Both of the proposed mechanisms, the Kerr effect and compressional forces, seem capable of accounting for the observations. Undoubtedly both mechanisms are operative but we cannot at present determine which one is most important. No direct connection has been demonstrated between the birefringence changes and the excitation process.

References

[1] A.V.Babakov, L.N.Ermishkin and E.A.Liberman, Nature 210 (1966) 953.
[2] J.W.Beams, Rev. Mod. Phys. 4 (1932) 133.
[3] L.B.Cohen, B.Hille and R.D.Keynes, J. Physiol. 203 (1969) 489.
[4] L.B.Cohen, B.Hille and R.D.Keynes, (1970, in preparation).
[5] L.B.Cohen and R.D.Keynes, J. Physiol. 194 (1968) 85P.
[6] L.B.Cohen, R.D.Keynes and B.Hille, Nature 218 (1968) 438.
[7] K.S.Cole and H.J.Curtis, J. Gen. Physiol. 22 (1939) 649.
[8] P.Debye, Polar Molecules (Chemical Catalogue Company 1929, reprinted, New York, Dover, 1958).
[9] E.H.Grant, S.E.Keefe and S.Takashima, J. Phys. Chem. 72 (1968) 4373.
[10] G.Hammes, Advan. Protein Chem. 23 (1968) 1.
[11] D.A.Haydon and J.L.Taylor, Nature 217 (1968) 739.
[12] H.Hendrickx, R.Verbruggen, M.Y.Rosseneau-Motreff and H.Peters, Biochem. J. 110 (1969) 419.
[13] B.Hille, J.A.Bangham and R.D.Keynes, (1968, unpublished).
[14] C.G.LeFèvre and R.J.W.LeFèvre, in: Technique of Organic Chemistry, ed. A. Weissberger, Vol. I, Part 3 (Interscience, New York, 1960).
[15] J.M.Mitchison, J. Exptl. Biol. 30 (1953) 397.
[16] J.W.Moore, T.Narahashi and T.I.Shaw, J. Physiol. 188 (1967) 99.
[17] R.M.Pytkowicz and C.T.O'Konski, Biochim. Biophys. Acta 36 (1959) 466.
[18] D.Rosen and A.M.Sutton, Biochim. Biophys. Acta 163 (1968) 226.
[19] F.O.Schmitt and R.S.Bear, Biol. Rev. Cambridge Phil. Soc. 14 (1939) 27.
[20] L.Stryer, Science 162 (1968) 526.
[21] I.Tasaki, L.Carnay, R.Sandlin and A.Watanabe, Science 163 (1969) 683.
[22] I.Tasaki, A.Watanabe, R.Sandlin and L.Carnay, Proc. Natl. Acad. Sci. U.S. 61 (1968) 883.
[23] I.Tinoco Jr., J. Am. Chem. Soc. 77 (1955) 3476, 4486.
[24] S.H.White, Biochim. Biophys. Acta 196 (1970) 354.

LIGHT SCATTERING CHANGES DURING
AXON ACTIVITY

L.B.COHEN
Department of Physiology, Yale University School of Medicine,
New Haven, Connecticut, USA

1. Introduction

By studying optical properties of axons during the action potential we are expressing an interest in the structural events that occur at that time. The elegant experiments of Cole, Hodgkin, Huxley, Katz and Keynes [1–4] provided the information necessary for understanding the ionic basis of the action potential. These experiments imply that some kinds of structural changes must occur during activity. But voltage-clamp experiments have given little information about structure, and therefore we have tried a different approach, that of studying changes in optical properties.

Our experiments began as an effort to extend the discovery of Hill and Tobias [5,6], who found that the amount of light scattered from crab nerves decreased reversibly during and following a train of action potentials. In the preceding article Bertil Hille has described the results of birefringence measurements. This paper is devoted to changes in light scattering. Light scattering is used to study the size and conformation of macromolecules [7] as well as volume changes in cells and cell organelles [8]. We have assumed that the light scattering changes in axons can be interpreted in terms of changes in conformation or size of some axon structure.

In our initial experiments we confirmed many of Hill's [5] findings and determined the time course of the 90° light scattering changes following single stimulations [9,10]. Because of a number of technical difficulties it was impossible to decide whether the light scattering changes in the crab nerve were related to the action potential itself or to the ionic currents and membrane permeability changes that underlie the action potential. We therefore attempted similar experiments in the giant axon of the squid, *Loligo forbesi* and *Loligo pealii*.

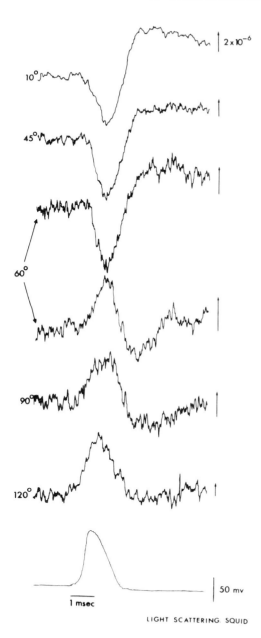

Fig. 1. The first six traces are changes in the light scattered at various angles from the giant axon of the squid *Loligo pealii* during propagated action potentials. The bottom trace is a representative action potential. In all figures the vertical arrow at the right of each tracing represents the change in scattering divided by the resting scattering per sweep. Here the amount is indicated to the right of the top arrow. Between 5,000 and 16,000 sweeps were averaged. The tracings were made from X-Y recorder plots of the output of the signal averager. The light-measuring apparatus responded to an instantaneous light change with a time constant of 50 or 96 μsec. The temperature of the bathing solution was $12-15°C$. Axon diameters were $475-600$ microns. Results from three axons are included. (L.B. Cohen and D.Landowne, unpublished results.)

After considerable effort we measured small changes in light scattering at several angles that occurred during and following the action potential (fig. 1). The first six tracings are the averaged optical records at the various angles, and the bottom tracing shows the concomitant action potentials. The results at $10°$ to $60°$ (for convenience called low-angle scattering) were qualitatively different from those at $60°$ to $120°$ (right-angle scattering), and accordingly the low-angle and the right-angle scatterings will be discussed separately. The angle at which the scattering change switches from the low-angle type to the right-angle type appears to vary from axon to axon, and the results shown in fig. 1 indicate that at $60°$ either type of change may be obtained, depending upon the axon. During the action potential, the change in scattering divided by the resting scattering was between 1:200,000 and 1:500,000. These results are about 100,000 times smaller than the changes reported by Ludkovskaya et al. [11], and therefore I feel that the changes which they reported were artifacts.

2. Low-angle scattering ($10°$ to $60°$)

To determine whether the scattering changes measured during the action potential are related to potential, ionic currents, or membrane permeability changes, combination light scattering and voltage-clamp experiments were carried out [12,13]. Fig. 2 illustrates the results of an experiment in which both hyperpolarizing and depolarizing potential steps were used. The top line represents the light scattering; the middle line, the potential; and the bottom line, the current. There was some sign of a small light scattering change during the hyperpolarizing step (on the left, fig. 2), and further experiments in which many more sweeps were averaged showed that there was a change which had the same shape as the potential step. Since there are only small currents and no permeability changes during the hyperpolarizing step, this scattering change apparently depended on potential. On the other hand, there was a large light scattering change during the depolarizing potential step (on the right, fig. 2), indicating that the scattering also depended upon either the ionic currents or the membrane permeability changes that occur during the depolarizing step [1,3]. Further voltage-clamp experiments showed that the large light scattering changes during the depolarizing step depended upon the ionic currents and not upon the permeability changes. When the experiment was arranged so that the only current was an inward "sodium" current, there was a light scattering decrease which had a time course nearly identical with the integral of the current. During an outward current, the light scattering increased, again with a time course similar to the integral of the current.

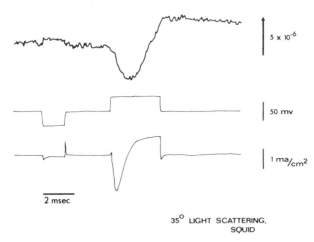

2 msec

35° LIGHT SCATTERING,
SQUID

Fig. 2. Low-angle light scattering changes in an axon from *Loligo forbesi* during voltage-clamp experiments. In the middle (potential) trace, the downward direction represents a hyperpolarizing potential step. There is a large scattering change during the depolarizing potential step. In the bottom trace, the downward direction represents an inward current. The light scattering record is the average of 800 sweeps. The chamber temperature was 15°C. The axon diameter was 870 microns. Light-measuring time constants were 100 or 150 μsec. (L.B.Cohen and R.D.Keynes, unpublished results.)

When the scattering angle was 10°, these scattering changes did not return to the baseline for more than 100 msec. The low-angle scattering changes are thus partly potential dependent and partly current dependent. The current-dependent changes occurred with a time course similar to the integral of the current, and they lasted for more than 100 msec.

3. Right-angle scattering (60° to 120°)

The right-angle light scattering change that occurred as a result of the action potential (fig. 1) appeared to have two components. One was the light scattering increase that occurred at about the same time as the action potential. The other (which is poorly illustrated in the time span of fig. 1) was a slow, long-lasting increase in scattering, persisting for 50 to 100 msec after the action potential.

Combination optical and voltage-clamp experiments were also carried out on the right-angle scattering. These experiments gave a result similar to the

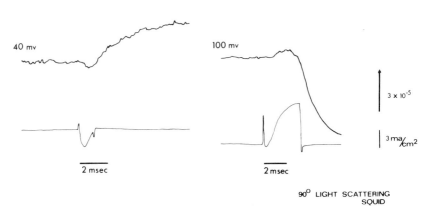

Fig. 3. Right-angle light scattering changes in giant axons from *Loligo forbesi* during voltage-clamp experiments. The top records are the light scattering; the bottom, the current density. Most of the scattering changes occur after current has ceased. The size of the potential step is given above the scattering records. Records from two axons are shown. The light scattering tracings are averages of 200 sweeps. Chamber temperatures were 12°C and 15°C. Axon diameters were 700 and 770 microns. The light-measuring time constant was 50 µsec. (L.B.Cohen and R.D.Keynes, unpublished results.)

low-angle experiments in that both current-dependent and potential-dependent scattering changes were found. The potential-dependent scattering change at right angles appeared to have a different origin from the potential-dependent change at low angles, because the right-angle change occurred more rapidly. Both of these light scattering changes appeared to be different from the birefringence change, because they were not affected by tetrodotoxin, while the birefringence change is made slower and larger by tetrodotoxin. The potential-dependent components may be due to orientation of membrane dipoles by the potential gradient, or to changes in membrane thickness or refractive index resulting from the potential. The right-angle scattering changes that depend upon current were qualitatively different from the low-angle changes. With a current of a few milliseconds' duration, the major scattering change, fig. 3, reached a peak following the end of the current pulse. The top traces are the light scattering and the bottom traces, the currents. Again, in the right-angle scattering, currents in opposite directions led to light scattering changes in opposite directions. The small light scattering change which occurred at the same time as the current may have been due to interference from the low-angle scattering. Using longer sweeps, we were able to measure the time course of the larger light scattering changes. These changes occurred with a time constant of 2-5 msec and returned to the baseline with time constants of 50—100 msec. The right-angle scattering changes are thus also partly potential dependent and partly current dependent, with the major current-dependent change occurring after the current flow.

4. Discussion

Our thoughts concerning the current-dependent scattering changes have centered around a consideration of the salt concentrations in the immediate neighborhood of the axon membrane. When there is an outward "potassium" current, the current across the membrane will be carried by outward-moving potassium ions. At all other points between the internal and external electrodes about half of the current will be carried by inward-moving negative ions. This transport number effect [14,15] will result in an increase in the KCl concentration just outside the axon membrane and a decreased KCl—K-isethionate concentration just inside the axon membrane. The KCl concentration just outside the membrane will remain high for some milliseconds because of the presence of the diffusion barrier presented by the Schwann 'cell structures [16—18]. Frankenhaeuser and Hodgkin [18] showed that excess potassium would disappear with a time constant that we found to average 30 msec. There is no such barrier on the inside of the axon membrane, and a diminished salt concentration just inside the membrane would disappear with a time constant of less than one msec. However, a slightly diminished salt concentration would persist at regions further inside the axon for longer periods.

If a light scattering change were directly related to the increase in KCl concentration in the space between the axon membrane and Schwann cell (Geren-Schmitt space), then the scattering change should occur as soon as the KCl arrives in the space and it should return to the baseline with a time constant of 30 msec. The current-dependent change in low-angle scattering occurred as soon as the KCl arrived in the space, but it lasted far longer than 30 msec. The time course of this current-dependent change could be modified by alterations in the external refractive index, and the modified time course was sometimes similar to the time course expected if the scattering change were directly related to the excess KCl. It thus seems possible that the low-angle, current-dependent change may in part result from the increased salt concentration in the Geren-Schmitt space. On the other hand, the right-angle scattering change was not complete for some time after the arrival of the excess KCl and therefore cannot be directly related to the excess. However, the excess KCl generates an osmotic gradient, and water will flow to neutralize this gradient. The resulting volume change might be expected to occur with a time constant of about 5 msec, and the return to the original size would have a time constant greater than 30 msec. These two time constants describe a time course similar to the time course of the right-angle scattering changes, and our first hypothesis was that these scattering changes were the result of volume changes in the Geren-Schmitt space. This hypothesis was tested by changing the major anion in the bathing medium from chloride to isethionate. The mobility of the isethionate was estimated to be about half that of the chloride, and this decrease in anion mobility would reduce a transport number effect by about 35%. However, in preliminary experiments, the size of the light scattering change was unaffected by the anion replacement, which seems to rule out a transport number effect. Since the right-angle scattering changes for identical inward and outward currents are equal in time course and size, it is unlikely that they are due to specific effects of either sodium or potassium ions. At the moment we have no satisfactory hypothesis to explain the right-angle scattering changes.

In spite of the fact that our understanding of the origins of the light scattering changes is incomplete, it does seem clear that those changes that we have found are either potential dependent or current dependent. I was disappointed that neither the light scattering nor the birefringence changes were dependent upon the impressive increases in membrane permeability which occur during the action potential and during depolarizing voltage-clamp steps. However, the experiments we have described have encouraged a vigorous search for rapid changes in other optical properties of axons, and already changes in the fluorescence of dyes added to axons [19,20] as well as changes in binding of vital dyes [21] have been reported. During the next decade many more changes in optical properties will be found, and I expect that some of these will be related to changes in membrane permeability; detailed studies of such changes should provide considerable information about the structural events which underlie the permeability increases.

Acknowledgements

These experiments were done with Dr. R.D.Keynes at the Laboratory of the Marine Biological Association, Plymouth, England, and with Dr. David Landowne at the Marine Biological Laboratory, Woods Hole, Mass., USA. Supported in part by Public Health Service grant number NB-08437.

References

[1] K.S.Cole, Arch. Sci. Physiol. 3 (1949) 253−258.
[2] A.L.Hodgkin, A.F.Huxley and B.Katz, J. Physiol. 116 (1952) 424−448.
[3] A.L.Hodgkin and A.F.Huxley, J. Physiol. 117 (1952) 500−544.
[4] R.D.Keynes, J. Physiol. 114 (1951) 119−150.
[5] D.K.Hill, J. Physiol. 111 (1950) 283−303.
[6] S.H.Bryant and J.M.Tobias, J. Cellular Comp. Physiol. 40 (1952) 199−219.
[7] C.Tanford, Physical Chemistry of Macromolecules (John Wiley, New York, 1961) p. 275.
[8] S.L.Orskov, Biochem. Z. 279 (1935) 250−261.
[9] L.B.Cohen and R.D.Keynes, J. Physiol. 194 (1968) 85−86P (abstract).
[10] L.B.Cohen, R.D.Keynes and B.Hille, Nature 218 (1968) 438−441.
[11] R.G.Ludkovskaya, V.B.Emeljanov and B.K.Lemazhikhin, Tsitologiya 7 (1965) 520−530.
[12] L.B.Cohen and R.D.Keynes, J. Physiol. 204 (1969) 100-101P.
[13] L.B.Cohen and D.Landowne, J. Gen. Physiol. 55 (1970) 144.
[14] L.Girardier, J.P.Reuben, P.W.Brandt and H.Grundfest, J. Gen. Physiol. 47 (1963) 189−214.
[15] P.H.Barry and A.B.Hope, Biophys. J. 9 (1969) 700−728.
[16] B.B.Geren and F.O.Schmitt, Proc. Natl. Acad. Sci. U.S. 40 (1954) 863−870.
[17] G.M.Villegas and R.Villegas, J. Gen. Physiol. 51 (1968) 44S-60S.
[18] B.Frankenhaeuser and A.L.Hodgkin, J. Physiol. 131 (1956) 341−376.
[19] I.Tasaki, L.Carnay, R.Sandlin and A.Watanabe, Science 163 (1969) 683−685.
[20] I.Tasaki, A.Watanabe, R.Sandlin and L.Carnay, Proc. Natl. Acad. Sci. U.S. 61 (1968) 883−888.
[21] S.V.Levin and D.L.Rosental, Academy of Sciences of the USSR, Institute of Cytology, collected articles, No. 13 (1961) 148−172.

CONTRIBUTIONS TO THE GENERAL DISCUSSION

ON THE FUNCTION OF Na-IONS IN THE TRANSPORT OF AMINO ACIDS IN EHRLICH CARCINOMA CELLS

Erich HEINZ

*Chemisch-physiologisches Institut der Johann-Wolfgang-Goethe Universität,
Frankfurt am Main*

In the last decade an increasing number of animal transport systems for organic molecules have been shown to depend on the presence of Na-ions. This holds only for active transport systems, whereas facilitated diffusion, e.g. that of sugars into muscle and red cells, or that via the so called L-system into Ehrlich cells, does not require Na-ions. It seems that all Na-dependent systems are sensitive to ouabain, whereas the others are not.

As to the mechanism by which Na-ions influence those transport systems, various hypotheses have been offered to explain it. The most plausible ones among these may be the following: (1) The 'catalysis' hypothesis, according to which the mere presence of Na-ions activates the coupling of the transport of the organic solute to metabolism [1] ; and (2) the 'co-transport' hypothesis, according to which the Na^+ moves jointly with the organic solute across the osmotic barrier, possibly forming a ternary complex with the carrier and this solute [2] . In this case the passive movement of the Na-ions down their electrochemical potential (ECP) gradient may cause an up-hill movement of the organic solute. Hence the transport of the organic solute would not be 'primarily' active, i.e. it would not be immediately driven by the affinity of a chemical reaction but by the ECP-gradient of the Na-ions. Metabolic energy production would be required for this transport only indirectly, namely to feed the Na-pump which maintains the driving ECP-gradient of Na^+.

I would like now to summarize the evidence and arguments favoring the one or the other hypothesis, taking the transport of some amino acids into Ehrlich cells as a representative example. It had been observed already long ago by Christensen et al. that the concentrative uptake of glycine by these cells is impaired after part or all of the extracellular Na^+ has been replaced by choline or K^+ [3] . More recently could it be established by kinetic studies that the shortage of Na-ions, much more than the excess of K-ions, is responsible for this impairment. It was shown that the reduction of the extracellular Na-ion concentration causes a reduction of the influx of amino acids, such as glycine, glutamate, aminoisobutyrate (AIB) and others, without noticeable delay [4–6]. Changes of the cellular Na-level by themselves did not affect the amino acid influx, except that cellular Na^+ concentrations higher than about 100 mM slightly inhibited it [5,7].

Meanwhile a direct positive coupling between amino acid transport and Na-entry, as it is postulated by the second type of hypothesis, has been demonstrated by the following evidence: (1) the uptake of amino acids by Ehrlich cells is associated with an extra uptake of Na-ions in almost stoichiometric amounts [6]. (2) After complete metabolic inhibition these cells still transport glycine uphill as long as a favorable gradient of Na-ions is maintained. The maximal accumulation ratio of glycine under these circumstances is almost directly proportional to the inverse distribution ratio of Na-ions. If the cellular Na-level is higher than the extracellular one, glycine is moved up-hill out of the cells [7]. This has been confirmed for AIB transport in the same cell species [8]. (3) The interaction between the movement of Na-ions and that of amino acids has been shown to be mutual; adding an excess of extracellular glycine so as to produce a high down-hill chemical potential gradient of this amino acid into the cell markedly accelerates the entry of Na-ions [7]. Hence there can be little doubt that the transport of those amino acids and the passive entry of Na-ions are energetically coupled. In addition, also the ECP-gradient of K-ions in the outward direction may contribute, to a minor extent though, to the accumulation of those amino acids; in other words, there may be some negative coupling between the movements of K-ions and amino acids [7].

The question now arises whether these findings necessarily exclude a direct coupling of amino acid transport to metabolism. Could it be that the gradient of the alkali ions contribute only a minor fraction, may-be accidentally, of the energy required for active amino acid transport, whereas the other, may be essential, fraction is derived directly from metabolic reactions? There is, indeed, evidence in favor of this assumption. Long before the Na-effect on amino acid transport was fully appreciated, we had observed that metabolic inhibition of Ehrlich cells depresses the *influx* of glycine, with little, if any, effect on the *efflux* coefficient [9]. The 'co-transport' concept postulates that the influx of the transported species is a function of the extracellular Na-level, as the efflux is a function of the cellular one [2]. We had later confirmed, as already mentioned, that the glycine influx is hardly effected by a rise in cellular Na^+ [1]. Since in the above quoted experiments on metabolic inhibition the extracellular medium was always in great excess over the cellular space, inhibition of the Na-pump should raise the cellular Na-level without appreciable change in the extracellular one. With the K-ions the situation is analogous. Hence metabolic inhibition, if it affected amino acid transport only by degrading the ion gradients, should be expected to strongly increase the efflux coefficient while leaving the influx almost unaltered, which is contrary to what has been found. Furthermore, at any given Na-ion gradient glycine is much more powerfully accumulated by respiring than by metabolically inhibited cells [7]. Even though in inhibited cells glycine was actively accumulated at favorable ion gradients, this accumulation never exceeded about 30% of that obtained with respiring cells at the same ion distribution. Does this indicate that 70% or more of the total energy requirement of the transport is drawn directly from metabolic reactions? Eddy [7] offers an alternative explanation, which would make any direct coupling of amino acid transport to metabolism quite unnecessary. He assumes that in respiring cells the Na-pump creates an Na-depleted region, or compartment, in the immediate neighborhood of the inner membrane face. Hence the effective gradient of Na-ions across the cellular membrane would be in reality much higher than one could expect by assuming that the overall cellular Na concentration is the same everywhere inside the cell. On the other hand, as far as during metabolic inhibition the Na-pump is paralyzed, the assumption that the Na concentration is the same near the membrane as it is in the bulk cytoplasm may be correct. This explanation, however, is tacitly based on some improbable suppositions: A Na-depleted compartment can arise only if there is some barrier against the bulk cytoplasm. This barrier must at the same time prevent the cytoplasmic Na from refilling the membrane-near compartment, and let the amino acids pass freely in order to permit their accumulation. Even then the low Na-level in that compartment can only be maintained temporarily, unless there is either a second Na-pump in the inner barrier to move the Na back into the bulk cytoplasm, or a shunt for Na-ions between the extracellular space and the inner cytoplasm, by passing the membrane-near compartment. There is no evidence to support these assumptions. In order to further test them Schafer et al. studied the transport of AIB in these cells with reversed gradients of Na and K, and in the presence of ouabain at concentrations low enough to permit some active transport of the amino acid, but high enough to paralyze the Na-pump. Even under such adverse circumstances AIB moved up-hill *into* the cell. Only if the inverted gradients of Na and K exceeded a distinct limit could an up-hill movement of AIB *out* of the cell be observed [8]. Hence, the Na-pump does not seem to be necessary to permit active amino acid uptake with inversed Na- and K-gradients, and there must be an additional driving force besides the ECP-gradients of these ions.

If a direct coupling between amino acid transport and metabolism exists, it must depend on Na-ions, because in the absence of this ion in the medium amino acid transport seems to stop completely. The Na-ions would thus have a dual effect on this transport, firstly by their ECP-gradient and secondly by activating the coupling between transport and metabolism. The mechanism by which these effects are brought about may be the same, though. Whereas the first effect of Na (and possibly of K) is easily accounted for by the assumed formation of a ternary complex, the interpretation of the second effect in terms of a simple carrier model is more difficult. The various possibilities in this respect may be conveniently illustrated using the phenomenological notation of irreversible thermodynamics [10] :

$$J_a = L_{aa}X_a + \sum_{i=1}^{2} L_{ai}X_i + L_{ar}A \ .$$

J_a is the total net flux of amino acid into the cell, X_a its (negative) ECP-gradient across the osmotic barrier of the cell. X_i are the (negative) ECP-gradients of Na- and K-ions, L_{ai} the appropriate cross coefficients, that connecting amino acid transport to Na^+-entry being positive, and that connecting this transport to K^+-entry being negative. A is the affinity of the chemical reaction to which the amino acid transport is directly coupled by the (chemo-osmotic) cross coefficient L_{ar}. Obviously changes of the Na-ion concentration may, besides changing X_i, affect A or the cross coefficients L_{aa} and/or L_{ar}. Since there is no evidence that A depends on the Na-ion concentration, or gradient, we may assume that Na-ions have an effect on the 'coupling coefficient' which is a function of various straight and cross coefficients. To relate such an effect to possible effects on the various parameters, the R-notation of the above equation may be more helpful [10] . For this purpose we divide the total flux of the amino acid into the active part, J_a^a and the leakage part, J_a^p; the basic equations are:

$$X_a = R_{aa}^a J_a^a + \sum_{i=1}^{2} R_{ai}J_i^p + R_{ar}^a J_r^a = R_{aa}^p J_a^p \ . \tag{1}$$

$$X_i = R_{ii}^p J_i^p + R_{ai}J_a^a \ . \tag{2}$$

$$A = R_{rr}^a J_r^a + R_{ar}^a J_a^a \ . \tag{3}$$

R_{aa}^a and R_{aa}^p are the straight resistance coefficients for the amino acid movement with the active carrier and by passive diffusion, respectively. R_{ii}^p are those of the passive penetration of the two alkali ions, and R_{rr}^a that of the metabolic reaction that is directly coupled to the amino acid transport. R_{ai}^p are the cross coefficients linking the passive movement of the alkali ions to the amino acid transport, R_{ar}^a that linking amino acid transport to the metabolic reaction with the affinity A. We assume that the passive ion movements are linked only to amino acid transport, so that eqs. (2) have only 2 terms each. We further assume that A is fixed for a given experimental condition, i.e., being zero during metabolic inhibition, and having a constant value in respiring cells. Finally, it is assumed that the passive movement (leakage) of amino acid is not coupled to any other movement so that $J_{aa}^p = X_a / R_{aa}^p$. Combining eqs. (1), (2), and (3), and dissolving for the total flux of amino acid we obtain, following and extending the procedure of Essig and Caplan [11]

$$J_a^a = \frac{X_a - \sum_{i=1}^{2}(R_{ai}/R_{ii}^p)X_i - (R_{ar}^a/R_{rr})A}{R_{aa}^a\left(1 - \sum_{i=1}^{2}R_{ai}^a/(R_{aa}^aR_{ii}^p) - R_{ar}^2/(R_{aa}^aR_{rr})\right)} \tag{4}$$

or, introducing the coupling coefficients q_i and q_r, i.e., $q_i = R_{ai}/\sqrt{(R_{aa}^aR_{ii}^p)}$ for the coupling of amino acid transport to the alkali ion movements, $q_r = R_{ar}^a/\sqrt{(R_{aa}^aR_{rr})}$, for the coupling of amino acid transport to the metabolic reaction,

$$J_a^a = \frac{X_a - \sum_{i=1}^{2}(R_{ai}/R_{ii}^p)X_i - (R_{ar}^a/R_{rr})A}{R_{aa}^a\left(1 - \sum q_i^2 - q_r^2\right)}, \tag{5}$$

and for total amino acid flux:

$$J_a = \frac{X_a}{R_{aa}^a\left(1 - \sum q_i^2 - q_r^2\right)} + \frac{X_a}{R_{aa}^p} - \frac{\sum_{i=1}^{2}(R_{ai}/R_{ii}^p)X_i + (R_{ar}^a/R_{rr})A}{R_{aa}^a\left(1 - \sum q_i^2 - q_r^2\right)}. \tag{6}$$

Of the two effects of Na, according to the foregoing, the first one would be, possibly together with K^+, to raise the two X_i, and the second one to raise q_r or R_{aa}^p. q_r would rise numerically if R_{ar}^a is increased or if R_{aa}^a and/or R_{rr}^a are reduced.

Let us try to visualize these formal relationships in terms of a convential carrier model. Any decrease of the mobility of the active but unloaded, i.e., amino acid-free, carrier across the osmotic barrier would obviously tend to increase R_{ar}^a, whereas a decrease of R_{aa}^a might result if the movement of the loaded carrier is accelerated. The latter effect might be brought about either by making the carrier-amino acid complex more mobile, or by increasing the affinity of this carrier for the amino acid. A decrease of R_{rr}^a might result if the rate limiting step between inactivation and final reactivation of the carrier is accelerated. A rise of R_{aa}^p would indicate a tightening effect of Na^+ on the membrane. Since this latter effect would tend to decrease the total influx, which is opposite to observation, it can be disregarded. It has previously been shown that the unidirectional influx of glycine responds instantaneously upon changes in extracellular Na^+ but is almost insensitive towards changes in cellular Na^+ [1]. This seems to justify the assumption that the effect of Na^+ on the coupling is located at the outer face of the osmotic barrier. Here it may, for instance, increase either the affinity of the active (and inactive) carrier for the amino acid, or the mobility of the complex between carrier and amino acid, either of which effect would - as has already been mentioned - tend to lower R_{aa}^a and, hence, to raise q_r. Finally Na^+ could be required for the final activation of the carrier as far as this occurs at the outer face of the osmotic barrier. This could be made more plausible by postulating that the activation of the carrier occurs in 2 steps:

1. energization without increase in affinity by a reaction with ATP or the like, inside the cell,

2. conformational rearrangement of energized carrier to restore its affinity for the amino acid without much change in energy content, at the outside of the cell membrane. If this second step requires prior binding of Na^+, the effect of this ion would be to decrease R_{rr}^a and, hence, to increase q_r, the metabolic coupling coefficient. At the present stage it would be otiose to carry these speculations further, at least before the direct coupling between the amino acid transport and metabolism is firmly established..

Another unsolved problem, probably closely related to the foregoing, concerns the effect of ouabain on the amino acid transport. It has been shown that this drug inhibits the amino acid transport at a time before major changes in the distribution of alkali ions between cell and medium are apparent. This seems to suggest that ouabain acts on the amino acid transport directly and not through degrading the Na^+ gradient. On the other hand there seems to be a close parallelism in all transport systems known between the requirement of Na^+ and the susceptibility toward ouabain; systems depending on Na^+ are sensitive to ouabain, systems independent of Na^+ are not. This obviously argues in favor of a close relationship between the effect of ouabain on the Na-pump and that on the amino acid transport. At present it is impossible to offer a common denominator for these seemingly conflicting observations.

References

[1] H.Kromphardt, H.Grobecker, K.Ring and E.Heinz, Biochim. Biophys. Acta 74 (1963) 549.
[2] R.K.Crane, Federation Proc. 21 (1962) 891.
[3] H.N.Christensen and T.R.Riggs, J. Biol. Chem. 194 (1952) 57.
[4] E.Heinz, in: Biochemie des Aktiven Transports (Springer-Verlag, Heidelberg, 1961) p. 151.
[5] H.Koch, Med. Dissertation, Frankfurt (1965).
[6] J.A.Schafer and J.A.Jacquez, Biochim. Biophys. Acta 135 (1967) 1081.
[7] A.A.Eddy, Biochem. J. 108 (1968) 195, 489.
[8] J.A.Schafer and E.Heinz, in preparation.
[9] E.Heinz, J. Biol. Chem. 225 (1957) 305.
[10] A.Katchalsky and P.F.Curran, Nonequilibrium Thermodynamics in Biophysics (Harvard Univ. Press, Cambridge, Mass., 1965).
[11] A.Essig and S.R.Caplan, Biophys. J. 8 (1968) 1434.

TEMPERATURE DEPENDENCE OF TRANSCELLULAR MIGRATION OF GLUTAMATE IN NORMAL AND NEOPLASTIC CELLS

R.STROM, P.CAIAFA, B.MONDOVÌ and A.ROSSI FANELLI

Institute of Biological Chemistry, University of Rome,
and *Center for Molecular Biology of the National Research Council, Rome*

1. Introduction

Neoplastic cells have been shown [1–6] to be more sensitive than normal cells to the effect of relatively high temperatures. As shown in figs. 1 and 2, the oxygen uptake of Novikoff rat hepatoma cells and of a number of human malignant tumor cells is heavily inhibited by exposure of the cells to 42–43°C.

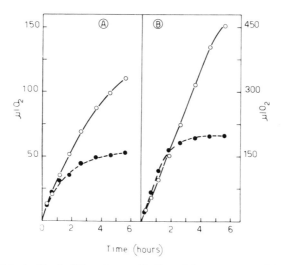

Fig. 1. O_2 uptake by Novikoff hepatoma cells. O_2 uptake was measured, in a concentional Warburg apparatus at 38°C ($\circ$ —— $\circ$) or 43°C ($\bullet$ - - - - $\bullet$), in the absence (A) or presence (B) of 0.015 M glucose + 0.013 M succinate.

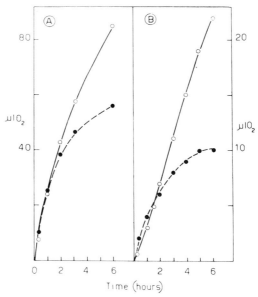

Fig. 2. O_2 uptake by human osteosarcoma cells (A) or rectum adenocarcinoma cells (B).
0.015 M glucose + 0.013 M succinate was added. Conditions and symbols as in fig. 1.

Also cells obtained from a minimal deviation experimental rat hepatoma
(Morris 5123) undergo a definite, although less marked, inhibition [4]. Incorporation of radioactive precursors into nucleic acids and proteins was also
severely decreased (table 1) in tumor cells at 42–43°C [5]. In regenerating
liver cells, which were used as controls, neither respiration nor DNA or RNA
synthesis were affected by the high temperature [2,5].

Respiration and DNA synthesis by cell-free suspensions from neoplastic
tissues were instead, as shown in table 2, not affected by elevated temperatures. This finding, and the peculiar sensitivity of neoplastic cells to agents,
such as the polyenic antibiotic filipin, which have a rather specific site of action on cellular membranes [4,5], have led us to suppose that the heat sensitivity of tumor cells might be due to an increased lability of the plasma membrane. This possibility was investigated by examining the effect of 'elevated'
temperature on transcellular migration of glutamate through a complex membrane of normal, regenerating or neoplastic hepatocytes on a Millipore filter.

Table 1
Influence of temperature on the incorporation of radioactive precursors into nucleic
acids and proteins in tumor cells

	Novikoff hepatoma cells			Morris 5123 minimal deviation hepatoma cells			Human osteosarcoma cells	
Pre-incubation temperature (°C)	38	42	43	38	42	43	38	43
Dis/min/μgDNA	776	40	36	530	320	195	85	32
Dis/min/μgRNA	387	–	44	70	–	58	–	–
Dis/min/μg protein	160	–	8	2700	1480	1075	–	–

Cell suspension was pre-incubated 2 hr in Eagle's medium at the temperature indicated.
Incorporation of ^{3}H-thymidine (0.6 μc/mg dry weight), ^{3}H-uridine (0.6 μc/mg dry
weight) and ^{14}C-amino acids (0.3 μc/mg dry weight) was performed by incubating the
washed cells in Eagle's medium at 38°C for 1 hr. DNA, RNA and proteins were isolated
prior to scintillation counting [5].

Table 2
Influence of temperature on O_2 uptake and ^{3}H-thymidine incorporation into DNA by
intact or disrupted Novikoff hepatoma cells

Pre-incubation temperature (°C)		38	43
μl O_2 consumed/hr/ 100 mg dry weight, after 90 min pre- incubation	Intact cells	400	125
	Sonicated cells	35	30
Dis/min/μg DNA	Intact cells	4000	42
	Cells disrupted by homogenization in hypotonic saline	50	60

For experimental conditions, see [4] and [5].

2. Materials and methods

Male Sprague-Dawley rats were used as the source of normal liver, regene-

Fig. 3.

rating liver, which was taken 24 hr after partial hepatectomy, and of Novikoff hepatomas. Isolated cells were prepared according to Birnie et al. [7] with the following modifications: the tissue was minced finely with scissors and washed several times with the incubation medium; the suspension of cells was passed through an 80 mesh nylon sieve with the aid of a plastic spatula, filtered through glass wool, suspended in 20 volumes of the incubation medium, washed 3 times by low-speed centrifugation (50 g), and resuspended in 20 volumes of the same medium by passage through a no. 2 gauge needle. Microscopic examination demonstrated that the cell suspension was homogeneous and without any gross damage.

The suspension fluid was either a potassium-free Krebs-Ringer bicarbonate buffer [8] diluted with $\frac{1}{15}$ of 0.154 M Na-glutamate, or a 0.3 M sucrose solution diluted with $\frac{1}{15}$ of 0.154 M glutamic acid neutralized to pH 7.2 with imidazole. The cell-coated Millipore filter was prepared by filtration on a water pump as described by Harris and Friedman [9] : the cells adhered to the filter and could not be removed by washing. The complex membrane was formed by two cell-coated filters sandwiched in an all-glass apparatus (fig. 3) similar to that described by the same authors [9] ; it separated a large compartment (200 ml) from a smaller one (20 ml). Both compartments were filled with the appropriate incubation fluid, and the whole apparatus immersed in a water bath at the desired temperature. Agitation was ensured by bubbling of air or of 95% O_2 + 5% CO_2.

Experiments were started by addition of 50 μl of a L-U-^{14}C-glutamate solution (New England Nuclear Corp., Boston, Mass.; 0.1 mc/ml, 1.5 mc/mg) to the larger compartment. Migration was followed by repetitive sampling of 100 μl from the smaller compartment, and scintillation counting in a Nuclear Chicago mod. 725 liquid scintillation system, after mixing with 20 ml of dioxane-naphtalene solution [10].

3. Transcellular migration in ionic medium

Normal liver cells, as well as cells from regenerating liver and from Novikoff hepatoma, followed, at 38°C, the same pattern reported in the literature for Ehrlich ascites cells [9,11] : the rate of migration of ^{14}C-glutamate into the smaller compartment remained constant over a period of at least 3 hr in the absence of any ionic gradient, but was significantly stimulated by addition of isotonic KCl-glutamate, added to the smaller compartment to a final K^+ concentration of 12 mM. The extent of stimulation was generally around 30–40% for all kinds of cells.

The various cells exhibited instead a different behaviour at higher tempera-

Table 3

Transcellular migration in ionic medium. The migration rate is expressed as increase per minute of the concentration of radioactive glutamate in the smaller compartment, i.e., as increase of dis/min/100 μl of the fluid of that compartment [6]

	Normal liver cells		Regenerating liver cells			Novikoff hepatoma cells			
	Exp.1	Exp.2	Exp.1	Exp.2	Exp.3	Exp.1	Exp.2	Exp.3	Exp.4
38°C	4.72	4.20	2.58	3.68	3.20	6.00	8.89	6.06	4.83
38°C + KCl	6.33	5.54	–	–	4.40	8.40	–	–	7.60
40°C	–	–	3.34	4.78	–	8.39	11.90	9.04	–
40°C + KCl	–	–	3.98	5.74	–	8.36	11.90	–	–
$R \dfrac{40°C}{38°C}$, no KCl	–	–	1.29	1.30	–	1.40	1.34	1.49	–
42°C	5.00	4.33	–	5.78	4.50	–	–	9.00	7.70
42°C + KCl	6.23	5.54	–	5.88	4.60	–	–	9.00	7.73
$R \dfrac{42°C}{38°C}$, no KCl	1.09	1.03	–	1.57	1.40	–	–	1.48	1.59

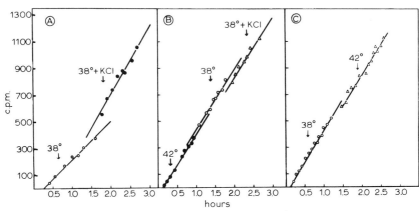

Fig. 4. (A) Effect of KCl on Novikoff hepatoma cells at 38°C in ionic medium. (B) Irreversibility of the temperature effect in Novikoff hepatoma cells. (C) Ineffectiveness of temperature increase in disrupted Novikoff hepatoma cells. In all cases, the same preparation of Novikoff hepatoma cells was used. In experiment (C), cells were disrupted, prior to the preparation of the membrane, by freezing and thawing 3 times.

tures. While the pattern followed by normal liver cells was scarcely or not at all changed, the rate of migration through Novikoff hepatoma cells was instead significantly higher at 42°C, or even at 40, than at 38°C, and stimulation by K^+ ions was no more evident at these temperatures (table 3). The enhancement by temperature was relatively fast, being complete within the equilibration time (about 10 min) and was not reversed by changing the temperature back to 38°C (fig. 4B). The behaviour of Novikoff cells pre-treated at 42°C is similar to that of the same cells disrupted by repetitive freezing and thawing: in both cases, the migration rate is high at 38°C, and is not influenced either by higher temperatures of by KCl addition (fig. 4C).

With regenerating liver cells, the migration rate was higher at 40°C than at 38°C, but it could still be enhanced by addition of KCl. At 42°C, instead, no further stimulation by KCl could be observed (table 3).

4. Transcellular migration in non-ionic medium

In an incubation medium devoid of any inorganic ion, i.e. in a 0.3 M sucrose solution containing glutamate and imidazole, membranes formed of normal or of regenerating liver cells show a characteristic behaviour, the rate

Table 4

Transcellular migration in non-ionic medium. The migration rate is expressed as indicated in table 3

	Normal liver cells			Regenerating liver cells		Novikoff hepatoma cells	
	Exp.1	Exp.2	Exp.3	Exp.1	Exp.2	Exp.1	Exp.2
38°C	4.65	4.04	8.31	8.90	5.00	6.54	6.40
38°C + NaCl	–	3.21	6.03	5.96	4.25	6.54	6.40
$R_{38°C}\frac{+\,NaCl}{no\,NaCl}$	–	0.79	0.73	0.67	0.85	1.00	1.00
42°C	4.89	–	–	–	–	–	–
42°C + NaCl	3.89	–	–	9.29	6.81	10.24	9.04
$R\frac{42°C}{38°C}$	1.12	–	–	1.56	1.60	1.56	1.41

of migration of ^{14}C-glutamate being significantly decreased by addition of NaCl to the sampling compartment (table 4). Preliminary experiments seem to indicate a non-specificity of the cationic species inducing this effect, K^+ being able to substitute for Na^+.

A temperature increase to 42°C produced only small, if any, effects with normal hepatocytes, while regenerating liver cells, responded with a marked increase of the migration rate.

With Novikoff hepatoma cells, no 'inhibitory' effect of alkaline cations was present, although a raise to 42°C resulted in a 'stimulation' of the migration rate of the same order of that seen with regenerating liver cells.

5. Discussion

Transcellular migration of glutamate, especially across an ionic gradient, is a complex phenomenon, where the effects of simple diffusion are superimposed to those due to facilitated transport and perhaps also to active transport. If only diffusion was present, migration rates would be affected by temperature through variations in the diffusion coefficients, according to the classical Arrhenius expression, viz.,

$$D = D_0 \cdot \exp - \frac{A}{RT}.$$

Diffusion activation energy (A) values known from the literature [12] range from 4.5 kcal/mole to $17-26$ kcal/mole. Brief calculation shows that such variations result in D_{42}/D_{38} ratios ranging from 1.097 to $1.42 - 1.70$. Theoretically, therefore, on strictly thermodynamic grounds, an increase of temperature from 38 to 42°C may, or may not, result in an appreciable (i.e., 10%) stimulation of the diffusion rate, according to the A value accepted.

The different behaviour of normal liver cells on one side and of regenerating or neoplastic hepatocytes on the other would anyhow require large differences in the diffusion activation energies for the different cell types. Moreover, a pure diffusion mechanism would explain neither the ineffectiveness of a raise in temperature on disrupted Novikoff cells, nor the irreversibility of 'stimulation' by heat in Novikoff hepatoma cells.

It is known that in many cases profound modifications occur, either in cellular or artificial membranes, at temperatures which are critical for the membrane considered [13–18]. Thermal transitions, in the $38-42^{\circ}$C range, have also been observed with pure lipid compounds, such as for instance lauroyl-1, 2-diglyceride [19], 2,3-dipalmitoyl-1-phosphatidylcholine [20,21], 2-oleoyl-3-stearoyl-1-phosphatidylcholine [18], cholesterol [18], and even more markedly with binary or multiple systems of lipid compounds [19]. These transitions are, in principle, thermodynamically reversible, but the reverse transition can take a long time to occur, as indicated by some experiments on synthetic phospholipids [22], or they may bring about some secondary irreversible process in the complex membrane structure.

Although establishment of an ionic gradient across the artificial membrane has clearcut effects on glutamate migration, the mechanisms underlying these effects are still obscure. The different behaviour of Novikoff cells, as compared to normal or regenerating liver cells, in a non-ionic medium is striking but totally unexplained. It is however of interest to notice how regenerating liver cells follow as a rule, with respect to ionic gradients and to temperature, a pattern which is intermediate between those of normal hepatocytes and of Novikoff hepatoma cells. It does not seem easy to discriminate qualitatively, in our conditions, between the behaviour of normal, but rapidly growing, cells, and that of neoplastic cells. It may however be conceived that membranes of the latter be characterized by a lability - to temperature and to membrane-damaging agents - which would result in the previously described [1–5] inhibition of the respiratory and biosynthetic activities of the cells themselves.

Acknowledgement

The authors wish to thank Mr. Vincenzo Peresempio for skillful technical assistance.

References

[1] R.Cavaliere, B.C.Giovanella, M.Margottini, B.Mondovì, G.Moricca and A.Rossi Fanelli, Rend. Accad. Naz. Lincei 42 (1967) 164.
[2] R.Cavaliere, E.C.Ciocatto, B.C.Giovanella, C.Heidelberger, R.O.Johnson, M.Margottini, B.Mondovì, G.Moricca and A.Rossi Fanelli, Cancer 20 (1967) 1351.
[3] B.Mondovì, G.Rotilio, R.Strom, A.Finazzi Agrò, R.Cavaliere, G.Moricca and A. Rossi Fanelli, Ital. J. Biochem. 17 (1968) 101.
[4] B.Mondovì, R.Strom, G.Rotilio, A.Finazzi Agrò, R.Cavaliere and A.Rossi Fanelli, Europ. J. Cancer 5 (1969) 129.
[5] B.Mondovì, A.Finazzi Agrò, G.Rotilio, R.Strom, G.Moricca and A.Rossi Fanelli, European J. Cancer 5 (1969) 137.
[6] R.Strom, P.Caiafa, B.Mondovì and A.Rossi Fanelli, FEBS Letters 3 (1969) 343.
[7] G.D.Birnie, H.Kroeger and C.Heidelberger, Biochemistry 2 (1963) 566.
[8] P.P.Cohen, in: Manometric Techniques, 4th ed., eds. W.W.Umbreit, R.H.Burris and J.F.Stauffer (Burgess, Minneapolis, 1957) p. 147.
[9] J.E.Harris and L.Friedman, Biochemistry 6 (1967) 2814.
[10] F.Snyder, Anal. Biochem. 31 (1964) 183.
[11] D.L.Oxender and H.N.Christensen, J. Biol. Chem. 234 (1959) 2321.
[12] W.D.Stein, The Movement of Molecules across Cell Membranes (Academic Press, New York, 1967) pp. 71 and 123.
[13] C.Huang, L.Wheeldon and T.E.Thompson, J. Mol. Biol. 8 (1964) 148.
[14] D.Chapman, The Structure of Lipids (Methuen, London, 1965).
[15] J.W.L.Beament, Brit. Med. Bull. 24 (1968) 130.
[16] D.Chapman, V.B.Kamat and R.J.Levene, Science 160 (1968) 314.
[17] D.Chapman and V.B.Kamat, in: Regulatory Functions of Biological Membranes, ed. J.Jarnefelt, B.B.A. Library, vol. 11 (Elsevier Publ. Co., Amsterdam, 1968) p. 87.
[18] D.Chapman, in: Thermobiology, ed. A.H.Rose (Academic Press, New York, 1967) p. 122.
[19] E.S.Lutton, in: Fatty Acids, ed. K.S.Markley, part 4 (Interscience Publ., New York, 1967) p. 2583.
[20] D.Chapman, R.M.Williams and B.D.Ladbrooke, Chem. Phys. Lipids 1 (1967) 225.
[21] L.L.M.Van Deenen, in: Regulatory Functions of Biological Membranes, ed. J. Järnefelt, B.B.A. Library, vol. 11 (Elsevier Publ. Co., Amsterdam, 1968) p. 72.
[22] D.Chapman and D.T.Collin, Nature 206 (1965) 189.

CALCIUM TRANSPORT IN CARDIAC MUSCLE

H.REUTER

Department of Pharmacology, University of Berne, Switzerland

1. Introduction

The cardiac cell membrane is highly permeable for calcium ions [1,2]. Passive distribution of calcium between both sides of the cell membrane, however, would require an internal concentration of this ion of at least 0.7 M, according to the equation

$$[Ca]_i = [Ca]_0 \exp - \frac{2VF}{RT} , \tag{1}$$

where the membrane potential, V, is 80 mV inside negative. But there is good evidence that $[Ca]_i$ is not higher than $10^{-8} - 10^{-7}$ M during relaxation of the muscle fibre, and even the total calcium concentration in cardiac tissue is only in the order of 10^{-3} M [1,3]. Therefore, some sort of 'active' extrusion mechanism has been postulated which keeps $[Ca]_i$ at this low level. The present report deals with some of the basic features of calcium transport measured in isolated cardiac preparations (guinea pig auricles) by means of the isotope ^{45}Ca [3]. A similar system of calcium transport has recently been described for squid axon [4,5].

2. Results

2.1. Effect of temperature and metabolic inhibitors

Rate constants of calcium efflux from resting guinea pig auricles have been determined at three different temperatures (3, 25, 35° C) between the second and fourth hour of the measurements. Fig. 1 shows an Arrhenius plot of the experimental results. Within the limits of experimental error the values could be fitted by a straight line. The apparent activation energy of calcium efflux calculated from this plot gave a value of 5.9 kcal/mole, corresponding

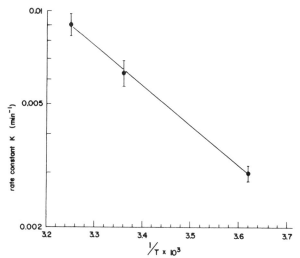

Fig. 1. Arrhenius plot of temperature dependence of calcium efflux from guinea pig auricles. Abscissa: reciprocal of absolute temperature, T, multiplied by 10^3; ordinate (log scale): rate constants, K (min^{-1}) of calcium efflux (mean $\pm$ S.E. of mean). (Data from [3].)

to a Q_{10} of 1.35. 2,4-dinitrophenol at concentrations of $5.5 \times 10^{-5} - 5.5 \times 10^{-4}$ M reversibly increased calcium efflux up to two-fold while ouabain $10^{-6}-10^{-5}$ M had no significant effect. These data provide some evidence that calcium efflux from isolated cardiac preparations unlike sodium efflux might be governed by a process which does not involve metabolic reactions.

2.2. Effect of external ions

The dependence of calcium efflux from cardiac preparations on external ion composition is qualitatively illustrated in fig. 2. The efflux decreased in calcium-free solution as well as in the absence of $[Na]_o$. More than 80% of calcium efflux from cardiac muscle is dependent on the presence of both of these ions in the bathing fluid under normal conditions. While Sr^{2+} can fully replace Ca^{2+}, Mg^{2+} has only a small tendency to displace Ca^{2+}. The effect of $[Na]_o$ on calcium efflux, however, is extremely specific since this ion cannot be replaced by Li^+, K^+, choline$^+$ or sucrose [3].

These results led to the assumption that $[Ca]_o$ and $[Na]_o$ might compete for some carrier which is activated at the outer surface of the membrane by both ion species. In this case total calcium efflux could be divided into a Ca-

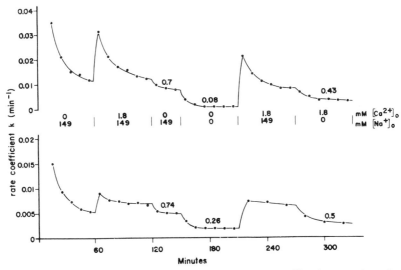

Fig. 2. The effects of removing $[Ca]_o$ and $[Na]_o$ on calcium efflux from a guinea pig auricle (upper curve) and a ventricular trabecula of a sheep (lower curve). Abscissa: time of ^{45}Ca-washout in min; ordinate: rate coefficient k (min^{-1}). Numbers within the curves indicate fractions of the preceding control efflux to which calcium efflux has been reduced. (From [3] by permission of J. Physiol.)

activated and a Na-activated component. Further experiments supported this hypothesis. It could be demonstrated that the Ca-activated component of calcium efflux increased when $[Na]_o$ was reduced and the Na-activated component increased upon reduction of $[Ca]_o$. Quantitatively, the respective sizes of both components of calcium efflux were dependent on the ratio $[Ca]_o/[Na]_o^2$ [3]. Further analysis of the data in terms of Michaelis-Menten kinetics indicated that the dissociation constant, K_m, of the Ca-carrier complex became larger with increasing $[Na]_o$ (table 1). In other words, the affinity of the carrier for Ca ($1/K_m^{Ca}$) decreased when the affinity for Na ($1/K_m^{Na}$) increased, the respective affinities being functions of the ratio $[Ca]_o/[Na]_o^2$. Because of the square of $[Na]_o$ in this ratio the affinity of the carrier for Na is about 1250 times less than the affinity for Ca in normal Tyrode solution.

The conclusion drawn from these experiments is that at the outer surface of the membrane 2 sodium ions and 1 calcium ion compete for a common carrier site. If this is correct the calcium concentration in the cardiac preparation should increase when $[Na]_o$ is reduced since net transport of calcium

Table 1

Average Michaelis constants, K_m, of Ca-activated and Na-activated components of calcium efflux from guinea pig auricles. K_m-values of Ca-activated component, K_m^{Ca}, were obtained with 3 different $[Na]_o$, those of Na-activated component, K_m^{Na}, with 3 different $[Ca]_o$. The high K_m^{Na} results from the square of $[Na]_o$ in the ratio $[Ca]_o/[Na]_o^2$ determining the respective size of each component. (Data from [3].)

Ca-activated component		Na-activated component	
$[Na]_o^2$ (mM)^2	K_m^{Ca} (mM $[Ca]_o$)	$[Ca]_o$ (mM)	K_m^{Na} (mM $[Na]_o)^2$
222001	1.34	7.2	3140
65001	0.67	1.8	1670
21601	0.42	0.45	770

Table 2

Calcium content of guinea pig auricles (μM/g wet wt. $\pm$ S.E.; n of each group = 6) in Tyrode solutions containing 100% and 25% NaCl. All preparations were first equilibrated for 1 hr in normal Tyrode (= 100% NaCl) solution. Groups 3 and 4 after another equilibration in 25% NaCl solution were transferred into normal Tyrode solution again for 15 and 30 min. (Data from [3].)

Group no.	1	2	3		4	
Solution	100% NaCl	25% NaCl	25%	100% NaCl	25%	100% NaCl
Equil.-time	60 min	60 min	60	15 min	60	30 min
Ca-content	1.70 ± 0.1	2.35 ± 0.2	1.90 ± 0.1		1.75 ± 0.1	

into the outward direction should be entirely dependent on the Na—Ca exchange across the membrane. The results listed in table 2 support this assumption. Reduction of $[Na]_o$ led to an increase in total calcium concentration in the tissue, while readmittance of sodium to the solution decreased the calcium content again. In these experiments calcium content in the preparations was determined by a fluorometric method [6].

2.3. Dependence of Ca influx on internal sodium

In cardiac muscle the sum of total internal sodium and calcium is only about 1/10 of the concentration of these ions in the external medium and most of the internal calcium is bound [1]. When, however, the carrier is similarly activated at the inner surface of the membrane as at the outer surface an

Table 3
Effect of $[Na]_i$ (mM/l fiber water) on Ca influx (μM/g wet wt. $\times$ 10 min) in resting
guinea pig auricles. Immediately after measuring ^{45}Ca-uptake for 10 min in normal
Tyrode solution or Na-poor solution the preparations were soaked in inactive Na- and
Ca-free solution for 25 min in order to wash extracellular space free of Ca without chang-
ing $[Ca]_i$ appreciably. (Data from [7].)

$[Na]_i$	12.5 ± 1.7	20.4 ± 2.5	40.5 ± 4.8	59.7 ± 6.6
Ca-influx Tyrode sol.	0.35 ± 0.02	0.42 ± 0.02	0.76 ± 0.05	0.92 ± 0.08
Ca-influx Na-poor sol.	0.56 ± 0.05	0.66 ± 0.03	1.05 ± 0.10	1.57 ± 0.09

increase in $[Na]_i$ could induce more carrier to move from inside to outside,
since the carrier is far from saturation by the internal ion concentrations [7].
This, however, should also provide more carrier to be loaded at the outer surface and hence an increase in calcium influx should be measured. $[Na]_i$ in the
guinea pig auricles was increased by rapid electrical stimulation or by cooling and reduced by increasing $[K]_o$. Immediately afterwards Ca-influx was
measured by soaking the resting auricles for 10 minutes in ^{45}Ca-containing
Tyrode solution with normal or reduced sodium content (NaCl replaced by
choline-Cl). Table 3 shows that Ca-influx from both solutions increased appreciably with increasing $[Na]_i$. Since calcium net efflux was inhibited in so-
dium-poor solution, increase in Ca-influx corresponded to an about equal increase in calcium content in the auricles, while calcium content increased only
slightly in preparations loaded with ^{45}Ca in normal Tyrode solution [7].

3. Conclusions

The interpretation of the results is that the energy for calcium efflux from
cardiac preparations is provided by the downhill movements of sodium and
calcium into the cell. In the outside solution both ions are present in much
higher concentrations than inside the cell. If sodium and calcium influx are at
least partially coupled with calcium efflux by means of a charged carrier, calcium could be transported uphill into the outward direction. Kinetically, some
type of facilitated diffusion mechanism would be in satisfactory agreement
with the present results. In such a system net outward transport of calcium
would result from Na-Ca exchange, while Ca-Ca exchange would shuttle calcium only forth and back. One possibility for explaining the low internal cal-

cium concentration in cardiac muscle on the basis of the present results could be given by the equation

$$\frac{[Ca]_i}{[Ca]_o} = \frac{[Na]_i^2/K_m^{Na_i}}{[Na]_o^2/K_m^{Na_o}} \exp \frac{zVF}{RT} , \tag{2}$$

where V is assumed to be -80 mV and $z = 2$.

The calcium ratio calculated from this equation for normal conditions is about 1:45000, corresponding to $[Ca]_i$ of less than 5×10^{-8} M. This value of $[Ca]_i$ is not an unreasonable estimation for resting cardiac preparations. According to eq. (2) $[Ca]_i$ should increase either when the ratio $[Na]_i^2/[Na]_o^2$ decreases or when the membrane is depolarized. The first condition would be given when the sodium pump is completely blocked or when $[Na]_o$ is reduced. An increase in total cellular calcium coinciding with a sustained contracture has been demonstrated in cardiac muscle during the application of large doses of cardiac glycosides or metabolic inhibitors [3,8], or when $[Na]_o$ was reduced [2,3]. The second condition is given when the membrane is depolarized by increasing $[K]_o$. Also in this case cardiac muscle develops contracture and cellular calcium may increase [2]. However, the effect of the membrane potential on this transport system is not yet settled [7].

This simple tentative explanation for calcium transport in cardiac muscle and also in squid axon [5] is attractive since under normal conditions it would be dependent energetically mainly on the sodium gradient and hence on the operation of the sodium pump.

References

[1] C.P.Bianchi, Cell calcium (Butterworth and Co., Ltd., London, 1968).
[2] R.Niedergerke, J. Physiol. 167 (1963) 515.
[3] H.Reuter and N.Seitz, J. Physiol. 195 (1968) 451.
[4] P.F.Baker, M.P.Blaustein, A.L.Hodgkin and R.A.Steinhardt, J. Physiol. 200 (1969) 431.
[5] M.P.Blaustein and A.L.Hodgkin, J. Physiol. 200 (1969) 497.
[6] H.M.Von Hattingberg, W.Klaus, H.Lüllmann and S.Zepf, Experientia 22 (1966) 553.
[7] H.G.Glitsch, H.Reuter and H.Scholz, J. Physiol. (in press).
[8] W.Klaus, Naunyn-Schmiedebergs Arch. Exptl. Pathol. Pharmakol. 246 (1963) 226.

STUDIES ON MESENTERY PERMEABILITY

D.TESI and W.G.FORSSMANN

Institute of Histology, Medical School, Geneva, Switzerland*

1. Introduction

One of the most important membrane systems involved in the separation of biological compartments is the capillary endothelium. Many physiological and morphological studies have resulted in the recognition of the similarity between capillary endothelial cells and mesothelial cells [1—8]. On the basis of this similarity, the easily accessible mesenteric membrane was used for the study of the diffusion kinetics of different substances [1—11]. The present work, based on both morphological and functional investigations, is to discuss whether the mesentery can be used as a model for capillary permeability studies.

2. Structure of mesentery

The peritoneum possesses a cell layer, the mesothelium, which seems to be of the same type as the endothelium of capillaries. The visceral mesothelium cells are characteristically arciform with a considerable enlargement around the nucleus. The cytoplasm is highly differentiated; a highly developed endoplasmic reticulum, mitochondria, vacuoles amd microvilli are found.

In these cells, however, few micropinocytotic vesicles and fine filaments inserting the cytoplasmic membrane at the side of the peritoneal cavity are found: such filaments are not present in the capillary endothelial cells.

Mesenterial mesothelial cells show also an endoplasmic reticulum and a cytoplasm more differentiated than that of an endothelial cell; still, these cells with their flattened form, resemble more the capillary endothelial cells than the visceral mesothelial cells which they are.

The intercellular gaps in the mesothelium are provided with maculae ad-

*Present address: Anatomische Institut, University of Heidelberg, 69 Heidelberg, Brennengasse 1, Germany.

herentes and occludentes. This is reminiscent of the structure of the intercellular gaps of the capillary endothelium [12].

A detailed morphologic description of mesentery has been published
elsewhere [13].

3. Permeability study

In our experiment a system similar to that of Ussing et al. [14] introduced
for study of frog skin permeability was used. The mesentery separates the
two compartments. On one side we add the tracer substance and then measure, as a function of time, the appearance of concentrations of substance on
the other side of the membrane.

Fig. 1 shows the passage of sucrose-^{14}C across mesenterial membrane.
After 10 sec, we already find radioactivity on the other side. It is demonstrated by radioactivity measurements that increased temperature results in a
more rapid diffusion across the membrane. Diffusion rates are shown for 17,
27 and 37°C.

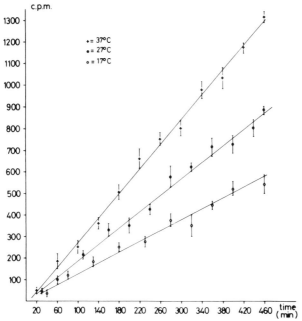

Fig. 1. Diffusion of sucrose-^{14}C across mesenterial membrane.

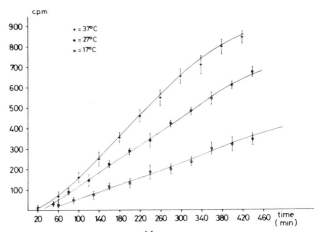

Fig. 2. Diffusion of inulin-^{14}C across mesenterial membrane.

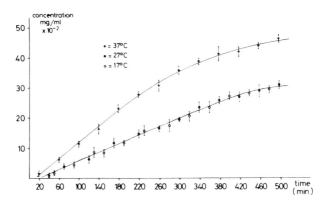

Fig. 3. Diffusion of HRP across mesenterial membrane.

The diffusion of inulin-^{14}C across the mesentery as a function of temperature is seen in fig. 2. With a decrease in temperature grows a decrease in
the rate of transmembrane diffusion. As for sucrose-^{14}C the results for 17°C,
27°C and 37°C are shown.

For peroxidase, the transmembrane diffusion curves are different from
those for sucrose and inulin.

Between 37°C and 27°C, there is a sharp difference in the rate of passage;

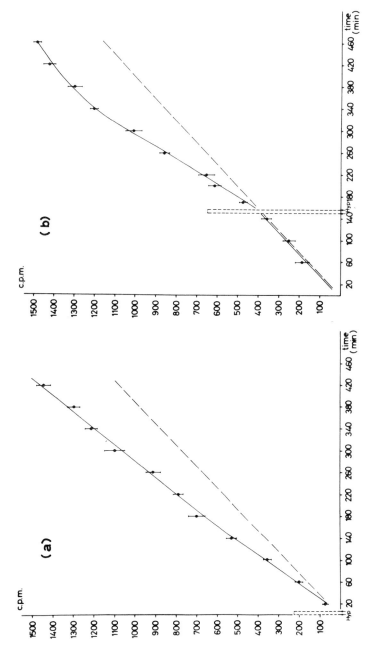

Fig. 4. Diffusion of sucrose-^{14}C across mesenterial membrane influenced by osmotic pressure. —— Osmotic pressure + 250 mOsm; - - - - Control 37°C. (a) Osmotic shock before tracer addition. (b) Osmotic shock after 150 min the tracer addition.

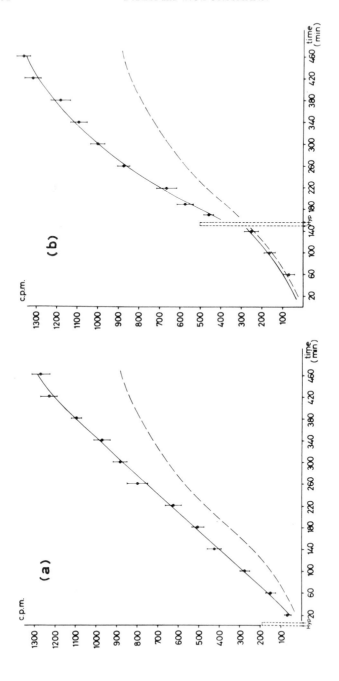

Fig. 5. Diffusion of inulin-^{14}C across mesenterial membrane influence by osmotic pressure. ——— Osmotic pressure + 250 mOsm; - - - - Control 37°C. (a) Osmotic shock before tracer addition. (b) Osmotic shock after 150 min the tracer addition.

between 27°C and 17°C we cannot discern a difference in rate with our present method (fig. 3).

In fig. 4a the diffusion kinetics of labelled sucrose across a mesentery previously subjected to osmotic shock by contact during 5 min with a 550 mOsm electrolyte solution are seen. Transmembrane diffusion is greatly increased in the normal 300 mOsm medium. This shows that there has been as a result of the osmotic shock an opening of some pores restraining normally the diffusion.

If after 150 min of diffusion under normal osmotic conditions, we shock the membrane with a 550 mOsm electrolyte solution, we find that the passage of labelled sucrose is also increased greatly (fig. 4b).

The same 5-min osmotic shock prior to the experiment also increased the passage of radioactive inulin (fig. 5a). If we subject the membrane to an osmotic shock after 150 min, the rate of passage of inulin-^{14}C is clearly increased (fig. 5b).

4. Discussion

Normal mesentery with its mesothelial cell border is morphologically analogous to vascular endothelial membrane. Therefore it has been suggested to be an adequate model for the study of capillary permeability. Morphological controls by phase contrast and electron microscopy, however, showed that the mesothelial cells are dissociated from the mesenterial membrane after less than 1 hr incubation in electrolyte solution. Thus structurally the mesentery membrane cannot be considered as a model for the capillary permeability. However the studies with the membrane after the dissociation of the mesothelium has been completed by equilibrating the membrane in electrolyte solution, gave quite correctly reproducible results of permeability study. Thus the membrane in question can be considered as a model for the study of interstitial permeability properties.

The results of this investigation show, in the mesentery membrane, interesting effects of permeability changes undergoing in variations of the molecular size, temperature and osmotic pressure. The fact that osmotic pressure changes can modify the permeability properties proves that the mesentery membrane can be used as an interstitial space model. Influence of osmotic pressure on non-cellular diffusion barriers has been described by Gliozzi et al. [15].

References

[1] D.L.Odor, J. Biophys. Biochem. Cytol. 2 (1956) 105–108.

[2] J.Staubesand and W.Schmidt, Z. Zellforsch. 53 (1960) 55–68.

[3] J.Staubesand, Z. Zellforsch, 58 (1963) 915–952.

[4] A.F.Baradi and J.Hope, Exptl. Cell Res. 34 (1964) 33–44.

[5] R.S.Cotran and G.Majno, Studies on the intercellular junctions of mesothelium and endothelium. Symp. Biophys. and Physiol. of Biological Transport (1965).

[6] R.S.Cotran, Elektronenmikroskopische Untersuchungen der normalen und gesteigerten Permeabilität des Mesothels und Endothels, in: Die Entzündungsgrundlagen und pharmakologische Beeinflussung, eds. R.Heister und H.F.Hofmann (Urban und Schwarzenberg, 1966).

[7] J.R.Casley-Smith, Quart. J. Exp. Physiol. 52 (1967) 105–113.

[8] R.S.Cotran and M.J.Karnovsky, J. Cell Biol. 37 (1968) 123–137.

[9] W.O.Berndt and R.E.Gosselin, Am. J. Physiol. 200 (1961) 454–458.

[10] W.O.Berndt and R.E.Gosselin, Am. J. Physiol. 202 (1962) 761–767.

[11] E.Brachet and E.Rasio, Biochim. Biophys. Acta 183 (1969) 162–168.

[12] M.J.Karnovsky, J. Cell Biol. 27 (1967) 213–236.

[13] D.Tesi and W.G.Forssmann, Verhandl. Anat. Ges. Anat. Anz. 64 (1970) 365–372.

[14] H.H.Ussing, Acta Physiol. Scand. 17 (1949) 1–37.

[15] A.Gliozzi, R.Morchio and A.Ciferri, Swelling and transport properties of collagen membranes (1969, in press).

ROLE OF BASEMENT AND CELL MEMBRANES IN THE MAINTENANCE OF THE INTEGRITY OF BLOOD CAPILLARY WALL

Jean-Maurice GAZAVE, Micheline ANCLA and Paulette CANU

Laboratoire de Physiologie Pathologique
de l'Ecole Pratique des Hautes Etudes, Paris

Until recently, permeability and resistance of capillary walls have been considered as a physiological question and although many studies have been done on the possibility of modifying this permeability and resistance with chemical compounds, few studies and theories have tried to find a correspondence between the constitution of capillary walls and their permeability and resistance.

The electron microscope gives a precise idea of the fine structure of the capillary wall. The capillary essentially consists of an uninterrupted tube of glycoproteins (basement membrane), the inside of which is covered by very flat cells (endothelial cells). This basement membrane is sometimes strengthened by other cells which are included in it (pericytes). The outside is strengthened in some parts by slabs of collagen fibres, and the whole by the cells of the surrounding tissues (fig. 1).

Thus, a chemical compound which passes through the capillary from the inside to the outside will meet: (1) the membrane of the endothelial cell, then the cytoplasm of this cell, and again the membrane unless the compound passes in between two endothelial cells; (2) the basement membrane which, as we have seen, is without interruptions (in the case of uninterrupted capillaries); (3) the membranes of the cells of the tissues surrounding the basement membrane or sometimes the space between two cells.

Although the methods for the measurement of the capillary permeability are numerous, they are not very precise, and it is more convenient to measure capillary resistance instead. In fact, both methods arrive at the same result, i.e. a measurement of the condition of the capillary wall [1].

In this study, we have considered the alteration of the capillaries during experimental scurvy of the guinea pig. The symptomatology of this condition presents many analogies with that of the human being [2].

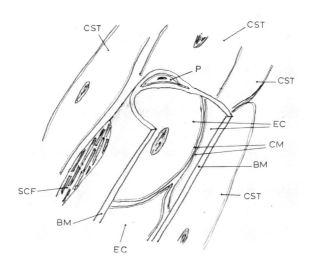

The diet used is almost entirely synthetic, composed of casein (6,5 parts), corn of maize starch (34 parts), cellulose (6,5 parts), saline mixture (1,75 parts) including: sodium chloride, magnesium sulphate, sodium phosphate, potassium phosphate, calcium phosphate, iron citrate, calcium lactate, vitaminized oils (2.25 parts, composed of equal amounts of cod-liver oil and maize seed oil), vitamin mixture (0.5 parts): thiamine, riboflavine, pyridoxine, nicotinic amide and para-aminobenzoic acid, and water [1].

This diet gives the animal serious scurvy which is often fatal after 15 days. Few animals are alive after 21 days. The animal loses weight and the resistance of the capillaries falls from 30 cm Hg to less than 10 cm with ruptures which provoke haemorrhages. There is increased activity of the thyroid gland and suprarenal cortex, and above all, a perturbation of the endochondral ossification, particularly visible at the chondro-costal junctions [1].

The most interesting feature is the decrease in resistance and rupture of the capillaries which denotes an important change in the constitution of the wall, because no abnormality in the blood crasis nor in the blood pressure is observed at this level.

This modification is the result of two chemical compounds: C factor (ascorbic acid) and C2 factor. The second is a flavanol whose chemical structure is incompletely understood. It is found in various plants, mainly in the juice

ERRATA

Permeability and function of biological membranes, edited by Liana Bolis, A. Katchalsky, R. D. Keynes, W. R. Loewenstein and B. A. Pethica

p. 356: The figure legend should read:
Fig. 1. BM: basement membrane; CM: cell membrane; SCF: slab of collagen fibres; EC: endothelial cell; P: pericyte; CST: cell of surrounding tissues.

p. 357: On the left-hand side of the figure the thin line should be marked E.

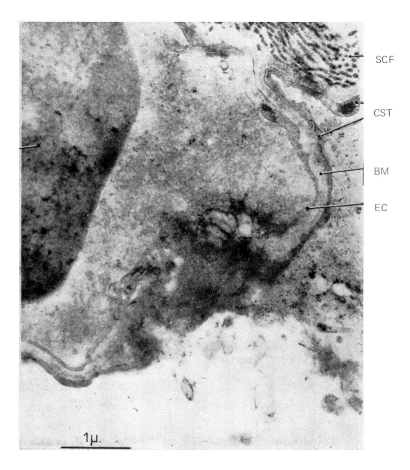

Fig. 2. Rupture of capillary (lung). E: erythrocyte.

of lemons and oranges, from which it can be extracted with pectic substances [3]. It can also be extracted from various animal organs in which it accompanies phospholipids [4].

A total of 50 guinea pigs were divided into 5 groups. All groups were fed with the above diet, but while the first group only received this diet, the remaining groups received the following additions to the diet: group 2: ascorbic acid (1 mg/100 g wt/day); group 3: ascorbic acid (10 mg/100 g wt/day); group 4: pectin extract from oranges containing approx. 0.5% C2 (200 mg/ 100 g wt/day); group 5: ascorbic acid (1 mg/100 g wt/day) plus pectin extract from oranges (200 mg/100 g wt/day).

The weight and the capillary resistance were checked throughout the experiments. After one, two and three weeks, some animals from each group were anaesthetized with "Rectanol", certain organs (lungs, kidneys, liver) were removed and treated with osmic acid for electron microscopy. Observation was centered on the capillaries. However, the thyroid gland, suprarenal cortex and chondro-costal junctions were examined by the optical microscope.

Examination with the electron microscope has shown that only the animals which received C and C2 factors in addition to the diet had no ruptures of capillaries. Moreover, their capillary resistance was normal and the aspect of thyroid gland, suprarenal cortex, and chondro-costal junctions did not show any abnormality, that is to say the animals were not suffering from scurvy.

In the other groups, all the animals, even those which had received 10 mg per 100 g of weight per day of ascorbic acid (which is a very important amount) showed capillary rupture (fig. 2). The capillary resistance fell and examination of their thyroid gland, suprarenal cortex and chondro-costal junctions showed typical scurvy lesions.

Therefore, neither ascorbic acid alone nor C2 alone can prevent rupture of the capillaries, but the combination of both does prevent rupture.

Ascorbic acid seems to be located in the basement membrane [2,5], and C2 factor, which attaches to the choline phosphate part of lecithin, is part of the constitution of the cell membrane. We know that the C2 factor increases the speed of reduction of dehydroascorbic acid to ascorbic acid with glutathione [6]. Their proximity suggests that the C2 factor is able, even at this level, to protect ascorbic acid.

References

[1] J.M.Gazave, J. Physiol. (Paris) 58 (1966) suppl. mo. 1, 128.
[2] H.Friederici, H.Taylor, R.Rose and C.L.Pirani, Lab. Invest. 15 (1966) 1442.
[3] J.M.Gazave, J.L.Parrot, A.Saindelle and P.Canu, J. Physiol. (Paris) 60 (1968) 251.
[4] J.L.Parrot, J.M.Gazave, P.Canu and A.M.Palou, J. Physiol. (Paris) 59 (1967) 278.
[5] I.Anotonowicz and E.Kodicek, Biochem. J. 110 (1968) 609.
[6] J.L.Parrot and J.M.Gazave, Compt. Rend. Soc. Biol. 145 (1951) 821–823.

INDEX